SISTERS IN LAW

SISTERS IN LAW

Women Lawyers in Modern American History

Virginia G. Drachman

781

HARVARD UNIVERSITY PRESS
Cambridge, Massachusetts
London, England
1998

Library of Congress Cataloging-in-Publication Data

Drachman, Virginia G., 1948–
Sisters in law : women lawyers in modern American history /
Virginia G. Drachman.
p.   cm.
Includes bibliographical references and index.
ISBN 0-674-80991-2 (alk. paper)
1. Women lawyers—United States—History.
I. Title.
KF299.W6D7   1998
340'.082—dc21   97-23490

For my daughters, Abigail and Eliza

Acknowledgments

I began this project over ten years ago. During that time, I have relied on and benefited from the help of numerous people.

I am indebted to a number of colleagues who generously took time from their busy lives to read all or portions of the manuscript and to share their ideas, including Mari Jo Buhle, David Chambers, Michael Grossberg, Dirk Hartog, Ann Lane, Elaine May, Carrie Menkel-Meadow, and Rosalind Rosenberg. A number of people gave me encouragement and ideas in the early stages of the project, including Barbara Brenzel, Ronald Chester, and Ellen DuBois. I am particularly indebted to two people, Nancy Cott and Martha Minow, whose careful and perceptive readings of the entire manuscript helped to sharpen my ideas and make this a better book.

During the early years of this project, I received generous support from both a Ford Fellowship from the American Council of Learned Societies and a grant from the Law and Social Sciences Program of the National Science Foundation (8810678). Tufts University assisted me through its Faculty Research Awards Program. The Schlesinger Library at Radcliffe College generously provided me with an office while I conducted my research there.

This book would have taken even longer had it not been for the invaluable help of numerous research assistants, including Sharon Ballard, Catherine Breen, Deborah Colson, Susan Cournoyer, Mark Fitzgibbons, Samantha Fox, Lauren Goldberg, James Lank, Jill Lepore, Dane Morrison, Daniel Perrone, David Rigoh, Audrey Rogers, Daneille Williams, and Julie Ann Zupan. Mary Hyde programmed the data in this book with her usual patience and insights. Tony Kaszowski served as an invaluable and patient computer consultant. Susan Buttrick, Mary-Ann Kazanjian, and Annette Lazzara helped keep the details of my life in order at Tufts, and Patty Dunn generously typed portions of the manuscript at a moment's notice.

I relied on the assistance of the staffs of numerous libraries around the country. In particular, Anne Engelhart, Barbara Haber, Diane Hamer, Pat King, Jane Knowles, Sylvia McDowell, and Eva Mosley were invaluable in their help and generousity during my years of research at the Schlesinger Library. In addition I would like to thank Mary-Ellen Jones of the Bancroft Library at the University of California at Berkeley; Judy Mellons of the Harvard Law School Library; Nancy Bartlett, Karen Jania, and the staff of the Bentley Historical Library of the University of Michigan; Susan Notar at the Office of Institutional Advancement of Washington College of Law; Amy Doherty at the George Arents Research Library of Syracuse University; and Margo Hargopian at Boston University. I am also grateful to the staffs of the Boston Public Library; the Pappas Law Library and Mugar Library of Boston University; the University Research Library at University of California at Los Angeles; the Chicago Historical Society; the Pusey Library of Harvard University; the Law Library of the New England School of Law; the Elmer Holmes Bobst Library of New York University; the Smith College Library; the Social Law Library; and the Yale University Law Library.

Portions of this book have appeared in the following publications: *Women Lawyers and the Origins of Professional Identity in America: The Letters of the Equity Club, 1887 to 1890* (Ann Arbor: University of Michigan Press, 1987); "The New Woman Lawyer and the Challenge of Sexual Equality in Early Twentieth-Century America," 28 *Indiana Law Review* 227–258 (1995); "Women Lawyers and the Quest for Professional Identity in Late-Nineteenth-Century America," 88 *Michigan Law Review* 2414–2443 (1990); " 'My "Partner" in Law and Life': Marriage in the Lives of Women Lawyers in Late-Nineteenth- and Early Twentieth-Century America," 14 *Law and Social Inquiry* 221–250 (1989); and "Entering the Male Do-

main: Women Lawyers in the Courtroom in Modern American History,"
77 *Massachusetts Law Review* 44–50 (1992).

I received conscientious and thoughtful editorial support from Aïda
Donald and Elizabeth Suttell at Harvard University Press. This book
has benefited from the careful eye of my copyeditor, Julie Carlson.

I have been extremely fortunate to enjoy special friendships in my
private life. In particular, Barbara Daley, Joy Kant, Sue Sand, and Peggy
Warren have enriched my life as we have raised our children and grown
older over the duration of this project.

I am motivated daily by my memories of Charles Brand, who, for six
brief years until his death, gave me, his daughter, the love I needed to
believe in myself.

My parents, Sally and Stanley Drachman, have given me their constant love and support. My father encouraged me intellectually when
he urged me to "reach for the stars." My mother, with her unique optimism, always made the stars seem within my reach.

This book has been a labor of love that I have shared with my husband, Doug. It was he who first suggested that I consider writing a
history of women lawyers, but my debt to him only begins there. He
brought his knowledge of the law to Chapter 1, which we coauthored,
and he is also the coauthor of Chapter 7. In addition, he has been a
patient and careful reader of every draft of this book. Although this
kind of project can test the limits of a relationship, in this case it has
deepened and strengthened our commitment to each other. He has
truly been, as one nineteenth-century woman lawyer lovingly described
her husband, "my 'partner' in law and life."

When I began this project I had one daughter in nursery school and
another in diapers. Today, Abigail is about to apply to college and Eliza
is in high school. Both have literally grown up with their mother working on this project. I lovingly dedicate this book to the wonderful young
women they are becoming.

Contents

Illustrations

Tables

SISTERS IN LAW

Introduction

"*D*ear Sisters in Law," wrote lawyer Jane Slocum to the women lawyers in the Equity Club in 1887.[1] Slocum was not alone in her use of this salutation to address her colleagues. Women lawyers in the nineteenth century frequently referred to each other as "sisters in law."[2] The phrase revealed women lawyers' consciousness that they were part of a distinct group of women, a community of women lawyers. In an age when women derived their identity from their place in the family, women lawyers defined themselves as sisters in the family of women lawyers.

The history of women lawyers is a powerful story of discrimination, integration, and women's search for equality and autonomy in American society. This book tells that story. It begins in the 1860s, when women first began to seek entrance into the legal profession. It follows women lawyers over more than half a century as they gained admission to most law schools, integrated all state bars, established professional careers, and tried to balance the traditional responsibilities of their private lives with the new demands of their professional careers. It ends in the 1930s, when women had achieved modest professional success and recognized the limits of their progress, a pattern that barely changed until the mid-1970s.[3]

I began this book over ten years ago, after completing a history of women doctors. I wanted to look for similarities between their history and that of women in another male-dominated profession. I discovered that along with the similarities, the history of women lawyers was distinct from the history of women in all other professions. The uniqueness of women lawyers is rooted in two major historical facts. First, more than any other profession women sought to enter in the nineteenth century, law was the most engendered and closed to women. Second, the legal profession was especially difficult to integrate because sexual discrimination was rooted in the legal system. Simply put, masculinity was part of the very foundation of the profession; it was fundamental to its principles, values, and culture.[4] A few simple numbers reveal the extent of the sexual discrimination and engendered nature of the legal profession. By 1920, women made up 86 percent of all schoolteachers, 66 percent of all social workers, 5 percent of all doctors, 4.7 percent of all scientists, and only 1.4 percent of all lawyers.[5]

But numbers do not tell the whole story. There were reasons unique to the legal profession that made it so impenetrable to women. Unlike medicine, in which women founded their own all-women's schools and hospitals in the mid-nineteenth century, until the very end of the century law had no separate all-women's institutions to ease women's entry into the legal profession.[6] Instead, access to the legal profession was obtained through male-controlled institutions: courts, bar associations, law schools, and law firms. Moreover, women lawyers faced an obstacle unique to women professionals: their profession made and interpreted the laws that denied women access to the rights of equal citizenship, including the practice of law. The very act of gaining admission to practice law demanded that women change the law of the land. Women had to persuade male judges and legislatures to reinterpret the male-constructed jurisprudence that made their entry into the legal profession not only unthinkable, but illegal.

As I examined the attempts of women lawyers to gain equality with male lawyers, I discovered that, more than any other group of professional women in nineteenth-century America, women lawyers linked their cause directly to the campaign for woman suffrage. Just as women suffragists claimed equal citizenship with men in order to win the right to vote, so nineteenth-century women lawyers claimed their status as citizens equal with men in order to justify their right to practice law. The demand that women practice law was almost as radical as the demand that women vote because its advocates dared to follow the suffragists' challenge—to place women in the public arena, independent of their domestic ties, and as equal citizens with men.[7] Nineteenth-century women lawyers did not duplicate the suffrage movement, nor did they create the broad organizational structure or attain the national attention that the suffrage movement did. Nevertheless, it is clear that women lawyers joined together in what they understood to be a community of "sisters in law" to overcome sexual discrimination in the legal profession.

As I uncovered the ways in which women lawyers sought the right to practice law and strived to carve their niche in the legal profession, I began to understand that the community of "sisters in law" composed a women lawyers movement. In the 1860s and 1870s in particular, the women lawyers movement shared some of the important characteristics of the nineteenth-century woman suffrage movement. Women lawyers articulated a body of shared ideas about the importance of reform of the American legal system; they advocated equal citizenship with men so that women could practice law; they supported each other through groups such as the Equity Club, the first attempt by women lawyers to organize nationwide; they urged the sexual integration of law schools; they publicly exposed sexual discrimination in the legal profession through law journals such as Myra Bradwell's *Chicago Legal News*; and they brought numerous lawsuits in order to integrate the bar. All of these efforts made up the women lawyers movement, which, like the woman suffrage movement, though on a much smaller scale, grappled with the question of women's power as defined by the law and the place of women in a male-constructed legal system.

As women tried to integrate the legal profession, they confronted a tension between their gender and professional identity, or what one nineteenth-century woman lawyer described as the burden of "double consciousness."[8] Few women lawyers escaped this burden. The pervasiveness of sexual discrimination in the legal profession forced women lawyers to reconcile continually their quest for sexual equality with their long-held belief in female uniqueness. As law students, for example, they considered whether they should speak out in the classroom like their male classmates or sit quietly as ladies. Once in practice, they made difficult professional choices between the visibility of courtroom practice or the privacy of office practice, and between the selflessness of charity law or the personal benefits of law for profit. They even struggled over what the proper woman lawyer should wear, especially when she was in the courtroom.

The tension between their gender and professional identity also intruded into the private lives of women lawyers, forcing them to make difficult decisions about marriage, motherhood, and health. Could they marry and have families like male lawyers did, or did they have to make sacrifices? Could they compete physically and mentally with male lawyers, or did they need to take special precautions? Their concerns reveal that nineteenth-century women lawyers debated these personal issues well before women sought equality in marriage in the early twentieth century.[9]

By the early twentieth century, nearly all of the institutional barriers to women's entry into the legal profession had crumbled, and younger women who entered law felt confident that they would not have to face the tension between gender and professional identity that had plagued nineteenth-century women lawyers. This generation of women believed that the new ideal of a meritocracy in the legal profession promised them a fair and equal chance to prove their ability and to succeed in the profession. Many also marched headlong into marriages, trusting that they would be better able than their predecessors to balance marriage and motherhood with their careers. An exceptional elite reached the pinnacle of professional accomplishment. But the majority of women lawyers achieved only modest success.

The optimism of the new women lawyers of the early twentieth century was also undermined by new and persistent forms of sexual discrimination. Although practically all law schools, including some of the most prestigious ones, were open to women by the early twentieth century, most women lawyers graduated from bottom-tier institutions. Corporate law firms, the new institutions of power and prestige in the early twentieth century, excluded women lawyers. Lucky women graduates achieved modest success as solo practitioners or found office positions as clerks or in law-related sectors of the economy. With the exceptional elite as the standard of success, however, even this modest achievement seemed a disappointment. By the 1930s, it was clear that double consciousness, identified more than half a century before and fostered by sexual discrimination, remained an inescapable burden for women lawyers—the legacy of their integration into the legal profession.

The history of women lawyers from the 1860s to the 1930s is part of the rich fabric of American culture. It is central to two broad areas of American historiography—the history of women in the professions, and the history of the legal profession.

Women's historians have paid a great deal of attention to women's entry into the public sphere.[10] But although they have looked at women in a wide range of professions, they have given little attention to women lawyers.[11] They have shown that nineteenth-century women first entered the public arena through separate all-women's institutions such as women's colleges and women's clubs. This trend was certainly true for women doctors, who entered medicine through their own medical schools and hospitals.

The history of women lawyers reveals a different story. In an era of rigid sexual separatism, nineteenth-century women entered the law through male-dominated institutions, thereby integrating the profession from the outset in the late 1860s and 1870s. Moreover, at the turn of the century, when women began to integrate American society and women doctors in particular began to dismantle their separate women's medical institutions, women lawyers had their first opportunity to study at law schools created specifically for them. As a result, women lawyers did not reap the benefits of the separate women's organizations of the nineteenth century. Nor did they face the tension women doctors encountered at the turn of the century between loyalty to separatism and the lure of integration.

The path of immediate integration taken by nineteenth-century women lawyers contrasted with the more typical route from separatism to integration followed by other women professionals. This study of women lawyers reveals that the model of immediate integration, which coexisted with the well-established paradigm of separatism to integration, is also part of the broad history of women's entry into the public arena.

Central to the immediate integration of women in law were their experiences as a minority in the profession. Although historians of the legal profession have begun to explore the entry of minorities into the law, they have essentially left women out of their interpretations of the development of the modern legal profession.[12] Lawyers in the 1860s were primarily solo practitioners who shared the values of small-town, protestant America. They were white, Anglo-Saxon, and male. By the early twentieth century, the profession had become more diverse. Minorities, particularly Jews and African-Americans, had entered the law, usually at the bottom of this highly stratified profession. A small elite of wealthy, American-born, protestant men who made up the leadership of corporate law firms and prestigious law schools in the nation's largest cities, however, still dominated the profession. This book places women into the diversity and inequality in the modern legal profession and shows that although a few reached the top of the professional hierarchy, most women lawyers joined ethnic and racial minorities on the lower rungs of the professional ladder.

Women's first challenge was to win the right to practice law. The legal history of this struggle has tended to begin and end with Myra Bradwell.[13] Historians of the law have emphasized the 1873 case of Bradwell v. State of Illinois because it was the first decision by the United States Supreme Court that foreclosed women's efforts under federal, constitutional law to gain the right to practice law. The focus on a single "great case" such as the *Bradwell* decision, however, eclipses the efforts of numerous nineteenth-century women lawyers who tested the limits of the law in state and federal courts. This book moves the judicial thought on women lawyers to center stage by examining the legal thought of nineteenth-century state court judges and the legal rhetoric of women lawyers as they sought to make sense of a gender polity in disarray. Issues of natural law; common-law rights; citizenship under federal, constitutional law; and equality are examined in order to understand why the keepers of the rule of law in American society denied women lawyers their basic rights, and, ultimately, how women lawyers gained the right to practice by forcing a reformulation of women's position in American law.

From the outset, I sought to cast a wide net around my subject, to provide a broad history of women lawyers that was national rather than local in scope. I have taken an inclusive approach, reinterpreting the experiences of well-known as well as barely known women lawyers within the broader contours of the story. Women lawyers were a diverse group. They came from large cities and small towns and from all sections of the country. At the same time, they were homogeneous. Women lawyers were, for the most part, white, middle-class, and protestant, though by the early twentieth century daughters of working-class immigrant families—and to a lesser degree, African-American women—had made their way into the profession. This is therefore primarily a study of white, middle-class women, though issues of race, ethnicity, and social class are important interpretive strands of the story. At the same time, my intent here is to look at the women lawyers themselves. I have not sought to measure them against male lawyers. Nor have I sought to compare them with the history of women in other professions, although as the context of the book warrants I draw comparisons at times, particularly to women doctors.

The sources I uncovered for this study were remarkably rich and diverse. They included the usual tools of a historian studying a group of professional women: manuscript collections of women lawyers, law schools, and professional organizations, as well as popular printed sources, including newspapers, magazines, short stories, and novels. (I have described the quantitative sources in Appendix 2.) I also relied heavily on the sources of the legal historian such as judicial decisions, statutes, legal periodicals, appellate court briefs, the *Martindale-Hubbell Law Directory*, and biographical directories of women lawyers published during the first half of the twentieth century. Among this diverse collection of sources, two stand out as unique and especially significant: the letters of the Equity Club, a correspondence club of women lawyers in the late 1880s, and the questionnaires of the Bureau of Vocational Information, completed by women lawyers in 1920. These two collections enabled me to portray in remarkable depth two groups of women lawyers—women lawyers of the late nineteenth century, and the new women lawyers of the early twentieth century.

Finally, I have sought at every turn to tell a story. Though I have relied at times on diverse sources and methods, this work is at its heart a narrative. It follows a clear chronological path, yet it weaves the important interpretive themes into the chronology to create an analytic tale. It begins with women's first efforts to enter the legal profession in the late 1860s and ends in the early twentieth century when a new generation of women lawyers, though finally part of the legal profession, recognized the limits of their progress. The result is a story that incorporates the major analytic themes in the history of women and the history of the legal profession.

Ultimately, the story of women lawyers in modern American history embraces both the limits and possibilities of sexual integration into the legal profession. From the very beginning, women faced discrimination as they struggled to enter the law. As the most engendered of all the male-dominated professions, the law put enormous obstacles, both structural and cultural, in women's way—obstacles that blocked them first as they broke into the profession and then as they sought to practice the law. But the history of women lawyers is not simply a story of discrimination. As closed as it was, the legal profession did not completely exclude women, and women overcame many of the barriers in their way. Despite their continual struggle to balance their gender and professional identity, women lawyers in the late nineteenth century and early twentieth century made their way in the profession. But the task was not easy, and their gains were modest, not monumental. Women never completely overcame the sexual discrimination that was so pervasive in the legal profession.

ONE

"A Sphere with an Infinite and Indeterminable Radius"

with Douglas Lamar Jones

*W*omen in late-nineteenth-century America did something that generations of women before them did not do: they sought and gained the legal right to practice law. The pioneer women lawyers who sought admission to practice law in late-nineteenth-century America, however, faced bleak prospects. Both legal precedent and social convention defined women as belonging to a "separate sphere" of society from men, and women rarely crossed the boundary into the male domain of public life.[1] In 1875, Chief Justice Edward G. Ryan of the Wisconsin Supreme Court typified these views by defiantly rejecting Lavinia Goodell's application for admission to the bar of that court. He stated that the court found "no authority for the admission of females to the bar of any court of this state . . . We cannot but think the common law wise in excluding women from the profession of the law . . . The law of nature destines and qualifies the female sex for the bearing and nurture of the children of our race and for the custody of the homes of the world and their maintenance in love and honor."[2] Chief Justice Ryan not only asserted the natural law view of woman's "separate sphere"; he also believed that admitting women as lawyers would "emasculate the constitution itself and include females in the constitutional right of male suffrage and male qualification. Such a rule would be one of judicial revolution, not of judicial construction."[3] This linkage of women's right to practice law with suffrage emerged as a major rationale of judges and lawyers who opposed admitting women lawyers.

By 1884, Justice P. Thayer of the Common Pleas Court of Philadelphia fashioned an altogether different and competing view of women's right to be admitted as lawyers. Ruling that Carrie Burnham Kilgore, a graduate of the University of Pennsylvania Law School, was entitled to be admitted to practice law, he observed that "if there is any longer any such thing as what old-fashioned philosophers and essayists used to call the sphere of woman, it is . . . a sphere with an infinite and indeterminable radius . . . Everywhere now she is permitted by the common consent of mankind to select and pursue her own vocation." Justice Thayer further asserted that the "revolution is over. It was so gradual that perhaps you did not observe it . . . But it is over."[4] Justice Thayer created a new conception of the woman's sphere metaphor, one with an "indeterminable radius" large enough to include as lawyers women, even married women who otherwise had no legal rights independent of their husbands or rights granted to them by statutes such as the married women's property acts.

Reflecting the legal principles of a gender polity in disarray, the opinions of Justices Ryan and Thayer starkly illustrate the extremes of the legal debate in late-nineteenth-century America about women in law. In the 1860s and 1870s, when women first began to seek the right to be admitted to practice law, male judges and lawyers, in case after case, adhered to the premise that women were not entitled to this right. The result of these cases on women lawyers was the emergence of an unprecedented judicial rationale for the exclusion of women from public life in America: the jurisprudence of separate spheres.[5] In the process, the old order defined the law as a masculine profession. Initially, the jurisprudence of separate spheres relied on the natural law argument that women, both historically and according to common law, occupied different spheres of action than men. Women, the argument went, were naturally intended to bear children and care for the home, not to participate in public life, particularly the legal profession. Over time, the arguments of the jurisprudence of separate spheres changed to rely less on a natural law view of women as separate from men. Instead, they gradually emphasized both that women had historically not served as lawyers and that because lawyers were officers of the court, women, who could not vote, were unfit to practice. Nevertheless, the ideology of separate spheres that women did not belong in the legal profession remained unchanged. Late-nineteenth-century judges struggled to develop a judicial rhetoric to rationalize women's secondary status in a potentially egalitarian constitutional regime. Paradoxically, the jurisprudence of separate spheres was created in response to a jurisprudence of integration, a new and competing judicial rhetoric that assumed that women were equal with men.

The jurisprudence of integration articulated an alternative vision of the legal role of women lawyers in American society. Contained initially in the speeches and writings of activists in the woman's rights movement, the jurisprudence of integration found a vibrant, new voice in the legal briefs of women lawyers who petitioned nineteenth-century courts for the right to practice law. By the 1880s, some state court judges had broken from the traditional view and held in favor of equal rights for women to practice law.[6] Together, these views articulated a legal justification for integrating women into the legal profession and more broadly into public life in America. In doing so, the jurisprudence of integration challenged the old order's limited and paternalistic vision of women in society. The competing lines of judicial thought—the jurisprudence of separate spheres and the jurisprudence of integration— influenced the direction and the success of women's efforts both to gain admission to practice law as well as to expand the emerging legal status of women in nineteenth-century America.

Law in the late nineteenth century was even more masculine than other male-dominated professions: it was characterized by an all-male bar, all-male judges, and the shared belief that law was the natural province of men, not women. In contrast, teaching and nursing were obvious areas of work for women to enter. Even the male-dominated profession of medicine was more open than law was to those women who emphasized their traditional roles as healers and caretakers. But the legal profession provided no obvious way for women to claim their place. In the 1860s and 1870s, when the profession was dominated by courtroom practice, the boisterous conflict and male camaraderie of judges and lawyers reinforced the notion that women did not belong in this most manly of professions.[7] Aspiring women lawyers thus turned to the ideological tradition of woman's rights—suffrage, equal rights, and full citizenship for all—for their guiding principles. The efforts of women lawyers to win the right to practice law became the women lawyers movement—a movement inextricably tied to the nineteenth-century woman's rights movement and a crucible for defining the rights of women in nineteenth-century American society.

The vitality of the women lawyers movement can be seen most clearly in the numerous lawsuits that women initiated between 1869 and 1901. In this period, women lawyers filed lawsuits to gain the right to practice law in at least seventeen states, sought the right to practice in the United States Supreme Court and the United States Court of Claims, and appealed two cases to the United States Supreme Court (see Table 1). These actions were not isolated incidents; they were part of a concerted effort by women to gain the right to practice law in late-nineteenth-century America. The women lawyers movement was not centrally organized with a nationally visible group of leaders like Susan B. Anthony and Elizabeth Cady Stanton, both of New York. Instead, it comprised individual women—some directly connected with the woman's rights movement, such as Belva Lockwood of Washington, D.C., and Myra Bradwell of Illinois, and others who were less so, such as Lelia Robinson of Massachusetts and Lavinia Goodell of Wisconsin. They systematically challenged the jurisprudence of separate spheres in lawsuits, in Congress and in state legislatures, seeking the right to practice law. This effort to redefine the existing norms and laws as to who should be permitted to practice law truly bound the pioneer women lawyers together.

Women in late nineteenth-century America gained admission to practice law in one of two ways. Some won decisions of state and federal courts. But by far the more common method was by passage of a state statute—or, in the case of the United States Supreme Court, the requirement of an act of Congress—that specifically permitted women to practice law. Even so, admission to lower courts, such as county courts, was often a prerequisite for admission to practice before a state supreme court. And either way, the task was not an easy one, for women had to persuade either male judges or male legislators that they were entitled to practice law. Between 1869 and 1899, thirty-five states and territories and the District of Columbia permitted women to practice law.[8] The United States Congress authorized women to practice law before the United States Supreme Court in 1879.[9] Although many state legislatures voluntarily admitted women to be licensed to practice law, a lawsuit or the threat of a lawsuit often galvanized state legislatures into allowing women to practice either by legislation or judicial decision. The ideas of the jurisprudence of integration, articulated most clearly in the lawsuits of women lawyers, shaped the efforts of women lawyers as they petitioned both the courts and the legislatures for the right to practice.

The jurisprudence of integration has its lineage in the woman's rights movement of the early nineteenth century. The personal experiences of early leaders of that movement reveal the inseparable connection. Sarah Grimké of South Carolina, for one, dreamed as a child of becoming a lawyer like her father and older brother, a dream that was never fulfilled. Similarly, Elizabeth Cady Stanton spent part of her childhood in her father's law office, both reading laws on marriage and property and discussing the legal rights of women with her father and his law clerks.[10] As they became adults, women like Stanton, Grimké, Susan B. Anthony, and Lucy Stone of Massachusetts, by working tirelessly in the abolitionist movement and later in the suffrage movement, helped to define an alternative to the separate spheres ideology that permeated American culture during the mid nineteenth century.[11] Lavinia Goodell, while still a student at the Brooklyn Heights Seminary, wrote to her sister in 1858 that she thought that "the study of law would be pleasant . . . [though] utterly impracticable." In particular, Goodell feared that her parents would disapprove of her desire to attend college, even though her father was an anti-slavery advocate, because her mother was "afraid I shall become identified with the 'woman's rights movement.' "[12]

Others tied the entrance of women into the legal profession directly to the woman's rights movement. As early as 1860, Elizabeth Jones of Ohio addressed the National Woman's Rights Convention, urging that "there be no proscription on account of sex [in the legal profession]." She believed that men in the legal profession would benefit from the "manners and morals" of women lawyers. But Jones also understood that women's place in law was not justified by their ability to civilize men. Talent, competition, and ability were to apply equally to aspiring women lawyers so that the marketplace, not a prohibition against women in law, would decide which lawyer was the best. These ideas became part of the foundation of the women lawyers movement as women tried to break into the all-male bar.[13]

Following the Civil War, the Radical Republicans in Congress re-shaped the social and legal landscape of southern states by passing what have become known as the Reconstruction amendments. The effect of these amendments on women's efforts to practice law was profound. The Thirteenth Amendment, adopted in 1865, ended the institution of slavery. The Fourteenth Amendment, adopted in 1868, sought to address the issue of citizenship by providing, in part, that "all persons born or naturalized in the United States and subject to the jurisdiction thereof, are citizens of the United States and of the State wherein they reside. No State shall make or enforce any law which shall abridge the privileges or immunities of citizens of the United States." The Fifteenth Amendment, adopted in 1870, guaranteed to freed blacks the right to vote. The hopes of Stanton, Anthony, and other woman's rights activists were dashed, however, because the Reconstruction amendments left the status of women as citizens or voters unchanged.

With the failure of the Reconstruction amendments to grant women the right to vote, the jurisprudence of integration expanded to include equal citizenship and voting rights for women. The adoption of the Fourteenth and Fifteenth Amendments to the Constitution, which extended equal political rights to freed African-Americans, also represented a turning point in the suffrage movement. With the exclusion of woman suffrage from the Reconstruction amendments, women in the 1860s became divided over the primacy of female versus African-American, male suffrage. The result was a split in the suffrage movement between the more radical National Woman Suffrage Association, which advocated immediate suffrage for women, and the more moderate American Woman Suffrage Association, which accepted African-American, male suffrage before woman suffrage.[14]

At issue was the complex question of the definition of citizenship for women under the privileges and immunities clause of the Fourteenth Amendment and whether women were entitled to citizenship and the right to vote under federal, constitutional law. The suffragists maintained that women were entitled to vote under the Fourteenth Amendment. Yet the women lawyers widened the debate over women's political rights in another way. By seeking the right to practice law, women lawyers also argued for an expansive conception of the Fourteenth Amendment, one that asked judges to decide that women lawyers were legally entitled to be part of the American polity. Akin to the right to vote, the right to practice law became a marker on the path to full citizenship for women. For women lawyers, gaining the right to practice law became a central tenet of their rejection of the jurisprudence of separate spheres.

The failure of Congress to grant women full citizenship and the right to vote provoked members of the suffrage movement to create in 1869 "a practical test" of their view that the Fourteenth Amendment gave women the right to vote. In the words of Susan B. Anthony, the suffrage movement moved the political debate from the "halls of legislation to the courts of final adjudication."[15] The more radical National Woman Suffrage Association adopted the position that the privileges and immunities clause of the Constitution already guaranteed to women the right to vote as well as full citizenship. Full citizenship for women, it was argued, was the basis of the right to vote. It only remained to test these principles in courts of law.[16]

A few women successfully registered to vote, but most officials turned them away when they tried to cast their ballots. Others were unable to register. Some of these women filed lawsuits against local officials claiming that they had a right to vote because they were citizens under the Fourteenth Amendment.[17] Women who later became lawyers, such as Marilla M. Ricker of New Hampshire and Catherine V. Waite of Illinois, tried to register to vote because woman's rights had been expanded by the Fourteenth Amendment. Susan B. Anthony's arrest and conviction in 1872 for attempting to register to vote two years after women had begun to try to do so remarkably failed to yield an appellate court decision on the Fourteenth Amendment, but they nevertheless became important symbols for the suffrage movement. After a highly publicized trial by jury in an upstate New York federal district court, the judge directed the jury to find Anthony guilty because the Fourteenth Amendment excluded women from the right to vote. Anthony did not appeal her case.[18]

At precisely the same time that suffragists asserted both at the ballot box and in the courtroom that women had the right to vote, women lawyers began their long campaign to win the legal right to practice law. Women lawyers like Myra Bradwell, Lavinia Goodell, and Belva Lockwood sought judicial decisions that would immediately entitle them to practice law.[19] Attacking the jurisprudence of separate spheres, women lawyers were at the center of this redefinition of the rights of women in the 1870s and 1880s. Their movement began with Bradwell's attempt to gain access to the Illinois bar and her unsuccessful appeal to the United States Supreme Court.[20] Bradwell was first, but she was not alone. Women lawyers followed her lead in quick succession, challenging the jurisprudence of separate spheres and, in the process, creating a jurisprudence of integration.[21]

Bradwell's journey through the Illinois Supreme Court and the United States Supreme Court was not as clearsighted as it first appeared. In 1868, Bradwell and her husband, James, also a lawyer, established the *Chicago Legal News*, a highly successful legal newspaper in Chicago.[22] Bradwell turned the *News* into one of the major journals of the nineteenth-century women lawyers movement, one that documented women's efforts to gain admission to practice law.[23] In order to practice law with her husband, Bradwell petitioned the Illinois Supreme Court in 1869 to be admitted as an attorney. Her petition revealed a mind steeped more in the principles of state, common law than in the tenets of federal, constitutional law. She stated, almost matter of factly, that she met the statutory requirements of admission—proper age, good moral character, and a successful examination by a lower court.[24] She claimed that the only issue was whether a woman was disqualified from receiving a license to practice law.[25] Following the lead of Arabella A. Mansfield, who was admitted to practice law in Iowa in 1869, Bradwell asserted that the most expedient way for the court to admit women in Illinois was simply to interpret the word "he" in the attorney licensing statute as including women.[26] Mansfield secured both the approval of local attorneys and the concurrence of a local judge, who agreed that the gender pronoun statute of Iowa permitted women to be admitted as attorneys.[27] Less than a year after Mansfield's admission to practice as the first woman lawyer in America, the Iowa legislature resolved any lingering ambiguity over women's right to practice law by amending its statute to include "women and colored persons."[28]

The Supreme Court of Illinois ignored the Mansfield precedent and rejected Bradwell's application because she was a married woman. Writing to her through the clerk, the court stated that Bradwell would not be bound by the obligations between an attorney and a client "by reason of the disability imposed by [her] married condition."[29] The court also resurrected the legal doctrine of the common law of coverture, in which married women had no independent legal existence from their husbands, and fit it to the new task at hand. Bradwell's efforts to gain the right to practice law were just beginning. But rather than arguing broad principles of the right of women to equality under the Constitution, she responded to the court with a narrowly argued Additional Brief that asserted the right of a woman to practice law based on Illinois statutes and common law.[30] Citing the noted nineteenth-century legal commentator Joseph Story on the law of agency, she argued that attorneys were agents who entered into contracts for services with their clients.[31] To Bradwell, married women, *femme couvert*, were agents at common law who could act as attorneys as did men.[32] She urged the court to conclude that married women were entitled to practice law in part because the married woman's property acts of Illinois permitted women to own property and to enter into contracts.[33] She also asserted that the admission of women to practice law was a beneficial public policy,[34] reminding the court that the legislature had already contracted with her as a married woman to publish the decisions of the Illinois Supreme Court in the *Chicago Legal News* "as if she were AN UNMARRIED WOMAN."[35]

The interplay between state, common-law arguments, and principles of federal, constitutional law in the Bradwell briefs seemed to assume a new and bolder meaning after the Bradwells met with Elizabeth Cady Stanton and Susan B. Anthony late in 1869.[36] Until that time, Bradwell's legal arguments had centered on her rights as a woman under state law, particularly the common law of coverture, not on principles of equality or citizenship under federal, constitutional law. Almost immediately following her discussions with Stanton and Anthony, it was as though Bradwell had finally grasped the constitutional implications of her claim. Amending her Additional Brief on January 3, 1870, she challenged the constitutional underpinnings of the jurisprudence of separate spheres.[37] She argued that she was entitled to practice law because of the protections of the Fourteenth Amendment and the "civil rights bill," tying her claim to the right extended by Congress to ex-slaves. She also advanced an equal protection argument, asserting that she had "the right to exercise and follow the profession of an attorney-at-law upon the same terms, conditions and restrictions as are applied to and imposed upon every other citizen of Illinois." She questioned the constitutional conception of the jurisprudence of separate spheres by claiming that she had been a citizen of Vermont, was a citizen of Illinois, and was also a citizen of the United States.[38] Asserting her rights as a citizen of the United States, she claimed that the Fourteenth Amendment protected her right to carry on a trade or profession in any state. In just a few sentences, Bradwell extended her attack on the jurisprudence of separate spheres to include not only state, common law but also federal, constitutional law.

The Illinois Supreme Court remained unpersuaded. Instead, it seized the opportunity to define the masculinity of the law in terms of the jurisprudence of separate spheres under common law. Ignoring the issue of whether a married woman could legally enter into contracts, the court held that "the sex of the applicant, independent of coverture, is, as our law stands now, a sufficient reason for not granting this license."[39] Although the court acknowledged that an attorney was an agent, it also ruled that an attorney was an "officer of the court" and that the legislature did not intend for women to hold such offices.[40] With the common law of coverture suddenly not an issue, the court searched for a variety of other reasons to reject Bradwell's claim of equality.

Directly confronting the relationship between suffrage and women's right to make and administer laws as attorneys, the court noted that "the right of suffrage has not been conceded."[41] Adhering to the natural-law view of women, the court said that "God designed the sexes to occupy different spheres of action, and that it belonged to men to make, apply and execute the laws."[42] *In re* Bradwell represented the decision of only one court. Its influence derived from the fact that it was the first decision by a state supreme court to grapple with the rights of women to practice law. It thereby outlined the basic tenets of the jurisprudence of separate spheres.

Central to the thinking of the jurisprudence of separate spheres was the belief that women naturally occupied "different spheres of action."[43] According to this view, it was the law of nature that women both lived in separate spheres from men and that the practice of law was closed to women. Justice Charles Lawrence in *In re* Bradwell enunciated perhaps the most common theme of the jurisprudence of separate spheres when he said that "God designed the sexes to occupy different spheres" and that men made and applied the laws.[44]

Other courts followed the same point of view. Invoking a similar natural law view of women, Chief Justice Ryan of the Supreme Court of Wisconsin asserted in the case of *Lavinia Goodell* in 1875 that the "law of nature destines and qualifies the female sex for the bearing and nurture of the children of our race and for the custody of the homes of the world and their maintenance in love and honor."[45] To Chief Justice Ryan, the profession of law was inconsistent with women's "sacred duties of their sex."[46] Ryan saw womanhood as having special qualities—gentle graces, quick sensibility, tender susceptibility, purity, delicacy, and subordination of hard reason to sympathetic feeling—none of which were qualifications for "forensic strife."[47] Justice Joseph Bradley of the United States Supreme Court echoed this same natural law view of women, asserting that "the paramount destiny and mission of women are to fulfill the noble and benign offices of wife and mother."[48] Similarly, Bradley emphasized the different spheres of men and women and that women were thus "unfit . . . for many of the occupations of civil life."[49] Justice Charles C. Nott of the United States Court of Claims went so far in 1873 as to state that the legislature may not even have authority over women's legal status because it was "by an unwritten law interwoven with the very fabric of society."[50]

Judges viewed the female character as "unfit" for the legal profession and therefore that women had to be protected by men in order to preserve their female sensibilities. Equally, male judges seemed to think that because of their delicate natures women were ill prepared for the "juridical conflicts of the courtroom."[51] They claimed that women were innocents who should be protected from the "brutish" and "obscene" side of life. In the words of Chief Justice Ryan, women had to be protected from "all the nastiness in the world," all the "unclean issues, all the collateral questions of sodomy, incest, rape, seduction, fornication, adultery, pregnancy, bastardy, legitimacy, prostitution, lascivious cohabitation, abortion, infanticide, obscene publications, libel and slander of sex, impotence, divorce: all the nameless catalogue of indecencies, *la chronique scandaleuse* of all the vices and all the infirmities of society."[52] It was "bad enough for men" to have to endure them, according to Chief Justice Ryan.[53]

Judge A. H. Young of the Hennepin County, Minnesota, court of common pleas took the natural law view of women a step further by arguing that married women had a natural inability to commit themselves to the "calling" of the law. In 1876, he rejected the application of Martha Angle Dorsett to be admitted to practice law even though

Dorsett had gained admission to practice in Iowa.[54] Reflecting the natural law view that the "part assigned to women by nature . . . [i]s inconsistent with" a career in law, Judge Young asserted that the domestic duties of women "prevented women from committing time to devote to a law practice."[55] Judge Young explicitly linked the limitations of women according to his view of natural law with the perception that women had insufficient time to devote to law practice. Women were even a threat to the profession because they would lower standards as they tried to both work full-time and care for their husbands and children.[56] Judge Young acknowledged that single women could practice law, but he refused to admit Dorsett without legislative action. Contradicting himself, he concluded that once a statute authorizing women to practice was passed, he had no doubt that the legal profession would "heartily welcome to its ranks [Dorsett] and others of like merit."[57] Judge Young seemed to believe that legislative action would miraculously overcome his concerns about women in the legal profession.

Judges tied the separate spheres argument to the common law. If courts had never sanctioned women to practice law, nineteenth-century judges could not create that precedent. Arguing that women attorneys were unknown in England but citing little evidence to support their view, judges literally created what they believed to be a common law tradition that was devoid of women lawyers.[58] Chief Justice Ryan put it succinctly: "We cannot but think the common law wise in excluding women from the profession of the law."[59] Justice Nott viewed the common law as requiring that a woman be responsible for the family and the home, a very traditional viewpoint. It was the founders of the common law, asserted Justice Bradley, who had developed the maxim that a woman had no legal existence apart from her husband.[60]

Some judges argued that the common law prevented married women from practicing law because women were not bound by either express or implied contracts without their husbands' consent.[61] Although many states had adopted statutes that permitted women to enter into contracts, judges reused the concept of the common law of coverture.[62] Justice Nott asserted that the common law of coverture regarded men and women as "one." He speculated that if a woman lawyer misapplied a client's funds or committed gross negligence or fraud, her husband could be sued at common law for what she had done as an attorney.[63] Unmarried women, in contrast, did not suffer the common law disabilities of married women, according to the judges. Thus unmarried women presented a dilemma for many judges because their rights were very similar to men's, except for the vote. Some judges overcame this inconsistency by claiming that because unmarried women were naturally destined to become wives and mothers, even they could not practice law.[64]

The jurisprudence of separate spheres strictly adhered to the judicial view that a court should not interpret the law to reach an outcome that the legislature had not specifically intended. For example, general statutory provisions requiring that the words "he," "him," and "his" apply equally to females were rejected under the separate spheres view. These judges would not revise the law on an issue of such great magnitude by resorting to formalities of statutory construction. By the 1870s, the discretion of state courts to admit women to practice law waned as the jurisprudence of separate spheres required that states enact specific statutes permitting women to practice law. Between 1874 and 1886, for example, ten states passed laws admitting women to practice law, whereas only three states admitted women by the discretion of a court. The statutory requirements reflected the limited conception of citizenship accorded to women in the late nineteenth century. Without an affirmative vote of the state legislature, so the argument went, women were not entitled to practice law.[65]

Judges expressed a far greater concern, one that linked the practice of law by women directly with the woman suffrage movement. In the 1870s, judges feared that admitting women to practice law would entitle them to vote. Although the separate spheres arguments were most common in the early 1870s, judges such as Chief Justice Ryan believed that if the court admitted women to practice law by "ignoring the distinction of sex, we do not perceive why it should not emasculate the constitution itself and include females in the constitutional right of male suffrage and male qualification."[66] Ryan's image of an "emasculated constitution" graphically revealed the depth of his feelings, as a man and as a judge, about the prospect of women becoming lawyers. The court in *In re* Bradwell also explicitly acknowledged that "it belonged to men to make, apply and execute the laws," not to women.[67] In rejecting the suffrage movement as a basis for justifying a change in the law, judges in the 1870s began to formulate a legal rationale that legitimated excluding women from full participation in government.

21

The volatile issue of suffrage for women and the jurisprudence of separate spheres merged as state and federal court judges explicitly linked the two. Ironically, late-nineteenth-century judges, despite their avowed efforts to separate law and politics, fused the political question of suffrage with women's legal right to practice law. Justice Lawrence, in *In re* Bradwell, anticipated the parallels between women being licensed to practice law and "that school of reform which . . . claims for women participation in the making and the administering of the law." Justice Nott stated in 1873 that admission to the bar "constitutes an office."[68] The judges who advocated the separate spheres argument were becoming concerned that women actually thought they were entitled to make and administer the law. Women, the judges realized incredulously, believed that they could participate in the courtroom as lawyers. Moreover, the judges came to understand that if women could become lawyers, they could become public officers, or even voters.

Bradwell pinned her hopes on an appeal to the Supreme Court of the United States: she sought a decision that would establish a constitutional right of equality for women lawyers. But a dramatic decision was not to be. In Bradwell v. State of Illinois in 1873, the court held that women were not entitled to the equal protection and privileges and immunities of the constitution of the United States to gain admission to practice law under the laws of the states.[69] Bradwell v. State of Illinois was argued and decided together with the Slaughterhouse Cases in 1873, the first judicial interpretation of the Fourteenth Amendment by the court.[70] The Slaughterhouse Cases turned on the issue of whether the city of New Orleans or private owners could regulate the operation of the city's slaughterhouses. Justice Samuel Miller, writing for the majority, articulated a dual conception of citizenship, one in which individuals had protections as citizens of the United States that were distinct from those guaranteed by the individual states.[71] With a common body of "privileges and immunities" placed outside of the protection of the federal government, Justice Miller narrowly interpreted the scope of the Fourteenth Amendment. The result was that the Fourteenth Amendment was not to be used, at least in the 1870s and 1880s, to achieve federal regulation of state interests.[72]

The jurisprudence of the Slaughterhouse Cases dealt a serious blow to the legal strategy of the women lawyers movement and its allies. By including the Fourteenth Amendment argument in her state court appeal at the eleventh hour, Bradwell preserved an appeal for the United States Supreme Court, but to no avail. Justice Miller, again writing the opinion in Bradwell v. State of Illinois, specifically referred to the Slaughterhouse Cases and the legal principles he expressed in that case: "The right to control and regulate the granting of [a] license to practice law in the courts of a state is one of those powers which are not transferred for its protection to the Federal government, and its exercise is in no manner governed or controlled by citizenship of the United States in the party seeking such license."[73] The court refused to understand Bradwell v. State of Illinois as a gender issue. Instead, it defined the problem for women lawyers as a licensing question like that regarding the New Orleans slaughterhouses, one that was ultimately controlled by each state. At one level, Justice Miller treated women equally; neither women nor slaughterhouses had protected federal interests under the Fourteenth Amendment.

This narrow conception of the Fourteenth Amendment had far-reaching effects for women. State and federal court judges construed the issue of women's right to practice law equally with men as strictly within the control of each state. Women were citizens of the federal system, but with rights different from men; they were also citizens of their states, with their respective rights. Those rights did not include the right to practice law unless specifically permitted by state statute, judicial decision, or state constitutional amendment. Because of the court's decision in Bradwell, women lawyers not only lost in their attempt to gain the right to practice law by judicial decision; they also had to overcome the power of a decision of the United States Supreme Court.

Matthew H. Carpenter, a senator from Wisconsin and an experienced constitutional lawyer, represented both Myra Bradwell and the New Orleans slaughterhouses in the Supreme Court. In the Bradwell case, he argued that if admission to practice law was open to all in one state, then the same should be true in every other state. But Carpenter made one significant concession in his argument before the United States Supreme Court. Seeking to allay the fears of the justices about the relationship between the right to practice law and the right to vote, Carpenter acknowledged that the right to vote was not a privilege or immunity controlled by the states; rather, it was a political right.[74] Carpenter tried to remove the volatile issue of suffrage from Bradwell's case, hoping to gain some ground on behalf of women lawyers rather than losing the case because of the suffrage issue.

Underlying Bradwell v. State of Illinois, however, was the majority's belief in state power within federalism. To Justice Miller, the licensing of women lawyers was similar to the regulation of slaughterhouses. In contrast, Justice Joseph Bradley's concurring opinion sharply focused on a legal rhetoric that used the separate spheres jurisprudence to curtail Bradwell's demand for equal rights. He argued that Bradwell had erroneously assumed that women were entitled to the privileges and immunities of citizens to engage in professional life. Tying Bradwell's constitutional claim to women's rights as citizens, Bradley concluded that "it is not every citizen of every age, sex and condition that is qualified for every calling and position."[75] Bradley anticipated the views of Judge Young of Minnesota that women were not qualified to become lawyers. Admission to practice law was not a constitutional right but a question of the power of the state to police its citizenry. Bradley concluded that so long as the state properly exercised its police powers, no abridgement of Bradwell's privileges and immunities had occurred.[76]

The concept of the legislature's police power emerged among jurists in the mid-nineteenth century as the major legal category for states to regulate the health, safety, and morals of their populace.[77] It was to the police power, which was a known and tested legal construct, that Justices Bradley, Stephen Field, and Noah H. Swayne gravitated in Bradwell v. State of Illinois. They were more comfortable with a decision that limited women's right to practice law by reason of the police power than with one that did so using the uncharted waters of the Fourteenth Amendment. The only dissent in Bradwell was by Chief Justice Salmon Chase, and it was delivered without an opinion.[78]

The effect of Bradwell was to turn the issue of women lawyers over to the state legislatures and state courts. The right to practice law, the court declared, was not one of the privileges and immunities of the Fourteenth Amendment, and it was not a right of citizenship in the United States.[79] Bradley's concurrence, however, underscored the fact that late-nineteenth-century jurists reacted aggressively to the arguments of women lawyers for a jurisprudence of integration. Myra Bradwell's state and federal court arguments and the decisions they spawned helped lay the groundwork for a jurisprudence of integration as well as for a new rhetoric among male judges responding to women's demand for equal rights.

Far from being the path-breaking decision that women lawyers and suffragists had hoped for, Bradwell v. State of Illinois reinforced the jurisprudence of separate spheres by shifting the licensing of women lawyers to the states. Moreover, although some state legislatures permitted women to be licensed as lawyers, no state court had yet concluded that women could practice law.

Virginia Minor took an approach as assertive as Bradwell's when she tried to obtain the right to vote by judicial decision. But Minor had a more clearly defined legal strategy than did Bradwell. Whereas Bradwell had asserted that her right to practice law was protected by her status as a citizen of the United States, Minor argued that she was entitled to vote because she was a citizen of the United States. The court disagreed with Minor as well. In deciding Minor v. Happersett in 1874, the court acknowledged that women were "citizens" of the United States, but it determined that the right of suffrage was not part of the Constitution at the time of the adoption of the Fourteenth Amendment.[80] The court noted that "women were excluded from suffrage in nearly all of the states."[81] It concluded with the refrain of the jurisprudence of separate spheres: only the legislature could change the law.[82] Had the Supreme Court held that women were entitled to vote, it would have radically changed the arguments that women lawyers faced in the next two decades because the jurisprudence of separate spheres relied on the fact that women were not citizens, could not vote, and therefore could not be lawyers. In response to the decision in Minor, suffragists called for an amendment to the Constitution that would guarantee women the right to vote.[83]

Women's efforts to expand the scope of citizenship under the Fourteenth Amendment to include the right to vote and the right to practice law did not stop with the decisions in Minor and Bradwell. Although a federal, constitutional decision establishing women as equal citizens with men still eluded them, women, especially lawyers, pursued state court remedies to seek a broadly expanded place for women. During the late nineteenth century, women went to court to continue to secure their rights to participate in public life: to vote;[84] to be a justice of the peace;[85] to be a notary public;[86] to serve as school district directors;[87] school committee members;[88] school officers;[89] and prosecuting attorneys;[90] and, of course, to practice law. But women continued to meet resistance in state courts. For example, in Massachusetts in 1871, the Supreme Judicial Court denied women the right to serve as justices of the peace because the justices concluded that the position was a judicial office, which was closed to women.[91] Though women legally served on school committees and on the state board of charity in Massachusetts, these limited rights were based on the separate spheres argument and what the justices saw as women's unique capacity to contribute to education and social welfare.[92]

A related position was that of notary public. By 1893, fourteen states permitted women to serve as notaries, whereas in twenty-one other states, women either could not serve as notaries or the law was unsettled.[93] Adhering to the jurisprudence of separate spheres, the Massachusetts Supreme Judicial Court prohibited women from serving as notaries because it viewed the position as a public office not open to women.[94] Similarly, the Tennessee Supreme Court held that although women were citizens, they could not vote and therefore could not serve as notaries.[95]

Women lawyers achieved little success in the courtroom in the 1870s, but they scored some victories. Six state legislatures admitted women to practice law by statutes and another six states and the District of Columbia admitted women to practice by approval of the courts. With the exception of North Carolina and the District of Columbia, all of these states were midwestern and western states, which tended to have more liberal policies on the role of women in law. Midwestern law schools admitted women, and some territories permitted women to serve as jurors.[96]

After the Supreme Court's decision in *Bradwell*, it was up to state legislatures to pass specific statutes authorizing women to vote. Even by the 1880s, it was rare for a state court to admit a woman to practice law without an enabling statute. State legislatures such as Illinois and Wisconsin admitted women to practice law, despite adverse court decisions, as did the United States Congress. Congress required that women lawyers be admitted to practice law for three years before the supreme court of their state or of the District of Columbia.[97] Belva Lockwood, who dedicated herself to integrating the state and federal courts, first sought admission to the United States Supreme Court in 1873. Chief Justice Waite, in an unpublished decision on Mrs. Lockwood's Case, denied her application for admission but invited the Congress to act on the matter.[98] The House of Representatives quickly passed the bill permitting women to practice law before the Supreme Court, but the same bill languished in the Senate from 1877 to 1879 before passing by a mere two-vote majority.[99]

This shift toward admission by legislation reinforced the disarray of the gender polity in the 1870s. Judges and lawyers did not know what to do with women lawyers or how to fit them into the prevailing conceptions of citizenship and suffrage, much less the practice of law. As a result, women lawyers were often excluded because they threatened the legal order.

With the 1880s came a sharper confrontation between the jurisprudence of separate spheres and the jurisprudence of integration. Women lawyers initiated a new series of cases to test the jurisprudence of separate spheres, with startling results. The rhetorical stridency of judges' natural law decisions became muted. Instead, judges reinterpreted the jurisprudence of separate spheres to be based on the inability of women lawyers to hold public office. One of the defining cases was Lelia J. Robinson's Case, decided in 1881 by the Massachusetts Supreme Judicial Court.[100] The *Robinson* decision explicitly tied the volatile political issue of suffrage to women's common-law rights to practice law. Chief Justice Horace Gray, later an associate justice of the United States Supreme Court, concluded that in Massachusetts an attorney was "almost" a public officer. To permit women to practice law implicitly granted them the right to vote. Although judicial concern over suffrage was typical in the jurisprudence of separate spheres, Chief Justice Gray handled the issue using legalistic terms rather than those of natural law. Gray elevated the concept of public office so that it was central to his decision. He held that an attorney was "very near" to being a public officer, making it seemingly impossible for women to be attorneys without winning the right to vote.[101]

But as suffrage became more of a legitimate political movement in the 1880s, and as some professional women gained equality, even this argument was challenged.[102] Lelia Robinson, for example, graduated from Boston University Law School with impeccable credentials. The fact that she could not find a job led her to apply to be admitted to practice before the Supreme Judicial Court of Massachusetts.[103] Robinson, with no apparent background in the woman's rights movement, quickly grasped the task at hand. She briefed her case meticulously, arguing for an expansive judicial construction of the 1876 Massachusetts licensing statute. She urged the court to interpret the word "citizen" in the licensing statute to include women. She pointed out that women in Massachusetts enjoyed a wide variety of rights as citizens, including the right to vote in certain elections.[104] Robinson argued that the legislative body of Massachusetts, the General Court, had constructive knowledge that women practiced law in other states when it revised the licensing statute in 1876. Moreover, she stated, the General Court did not intend to restrict the practice of law to "those possessed of full political rights only"; rather, it intended to include women. She anticipated the issue of whether an attorney was a judicial officer, arguing that an attorney was "a *local office* of an *administrative* character."[105]

The Supreme Judicial Court asked the Bar Association of the City of Boston to brief the legal issues in opposition to Robinson.[106] The bar brief, prepared by Boston lawyers Robert Morse, Jr., and Herbert L. Harding, applied the federal, constitutional arguments in the Supreme Court's *Bradwell* decision directly to the state law issues that she had raised. They employed the same dual conception of citizenship as was used in the *Slaughterhouse* and *Bradwell* cases, but they applied it to an analysis of the meaning of the word "citizen" under Massachusetts law.[107] Arguing for a narrow interpretation of "citizen," they believed that the 1876 licensing statute encompassed adult males who were entitled to vote.[108] According to the bar brief, an attorney was an officer of the court and was dependent on the court for admission to practice. They found no legislative intent in the past century "to throw the privilege [of law practice] open to women."[109] Rather, they argued, the rules for admission revealed a tendency to reverse the "levelling" of the barriers of bar admission, which was most likely a reference to the bar's efforts to control the admission of immigrants to law practice. More importantly, the bar brief rejected the view that the Fourteenth Amendment entitled women to be lawyers. Just as the right to vote was controlled by statute, so too was the right to practice law.[110] Morse and Harding recommended that the issue be resolved by the legislature, not the courts.

Robinson responded to the bar brief with unusual vigor. Despite the

Supreme Court's decisions in *Slaughterhouse* and *Bradwell*, she urged the court to adopt a broad conception of citizenship under Massachusetts law. Robinson attacked the dual conception of citizenship, arguing both for equal rights and a broad interpretation of the licensing law. Revealing a strikingly modern conception of discrimination theory—one that linked race, disability, and gender—she asked rhetorically if the court had the power to "refuse to admit a black man on account of his color; a man in such confirmed ill health that he is unable to stand when he addresses the court, on account of his physical weakness; a man who had lost both hands, because he could not write his name."[111] Robinson's comparison of women's right to practice law with that of African-American men was familiar to other women lawyers.[112] When Ada H. Kepley was refused admission to practice law in Illinois in 1870, an African-American man received his license the same day.[113]

Robinson, however, was pragmatic about women's right to vote: she argued that the right to practice law need not be linked with suffrage. Like Matthew Carpenter, Myra Bradwell's attorney, she rejected the bar's fears of judicially declared suffrage, charging that the bar was trying to "frighten" the court. This line of thought revealed the realistic side of the jurisprudence of integration. Winning the right to practice law by a court decision was a milestone and became a step toward the ultimate goal of suffrage for women. But it was not made without a sacrifice.[114]

Robinson's supplemental brief used language cultivated from her roles as both a woman and a lawyer. To chastise the "gentlemen of the Bar Association" for raising the issue of female suffrage and office holding, Robinson used a domestic metaphor common among women. She likened the bar's arguments to those of the "wily nurse" who scared a child into "subjection" so that the child would not "develop some will of its own."[115] She criticized the bar association for quoting the "angry words" of Wisconsin Chief Justice Ryan in his 1875 *Goodell* decision. In that case, Ryan had expressed the fear that a judicial decision admitting women to practice law would result in a "sweeping revolution of social order." Robinson pointed to the use of this quotation by the bar association as fomenting rage rather than keeping to the point in question— "as women are often accused of doing in argument."[116] Moreover, Robinson argued, women in other states practiced law without creating the feared "social revolution."[117]

Robinson's briefs and her claim that her task before the court was to argue law, not "questions of policy" displayed both her realism and her understanding of the law of the woman's rights movement. Although she was conscious of being the first woman to petition for admission to the bar in Massachusetts, of bringing a "test case," and of using the language of legal discourse familiar to other proponents of woman's rights, she was also tentative. She expressed the hope that her case, if successful, would be "a help to women without being an injury to the community."[118] Robinson's brief illustrated a legal mind breaking free from the constraints of the jurisprudence of separate spheres. Trained in the classical legal thought of the nineteenth century, Robinson advocated creative judicial activism on behalf of women, but she tempered her views with the knowledge of the limits of judicial thought and action in nineteenth-century Massachusetts.

Robinson lost in court, but she nevertheless secured her victory when Massachusetts adopted a statute specifically permitting women to practice law on the same terms as men. Robinson gained admission to practice the following year, and thereby crossed, as she put it, "the grand Rubicon which made me a full fledged attorney." The Bar Association of the City of Boston, however, did not accept women members until 1916.[119]

The *Robinson* decision had an immediate effect on cases in other state courts. The supreme court of Oregon cited the *Robinson* case approvingly as the jurisprudential benchmark justifying the denial of women's admission to practice law. The supreme court of New York also decided against the right of women to practice law. Citing the *Robinson* case, the New York court concluded that the legislature authorized only "male citizens" to practice law.[120]

Ironically, during 1882, the same year that Massachusetts passed a law permitting women to practice law, the neighboring Connecticut Supreme Court interpreted its attorney licensing statute in the case of *In re* Hall, holding that women could practice law.[121] Ruling on facts strikingly similar to those in the *Robinson* case, Chief Justice John Duane Park held that the Connecticut licensing statute's use of "persons" applied equally to men and women. The jurisprudence of integration, which women lawyers had advocated since 1869, finally became ratified by this judicial decision. The jurisprudence of integration was not a new idea. Women lawyers and woman's rights activists had advocated the jurisprudence of integration since at least 1869: it was just a matter of time before state court judges agreed.

Between 1882 and 1893, the jurisprudence of integration suddenly gained judicial acceptance. The legal decisions of this period represented one of American women's first successes in using the judicial system to change radically their legal status. *Hall* was one of five decisions between 1882 and 1893 that admitted women lawyers by judicial decision rather than legislative statute. Courts in Connecticut, Pennsylvania, Colorado, New Hampshire, and Indiana expanded the rights of women to entitle them to practice law.[122] Classical legal thinkers' concern that only the legislature could change the law received barely a mention in these rulings. It is remarkable that these five cases addressed the same issues as did the cases denying women the right to practice law, yet the courts came to opposite conclusions.

The *Hall* case is the best example. Mary Hall had studied law, passed the examination of the Connecticut Superior Court, and sought only a determination that a woman could legally be admitted to practice. The bar of Hartford County recommended the admission of Hall subject to a decision of the Supreme Court, which set up another test case in a state court. George McManus of the Hartford bar argued in a straightforward manner for Hall that the common law and legislative history of Connecticut have given to "women equal right, scope and opportunity with men whenever possible." Pointing out that women preached in pulpits, practiced medicine, taught in public schools, and acted as executors, guardians, trustees and overseers, McManus argued that the Connecticut state constitution did not prohibit women from any public duty. If Connecticut even permitted "soulless corporations" to act in a fiduciary capacity, why not allow women to be lawyers?[123] In contrast, George Collier, also of the Hartford bar, restated the jurisprudence of separate spheres: women were not specifically permitted to practice law; only the legislature could change the law; a lawyer was a public officer; and the court should follow the precedents of the two *Bradwell* cases, the *Goodell* case, and the *Lockwood* case.[124]

Chief Justice Park rejected Collier's position—and with it the entire jurisprudence of separate spheres. In broad language that expanded the rights of women, he held that women in Connecticut could be admitted to practice law. He defined the question as one of statutory construction: did the Connecticut licensing statute include women? Park argued that because the last revision of the 1875 Connecticut licensing statute included the words "such persons," it therefore was passed with the knowledge that women were practicing law in other states.[125] Park presumed the legislators to have acted with that knowledge because no words of limitation were inserted. He further stated that "all statutes are to be construed . . . in favor of equality of rights." For Park, if a statute did not express a clear limitation on liberty, that limitation did not exist.[126]

Chief Justice Park confronted directly the issue of officeholding. The attorney as an officeholder was a minor issue in Park's opinion. He concluded, in a remarkably realistic appraisal of the status of the nineteenth-century lawyer, that if "an attorney is to be regarded as an officer, it is in the lower sense."[127] With a deft stroke, Park undercut the opinion of Chief Justice Gray in *Robinson* by defining a lawyer as a "lower" sort of officer. Park swept aside the precedents of the jurisprudence of separate spheres, becoming the first judge in America to declare that a woman could be admitted to practice law by judicial decision.[128]

The *Hall* case represented a major departure in how American judges viewed their roles within the legal system. Rejecting classical legal thought, the court in *Hall* broke the pattern of reliance on the legislature and decided the issue of woman's rights on the grounds of equal protection of the laws: "We are not to forget that all statutes are to be construed, as far as possible, in favor of equality of rights."[129]

As early as 1869, women lawyers had persistently argued this very position as well as the view that courts had the power to admit women lawyers. Classical legal thought notwithstanding, Myra Bradwell, Lelia Robinson, Belva Lockwood, and Mary Hall had all acted on the belief that courts could integrate the legal profession by judicial decision. Although only Mary Hall was successful, the women lawyers movement sought to empower judges to give more rights to women. The jurisprudence of separate spheres, in contrast, had spoken to fears of an expansion of woman's rights—whether to become an attorney or to vote—by judicial decision. Yet in the 1880s and early 1890s, this classical legal thought had eroded as courts plainly saw the reality of women practicing law.

As Chief Justice Park recognized that "women in different parts of the country are and for some time have been following the profession of the law," the jurisprudence of separate spheres was not only rejected, it was also ridiculed.[130] The paradox of the jurisprudence of separate spheres became obvious. As legislatures began to admit women to practice law, the advocates of a jurisprudence of separate spheres could no longer justify women's subordinate status. Judge P. Thayer of the Court of Common Pleas of Philadelphia observed in 1884 that "positive legislation has everywhere broken down the barriers [for women]."[131] To Judge Thayer, a woman was no longer a "plaything or a drudge, or compelled to bound her aspirations by the nursery or the parlor."[132] Thayer observed that women pursued vocations without sacrificing status or social standing; held national and state offices; practiced law in at least thirteen states, two territories and the District of Columbia; and had been admitted to practice before the United States Supreme Court. Thayer's perspective was clear: the "revolution is over."[133]

As the issue of women in law arose more frequently, judges disagreed more often with their predecessors. Central among the points of contention was whether an attorney was an officer of the court. If this was true, women could not be admitted to practice because only males could be officers under the laws of the states. This was the lesson of *Robinson*. Chief Justice Gray had redefined the issue of women in law by rejecting the natural law thinking of the 1870s, which had relegated women to the household, and he had concluded that officeholding prevented women from exercising the right to practice law without a specific statutory mandate. The *Hall* decision undermined *Robinson* by dismissing in but a paragraph the idea that lawyers were public officers. Park's view of nineteenth-century law practice was certainly more realistic than that of Chief Justice Gray. Gray had presented a romanticized view of the lawyer as well as the lawyer's role in the courtroom—a perspective that was slowly fading, even in Boston.[134]

In 1889, Marilla Ricker and Lelia Robinson came together with Chief Justice Charles Doe of New Hampshire to resolve with unparalleled legal erudition and clarity the issue of whether an attorney was a public official. Ricker petitioned to be admitted to practice law in New Hampshire. Almost twenty years earlier, Ricker had registered to vote in New Hampshire, but her vote had been refused at the ballot box because she was a woman. She had been admitted to the bar in the District of Columbia, practiced there, and sought admission in New Hampshire. Ricker prepared her own brief, citing both cases and statutes providing for the admission of women.[135]

Robinson assisted Ricker in her application, preparing a supplemental brief for the court. Robinson's brief focused on two points: that the words "person" or "citizen" should be interpreted to include women; and that the decision in *Hall*, together with the knowledge of the Massachusetts statute of 1882, meant that the New Hampshire licensing statute passed in 1883 had been intended to include women.[136]

In the hands of Chief Justice Doe, the decision in *Ricker's Petition* transcended the briefs of Ricker and Robinson. Forty-eight pages long, Doe's opinion directly challenged the jurisprudence of separate spheres, in particular the decision of Justice Gray in the *Robinson* case. Doe concluded that an attorney in New Hampshire was not a public officer and that women were not prohibited from being lawyers at common law. Chief Justice Doe's learning was prodigious. He cited cases from American jurisdictions and seventeenth-, eighteenth-, and nineteenth-century English cases and statutes. No opinion of the nineteenth century on the admission of women to practice law matched Doe's for thoroughness.

Doe turned the decision in *Robinson* on its head, concluding that the attorney "is not generally regarded as a public officer."[137] He defined the issue not as whether women were excluded because the lawyer was an officer of the court but as whether the nature of the employment disqualified women.[138] Doe moved the discussion from the subjective label "officer of the court" to an objective test of whether an attorney performed actions that could not be done by women.[139] Doe held that women were excluded from acting as attorneys only for those offices defined by state law to require electoral and official power. Because of Doe's preeminence as a jurist, his opinion carried substantial weight as precedent. Lelia Robinson claimed victory, and the news traveled fast as she celebrated her success with her friend, Catharine Waugh McCulloch, an attorney in Illinois and a longtime supporter of woman's rights.[140]

With state courts in Connecticut, Pennsylvania, and New Hampshire holding that women could practice law, it was not surprising that a western state such as Colorado followed their lead. When Mary Thomas petitioned to be admitted as an attorney in Colorado, Chief

Justice Joseph C. Helm of the Colorado Supreme Court readily held in favor of her admission in 1891.[141] Like Chief Justice Park in the *Hall* case, Helm rejected the decisions of the jurisprudence of separate spheres. In a remarkable break with other nineteenth-century jurists, he refused to "indulge" in the paternalistic, natural law argument that women were not physically capable of being lawyers. Similarly, he refused to decide the case on the "historic" common law or on usages in England or America; instead, he preferred to examine the past fifty years of the legal status of women. Helm also clearly understood the limits of the jurisprudence of separate spheres. He noted that each decision against admitting women to practice was followed by a statute permitting them to do so.[142]

Chief Justice Helm emphasized the sexual integration of women in nineteenth-century America. As a result, he held that the word "person" in the licensing statutes included women.[143] But were attorneys "*civil officers*" such that women, who could not vote, could not be admitted as attorneys? Like Chief Justices Park and Doe, Helm held that attorneys were not civil officers per se. Although Helm acknowledged that attorneys were in some sense "officers of the court," in his view they performed only a "*quasi* public duty." Helm realistically assessed the profession of law as "a purely private matter . . . secured solely for the advancement of private interests." Lawyers who served as prosecuting attorneys were either elected or appointed independently of their admission to the bar.[144] By distinguishing lawyers from elected officials, Helm easily removed the suffrage argument from the case and advanced the jurisprudence of integration.

Justice Leonard J. Hackney of the supreme court of Indiana agreed with the *Hall*, *Ricker*, and *Thomas* decisions in his 1893 opinion on *In re Petition of Leach*.[145] Hackney focused more closely on the right of every citizen to choose a vocation, regardless of sex.[146] "Citizenship belongs to women," said Hackney, who rejected the need for the legislature to pass a statute enabling women to practice.[147] Hackney resolved easily the issue of whether an attorney was a full civil officer or simply an officer of the court by concluding that the court was required to admit women as lawyers. This position was consistent with the laws of the state.

The ideas of the jurisprudence of integration gained momentum and by 1890 reflected a broader conception of woman's rights. As women began to attend law school, practice law, and participate in public life, judges and legislatures observed these changes in the gender polity and sought to bring the legal order into its proper balance. State courts began to admit women to practice law at their own discretion. Between 1888 and 1923, twenty of thirty-one state courts had admitted women to practice either independently or by court decision.[148] Only a few remaining states represented the last gasp of the old order. After 1900, southern states such as Maryland, Tennessee, Georgia, and South Carolina tenaciously clung to the principles of the jurisprudence of separate spheres, admitting women to practice law only after legislative action. In 1901, the supreme courts of Maryland and Tennessee refused to integrate women into the legal profession by judicial decision. Delaware took the logic of the jurisprudence of separate spheres to its ultimate conclusion by refusing to admit women lawyers until 1923, when it amended its constitution following passage of the Nineteenth Amendment. Nevertheless, the jurisprudence of integration had become the dominant perspective on the role of women in law in 1900. The struggle to gain the right to practice had effectively been won by the turn of the century.

Ironically, the women lawyers movement possessed an inherent contradiction; it was willing to accept women's right to practice law without women possessing the right to vote. Mary Putnam Jacobi of New York, a well-known doctor and suffragist, saw this contradiction as "intrinsic[ally] absurd"; she apparently preferred to tolerate a "rational delay" of the right to practice law until women had gained equal citizenship with men.[149] Women lawyers such as Bradwell and Robinson disagreed. They understood that the practice of law was only a part of a broad movement to achieve equal rights, one that also encompassed gaining admission to law schools on a par with men. Undeterred by their inability to win the right to vote and gain equal citizenship, nineteenth-century women lawyers expanded woman's rights to legal education by using the same determination and acumen that won them the right to practice law.

TWO

"I Was the Only Woman in a Large School of Men"

$\mathcal{I}$n 1868, Lemma Barkaloo of Brooklyn, New York, applied for admission to the law school of Columbia University. When her application was denied, she turned her sights westward and in 1869 entered the law department of Washington University in St. Louis. Though Barkaloo never completed her studies, she was part of the pioneer generation of women who broke the sexual barriers to American law schools. In the 1870s a number of women turned to law schools in order to study law.[1] Their efforts were not isolated and spontaneous, but coincided with and drew strength from women's attempts to gain admission to practice law. Barkaloo entered Washington University Law School in 1869, precisely when Arabella Mansfield gained admission to the Iowa bar and Myra Bradwell was rejected from the Illinois bar. Moreover, several of the women who had initiated cases to gain the right to practice law, including Lelia Robinson and Belva Lockwood, were also among the first women to enter law school. Women seeking to enter law schools encountered resistance similar to that for women's entry into the bars: the closed, rigid traditions of the eastern states contrasted with the open, flexible egalitarianism of the western states and territories; and sexual discrimination persisted tenaciously in the face of growing sexual integration.

Women's entry into law schools in the 1870s and 1880s was part of a broad movement among nineteenth-century women to gain access to higher education.[2] In the years following the Civil War, several women's colleges opened in the Northeast, including Vassar, Wellesley, Smith, and Bryn Mawr. The Morrill Land Grant Act of 1862 accelerated the founding of universities in the Midwest, which were open to both men and women. In 1870, although women were excluded from over 340 colleges, 239 colleges were either coeducational or open to women only. By 1890, 681 (63 percent) of the 1082 colleges in the country admitted women.[3]

The opening of colleges to women sparked a heated controversy over the place of higher education in women's lives. Its advocates claimed that education made married women better wives and mothers and gave single women the tools they needed to be self-supporting. Critics, echoing the same arguments found in the jurisprudence of separate spheres, voiced concern about the independence that higher education offered women and the threat that it posed to the traditional relations between the sexes. Some envisioned higher education for women as a serious assault on marriage and the family. Others feared that it would provoke an exodus of women from the home into the workplace.

At the root of the criticism was the prevailing theory that women were biologically inferior to men and could not withstand the physical and mental demands of higher education. Dire consequences—physical weakness, emotional breakdown, sterility, even death—awaited the young woman who failed to heed her unique physiological needs by pushing her intellectual pursuits too far.[4] Such was the apparent fate of Lemma Barkaloo. Though she died tragically in 1870 of typhoid fever, her death was attributed to "over-mental exertion."[5]

The man most responsible for popularizing the biological dangers of higher education for women was Dr. Edward H. Clarke, a Harvard University physician. In 1873, Clarke published *Sex in Education; or, A Fair Chance for the Girls*, which explained the supposed weaknesses of female physiology to the general reader. Clarke warned that women's reproductive physiology made it unsafe for women to undertake any intellectual activity with the same rigor as men. Excessive study, he explained, diverted energy from the female reproductive organs to the brain, causing a breakdown in women's health and threatening the health of future generations.[6]

To advocates of higher education for women, *Sex in Education* was particularly alarming because of its widespread popularity.[7] With seventeen printings in thirteen years, *Sex in Education* placed even the most ardent supporters of higher education for women on the defensive. In the years immediately following the book's release, the president of Smith College anxiously defended his school against Clarke's arguments in his annual reports to the board of trustees. Even M. Carey Thomas, president of Bryn Mawr College, acknowledged that she did not know when Bryn Mawr first opened "whether woman's health could stand the strain of education. We were haunted in those days by the clanging chains of that gloomy little specter, Dr. Edward H. Clarke's *Sex in Education*."[8]

Sex in Education reached beyond the boundaries of the elite women's colleges in the Northeast to large public universities such as the University of Michigan. One local bookseller in Ann Arbor, Michigan, sold over two hundred copies of the book in a single day. Olive San Louie Anderson, one of the first female students at Michigan, reminisced about the effect of the book on the university community. "Dr. Clarke's book was discussed by more than the girls in Clinton Street. The boys read it and delivered their opinion at length among themselves. The president and the faculty read it, and shook their heads doubtfully about the 'experiment in coeducation.' "[9]

Women's attempts to enter law schools also coincided with a time of important transition in the legal profession. Standards of legal training were informal and ill defined in the 1870s. With only twenty-one law schools in the country, most aspiring lawyers relied on the apprenticeship system, which dated back to colonial times, for their training. A student read law with a practicing attorney prior to examination by a local bar committee.

In fact, early efforts at founding law schools were few and often unsuccessful. Litchfield Law School, founded in Connecticut in 1784, was the first law school in the country, and in the early nineteenth century, several additional law schools opened, including Harvard in 1817, Yale in 1824, and the University of Virginia in 1825.[10] Several law schools, however, were remarkably short-lived ventures. Princeton opened and closed a law school three times between 1825 and 1846 before it finally gave up the endeavor in 1852. Columbian, later George Washington, had a law school that lasted only one year, from 1826 to

1827. Similarly, New York University opened a law school in 1838 that closed in 1839. By 1840, there were only nine university-affiliated law schools in the country. Apprenticeship retained its status as the primary mode of preparation for the law.[11]

In the mid-nineteenth century, however, as institutionalization began to reshape the legal profession, law schools began to emerge as the more rigorous, formal, and prestigious path into the profession.[12] Beginning in the 1870s, education in law schools gradually became an alternative to the apprenticeship system. But standards were informal and varied widely among law schools. High school graduates could enter most law schools without a college degree. Although some students took a few college courses between high school and law school, most students, even those at elite institutions such as Harvard, Columbia, and Yale, went directly from high school to law school. There they spent a year or two attending lectures by practicing attorneys. As soon as the lawyer-to-be had acquired legal training, whether in a law school or through an apprenticeship, he or she took an oral exam and, upon passing, gained admission to the bar. The exam was quite casual and unregulated. In 1870, only New York required a written exam; all other states administered an oral exam. Not until 1878 did a state—New Hampshire—establish a permanent examining committee.[13]

The ascendancy of law schools during the second half of the nineteenth century had a powerful effect on women seeking to enter the legal profession. Of their two choices for preparation, apprenticeship or law school, apprenticeship certainly offered the simpler, more comfortable path. A woman whose father or husband was a lawyer could study law within the context of her family, enjoying the privacy and protection of that family connection. In contrast, a woman who attended law school left her home and the support of her family and ventured forth into an unfamiliar and impersonal world dominated by men whom she did not know and by rules and regulations that she had little power to challenge.

Women who sought a law school education had a harder road to follow than did women who wished to enter medicine. Most nineteenth-century women doctors attended all-women's medical schools and hospitals, such as the Woman's Medical College of Pennsylvania in Philadelphia and the New England Hospital for Women and Children in Boston. These nineteenth-century women's medical institutions combined female culture with medical study to provide aspiring women doctors with a supportive and nurturing environment where they could learn medicine apart from men. They also provided women doctors with their own professional workplace in an era when it was all but impossible for a woman doctor to find acceptance in any male-run medical institution.[14]

At least until the very end of the nineteenth century, there were no separate law schools for women. Aspiring women lawyers had no choice but to brave the lonely, often hostile environment of the male-run law schools. The possibility of institutional integration motivated them to sacrifice the comforts of apprenticeship and take on the challenges of law school education.

Although major changes in the patterns of legal education in America were under way, the idea of coeducation unleashed a strong negative response from the leaders of elite law schools in the Northeast who wanted to preserve the all-male character of their schools. The most prestigious law schools in the country, such as the University of Pennsylvania, Yale, Columbia, and particularly Harvard, resisted admitting women. When women first tried to integrate these institutions, they were soundly refused. In 1868, three women, including Lemma Barkaloo of Brooklyn, were rejected from the law school at Columbia University.[15] George Templeton Strong, a trustee of Columbia College and a founder of the law school, disgustedly recorded the event in his diary. "Application from three infatuated young women for admission to Law School," he noted disdainfully. "No woman shall degrade herself by practicing law, in N.Y. especially, if I can save her. I think the clack of these possible Portias will never be heard at Dwight's moot courts. 'Womens' Rights-women' are uncommonly loud & offensive of late. I loathe the lot."[16] As early as 1868, Strong understood the close connection between women's drive to study and practice law and the goals of the woman's rights movement.

Leaders of other elite law schools shared Strong's hostility toward the admission of women to law schools. In 1871 Carrie Burnham and Helen Sawyer confronted this sexual discrimination when they applied to the prestigious law schools at University of Pennsylvania and Harvard. Burnham, then a single woman in her early thirties, had been reading law since 1865 with her future husband, Philadelphia lawyer and advocate of woman's rights Damon Young Kilgore. With his encouragement, she sought entry to the law school at the University of Pennsylvania.

Burnham's application set off a wave of opposition to the idea of women intruding into the exclusive male community of the law school. Some faculty members simply could not comprehend the possibility of a woman practicing law. Others vehemently opposed the presence of women at their law school. Law school dean E. Spencer Miller, appalled by Burnham's application, unleashed a venomous response that revealed the depth of his sexism and racism: "I do not know what the Board of Trustees will do, but as for me, if they admit a woman I will resign for I will neither lecture to niggers nor women."[17]

In the same year, 1871, Helen Sawyer applied to enter the law school at Harvard and was unanimously rejected. In response to the overwhelmingly negative reaction of the authorities at Harvard, the *Woman's Journal*, a leading publication of the nineteenth-century woman movement, tried to cast an optimistic light on the situation and urged women to be patient and persistent.[18] But the *Journal* seriously underestimated the strong feelings against women at Harvard, which still excluded women twenty years later when the *Journal* once again addressed Sawyer's rejection. Recalling the incident in 1891, a Boston lawyer, Mary Greene, suggested that the reason that Sawyer was rejected in 1871 was that the faculty at Harvard could not tolerate the idea of forcing male students to share the law library with women. It "seemed to the faculty such an insurmountable mountain of difficulty that they could see no way of getting around it."[19]

Library privileges aside, the animosity against women at Harvard ran much deeper. Indeed, its leaders had significantly more on their minds than the allocation of library resources when they rejected Sawyer. The question of coeducation raised by Sawyer's application in 1871 came just two years after the university's new president, Charles Eliot, had begun his campaign to make Harvard the premier law school in America. To achieve this goal, Eliot pinned his hopes on the educational innovation of the case method, whereby students read legal decisions organized by principles of law rather than relying solely on lectures and treatises. With his new dean of the law school, Christopher Langdell, Eliot replaced the traditional lecture method of legal education with this pedagogical reform, which the two men believed would bring the systematic, objective characteristics of scientific inquiry to the study of law. Immersed in this crusade to transform Harvard Law School into a beacon of scientific training in law, they were unwilling to be steered off course by the controversial reform of coeducation posed by Sawyer's application.[20]

Even with an influential male advocate, women fared no better at Yale. In 1872, George G. Sill, a Yale graduate of 1852, advised a young woman who wished to study law in his office to first enroll at Yale for a year. In a letter to one of the faculty at the law school, Sill expressed dubious support for women law students at his alma mater. "Are you far advanced enough to admit young women to your school?" he inquired. "I am in favor of their studying & practicing law, provided they are *ugly*." The leaders at Yale, however, did not share Sill's views and simply let the matter die "upon the table."[21]

The law schools in the District of Columbia adopted the same closed, discriminatory approach to women as did the elite law schools of the Northeast. In 1869, George W. Samson, the president of the newly formed law class of Columbian College, later George Washington University, invited Belva Lockwood to attend the opening lecture of the law class with her husband. But the support of the law school's president was not enough to overcome the strong opposition of the faculty, who feared that Lockwood's presence would "distract the attention of the young men." Ultimately, the faculty prevailed; they voted formally to deny Lockwood admission because she was a woman.[22]

Lockwood found another opportunity to study law the following year when National University Law School opened and admitted women on an equal basis with men. Lockwood enrolled along with fourteen other women. But the male students did not share the school's progressive view toward women. The "growl by the young men" quickly turned the once friendly and progressive law school into a place that discriminated against women. At first the women students were told they could no longer attend lectures, although they would be permitted to complete the course of study. By the end of the two-year course, National University Law School had become so inhospitable to women that only Lockwood and one other woman remained. When it was time for them to graduate, they learned that they would not be permitted to sit on the stage with their male classmates or receive their diplomas. National University Law School was so reluctant to issue diplomas to women that Lockwood did not receive her degree for three years, and then only after she wrote angrily to Ulysses S. Grant, then President of the United States as well as president of National University. "Sir, You are, or you are not, President of the National University Law School," she wrote. "If you are its President, I desire to say to you that I have passed through the curriculum of study in this school, and am entitled to, and demand, my diploma. If you are not its President, then I ask that you take your name from its papers, and not hold out to the world to be what you are not."[23]

Lockwood's bold persistence paid off, and she received her degree within a week. Still, this was but a small victory because it was clear that women were no longer welcome at the National University Law School.[24] In addition, Georgetown Law School was also closed to women. Lockwood had unsuccessfully tried to attend some classes there after she had been denied her diploma from National University. With Georgetown, National University, and Columbian College all closed to women, the only law school willing to admit women in the District of Columbia was Howard University, and it did so with great reluctance.

Howard University was a product of the Reconstruction era's commitment to educating newly freed African Americans. With the support of the Freedmen's Bureau and Radical Republicans in Congress, the school opened in 1867 with General Oliver Otis Howard, director of the Freedmen's Bureau, as its president. Two years later, the law department opened under the direction of John Mercer Langston. An ex-slave who had graduated from Oberlin College and the Theological Seminary of Oberlin, Langston had read law with Philemon Bliss, a white newspaper editor and antislavery advocate in Elyria, Ohio. Langston's accomplishments made him the ideal symbol for the law school of African-American intellectual ability and achievement.[25] Run by men who were committed to racial equality and integration, Howard University was open to both black and white students. In addition, the school was open to men and women equally. Thus Howard was the first law school in the country to accept applicants regardless of race or sex.

Despite the university's formal commitment to sexual integration, not everyone there supported coeducation. The medical school faculty was divided over the wisdom of admitting women. The anatomy professor, for one, did not give women medical students the materials they needed to perform their dissecting assignments, and he tolerated his male students' "ill treatment and insults" toward them. For decades, female students were passed over for clinical and laboratory appointments as well as for positions at the Freedmen's Hospital.[26]

The medical school at Howard was not alone in its discrimination of women students. From the beginning, Howard's law school also resisted the university's commitment to coeducation. Mary Ann Shadd Cary, an African-American widow from Washington, D.C., and onetime antislavery activist, was the first woman to enter the law school when she enrolled in 1869, but she was not permitted to graduate because of her sex.[27] Charlotte E. Ray fared better in 1872, but not because the law school had changed its views on women.[28] The daughter of prominent leaders in the underground railroad in New York, Ray studied at the Institution for the Education of Colored Youth, a school founded by Myrtilla Miner, a white woman who devoted her life to the education of young black children. After graduating, Ray taught in the normal and preparatory department at Howard University. While she taught at Howard, she registered in the law department of the University. But Ray did not take the school's policy of coeducation for granted. Aware of the school's reluctant commitment to the principle of sexual equality, she disguised her sex by applying as C. E. Ray, rather than Charlotte Ray. The school admitted her, unaware that she was a woman, but from the moment her true identity became known, her presence aroused curiosity and attention.

Even after Ray was accepted into the daily life of the law school, her presence continued to provoke surprise. A visitor to Howard in 1870, listening to Ray deliver a paper on corporations, was impressed that "a colored woman" had written a thesis that was "not copied from the books but from her brain, a clear, incisive analysis of one of the most delicate legal questions."[29] Nevertheless, when Ray graduated from Howard in 1872, she became the first woman, black or white, to graduate from Howard Law School and the first black woman in the country to earn a law degree. A decade later, Phebe Hanaford included Ray in her book, *Daughters of America*, which chronicled women of accomplishment in the nineteenth century. But by the time Hanaford described Ray's "fine mind" and wrote that she "deserves success," Ray had given up law practice in Washington because of the discrimination she had encountered and had become a teacher in Brooklyn, New York.[30] Despite Howard's so-called open policy toward women, only eight more women, including Mary Cary, graduated from the law school before the turn of the century.[31]

With the elite law schools of the Northeast and all but the reluctant Howard University in the nation's capital opposed to coeducation, women turned to the West to find acceptance into law schools.[32] In 1868, the year that Columbia University refused to admit Lemma Barkaloo because she was a woman, several law schools in the West came out in support of coeducation. At the University of Iowa, there was "no objection whatever" to opening the law school in 1868 to men and women on an equal basis.[33] Similarly, at Washington University, the faculty considered the matter and agreed wholeheartedly that women of good character and intellect should be accepted into the law school.[34]

Barkaloo left her family in Brooklyn and entered the law class of Washington University in 1869, setting an example for others, like Phoebe Couzins, to follow. While Barkaloo and Couzins studied law at Washington University, Ada Kepley entered the Union College of Law, later the law school of Northwestern University, in Illinois, and graduated in 1870 to become the first woman to receive a law degree in the country. That same year, the law school at the University of Michigan opened to women. The admission of women to the University of Michigan was significant because it was the premier law school in the Midwest and the largest law school in the country.[35] Though Michigan did not introduce the case method until the turn of the century, it nevertheless offered a rigorous program of traditional lecture instruction.

Meanwhile, as the trend toward coeducation in law schools spread in the West, one large university, Boston University, bucked the tide in the East when it opened in 1872 to both men and women.[36] Progressive in its acceptance of women, Boston University Law School nevertheless was founded with the pedagogical goal of preserving the traditional lecture method in the face of Harvard's innovation of the case method just two years earlier. Although women at Boston University did not have access to the newest methods of legal pedagogy available to men at Harvard, they nevertheless found in Boston University a top-notch law school with its own mission of educational reform. It was the first law school in the country to require an admission exam before entry, preceding Harvard by four years. It was also the first law school to design a three-year course of instruction: Harvard had introduced only a two-year course of study the year before, and many other law schools required only one year.

Although during the 1870s important victories for women's legal education were garnered in the West, California's Hastings law school in San Francisco opened to women in 1879 only as a result of a lawsuit by two of its women students. With no explicit statement restricting admission to men only, Clara Shortridge Foltz and Laura de Force Gordon caught the school off guard when they sought admission.[37] After two days of confusion, during which Foltz attended classes, the board of directors issued a formal policy barring women from the school. Foltz and Gordon were not deterred. They sued Hastings College of the Law, arguing that the college was part of the University of California system, which was already open to men and women equally.[38] Though the prospect of two women lawyers defeating a powerful law school seemed bleak, Foltz and Gordon were so effective in their arguments that they impressed both the judge and the attorney for the school.[39] Also in their favor was the sentiment of the California legislature, which had recently voted to deny the restriction of women from any profession or department of the state university. Foltz and Gordon ultimately won their suit, thereby opening a major, western university law school to women.[40]

With mixed results, women continued to press for more opportunities for legal education during the 1880s. Some schools held onto their exclusionary policies. In Washington, D.C., Columbian College, which was thriving as a night school for government clerks who wished to pass the bar exam, reconsidered the admission of women. In 1883, the trustees expressed their willingness to admit women, but the strong resistance of the law faculty prevailed.[41] Harvard and Columbia escaped the issue in the 1880s because no women applied to their law schools, but the story at the University of Pennsylvania and Yale was very different.

The admission of women into the law school at Yale in the nineteenth century was accidental and temporary. In the fall of 1885, Alice Rufie Jordan applied to the Yale Law School.[42] Jordan was a highly qualified candidate with a Bachelor of Science degree from the University of Michigan. In addition, she had studied for a year at the law school there and had been admitted to the Michigan bar in June 1885. Initially,

Jordan had considered finishing her law training at the Union College of Law in Chicago. Armed with a letter of introduction from Judge Thomas M. Cooley of the Michigan Law School, she had visited Chicago and had even met with Myra Bradwell, then editor of the *Chicago Legal News*. But ultimately Jordan set her sights on Yale, and she arrived in New Haven in the fall of 1885 to enroll for her senior year. Yale did not want to accept Jordan, but Jordan shrewdly pointed out that there was no written policy that specifically excluded women from the law school. "You'll have to admit me," Jordan calmly told the registrar who tried to prevent her from enrolling. "There isn't a thing in your catalogue that bars women."[43] Caught off guard, the university admitted Jordan, the first woman to study at Yale Law School. An article in the *Chicago Legal News* hailed "old conservative" Yale's decision to admit the "gentle, intellectual and talented woman" and praised Yale for opening the doors of its law school to women.[44]

But the reform was more apparent than real. At every turn, Yale tried to discourage Jordan. To encourage her to quietly leave the law school, the university initially promised to refund her money if she withdrew. When it became clear that Jordan planned to stay, the school took steps to diminish Jordan's presence. Against the advice of the dean of the law school, Noah Porter, president of the university, refused to list Jordan's name in the *Annual Catalogue of the College*. Still, Jordan persisted against the resistance she encountered, and she participated fully in student activities and met all obligations. Ultimately, Jordan graduated with her male classmates and became the first woman to receive a law degree from Yale.

The leaders of the school shared a strong desire to protect the school from sexual integration in the future. With this in mind, they amended the *Annual Catalogue* to state unambiguously Yale's restrictive policy: "It is to be understood that the courses of instruction are open to persons of the male sex only, except where both sexes are specifically included."[45] Mary Greene remembered that the dean of the law school, Francis Wayland, sent a copy of the new catalogue to a friend of hers with an explanatory note: "This is intended to prevent a repetition of the Jordan incident."[46] Only a year after Jordan applied, Yale returned to its men-only status, having deliberately slammed its doors on aspiring women lawyers.

Unlike the temporary victory at Yale, the opening of the law school at the University of Pennsylvania to women was a permanent reform. Carrie Burnham, who had applied unsuccessfully to the University of Pennsylvania in 1871, finally pried the doors of the law school open to women a decade later.[47] Since her initial rejection from the law school, Burnham had encountered further sexual discrimination that had significantly influenced the direction of her life. Twice, in 1873 and 1874, she had applied to take the state bar exam, having read law with her mentor and future husband, Damon Kilgore, and both times she had been denied entrance because of her sex. The discrimination she encountered from the Pennsylvania Board of Examiners, following as it did on the heels of her exclusion from the University of Pennsylvania, provoked Burnham to become interested in woman's rights. For several years during the 1870s she linked the cause of women lawyers directly with the woman's rights movement, using her legal knowledge to campaign for woman suffrage.

In 1876, Carrie Burnham married Damon Kilgore and settled down for a few years to raise a family. But shortly after the birth of her second daughter, she resumed her goal of studying law at the University of Pennsylvania. Her return to the law school a decade after her first application, this time as Carrie Burnham Kilgore, reignited a controversy about women's place in the law school. But this time, as the wife of a lawyer, she was more successful in gaining entry. On the opening day of classes in the fall of 1881, her husband purchased the necessary tickets for her attendance at the first semester lectures. He also accompanied her to the opening lecture, thereby supporting her on that first day of classes.

Kilgore gave up her husband's protection very quickly, however; she went to her classes unescorted on the second day. As she left the lecture hall, she received a letter from the board of trustees that defined the limits of her acceptance. Though she would be permitted to attend all classes and take the exams, the university would not guarantee that it would officially award her a degree. Undaunted, Kilgore continued her studies and discovered that once she was part of the student body, she was treated with courtesy and respect by her fellow classmates as well as by her professors. In 1883, despite the dire warnings of the board of trustees, she became the first woman to graduate from the law school. Her accomplishment, Kilgore recalled fondly, "was familiarly said to be 'the greatest victory since the [C]ivil [W]ar.'"[48] The following year she was finally admitted to the Philadelphia bar, and in 1886 she was admitted to practice before the supreme court of Pennsylvania.

This small group of women, from Kilgore in Philadelphia to Foltz and Gordon in San Francisco, was part of the first generation of women in America to attend law school. As a group, they shared certain experiences. They knew what it meant to be pioneers—that is, to be among the first to face the daunting task of breaking cultural taboos and institutional barriers to attend law school among men. They also experienced firsthand what it meant to give up the comforts of female friendship and to interact in a community without women. In an era that defined ideal womanhood in terms of domesticity and separate spheres, this first generation of women who studied law helped broaden women's place in society.

But there was also much that distinguished these women from each other. Their motives for applying to law school were diverse, spanning the spectrum from professional goals to personal fulfillment. Some had been teachers who had found their work, although socially acceptable, to be arduous and unfulfilling. Emma Gillett, for one, quit teaching and entered the law school of Howard University: "I taught school ten years and found myself growing tired, nervous, and unhappy, and moreover earning a mere pittance, never over $500 a year. The outlook was discouraging and I resolved to carry out an idea that had existed *in nubibus* in my mind for years and to study law."[49] Gillett was not alone in her frustration over teaching. Almeda Hitchcock found teaching "very trying" and gave it up after only one year for "more congenial work" in her father's law office before entering the University of Michigan.[50] Similarly, Letitia Burlingame left teaching to study law because her "health demanded a change." Although friends echoed Dr. Clarke's dire predictions and warned her that the study of law would destroy her health, Burlingame claimed that her health "steadily improved" after she entered law school "so that I am now stronger than ever before."[51] Other women left teaching because they found it too confining. Bristling under the limits of her narrow education, Margaret Wilcox asked: "Why should women be satisfied with just enough scholarship to earn a livelihood?"[52]

Not all women studied law as an alternative to teaching.[53] Some women who were married to lawyers sought to learn the law so that they could work with their husbands. At her lawyer husband's suggestion, Emma Haddock entered the law school at the University of Iowa after she confided to him that she was bored with the duties of housework. Ada Kepley, also married to a lawyer, read law with her husband and then entered the Union College of Law in Chicago. Margaret Wilcox, who had left teaching to further her education, entered the law school at the University of Michigan with her husband.

Other women entered law school as a way to link their personal situation to the quest for women's political and legal rights. Phoebe Couzins, for one, was motivated by her desire to expand women's opportunities and influence in American society. She entered Washington University "to open new paths for women, enlarge her usefulness, widen her responsibilities and to plead her cause in a struggle which I believed was surely coming."[54] Mary Greene went to Boston University after she discovered how little she understood about her personal finances and legal affairs. "I was most woefully ignorant of the very first principles of our common law," she recalled.[55] She understood that other women suffered from the same lack of legal knowledge as she. For Greene, studying law at Boston University was a way both to protect herself in her future legal and business dealings and to help other women with the same needs.

More than any other woman in this early group of law students, Lelia Robinson reveals how important it was that women had access to legal education by the 1870s.[56] Married at the age of seventeen, she built a successful career as a journalist in Boston. But her marriage fell apart, and unlike other women of her day who endured failed marriages in silence, Robinson filed for divorce, accusing her husband of adultery and petitioning the court to permit her to resume her maiden name. Fresh from her divorce, Robinson entered Boston University Law School, determined to find a new career to support herself and intent upon learning about the laws of marriage and divorce.

Once in law school, women's minority status shaped their experiences in a variety of ways. Some endured outright hostility, others encountered curiosity and disbelief, and still others enjoyed support and friendship. Foltz was one of the unlucky ones; she suffered the scorn of her male classmates during her brief experience as a student at Hastings law school. They resented her presence and made her feel unwelcome by maliciously mimicking her every move. As Foltz recalled: "The first day I had a bad cold and was forced to cough. To my astonishment every young man in the class was seized with a violent fit of coughing . . . If I turned over a leaf in my note book every student in the class did likewise. If I moved my chair—hitch went every chair in the room."[57]

Carrie Kilgore fared much better at the University of Pennsylvania. Administrators expected such a disorderly response to Kilgore's presence that they considered the idea of seeking police protection. Their concern proved to be unfounded. Kilgore recalled receiving only the "utmost courtesy" from her professors and fellow students.[58]

Some women escaped the overt hostility of men but were viewed as curious oddities. Alice Jordan not only encountered the stares of her professors and classmates when she appeared before the moot court at Yale—she also endured a throng of curious men and women as well as newspaper reporters who turned out to watch the first such performance by a woman at the prestigious university. Initially shy before the crowd, Jordan argued well and won the approval of the spectators. "She read with vivid emphasis and determination, in a rich contralto voice, and when she got over her nervous bashfulness she made an excellent impression," commented one newspaper reporter.[59]

Curiosity became amazement at Howard University Law School, where assumptions about race combined with those about sex. One reporter at the annual examinations in 1870 was transformed by the performance of the students, "all colored people, one of them a lady." Listening to their answers, he likened the two major technological discoveries of the nineteenth century, the telegraph and the steam engine, to another "wonderful" discovery—"the capacity of the freed people for all the duties of the highest citizenship."[60] That same year, a trustee of the school felt compelled to admit his surprise that "a colored woman," Charlotte Ray, had written an intelligent thesis.[61]

In the 1880s, six more women graduated from Howard University. The graduation in 1883 of Mary Cary, who had been denied a diploma at Howard in 1869 because she was a woman, reveals how far the school had progressed on the issue of coeducation. But women at Howard still encountered resistance. Eliza Chambers, who graduated from the law school in 1886, recalled a few years later that the faculty had deliberately omitted her name from the list of students recommended to take the bar exam because she was a woman.[62]

Some women among this pioneer generation of law students were fortunate enough to escape the resistance that Chambers and others endured. Schools in the West were the most welcoming. At Washington University, the law professors enthusiastically supported coeducation. They not only warmly welcomed their first female students, Barkaloo and Couzins, they also lent them readings throughout the semester and praised the women publicly when they graduated. Their support did not go unnoticed. At the end of her studies, while publicly thanking her professors for their help, Couzins revealed her dependency on their benevolent paternalism: "To one whose soul has been sadly torn and bruised by endless friction with the carping spirits and narrow minds of today, this kind and fatherly anointing oil fell upon troubled waters."[63]

Similarly, Emma Haddock enjoyed "the greatest courtesy" from her professors and classmates at the University of Iowa. When she graduated in 1875 as the only woman among almost a hundred men, she was one of ten students chosen to represent her class at commencement. After graduating from law school, Haddock returned for another year of advanced studies, and when she completed the year she was once again chosen by her classmates, this time as the sole representative, to speak for the class.[64]

Tiera Farrow, the only woman student among more than eighty men at the Kansas City School of Law in 1895, was fortunate to find one male classmate to ease her entry into the school. She recalled what it was like to enter the classroom on her first day. "All talk ceased . . . Every eye of those more than eighty men was turned toward me . . . Then one young man who had seen me almost daily on the street cars, came toward me, introduced himself . . . And how much I appreciate his friendly gesture he will never fully realize." From that day on, Farrow sat next to two classmates who escorted her home in the evenings and became her loyal friends. Still, she did not escape teasing by many men in her class who loved to remind her that, according to "Blackstone's Law," women were merely the chattel of men.[65]

Lelia Robinson was neither hindered nor helped by the administrators and faculty of Boston University Law School. The dean, Judge Edmund Bennett, introduced her to no one and gave her no advice on even the smallest matters such as where to sit in class, even though he knew that the students were seated alphabetically. As the only woman among 150 male classmates, Robinson was left to make her own way.

With no social guidelines to follow, Robinson rejected the reserved, demure behavior expected of a nineteenth-century lady toward men she did not know and instead adopted an outgoing and sociable persona. Rather than withdrawing to the back of the classroom, she took a seat in the front row, and rather than waiting for formal introductions, she initiated conversation with her classmates. Her friendliness disarmed her male classmates, who were initially uncomfortable in her presence. But her outgoing manner and ability to transcend the etiquette that distanced men from women put them at ease, and they accepted her and warmly referred to her as a "good fellow." A decade after she graduated, she recalled that "I was not permitted to realize or remember the fact that I was the only woman in a large school of men. I was simply a student like the rest."[66]

By the time Jessie Wright began her studies at Boston University in 1887, the same dean who had treated Robinson with benign neglect treated her with patronizing interest. "Judge Bennett . . . used to smile on me benignantly about three times a term during the three years I was in the school," Wright recalled, "and ask me how I liked the law."[67] The following year, Mary Greene, the only woman in her law school class, had no trouble earning the respect and admiration of her classmates and professors. "Uniform kindness and courtesy have characterized the behavior of my fellow students. Nothing at all unpleasant or disagreeable to me ever occurs," she explained.[68] One of her classmates even confided in her that he believed women lawyers could serve the needs of women clients much better than men could.[69] Ultimately, Greene ranked second in her class of twenty-eight men and graduated magna cum laude in 1888. Still, both Greene and Wright had to tread carefully, and they worked hard, just as Robinson had done, to make the men around them feel comfortable in their presence. When asked by Dean Bennett about how well she liked law school, Wright deliberately exaggerated her enthusiasm for the law. When confronted with the necessity of discussing delicate legal issues with her classmates, Greene avoided the potentially awkward situation by approaching the topics in a direct, businesslike manner.[70]

By the 1880s, the presence of women at Union College of Law had generated an undercurrent of sexual electricity in the classroom that transcended the dull, dingy conditions of the school. Students attended daily lectures from four different professors. But the facilities of the law school were meager at best. All lectures occurred in one dark classroom, where the desks were old, the floor was dusty and unswept, and the outside noise often drowned out the voices of professors and students. Moreover, the law school had no library, no study room, and no books to borrow.[71]

But the social interaction among the male and female students transcended the school's meager facilities. Students passed notes back and forth to each other during recitations and engaged in playful flirtatiousness "as though the school were equally co-education." Catharine Waugh McCulloch reflected years later on the social atmosphere that took over the classroom during 1886, her first year: "We were a little shocked in recitations, however, by so much horseplay, perhaps better call it 'colt-ishness,' the equal of which I never witnessed since except once at the Ladies Night session of the 'highbrow' Chicago Law Club."[72] Mc-Culloch must have overcome her initial shock, however, for she struck up a romance with a fellow classmate, Frank McCulloch, and ultimately married him.

McCulloch also became a strong advocate of the social benefits of a coeducational law school experience for both male and female students. The presence of women in law school, she argued, prevented young men from falling victim to the lures of urban vice. "A lonely young man in a professional school, far from home . . . sometimes finds it hard to cling to his ideals of personal sobriety and purity . . . If in his absence from all women relatives and friends he sees women classmates who are congenial, wholesome and intelligent, he does not hunt the opposite."[73] At the same time, McCulloch strongly argued that coeducation enabled women to work with men as equals, thereby encouraging them to give up the romanticized notions they might have about men and to view them more realistically. "For a woman who may have led a cloistered life, the first man she glimpses may decide her fate and perhaps unwisely. But to work and recite with 100 or 200 men, thin and fat, tall and short, dumb and brilliant, may destroy the unknown man of her dreams but better still disclose man as a human being, a good comrade, an equal."[74]

Like the Union College of Law, the University of Michigan also welcomed women into its law school. Two women enrolled in the law class in 1870, creating very little commotion. In contrast to the male students in the medical school, who had ridiculed the women in their classes, most of the male law students welcomed their female classmates.[75] Students of the Webster Society led the way.

The Webster Society was a literary club run by the law students at the University of Michigan. Its members were committed to the idea that literary culture was essential to success in professional life, and they met weekly for discussions, orations, and music. The members were student leaders in the law school, and they set an example for their fellow classmates regarding the treatment of women law students. As early as 1874, they invited their female classmates to join the Webster Society. The following year they chose a woman law student to read an essay at the society's annual public exercises, and they elected another woman law student to be secretary of the society. "Every courtesy was ungrudgingly extended to us," one female graduate of the law school recalled years later.[76]

Over the years, the male law students at the University of Michigan followed the Webster Society's lead and welcomed their female classmates' participation in student life. In 1885, they chose Letitia Burlingame to be class poet, and they elected her classmate, Mary Merrill, class secretary.[77] In 1888, law student Almeda Hitchcock reflected on the consideration that she received from her male classmates. "The life here at college has been all that one could ask for," she wrote shortly before she graduated. "My classmates have treated me with respect and kindness. Not an unpleasant thing has occurred in my college life."[78] Law school graduate Martha Pearce echoed Hitchcock's remarks: "We had received a hearty welcome from our brothers in law to their moot courts and debating clubs and had found that they forgot all troublesome distinctions just to the degree that we ourselves ignored them."[79]

The women law students were received graciously by their teachers as well. In his commencement address in 1873, University of Michigan law professor Charles A. Kent went out of his way to praise the two early women graduates for their superior scholarship. And with an eye to the critics of coeducation, especially Dr. Clarke, he publicly recognized their excellent health, which, he claimed, held up as well as that of their 120 male classmates.[80]

This support was not reserved solely for graduation formalities. The faculty also tried to make the women in the law school feel welcome and safe while they were students. "Judge Campbell's scholarly and be-nign face smiled upon us from the desk at regular intervals," Jane Slocum recalled. Referring to Campbell and Judge Thomas M. Cooley, then dean of the law school, she continued: "The generous interest of these distinguished jurists will never be forgotten by the grateful women who were treated not only as students who were welcome there, but as friends whom they were glad to aid in their life work."[81] Cooley worked with Cora Benneson, for example, as she undertook graduate studies beyond her law degree. Her master's thesis on "Republican Constitu-tions" was completed with the joint cooperation of faculty from the law school and the literary department, with whom Benneson worked from 1880 through 1883.[82]

Even while being supportive and kind, some of the professors were also patronizing, if not condescending, to the women students. Burlin-game, a graduate of the law school in 1886, recalled that although her University of Michigan law professors welcomed and encouraged the women students, they did not always demand as much of them as they did of the men. One professor in particular, she explained, used to "arouse my indignation by picking out easy questions to ask us women."[83] Another professor made it clear to Ada Bittenbender that he did not believe women were fit for the demands of courtroom work.[84] Even Cooley was originally condescending and skeptical at the same time that he accepted women students. In a letter to the president of Cornell University in 1871, the year before Slocum arrived on campus, he re-vealed his ambivalence toward the new female students: "The number who come is small, and for the most part of the unlovely class, some of them afford the boys some amusement."[85] Still, Cooley acknowl-edged that women not only could compete academically with the male students but also were often held to higher standards: "You are misin-formed if you are told the standard for admission is lowered. The ten-dency has been in the other direction."[86]

Cooley's ambivalent views did not seem to interfere with his respect-ful treatment of the women law students. For her part, Slocum was aware of only courteous and kind treatment from Cooley. In a letter to him, she freely expressed her deep gratitude for his respect and kindness toward her: "It would in any case be impossible for me to express the gratitude which I feel for all your kindness and courtesy and for the advantages I have been permitted to enjoy here. One cannot know what a little cordial help is to any woman who tried to do something out of the beaten tracks, which makes people look with cold criticism if not with suspicion upon every motive and act, so you will never know how your abundant kindness will be treasured."[87]

Years after Judge Cooley confessed his initial fears, female graduates continued to speak appreciatively of their treatment at the law school. In 1889, Benneson summarized the goodwill the women students enjoyed from both the faculty and male students. In an essay she wrote for the *Woman's Journal* entitled "Life of Women at Michigan University," she explained that the women students took their place beside their male classmates "as if no lengthy discussion had ever been held in regard to the fitness of co-education."[88]

Although the spirits of the women law students at the University of Michigan were high, their numbers remained low. In 1870, when the school admitted its first two women, there were more than six hundred male students in the law school. In 1872, Jane Slocum was one of only three female students among 327 men in her class and over 670 men in the entire law school. In 1886, there were seven women in the law school, the largest number of female students since women were first admitted in 1870. But for almost four decades thereafter, the number of women at the law school did not reach seven again. Overall, during the first two decades of coeducation at the University of Michigan, 1870 through 1890, 7,532 men and only sixty-two women enrolled in the law school.[89] Judge Cooley's description of the situation in 1871 still held true by 1890. The numbers of women at the law school were so small that their presence was a matter "of entire indifference."[90]

Even though the male law students at the University of Michigan accepted women into their classes, it was not easy for most young women in the late nineteenth century to attend law school in an environment dominated so heavily by men. In 1884, shortly before she left her home in Joliet, Michigan, for Ann Arbor, Burlingame worried about going to the University of Michigan precisely because she knew there would be so few other women law students. "With my dreadful bashfulness, which age seems very little to banish, I realize what a trial a course in the University, in a large class with few, if any, ladies will be, but I guess grit will conquer shyness, for I feel that I can really make a successful lawyer let me once get admitted to the bar."[91]

The lack of female friendship was not the only problem that women

Laura A. Woodin LeValley with her male classmates at the University of Michigan Law School, 1882.

law students faced; they also had to negotiate carefully the social rules that dictated their proper interaction with their male classmates. At Boston University, Robinson had overcome her loneliness while preserving her respectability by behaving in an outwardly friendly way that earned her the label of "pal." Burlingame found a different solution to the same challenge—her mother lived with her in Ann Arbor. While Letitia attended law school, her mother ran a boarding house for students of the university. In this way, Letitia's mother recreated a home away from home for her daughter, thereby protecting her from the loneliness and dangers young single women faced when living alone in a city.

In doing this for Letitia, the Burlingames temporarily broke up their nuclear family. Letitia's mother left her husband for almost two years in order to stay with her daughter. This was no small sacrifice. Letitia recalled how difficult the breakup of her family was, particularly for her mother. "Such a general breaking up at home and leaving Papa behind awakened sad thoughts . . . Thus sadness was mingled with joy, for I knew it was all done for me, and Mama cried for hours as if her heart

Thirtieth anniversary reunion of the University of Michigan Law School, 1911, with Leona Taylor Lounsbury (no. 4) and Laura A. Woodin LeValley (no. 20).

would break."[92] The enormity of this sacrifice reveals the lengths to which Letitia's parents were willing to go to enable their daughter to attend law school at the University of Michigan.

The women law students at the University of Michigan enjoyed cordial relationships with most of their male classmates, but they found their deepest friendships and strongest support among each other. During the summer after her first year at law school, for example, Burlingame established strong friendships with several other women lawyers and law students. "Those were golden hours," she recalled. "How I feel refreshed and strengthened by the sympathy of kindred minds."[93]

Burlingame was particularly close to Martha Pearce. "It will be a long while before I shall find another friend in whom I can confide so unreservedly," she wrote in the midst of her second year of law school.[94] Moreover, these friendships lasted well beyond the days the women spent together in Ann Arbor. Three years after she graduated from law school, Burlingame wrote to her fellow classmate, Rebecca May, then practicing law in Topeka, Kansas, to invite May to join her in practice. Unfortunately, Burlingame and May never had the opportunity to work together because Burlingame became ill just two weeks after she wrote to May and died seven months later.

During their years together in Ann Arbor, Burlingame, Pearce, and May, along with three other women—Margaret Wilcox, Almeda Hitchcock, and Corinne Douglas—built a small community of women lawyers. Unlike Robinson at Boston University, Kilgore at the University of Pennsylvania, or Ray at Howard, the women at the University of Michigan, at least by the late 1880s, were not alone. In the fall of 1886, this small group of women formalized their friendship and its social benefits. Burlingame, Pearce, and Wilcox invited the new women law students, or lady "Freshies," to Burlingame's home for a "coed spread," as such dinners were called at the University of Michigan. Burlingame and her friends borrowed the idea from the women of the literary department who had initiated the tradition of inviting new female literary students to a special annual dinner. The female medical students had already adopted the tradition.

In the fall semester of 1886, there were seven women law students—the largest number since women were first admitted in 1870—and two female alumnae living in Ann Arbor. Of this group, seven gathered at Burlingame's home to celebrate the start of the academic year and welcome the new students. By the end of the evening, the group had formed a women lawyers' club, the Equity Club, and had chosen Burlingame as chair and Pearce as corresponding secretary.[95]

The creation of the Equity Club revealed just how far the situation for women law students at the University of Michigan had progressed. After so many years of studying law alone among such a large number of men, there was finally a nucleus of women law students large enough to come together and define themselves as a group. Though their numbers were still extremely small, the seven women law students at the University of Michigan finally had a female community to ameliorate their loneliness and alienation. The Equity Club became the center of the member's social lives. They met regularly to chat and to discuss issues such as the duty of women lawyers to society. Topics such as this were never addressed by their professors or male classmates. Away from their classrooms and the presence of men, women law students used the Equity Club as the one place where they could come together and define the issues that were important to them.

Although the Equity Club played an important role in the life of the women law students and lawyers in Ann Arbor, it had a broader goal. From the beginning, its founders wanted the group to become a correspondence club for all women lawyers and law students in the country. In doing so, they sought to transcend the geographic distance that kept women lawyers apart, to bring them together into a community of friendship and professional support much like the one they enjoyed at Michigan. As it helped women lawyers articulate the professional challenges they confronted in the legal profession, the Equity Club also pushed the women lawyers movement beyond its focus on integrating the bar and law schools to include broader professional and social issues.

Women were attracted to the club as an antidote to their professional loneliness and isolation. Here they found what Pearce touted as "sympathy and encouragement" from each other. "What can be so refreshing to an aspiring soul, that has been stifled in a narrow conventionalism as to be simply understood?" she asked rhetorically in her first letter as corresponding secretary in 1887.[96] These were compelling words to women such as Robinson, Greene, and Wright, all of whom had endured loneliness at Boston University Law School, as well as to others including Kepley and Gordon. It is not surprising that these women, who had suffered sexual discrimination and alienation as they blazed paths for women in legal education, flocked to the Equity Club. Gordon echoed Pearce's words: "There is a certain 'moral support' in the confiding sympathy of brave-souled, warmhearted women, who have dared and suffered in kind with ourselves, which becomes a *tower* of *strength* to nerve the heart and sustain the brain when both are taxed to the utmost as is often the case in the practice of our grand profession."[97]

By the end of the 1880s, women law students were no longer isolated pioneers. Many discovered each other through the Equity Club. Much had changed since 1869 when Kepley and Barkaloo had become the first two women to enroll in law school. At that time, there were 1,200 law students in twenty-one law schools.[98] In the two decades that followed, women's options for formal legal education had expanded considerably. Women gained access to law schools throughout the country—from Boston University in the Northeast and Howard in the nation's capital; to the University of Michigan, the University of Wisconsin, and Iowa University in the Midwest, to Hastings College of the Law in California. The range of possibilities meant that women could actually make choices when it came to selecting a law school. Almeda Hitchcock, for one, discussed her options with her father, a lawyer in Hawaii, and then requested catalogues from a number of schools. Together, they reviewed the schools, narrowed the choices to University of Michigan and Hastings in San Francisco, and ultimately decided upon Michigan.[99]

But sexual discrimination persisted as many law schools successfully fought back the tide of coeducation. Both Yale and National University Law School excluded women immediately after each school permitted one woman to graduate. In addition, all of the elite northeastern law schools except the University of Pennsylvania remained closed to women. Moreover, even at the coeducational law schools, men continued to outnumber women dramatically. By 1890, women were but a minute fraction of the 4,500 law students in the sixty-one law schools across the country.[100]

Still, the women who studied at these law schools in the 1870s and 1880s benefited firsthand from the progress of sexual integration in legal education. As their numbers grew steadily from 5 in 1870, to 75 in 1880, to 208 in 1890, these pioneer women lawyers fueled the growing women lawyers movement. As they broke the barriers to law schools and won the right to practice law, they turned their attention to the next challenge, that of forging a career in the legal profession. Individually, and together as part of the women lawyers movement, these pioneer women lawyers faced new forms of sexual discrimination and professional opportunities. As they strived to balance their gender and professional identities, some joined the Equity Club, which by the late 1880s had emerged as one of the most inspirational voices of the women lawyers movement.

THREE

"Sweeter Manners, Purer Laws"

*I*n the 1880s, Lelia Robinson, having broken the barriers to legal education and law practice in Massachusetts, offered women advice on how to succeed in the legal profession. "*Do not take sex* into the practice. Don't be 'lady lawyers.' Simply be *lawyers* and recognize no distinction—no existence of any distinction between yourselves and the other members of the bar . . . You can take this stand and yet in no wise cease to be ladies—true ladies in every sense of the word."[1] But Robinson's contemporary, Sara Killgore Wertman, who paved the way for women to study and practice law in Michigan, saw the situation differently. Wertman urged women lawyers to emphasize their femininity and to claim their special place as women in the legal profession: "Woman's place in the practice of the law, as elsewhere, is not so much to bring to it wisdom and justice, as the purifying graces,—lifting the profession to higher and nobler purposes than the selfish aggrandizement that now characterizes so much litigation."[2]

Robinson and Wertman underscored clearly that the Victorian woman lawyer of the late nineteenth century straddled two worlds. As a woman, her place was at home and her role was the caretaker of domestic and family concerns. As a lawyer, her place was in the office and the courtroom and her task was to protect justice and freedom. As a woman she was to be modest, sentimental, and caring; as a lawyer, she was to be assertive, rational, and objective. Martha Pearce, the secretary of the

Equity Club, identified this conflict between gender and professional identity as the burden of "double consciousness" that confronted every "*woman* who wishes to be a *lawyer.*" The burden of double consciousness influenced every aspect of women lawyers' professional lives: the type of practice they chose; their relationship to social reform; whether they entered the courtroom or remained in the office; and how they dressed. It even challenged them to justify the very existence of their legal careers. Long after women had won the right to practice law and had gained admission to law schools, women lawyers continued to face the challenge of defining a comfortable space for themselves within the male-dominated legal profession. Although admission to the bars and to law schools represented institutional victories of great magnitude in nineteenth-century America, arguably the greater task for women lawyers was to overcome the burden of double consciousness.[3]

The burden of double consciousness derived from the inescapable fact that every aspect of the legal profession embodied male culture.[4] Men made the laws, and male judges interpreted them in a way that reflected men's needs, biases, and perceptions of a just society. Moreover, most male lawyers and judges viewed women lawyers as interlopers simply because of their sex. With male lawyers and judges acting as gatekeepers, women lawyers represented a new regime that threatened the male hegemony of the legal profession. Thus gender and professional identity did not easily merge because women lawyers were forced to confront both a male cultural system and their own identity as women. Women lawyers had to navigate a profession generally at odds with who they were professionally at the same time that they had to rethink where they fit within nineteenth-century gender relations. This was the burden of double consciousness.

From the moment women began to break into the legal profession, they encountered this burden. It is true that the reality of many women's lives did not fit the idealized image of the domestic, modest, pure woman in the late nineteenth century. Poor and working-class women, immigrant women, and newly freed, African-American women worked outside the home simply to survive. But women of color, women from working-class backgrounds, or women who had recently immigrated did not enter the legal profession in any substantial numbers until the turn of the century, when part-time law schools for women made it possible for them to study law at night while holding a job during the day. Although Howard University was open to African-American women, barely a handful graduated in the nineteenth century after Charlotte Ray and Mary Ann Shadd Cary. The earliest women lawyers were overwhelmingly white, economically comfortable, and American-born. Their new professional lives conflicted sharply with the traditional feminine roles demanded of women of their economic and social station. Although this challenge faced all professional women of their day, the situation was most acute for women lawyers.[5] As they grappled with the tensions and contradictions in their lives, women lawyers began to define the parameters of professional identity for nineteenth-century women in law.

But a nineteenth-century woman lawyer did not have to shoulder the burden of double consciousness alone. By the late 1880s, she could turn to other women lawyers in the Equity Club, the organization that women law students and lawyers had founded in 1886 at the University of Michigan. In the late 1880s, the Equity Club emerged as a major asset to the women lawyers movement. By preserving sisterhood and nurturing female gender roles in a bastion of male lawyers and law students, it provided the best available mechanism for women lawyers, scattered around the country, to explore the paradox between their gender and professional identities.

Though it lasted only four years and attracted just thirty-two members, the Equity Club held a special place in the history of nineteenth-century women lawyers. It was the first national group of women lawyers in American history, and it even had several European members. Larger and longer-lasting women's legal institutions followed, including county, state, and national women's bar associations and legal sororities, but the Equity Club marked the budding of professional identity among women lawyers in the late nineteenth century.[6] Founded during the second half of a decade in which the numbers of women lawyers in America grew from seventy-five in 1880 to 208 in 1890, the thirty-four members of the Equity Club represented a significant proportion of all women lawyers in America to 1890.[7] Through their letters, they shared their experiences as they sought to tackle the difficult task of preserving their femininity while creating a professional identity.

From the beginning, the founders of the Equity Club encountered the burden of double consciousness. The very naming of the club challenged them to defend their femininity while championing their professional identity. The founders wanted a name that would convey the club's unique commitment to women lawyers without offending the male lawyers and law students who were their friends and supporters. Their professor of equity at the University of Michigan, Harry Burns Hutchins, provided them with the inspiration for the name. His statement, "Equity has been the saviour of woman," conveyed the message that they wanted, and the Equity Club was so named.[8]

In speaking of equity, Hutchins reached back to the historical roots of equity law in fourteenth- and fifteenth-century England. The law of equity emerged during this era of English legal history because the common law courts were unable to respond to the growing social and legal problems of an increasingly complex English society. Equity was not an alternative system of justice in competition with the common law. Rather, it was a complementary court of law designed to supplement the common law. When the rigidity of the common law courts threatened a legal but heartless decision, one turned to the equity courts for fairness and flexibility.

When Hutchins spoke of equity as the savior of woman, he evoked the popular notion of the equity court as moderating the common law court. Indeed, the law of equity embodied the very qualities of femininity as conceived by Hutchins's generation. The law of equity offered mercy, whereas the common law courts promised rigid and pure legal outcomes. In fact, it was a woman, Shakespeare's Portia in *The Merchant of Venice*, who symbolized these very ideals. Her soliloquy in court when she pleaded to Shylock, "We do pray for mercy . . . [t]o mitigate the justice of thy plea," embodied the pure expression of equity law.[9]

In their search for a name for their group, the founders of the Equity Club found a symbolic place within the law of equity. They expanded the concept of equity beyond the law and infused it with their vision of women lawyers' professional place. Their particular interpretation of equity provided them with justification for their unique role within the male-dominated legal profession. Just as the equity court system supplemented the common law, so too the founders of the Equity Club envisioned themselves and other women lawyers as complementing, rather than competing with, male lawyers. As a law student, Letitia Burlingame even decided to specialize in equity law precisely because she believed it to be less antagonistic than the common law—that is, because she thought it was "a very nice subject for a lady to pursue."[10]

The founders of the Equity Club strived to preserve their femininity as they established their professional identity. Whereas men claimed that the practice of law demanded an objective mind, most nineteenth-century women lawyers insisted that law required an understanding heart as well. By calling their organization the Equity Club, its founders assumed the accommodating role of Victorian womanhood, thereby reassuring men and women alike that women lawyers would complement their male colleagues, not compete with them.

Having settled on the name for their organization, the founders of the Equity Club invited sixty-two women to join. Requirements for membership were simple: an annual letter that described the author's experiences or views on being a woman lawyer and annual dues of twenty-five cents, which covered the costs of postage, stationery, copyright, and printing.[11] Martha Pearce, the corresponding secretary, collected the letters and prepared them for circulation among the members. The original plan, to publish the letters each year and to distribute a copy of the printed collection to each member, encountered financial problems. Hampered by a lack of funds in the club's first year, Pearce had to send out the original letters. One by one, individual club members received the collection of letters for 1887 and often held onto them until they made personal copies before they sent them on to others. With an increase in the dues in 1888, Pearce was able to publish the letters as the *Equity Club Annual* and wrote an extensive secretary's report describing the club's founding as well as its purpose, organization, and structure.

The time involved in producing the *Equity Club Annual* in 1888 discouraged Pearce from continuing in her position as corresponding secretary. At the same time, she was disheartened by the decline in members. "The letters [I] longed for never came," she lamented.[12] In 1889, Pearce called for someone to replace her, but no one volunteered to take on her job. As a result, the *Annual* was not published in 1889 and 1890. Instead, the letters were copied into a letter book and the original letters were circulated as they had been in 1887.

During the four years of the Equity Club, thirty-two women participated, writing a total of sixty letters. Membership varied by year. Of the sixty-two women who were invited to join in the first year, fourteen responded with letters; of that group of fourteen, ten were either alumnae or students of the University of Michigan Law School. But word of the Equity Club spread quickly, and in 1888, sixteen new members joined. Six members remained from the year before, but eight dropped out, bringing the total membership for the club's second year up to twenty-two. That year, 1888, marked the peak of membership in the Equity Club. In 1889, there were no new members and ten women dropped out, leaving only twelve women in the Equity Club. In 1890, the last year of the club, two new members joined, but they were part of an even smaller group of eleven members. Despite the turnover in membership, there was some continuity as well. Nine women were members for at least three years, five of whom were members all four years. Of this group of five, three were among the original founders in 1886. Lelia Robinson and Mary Greene of Boston were the other two.

The thirty-two women who composed the membership of the Equity Club shared certain characteristics. All were white, American-born (except for the European members), and middle class, which reflected the fact that they lived in an era when women lawyers, and male lawyers as well, made up a homogeneous profession. In other ways, the members of the Equity Club were a diverse group. They came from urban centers such as Boston and Chicago; smaller cities such as Omaha, Nebraska, and Iowa City, Iowa; and small towns such as Hutchinson, Kansas, and Tiffin, Ohio. In addition, there were three European members—one each from England, France, and Switzerland. The members lived throughout the country from Massachusetts to California, but a majority of twenty were from the Midwest and West, where law schools and state bars had a tradition of accepting women; only seven lived in cities and towns in the East. Nine lived in large cities—three each from Boston, Chicago, and Washington, D.C., where women already worked in social reform, the professions, and other activities in the public arena.

The women who joined the Equity Club ranged in age from their mid-twenties to their late fifties. At one end of the spectrum were young women in their mid-twenties who were embarking on their legal careers. Most of the Equity Club members were in their thirties and forties. They had completed their legal training and had settled into the pattern of their adult lives, whether it was legal practice, reform work, or care of home and family. Only two members, Belva Lockwood and Catharine Waite, were in their fifties. Age fifty-seven and fifty-nine, respectively, they were the Equity Club's link with woman's rights activists in the mid nineteenth century.[13]

An impressive number of Equity Club members were leaders in breaking barriers in the legal profession. Lelia Robinson, Sara Killgore Wertman, and Ada Kepley, the first woman to earn a law degree in America, were all members. So were Ada Bittenbender, Mary Greene, and Almeda Hitchcock, the first women admitted to the bars of Nebraska, Rhode Island, and Hawaii, respectively. Several club members broke ground in other ways. Emma Gillett, a founder of the Washington College of Law in Washington, D.C., was a member, as was Laura de Force Gordon, who sued the University of California with Clara Foltz to open Hastings College of Law to women. Indeed, all but a handful of members were graduates of law schools. In an age of transition from apprenticeship to formal legal education, many Equity Club members were part of a small vanguard within the legal profession who had gone to law school.

Although their professional identity distinguished Equity Club members from most women in nineteenth-century America, their involvement in reform activity connected them with many other reform-minded middle-class women of their day. Eighteen of the twenty-nine members who lived in the United States were involved in reform activity, including suffrage, temperance, social purity, and educational reform. With most of their reform work focusing on laws governing marriage, divorce, rape, and age of consent, the majority of women lawyers in the Equity Club clearly allied themselves with the broad quest for woman's rights. Some Equity Club members even held leadership positions in the woman's rights movement, particularly in the suffrage and temperance movements. Bittenbender, for one, served as legal counsel for the Woman's Christian Temperance Union; Gillett and Gordon were leaders in the suffrage movement in Washington, D.C., and California, respectively; McCulloch and Kepley were suffrage and temperance leaders in Illinois; Waite published the progressive *Chicago Law Times*, which promoted a broad platform of women's legal rights; and in 1884 and 1888 Lockwood was the candidate for President of the United States for the Equal Rights Party on a platform of equal legal rights for men and women. These Equity Club members expanded the parameters of the woman's rights movement by bringing their knowledge of the law to the question of women's legal rights. By providing their legal expertise to the suffrage and temperance movements, as well as to other legal reforms such as women's property rights and custody rights, the members of the Equity Club became important contributors to the women lawyers movement as well as to the woman's rights movement.

The women lawyers of the Equity Club communicated once a year through letters to ask questions, give advice, express their hopes and fears, and share the successes and setbacks in their professional and personal lives. Although a few were tentative about what they wrote, perhaps because they were intimidated somewhat by the accomplishments of some of the members, they all participated enthusiastically and expectantly. The long silences between their annual letters tested their patience. But their persistence revealed their need for each other and their reliance on the Equity Club at a time when they had few if any other opportunities to share their thoughts with other women lawyers. Moreover, their letters from year to year revealed a remarkable continuity in their subject matter as they responded to each other's queries, though a year or more later. Members shared with each other some of their most significant professional and personal moments. Some graduated from law school, others passed the bar, and still others had important legal victories. A few married, one had a baby, and others had to stop work to care for sick relatives. As they communicated these events with each other from year to year, Equity Club members created a strong internal network of support. They were candid and trusting as they addressed controversial professional matters and asked each other for advice. They were not afraid to disagree, but they always did so with respect and good humor. And they willingly shared some of the most intimate details of their personal lives.

Topics the Equity Club members discussed in their letters revealed the stresses and tensions in their public and private lives. They sought each other's advice on a range of questions, including how to succeed in the business of law while preserving their ties to charity and reform, whether women lawyers belonged in the courtroom as well as in the office, and how to dress as lawyers while retaining their femininity. Although the specific issues were diverse, the burden of double consciousness was a common theme. As the women lawyers in the Equity Club shared their concerns, they found that they could not escape the nagging dilemma of balancing their gender and professional identity.

One of the first questions the women lawyers of the Equity Club considered was how to justify their professional lives. This was no simple task. Nineteenth-century women lawyers understood that they had to explain why it was appropriate that they, as ladies, should move out of their traditional arena of the home and enter the male domain of the legal profession. Women lawyers in Ann Arbor had first raised the issue at a meeting in 1887 when they discussed the question: "What Is our Duty as Women Lawyers in Society?" Some believed that their professional role dictated their obligations and that they should simply "peg along at [their] business, that is, the Law." Others argued that as women they had an obligation to "make a special effort . . . for other women besides [themselves]."[14]

Nineteenth-century women lawyers were divided along both sides of the issue. Some justified their careers by emphasizing the uniqueness of their gender identity. They insisted that they would be the special advocates of women's legal rights and that they would protect women's modesty and listen sympathetically to their legal problems. In fact, they argued that only women lawyers, precisely because of their sympathetic and maternal nature, could adequately protect women's legal rights. Other women lawyers rejected the nineteenth-century emphasis on sexual differences and denied their uniqueness from men. Instead, they focused on their professional identity and claimed that they entered law for precisely the same economic, intellectual, and professional reasons as men. Nevertheless, the task of justifying their legal careers forced all women lawyers, regardless of their point of view, to face the conflict between their gender and professional identity.

The task was not unique to women lawyers. Thousands of women of the era were struggling to extend the boundaries of their lives beyond the home. The efforts of nineteenth-century women to move into the public sphere took many forms, from reform activity such as temperance and suffrage to entry into higher education and the professions. As nineteenth-century women sought to forge public lives, they typically relied on the notion of their uniqueness from men to justify their departure from the home. Taking advantage of the popular belief that they were naturally domestic, modest, and pure, they argued that they had a special mission in the public sphere—to bring the virtues of the home to the world outside. Club women insisted that their reform efforts on behalf of kindergartens, park beautification, and temperance were all inspired by their womanly desire to protect their families. Women seeking higher education argued that they needed separate women's colleges, like Smith and Wellesley, so that they could learn the art and science of domesticity. Women justified their entry into the so-called women's professions of teaching and nursing by arguing that these fields demanded the feminine qualities of caretaking and sensitivity.

Nineteenth-century women also used this argument of female uniqueness to justify their entry into male-dominated professions. As early as midcentury, women doctors explained that their medical careers were simply a natural extension of their womanly responsibility to care for the health of their families. In addition, they argued that precisely because they were women, only they could truly understand the pain and suffering other women endured from gynecological problems. Moreover, they insisted that they could protect the modesty and virtue of a sick woman, whereas the presence of a male physician threatened those qualities. In an age that placed a high value on feminine modesty, women doctors argued that women often chose to endure their pain rather than seek the care of a male doctor. As one nineteenth-century woman doctor said: "In many a case of long-standing and great suffering, my colleagues and I have inquired how the patient could have so long remained without treatment and have been answered, 'Oh, I *could not* go to a man.' "[15]

Many nineteenth-century women lawyers followed the example of women doctors and relied on the argument of woman's uniqueness to justify their place in the law. But it was not so easy to argue that the practice of law was a natural extension of woman's proper place. Women could claim a special role in medicine because compassion, caretaking, and sensitivity were part of medical care. But the heart and the head did not work together as closely in law as it did in medicine. Rather, Victorian-American society saw law as a profession that demanded not only cold objectivity and the mastery of facts, but also cunning, toughness, and the ability to deal with a sordid world. In contrast to the practice of medicine, which occurred in a hospital where the worthy sick received treatment, law practice occurred in a boisterous courtroom where criminals and individuals of ill repute were brought to justice for their deception, greed, and crime. As one man explained: "I hardly think the nature of woman is very well adapted to the practice of law. It does not call into play the higher and better faculties. There is a good deal of cunning and pretense, a good deal that is along the lower lines of conduct; not much opportunity for generosity or nobility."[16] Some women lawyers agreed with this view. "Of her right, heaven given to heal the sick, to soothe pain and suffering, there is, there can be no question," explained Corinne Douglas. "There does not exist the same urgent need of a lady lawyer as a lady physician."[17]

Other women lawyers were unwilling to make that concession. They argued, instead, that just as women had a unique role in medicine, so they also had a special place in the law. Following the example of other women of their day, they based their claim on the notion of female uniqueness. Like women doctors, they turned the emphasis on female modesty to their own advantage. Mary Greene claimed that the importance of preserving female modesty made legal study an even more appropriate endeavor than the pursuit of medicine. "A woman's position in a law school can never expose her to the unpleasant features of a course of *medical* study in a mixed school, which so many hundreds of women are now pursuing."[18]

In addition, Greene claimed that women needed legal counsel from women lawyers in the same way that they needed medical care from women doctors. "Just as many women would prefer to consult a woman physician because they could talk freely and be more sure of sympathy, so they would for the same reasons, consult a woman lawyer," she argued. Greene based her argument on her own experience with widows who had been "duped and deceived" by friends they had trusted. Greene explained that these poor women would come to her "when it was too late for any remedy" and after sharing their situations with her would say in despair: "Oh if I had only known as much as I do now. If I could only have gone to someone who would give me sympathizing counsel, how much richer and happier I should be."[19]

Emma Haddock told a similarly heartrending story about a widow in Louisville, Kentucky. "Her face haunts me yet," Haddock wrote. She "came to me" and said: "Oh, Mrs. Haddock, you can never know the loss and trouble, and indeed in many cases great suffering which comes to us women who have no idea of business. We are so helpless, and with many of us the loss of husband means the loss of all property, and we are thrown without means, and without knowledge, upon our own resources."[20]

Even male lawyers sometimes recognized how difficult it was for women to seek legal counsel from a man. One of Greene's male colleagues claimed that after witnessing the suffering of women who had hesitated to talk to a male lawyer, he "felt sure that they might have been helped much sooner had they had an opportunity to consult a woman in whose legal knowledge and ability they had confidence."[21]

Women lawyers argued that they would do more than protect women's modesty and listen sympathetically to their legal problems; they would be advocates for women's legal rights as well. They claimed that because laws were made by men, men could not sufficiently protect women. Tiera Farrow discovered this fact while she was a law student at Kansas City School of Law. "Laws, from time immemorial, I realized, were made by men, and were interpreted through the courts by lawyers and judges of the male sex. More and more I began to see existing laws through the eyes of a woman in a man's world."[22] Laura de Force Gordon agreed. "Our laws are, in many instances, inimical to the well-being and interests of women," she explained, insisting that there was an "absolute necessity of women having a woman lawyer if they hope to secure a just and equitable interpretation of the statutes at the Bar of Justice."[23] Margaret Wilcox agreed, emphasizing the importance of women lawyers representing women in criminal court. "What [is] more fitting," she asked rhetorically, "than that a woman, trained in legal reasoning, a member of the local bar" be present in criminal court to protect "the needs and rights of members of her own sex in law."[24]

The argument that women lawyers would protect the legal rights of women drew its strength from the prevailing belief that women were naturally different from men. Most men pointed to women's sentimentality as proof that women were unfit to be lawyers, but women lawyers argued that men's objectivity and inexperience with domesticity made them unfit to represent the legal needs of women. According to this view, only women lawyers, precisely because of their sympathetic and maternal nature, could adequately protect women before the law.

One of the fullest elaborations of this argument came from Martha Strickland, a lawyer in Detroit. In her 1891 essay "Woman and the Forum," published in the popular legal journal the *Green Bag*, Strickland argued that sexual differences between men and women made it impossible for men ever to understand fully the needs of women. "The differences between man's nature and woman's nature are a bar, eternal as are Nature's laws, to the equitable administration of justice for humanity by men alone. Men cannot know all the subtle springs of feeling and action hidden within woman's complex organization. They cannot measure her needs by their own."[25] Strickland argued that male lawyers represented and judged women in court according to men's perceptions of women's needs. Moreover, she argued that American law was the creation of men who had infused it with what she said was a one-sided male view of justice and human needs. "Woman's legal rights have been brought to the bar of masculine knowledge and manly chivalry," she argued.[26] "The result is that women have suffered . . . [because the] complete appreciation of needs and innate sympathy with wants which members of one sex alone can have for one another, and which is the golden heart of justice, has been wanting [in] his adjudications."[27] The result, according to Strickland, was obvious. Men lawyers could never truly represent and protect women's legal rights; only women lawyers could. "I am merely saying that there are some things that men do not know, that men cannot learn, and that women do know," she wrote.[28]

Strickland explained that, as a lawyer, she knew firsthand that women did not receive fair treatment from male judges. Male judges, she asserted, not only interpreted laws made by men, but passed judgments reflecting men's needs as well. As one example, Strickland described a child custody case in which a judge ignored the law and awarded the child to the father. Although the burden of proof was on the father to prove the mother's incompetence, and although the judge had declared the mother perfectly competent, he nevertheless awarded the child to the father. In doing so, the judge unjustly favored the rights of the father. He revealed his male bias when he explained that the father "appears to love the child, and I think would suffer very much in giving it up."[29] In this case, the decision handed down by the male judge exposed him to be as subjective and sentimental as men claimed a woman lawyer would be.

Of course, in many cases judges did award custody of children to the mother rather than the father. But even then, according to Strickland, judges were still unable to understand the practical needs of women. She knew of numerous cases in which judges awarded the father at least two-thirds of the property acquired during the marriage, whereas the mother, who had to support herself and her children, received barely a third. This division of property, according to Strickland, did not prove that the judge was hard-hearted, but rather that he could only appreciate the man's point of view. "The judge is familiar with the wants of men in the business world; he knows the need of the man for capital," Strickland wrote. "Without meaning to be heartless or unfair, he, because of his incompetency to view the situation of the woman from the standpoint of experience, fails in complete equity."[30] The only way to rectify the male bias inherent in the legal system, according to Strickland, was to include women lawyers, who would bring their womanly view to balance that of men's. Echoing the Victorian view that men and women made different but complementary contributions to society, Strickland concluded that the acceptance of women into the legal profession would create a balanced and harmonious system of justice in which male and female views would complement each other. "The two shall form a perfect whole, each supplementing the other, and giving each to the other the benefit of a different organization and a different experience."[31]

Women lawyers claimed that they would do more than protect women before the law; they would also make an essential contribution to the legal profession as a whole. Championing the virtues of gender differences, women lawyers argued that their unique values and skills would provide a needed balance to the male view so dominant in the legal profession. The result would be a purer and more virtuous profession better able to serve the needs of men and women alike. In particular, women lawyers argued that whereas male lawyers paid close attention to the business side of law, women lawyers had a uniquely feminine mission to protect women and to expand the ethics of the law. The result, wrote Ada Kepley, would be "sweeter manners—purer laws."[32] Sara Killgore Wertman agreed. Men entered the legal profession for money and power, she explained. One need only look at "the wrecks of manhood strewn all along the shoals of this occupation to tell plainly how much *principle* has been sacrificed for success."[33] Women lawyers, Wertman believed, would elevate the legal profession beyond the crass materialism of male lawyers and transform it into a profession built upon a foundation of purity and ethics. "Ours [is] the part to give to the profession the love-lit hues of Christ's teaching so beautifully set forth in the 'Golden Rule.' "[34]

Some male lawyers agreed that women would bring a civilizing influence to the profession. One male lawyer explained that his personal experience with a woman lawyer persuaded him that women in the law would help preserve a "high standard of professional courtesy."[35] Another male attorney echoed this view, explaining that "if there were more lady lawyers, there would be more gentlemanly lawyers and fewer shysters."[36]

Not all women lawyers concurred with this view. Some approached the burden of double consciousness differently, insisting that professionalism, not femininity, must take precedence. To these women, it was not so easy to combine the virtues of true womanhood with the values of the legal profession. They believed that although a woman lawyer could be a lady at home, in the office or courtroom she must sacrifice her femininity for the good of her professional career. This was the point of Robinson's message when she advised women not to be "lady lawyers" but to "simply be *lawyers*."[37]

Other women lawyers agreed with Robinson's approach. Florence Cronise challenged Kepley's claim that women lawyers would bring "sweeter manners—purer laws" to the profession: "I cannot agree nor feel any sympathy with our sisters of the Equity Club who think woman's mission into the professions is to purify." Describing herself as "too matter of fact" to tolerate such sentimental visions of womanhood, Cronise claimed that female sentimentality had no place in the legal profession and that women lawyers must totally eliminate it from their practice of the law.[38]

At every turn, nineteenth-century women lawyers faced the gnawing problem of how to be at once a lady and a lawyer. For example, the matter lay at the very center of the debate over the place of philanthropy and reform in their professional lives. Victorian-American society made a clear distinction between business and charity. Business was defined as men's domain because it demanded the objectivity and hard-heartedness believed to be inherent in manhood. Charity and reform were accepted as part of women's domain because they relied on the supposedly womanly virtues of caretaking, selflessness, and sentimentality. This sharp division between men's business and women's charity and reform created another source of tension for women lawyers in the late nineteenth century. As women, it was their obligation to engage in charity and reform. But as lawyers, it was more acceptable for them to restrict themselves to business and professional concerns.[39]

Proponents of the traditional side of the debate argued that women lawyers should limit themselves to the more feminine work of charity and reform. This view made its way into the popular culture in the short story "The Lady Lawyer's First Client," written by Thomas Wharton and published in 1885 in the widely read, middle-class *Lippincott's Magazine*.[40] In the story, a woman lawyer, Ellen Tarbell, defended Mrs. Stiles, a poor widow with four children who had suffered an injury as she had attempted to board a train. Mrs. Stiles was permanently lamed as a result of the accident, and she could no longer operate a sewing machine, her sole means of support. As Mrs. Stiles's attorney, Mrs. Tarbell sued the railroad company for $10,000 in damages.

Tarbell's case was strong. The facts were on her side, and even the judge discreetly indicated his support of her argument. But the defense lawyer, Mr. Pope, sought to discredit Tarbell by accusing her of taking what he called "the romantic view of the matter." Linking romance with womanhood, Pope argued that such emotions belonged at home but had no place in the public sphere, certainly not in the courtroom. "Romance, gentlemen, breathes its tender and refining influence about the domestic fireside . . . But romance outside of the home-circle cuts but a sorry figure; it is very dangerous for it to stray out of doors into the rough arena of life,—into the street, gentlemen,—where there are street-cars."[41] The antidote to the romance that women lawyers inappropriately brought into the courtroom, Pope argued, was pure, objective law. "We must look at the evils of life from the strictly legal point of view when they come into court," he insisted. If the jury viewed the case solely from the perspective of legal doctrine, they would "make short work," he contended, "of romance."[42] In Pope's view, only pure objectivity, the domain of manhood and the antithesis of feminine emotions, belonged in the courtroom to grapple with the matters of the railway company, and by implication, all matters of big business.

But if the legal problems generated by the growth of commercial capitalism were naturally the domain of male lawyers, Pope still saw a place in the legal profession for women lawyers. Women's inherent emotions suited them perfectly to champion the cause of the poor and powerless in society. "Let her preserve that beautiful sympathy which is one of the chiefest ornaments of the female sex," he said. "It will bring to her a thousand cases of injustice and oppression which we hardened lawyers of the other sex have lost—if we *ever* had it—the instinct to detect. It will lead her and her sisters to find justice and consolation for innumerable victims of wrong-doing, whose hopes of obtaining redress might have seemed poor and empty to us less inspired practitioners. No one, no man . . . will be sorry to see the law vivified by a spark of that genius, that inexplicable instinct by which women know what is right and make right to be done, where men fail and fail again."[43] In the end, Tarbell's client was persuaded by Pope's argument, withdrew her case, and settled with the railroad company out of court.

The message of the Victorian view was clear. There were two separate divisions within the legal profession: the world of industrial capitalism and big business, what Pope had referred to as the "rough arena of life";[44] and a distinct arena of generosity and charity. Only male lawyers, the champions of cold facts, objectivity, and cunning, belonged in the former. Coexisting in Pope's scheme was another arena, one of philanthropy and sacrifice, where women lawyers dominated by bringing their moral superiority to the legal profession.

There was little consensus among nineteenth-century women lawyers over the place of philanthropy in their professional lives. Strickland offered a reinterpretation of the Victorian view, claiming that it was women lawyers' obligation to bring morality and virtue to all areas of the law. From this point of view, women lawyers belonged in commercial law and criminal law as much as they belonged by the side of the poor and dependent. Other women lawyers adopted the male lawyer's model of success, arguing that law and charity could not mix. They urged women lawyers to avoid the distractions of charity and reform because it was more difficult for women than men to establish successful legal careers. Lelia Robinson expressed this view in a 1888 letter to the Equity Club: "Anything whatever that lures the woman attorney away from her office should be put aside—must be put aside—if women are ever to establish themselves as a recognized element of the bar of this country."[45]

Some women lawyers shared Robinson's point of view. "A lawyer cannot devote any great amount of energy to anything else and make headway in the profession," explained Ellen Martin. "Law is a severe task master and demands undivided allegiance."[46] Emma Gillett also followed this disciplined approach to work. "I have endeavored to do thoroughly and conscientiously whatever I have had to do, to stick to my profession and not be lured into any class of philanthropic or other work," she wrote.[47] Florence Cronise agreed. "No thought of being a public benefactor ever entered my head," she explained. "I cannot accept sentimental views of woman's mission—this world is plain, hard facts, sentiment may be beautiful to look at and indulge one's thoughts in occasionally, but it will earn no bread and butter, accomplish no genuine good and should be set aside for holiday narrations and not allowed to show itself on our hard work days."[48] Emma Gillett was particularly impatient with charity and sentimentality. "Nothing is more wearing than sympathy," she wrote. "I have cultivated a hardness of heart. I can listen to distressing things unmoved, visit the dying and sleep soundly after it."[49] This businesslike approach to the law left little room for acts of charity and benevolence. "Charity clients should be shunned unless in extreme cases," she continued. "They have no more right to a lawyer's services for nothing than a washerwoman's."[50]

Women like Gillett, Martin, and Cronise linked charity with the sentimentality of womanhood and hard-heartedness with the objectivity of the law. In doing so, they created an equation that left no room for philanthropy or benevolence in their professional lives. It seems that with clear consciences and with what they believed to be women's best interest foremost in their minds, they chose career over compassion and self-interest over social reform. But to these women, charity was not simply a matter for each woman lawyer to reconcile with professionalism as she saw fit. It was an important issue for the entire community of women lawyers. "It concerns us all," Gillett wrote, when a woman lawyer permitted charity work to push her "beyond her strength and fail in her work."[51] From this point of view, the question of charity work became a political issue, a test of each woman's commitment to the cause of women lawyers. Thus, the woman lawyer who took on charity work indulged in sentiment at the expense of her own professional advancement and the best interests of all women lawyers. In contrast, the woman lawyer who rejected charity work proved her personal commitment to her own professional success as well as her political allegiance to the larger cause of women in law.

Not all women lawyers were willing to exclude philanthropy from their professional lives. Instead, they sought to bring sentimentality and caretaking into their practice of the law. In doing so, they posed an alternative model of practice that was rooted in the values of ideal womanhood. They argued that the politically appropriate act was to incorporate charity and reform into their professional lives. Unlike Cronise and others who defined individual business success as the ultimate goal of the woman lawyer, these women lawyers shared the view that society came before self, and they urged others to put charity and reform at the center of their professional lives. "There is something besides law to be studied," claimed Marion Todd in 1888. "It is human justice." Referring to the poor women and children who toiled in factories and sweatshops, Todd, active in the Populist movement, insisted that women lawyers had an obligation to use their legal expertise to help the victims of industrial capitalism.[52]

Todd was not alone in her call to women lawyers to help others. Early in her career, Clara Foltz earned a reputation for her humanity and sympathy. Although her friends warned her about the inappropriateness of charitable deeds, Foltz aided many impoverished clients. "I kept myself continually impoverished by what my friends declared was unwise generosity."[53] Far from heeding their admonitions, she became a leading advocate of penal reform and spearheaded legislation that created a public defender system in California.

Even Robinson, who warned women lawyers to avoid distractions, devoted much of her time to helping others through the law. She counseled immigrant and working women at the Women's Educational and Industrial Union in Boston, and opened her office from two to four o'clock on Saturdays to poor women unable to pay her fee.[54] In addition, Robinson tried to remedy the inaccessibility of law to women by writing popular legal books. Her two books, *Law Made Easy: A Book for the People* and *The Law of Husband and Wife*, were written in a clear, straightforward style so that women as well as men could familiarize themselves with what she believed to be the most important legal matters to lay people.[55] Robinson was also aware of women lawyers' tenuous position in the legal profession. She helped to organize the Portia Club, a small women lawyers' club in Boston, as well as the Pentagon Club for women lawyers and other professional women in medicine, teaching, theology, and journalism.[56]

Some women lawyers went beyond legal charity and made social reform an integral component of their professional careers. Margaret Wilcox argued that there was a great need for the services of women lawyers among women's reform movements, particularly the temperance movement. Catharine Waugh McCulloch agreed. She worked hard on suffrage and temperance, even though she admitted that "Miss Cronise'[s] advice about sticking to law business is excellent."[57] McCulloch's male colleagues continually badgered her to give up her reform work. "It's about time you made up your mind whether you are going to be a lawyer or a temperance and suffrage evangelist," one male lawyer told her. He was not the only one to pressure her. McCulloch explained that "another lawyer on the same floor [of her office building] who has often caught me surrounded by women, posters, literature, or invitation cards . . . said, 'What is there to hinder you from being a good lawyer . . . ? [Y]ou waste your time working for these women who would probably consult a man rather than you if they had a paying case.' "[58]

Despite the friendly warnings to work only for paying clients, McCulloch preferred Wilcox's vision, admitting that "it is difficult for me to resist outside pressure to help in church, temperance, and suffrage work."[59] In contrast to Cronise, who deliberately excluded anything of "a public character" from her "law business," McCulloch devoted her legal expertise and professional connections to social reform work and became a leader on behalf of a range of women's causes, including temperance, suffrage, jury duty, and women's custody rights.[60] Other women lawyers shared Foltz's and McCulloch's commitment to reform. Ada Kepley, an ardent supporter of temperance, gave legal advice to the Woman's Christian Temperance Union for many years.[61]

Ada Bittenbender supported herself by serving as legal counsel for the Woman's Christian Temperance Union. With an annual salary of $1,500, she proved that a woman lawyer could make her political convictions pay. "We who have taken up 'side issues' receive many a rap . . . from you who have not or who have ceased to do so . . . But as for myself I believe I am drawing nearer to a successful professional career than would have been the case had I stuck entirely to my office and the court practice." She explained that her temperance work had led to her position as attorney for the Woman's Christian Temperance Union. Moreover, her position as attorney for the temperance union was far from professionally stifling. This "dabbling in side issues" had brought her into contact with many powerful male lawyers and politicians in Washington, D.C., and had thus made her a more influential lawyer than she otherwise would have been.[62]

Women like Bittenbender and McCulloch stood at the opposite end of the spectrum from Cronise, Gillett, and others on the place of charity and reform in women lawyers' professional lives. Over the course of the nineteenth century, women lawyers continued to be divided on the issue. As a result, the question of how a woman lawyer should practice remained unresolved and continued to confront every woman lawyer who embarked on a career, reminding them of the enduring tension between their gender and professional identity.

To many women lawyers, the burden of double consciousness created an even more perplexing problem when it came to choosing a type of practice. According to the custom of the era, women lawyers in nineteenth-century America had to choose between what Bittenbender so crisply labeled "court practice" and "office practice."[63] The choice was agonizing for some women, easy for others. An office practice centered around drafting legal documents such as wills, deeds for real estate conveyancing, and contracts. In contrast, a court practice focused on the trial of civil or criminal cases in state and federal courts. Trial practices were an integral part of the mechanism for dispute resolution in the nineteenth century, and attorneys' reputations depended on their successes in the courtroom.

The importance of courtroom practice created a problem for nineteenth-century women lawyers because the prevailing notion of separate spheres for men and women dictated that women's proper place in the legal profession was the office. Office practice mirrored the work of the home; it demanded the same focus on organization and efficiency that was expected of the nineteenth-century housewife. Moreover, office practice, like housewifery, took place behind closed doors rather than in the public arena of the courtroom. In striking contrast, the courtroom was the epitome of the male domain in the legal profession. Unlike the office, where lawyers handled private matters such as real estate closings and wills, the courtroom was the place where lawyers encountered the most sordid elements of society. The courtroom resembled a saloon, with its spittoons and its tradition of all-male culture.

Women rarely entered a courtroom in the late nineteenth century except to serve as witnesses, defendants, or litigants. Perhaps a court reporter was female, but judges, jurors, court personnel, or opposing lawyers were rarely, if ever, women. Here, in this most public site of legal practice, male lawyers squared off against each other in merciless legal combat. Before judge and jury, they flaunted their most manly qualities—assertiveness, combativeness, competitiveness, and hard-hearted objectivity.[64]

Most male lawyers viewed women lawyers in the courtroom as trespassers in their male domain. They agreed with Judge Ryan of Wisconsin that this arena of legal combat, where lawyers confronted "all the unclean issues" of society and where only the strongest among them survived, was no place for a woman. When Ryan blocked Lavinia Goodell's efforts to be admitted to practice in 1875, he was not thinking of a gentle office practice in which educated yet genteel women drafted exquisite wills and deeds. Rather, he knew all too well that law practice meant the rough and tumble of the courtroom, where murderers, rapists, and other criminals frequented its halls. By rejecting Goodell's application to be admitted to practice law, he had hoped to prevent the integration of his traditional conception of female culture with the seamy side of the male culture of the courtroom. The jurisprudence of separate spheres, as Ryan and others had constructed it, contained the unstated assumption that the courtroom was a male preserve, but for good reason; to protect women from the vulgar life that lurked there.[65]

At the same time that male judges and lawyers argued that woman's modesty and purity made her unfit for the sordid work and combative atmosphere of the courtroom, they also claimed that when a woman lawyer entered the male world of the courtroom, she lost her femininity and became the embodiment of temptation and sin. Stripped of the protection of her modesty and purity, woman's seductive nature took over in the courtroom and threatened to destroy the serious work of the male lawyer—that is, the rational quest for truth and justice.

This notion of the woman lawyer as a seductress evoked trepidation among many male lawyers and judges. At the root of their fear was their understanding that traditional rules of legal combat could not prevail in a contest between a male and a female attorney. Nineteenth-century etiquette made it impossible for any proper gentleman to launch a full-scale legal attack on a woman lawyer in open court. And without his so-called manly right to attack, he was left defenseless against the feminine wiles of his female opponent. The image of a woman lawyer standing before a male judge and an all-male jury struck fear in men's hearts. One male lawyer, speaking against the admission of women to the Georgia Bar in 1884, expressed this fear when he said: "We can imagine a pretty woman, who is a good talker, having some influence with a jury of men."[66] More than twenty years later, another male lawyer, lamenting the "danger of a female invasion" into the legal profession, echoed this same concern that "a handsome and seductive advocate would have it all her own way with a susceptible jury."[67]

A cartoon in the late 1880s, entitled "The Dangerously Pretty Lawyer," illustrated the fear of many male lawyers that their careful preparation and rational arguments could not stand up against a woman lawyer's seductive and alluring ways. The cartoon pictured a pretty, young, woman lawyer—the embodiment of purity, grace, and femininity—standing before a male judge. "Gentlemen of the jury," the caption read, "Can you look me in the eye and say you believe my client guilty?" One glance at the client, a wicked-looking man with apelike features, evoked the racism of the era and immediately told the reader that the client was indeed guilty. His sly grin contrasted sharply with the sincere expression on the pretty lawyer's face. The message of the cartoon was clear. In spite of his strong rational arguments, the male attorney would be no match for "the dangerously pretty lawyer." With her feminine wiles, she would influence the judge and jury, no matter how wise and respected, to forget their objectivity and free a guilty and dangerous man.[68]

Many male lawyers expressed hostility or ridicule toward women in the courtroom, but others conveyed their concern with a more paternalistic voice. They argued that women's inherent sentimentality, so important in other arenas of life, made them emotionally unsuited to make the tough decisions demanded of the lawyer in the courtroom. Emphasizing woman's inability to overcome her "heart and sympathies," one male judge argued that a woman had no place in the courtroom because "the last thing" she would consider in any case "would be the law and justice."[69] This was precisely the problem the fictional Ellen Tarbell had as she tried to win damages for her injured client from the railroad company in "The Lady Lawyer's First Client." As Mr. Pope, the

"The Dangerously Pretty Lawyer," cartoon glued onto inside
cover of the Equity Club Annual, 1888.

lawyer for the railroad explained, Tarbell's "romantic view of the matter"
had no place in the courtroom where matters of law were determined.[70]

Not all nineteenth-century men opposed women lawyers' presence
in the courtroom. A few even supported women lawyers, arguing that
precisely because of their femininity they would bring civility and decorum to the courtroom. They surmised that in the presence of a woman
lawyer, male lawyers would give up their rough ways for the manners
of gentlemen. According to one reporter, this was precisely what occurred in 1870 in the courtroom in Rockford, Illinois, in the presence
of Alta Hulett, who was preparing to practice law. "We observed fewer

boot soles resting upon tables and railings, and less lounging in uncouth attitudes than usual, while we remarked an unwonted spruceness of attire, and evidence of more than ordinary attention to their back hair."[71]

Women lawyers had their own opinions about their place in the courtroom, and once again, there was no consensus on the matter. Some supported the notion of a sexual division of labor in law practice and accepted the courtroom as belonging to men and the office as appropriate for women. Corinne Douglas expressed this view in 1887: "The law business that will fall most naturally into [woman's] hands is that not less honorable and more remunerative if less public, class known as 'office work.' Here her careful attention to detail, added to equal training will give the average woman an advantage over the average man. Surely it is better to make a deed over which there can be no litigation than to twist a meaning favorable to one's client out of one unskillfully drawn."[72]

Chicago attorney Mary Ahrens was one such woman lawyer who made it her "special object" in her law practice "to settle without litigation all cases which with justice to clients can be kept out of court."[73] Similarly, Emma Gillett did "principally office work," which included preparing wills and conveyances, performing notarial work, and supervising accounts and correspondence.[74] Mary Hall of Hartford, Connecticut, limited her practice almost entirely to office work and gave her court work to her male colleagues. With a practice made up almost exclusively of women, she mirrored the image of the ideal woman lawyer who worked carefully yet unobtrusively in an office for the benefit of other women.[75]

In some ways, an office practice was the easiest route for a woman lawyer to follow. Opening a law office was a relatively simple matter. Rooms were rented and furnished with a desk, a few chairs, diplomas, and books; and business cards were sent out. This was a common experience of women lawyers who opened office practices in eastern cities such as Boston and in the Midwest.[76] But once they opened their offices, women lawyers began to face the "doubtful future" as they waited for business.[77] Ellen Martin, a Chicago lawyer, put her finger on the problem: "People with desirable business are slow to entrust it to attorneys without experience . . . [so that] experience must be acquired from poor paying business, and it takes a long time to get upon a self-sustaining basis."[78] Lelia Robinson agreed, pointing out the importance of "patience" and "study"[79] for the beginning woman lawyer because clients were "reluctant to trust any but 'grey hairs.' "[80]

For some women lawyers, patience paid off, and they built successful office practices. Emma Gillett of Washington, D.C., deliberately chose office work over court practice because she believed that her health would not permit her to undertake the strain of jury trials.[81] She turned her skills to probate and other office work and built a successful private practice.[82] Similarly, Catharine Waugh McCulloch always paid her rent on time, never borrowed money, moved to a better office, and believed that she was "doing as well as any other young lawyer in [Rockford, Illinois]."[83] In general, despite their slow and modest beginnings in practice, many women believed that they were faring as well as male lawyers just starting out and were making as much money. Ellen Martin believed that women made their practices into "paying businesses" within two years, the shortest time calculated for men.[84]

Yet success could easily elude the patient and persevering woman lawyer in her office because, as Ellen Martin understood so clearly, a profitable law practice came from businesspeople, most of whom were men. Women lawyers lacked general business knowledge and contacts compared with male attorneys who had ready access to clubs and public places. Unless they had their own family businesses or acquaintances with businessmen, women lawyers were likely to struggle in their careers. This need to rely on business contacts placed women lawyers at a decided disadvantage, particularly when compared to women doctors. Women doctors could rely on the women of their social class to come to them as patients because the wife in a bourgeois family typically chose the family's doctor. In contrast, women lawyers could not rely on middle-class married women to choose them as lawyers because husbands, not wives, were responsible for business and legal matters and typically selected the lawyer for the family.[85]

Even if she had the necessary business contacts, a woman lawyer who restricted herself to office work was not assured of a successful practice; although an office practice could be remunerative, court practice provided a steady business. In truth, most nineteenth-century women lawyers had to enter the all-male courtroom if they wanted to achieve financial success. Many, like Bittenbender, who had a successful court practice in Nebraska, rejected the notion that women lawyers belonged only in an office.[86] Some explained that they could not sufficiently serve their clients outside the courtroom, whereas others admitted that they preferred the activity and publicity of the courtroom to the privacy of the office. Still others appreciated the lucrative financial rewards of courtroom work. Florence Cronise built a successful trial practice in Ohio, gaining "a comfortable income and a success comparing favorably with that of the young men entering the profession at the same time."[87] Letitia Burlingame embraced courtroom work for all of these reasons. "I am just wicked enough to prefer courtroom work," she confessed. "Skillful questioning and honest logic have charms for me that filling in prescribed forms with parrot-like precision never could have." Explaining that "women [lawyers] ought to go into the courtroom" to speak on behalf of their female clients, she asked rhetorically: "Where are they needed more?"[88] But the reality of Burlingame's practice suggests that her enthusiasm for the courtroom was motivated more by financial realities than by lofty ideals. "More courtroom than office work falls to my share," she explained. In one month alone, she earned $110 from court cases, "not one cent of which is from office practice."[89]

Other women lawyers moved into the courtroom more cautiously. Almeda Hitchcock, in practice with her father in Hilo, Hawaii, preferred to stay in the office whenever she could, but when her father went out of town, she "screw[ed] up [her] courage to the sticking point," went to court, and won her case.[90] Like Hitchcock, Robinson also had to overcome her fear of the courtroom. Believing that office work was the appropriate arena for women lawyers, she started out in Boston with high hopes of establishing her own office practice. But her expectations soon dissolved as few people sought her legal advice. "In my own case, I very emphatically chose office practice, but it didn't choose me in any encouraging way." Robinson tried to build an office practice for three and a half years, but "business came in very slowly . . . and consisted mostly of small and rather hopeless claims for collection."[91] Moreover, she referred her litigation cases to male lawyers, which reduced her fees even more. Robinson finally faced the hard truth that she could not support herself in this manner and took the bold step of moving to Seattle because she had heard that views on women were more liberal there than in the Northeast.

Robinson's move west opened up doors to her that would have been unimaginable in Boston. A male judge befriended her and encouraged her to do courtroom work. To help her get started, he appointed her as counsel for a prisoner. "With fear and trembling," she defended her client before a judge and jury and learned firsthand that she "could do the work" she had once deemed the sole domain of her male colleagues.[92] With just a little help, Robinson succeeded in establishing a lucrative law practice that combined both office and courtroom work.

Still, Robinson's professional success could not replace the loneliness she felt for her family. After barely a year in Seattle, Robinson gave up her thriving practice and the professional freedom she enjoyed and returned to Boston to resume her practice near her family. She was now a wiser, more confident, and more practical attorney who recognized the importance of courtroom work for protecting her clients and advancing her public reputation. Her experience in Seattle paid off. In one two-week period in Boston, she tried two cases in court, won them both, and earned $50 for her work.[93]

Although women lawyers like Burlingame and eventually Robinson enthusiastically embraced the challenges of the courtroom, other women lawyers did not find the courtroom so hospitable. They often tolerated rudeness and outright hostility from male lawyers and judges who deliberately tried to antagonize women lawyers and make their presence as uncomfortable as possible. This was Catharine Waugh McCulloch's experience in her early years of practice as a young, single woman in Rockford, Illinois. Even though most of the male lawyers she encountered at the Rockford courthouse treated her with respect, one viewed her with unveiled hostility. "Let me once meet Miss Waugh in a case and I will wipe the floor with her," he threatened. But in his encounters with McCulloch in court, this lawyer masked his aggression with a feigned friendliness. "To my disgust," she related, "he referred to me in open court several times as 'Kitty' so that an outsider would have thought us great friends." To McCulloch, such familiarity breached the boundaries of professional and social etiquette, and she boldly admonished her antagonist for his rudeness. "I told him with intense coldness that when he found it necessary to address me, he should call me Miss Waugh, as only my family and friends were privileged to call me by my home name." McCulloch's strong defense of her reputation in open court must have surprised her antagonist, for as she described the confrontation, "he actually blushed, for the first time in his life, much to the edification of listeners."[94]

Other women endured even more vicious treatment from men in the courtroom. More than any other example, the case of attorney Kate Kane revealed the sexual discrimination women lawyers suffered from male judges who were hostile to women's presence in the courtroom. Kane had been practicing law in Milwaukee since 1878 when she passed the Wisconsin bar. Single and without relatives nearby, she nevertheless built a successful private practice that often brought her into the local courtroom and earned her respect among her professional peers. But for several years, she had suffered under the rude, if not vicious, treatment of Judge Mallory of the municipal court. "I have been conscious for some time that Judge Mallory has been trying to drive me out of his court," Kane explained. "He has continually insulted and misused me, but I bore it because I thought no one else noticed it but myself, although clients, whose business I have solicited refused to employ me, stating that cases would suffer because I did not receive fair treatment." Other lawyers might not have tolerated this treatment, but Kane had little alternative. As a young, woman lawyer, she was well aware that she had no choice but to tolerate Judge Mallory's indignities because she had "to begin at the bottom."[95]

The situation finally became unbearable when Judge Mallory ignored a prisoner's request that Kane defend him and assigned the case to a male attorney instead. "Even the prisoner in the box looked at me with pity, to say nothing of the other people in the room," explained Kane. Furious, Kane left the courtroom and retreated to her office. That afternoon, still in a rage, she returned to the courtroom, reached for the glass of water on Judge Mallory's table, and threw it in his face. "Arrest this woman," Mallory shouted, as court officers seized Kane with such roughness she was left black and blue, fined $50, and "dragged to jail."[96]

The incident created an uproar that spread well beyond the city of Milwaukee and that raised questions not only about Kane but also about the fitness of women lawyers in general. The New York Times followed the story daily, reporting that Kane was "becoming demented" and that her "attack upon the dignity of the judicial bench was feminine." The New York Times revealed a blatant double standard regarding what it defined as acceptable courtroom behavior for male and female lawyers. It acknowledged that male lawyers often expressed their anger in court by throwing objects at each other. "It sometimes happens that arguments in the shape of inkstands, heavy law-books, and even cuspidors [spittoons], become so thick-flying in a courtroom that the spectators seek safety in flight or under desks and tables." According to the *New York Times*, this was tolerable manly behavior in the course of courtroom combat, whereas Kane's behavior was unacceptable and "decidedly feminine." What distinguished Kane's aggressive behavior from that of her colleagues, in the view of the *New York Times*, was that she assaulted a judge rather than another lawyer. In reality, Kane had exhibited the same aggressive behavior that was tolerated among her male colleagues, · but the *New York Times* created a distinction that permitted the paper to define her actions as "an outrageous breach of judicial decorum" while tolerating the aggressive outbursts of male lawyers as acceptable, professional behavior.[97] The *New York Times* failed to understand that Judge Mallory abused his power and that in the nineteenth-century courtroom Kane defended her impugned honor as others might well have done.

In Kane's situation, there was no way to balance gender and professional identity; she was trapped by the burden of double consciousness. As long as she behaved like a lady, quietly accepting Judge Mallory's hostile treatment of her, her courtroom career was doomed. But when she lashed out aggressively in court like her male colleagues often did, she was defined as unstable, feminine in the most negative sense, and unfit to practice law. Although Kane's situation may have been extreme among women lawyers of her day, it revealed how important it was for nineteenth-century women lawyers to preserve their femininity as they cultivated their professional identity. If, as in Kane's case, a woman lawyer stepped over the boundaries of acceptable feminine behavior, her career and professional reputation would suffer.[98]

Not all women lawyers encountered the intense degree of sexual discrimination that Kane endured. But there was a problem that every woman lawyer, no matter how acquiescent and demure, encountered once she crossed the threshold to the courtroom: what she should wear to court. The burden of double consciousness required every woman lawyer to show with clothing how she balanced her femininity with her professional identity. Before a woman lawyer left her home each day, she had to choose carefully an outfit that would convey at once seriousness and softness, objectivity and sentimentality, professionalism and femininity. Although fashion may have been a frivolous pastime for the leisured woman with money to spend, for the woman lawyer in the late nineteenth century, it was a serious matter that embodied the broader social issues of woman's place in the legal profession and in society at large.

Most women lawyers in the late nineteenth century chose suits and dresses that successfully balanced the demands of femininity and professionalism; indeed, women's suits incorporated some of the materials, techniques, and design elements of men's clothing.[99] Typically, they selected a simple, black outfit accented with jewelry or lace. The simplicity and dark colors of women lawyers' outfits mirrored the suits of men lawyers and revealed women lawyers' professional identification with their male colleagues. The extra adornments women lawyers carefully applied conveyed the message that although the women were certainly lawyers, they were still ladies. Moreover, this outfit assured them the respect due the most proper of ladies, for it followed the advice to women in etiquette books to avoid the frills of fashion and to dress neatly, simply, and comfortably.[100]

Belva Lockwood wore clothes that reflected this balance. She could be "a butterfly of fashion" when socializing with other women. At a meeting of the International Council of Women, she wore a pink satin dress adorned with black lace and pearls.[101] But in her professional life, she dressed with restraint, carefully balancing her soft and serious sides. She usually wore a plain black dress accentuated with lace or ruffles at the neck and wrist. To soften her appearance even more, she sometimes wore flowers in her hair, and as a clear testimony to her domesticity, she wore a gold brooch in the shape of a scissors and a thimble.[102] Clara Foltz and Laura de Force Gordon struck a similar balance between femininity and professionalism when they appeared in court in 1879 to defend their right to attend Hastings College of Law. Foltz wore a black silk business suit trimmed with velvet and lace, a gold brooch at her neck, and golden butterflies attached to bands of black velvet at her wrists. Gordon wore a black silk dress "with some suggestions of masculinity in the make, white linen cuffs, [and] simple gold jewelry."[103] It was important to women lawyers like Lockwood, Foltz, and Gordon that they find the successful balance between business and beauty in their clothing, for the press watched them carefully to report their appearances to an ever curious public. Often the descriptions revealed less than an objective reporter's eye. In the case of Foltz and Gordon, for example, a reporter described their outfits objectively but elaborated on their hair with unrestrained metaphors and exaggeration. Foltz's braids fell "backward from the crown of her head like an Alpine glacier lit by the setting sun," and Gordon had "curls enough to supply half the thin-haired ladies of San Francisco with respectable switches."[104]

Nineteenth-century women lawyers had little problem balancing their femininity and professionalism through their dresses and jewelry, but they faced a more perplexing problem in the question of what to do about their hats. This was a serious concern to every woman lawyer who entered the courtroom. It was not so easy for women lawyers to model their courtroom behavior after male lawyers, who respectfully removed their hats when they entered a courtroom. Because a hat was part of the appropriate attire for a nineteenth-century lady who ventured forth in public, social convention dictated that women lawyers— as ladies—wear their hats when they entered the courtroom. Here was the burden for the nineteenth-century woman lawyer. As a proper lady of her day, social etiquette required that she wear a hat in public. But as a lawyer, professional etiquette demanded that she remove her hat when she entered the courtroom. As a result, the question of the hat once again confronted women lawyers with the enduring challenge of reconciling their traditional role as women with their new professional identity as lawyers.[105]

Lelia Robinson first raised the problem of the hat in 1888. "Shall the woman attorney wear her hat when arguing a case or making a motion in court, or shall she remove it"?[106] Robinson's personal answer to the question was clearly in favor of the hat. She always wore a small hat "set back from her face" in court, just as she did in other public places. "It is surely no mark of disrespect to the court for a woman to appear at the bar in her bonnet, which it is customary for her to wear in church," she explained.[107] Robinson's strategy was simple. Her hat conveyed the message that even though she had entered the courtroom, she still adhered to the conventions expected of the proper lady of her day. But when another woman lawyer, younger than she, criticized her for wearing a hat in court, Robinson became so perplexed over the issue that she sought the opinion of other women lawyers. "Is there any good reason why a woman who is trying a case should bare her head—and with no chance to look in a mirror to see if her hair is straight, or rather to see if it is still in curl?" she asked.[108]

Robinson's query set off a discussion among women lawyers that revealed, once again, that there was no simple answer. McCulloch rejected Robinson's approach. Embracing the principle of equality between the sexes, she argued that women lawyers should follow the lead of male lawyers. "Some seem to think that a bonnet is absolutely necessary on a woman's head to redeem her from the curse deserved for lifting up her voice on the rostrum . . . but I object on principle." McCulloch agreed. Just as a man removed his "overcoat, stovepipe hat and mittens" before addressing a judge and jury, it was the woman lawyer whose "rubbers, gossamer, bonnet, veil and gloves [were] left at the door" who was "in speaking trim."[109] This was Gordon's approach when she went to court in 1879. With the press following her every move, she wore a "straw hat with saucy feather and velvet surrounds" into court but removed it before she spoke.[110]

Nineteenth-century men who engaged in the hat debate seemed to take this side as well. As early as 1876, a man raised the issue in Myra Bradwell's *Chicago Legal News*. Under the pseudonym of "E. Quality," the author, a self-described supporter of "complete legal and political equality of the sexes," argued that women lawyers should follow the same "court-room etiquette" as their male colleagues. "Would it not be more in keeping with their new office if . . . the lady lawyers would remove their hats, and address the court with head uncovered as the gentlemen members of the bar are compelled to do?" he asked.[111] This was also the view of author Thomas Wharton, whose fictional attorney in "The Lady Lawyer's First Client," Mrs. Tarbell, removed her tweed walking hat "very quickly in the court-room," understanding it was "impossible for her to remain covered before the bench of judges."[112]

Robinson and McCulloch presented dichotomous views on the hat question, but other nineteenth-century women lawyers took less extreme positions. Letitia Burlingame had no set rules. Instead, she let the particular situation dictate her decision. "I do not like to keep my head covered," she explained, "and feel sure that I shall never wear my hat when conducting a case, but if I were just going to make a motion or something of that sort, then I would."[113] To other women lawyers who were trying to determine whether to wear their bonnets in the court-room, her advice was simply, "Why, yes, if one prefers."[114] Margaret Wilcox, from Milwaukee, Wisconsin, echoed Burlingame's belief in a woman's right to choose whether to wear her hat. "Let no one lay down the law," she wrote. "Mind I give you all fair warning that I shall wage unending warfare for the freedom of women lawyers . . . I maintain it is the inalienable right of each lady to follow her 'own sweet will.' "[115]

The debate over the hat demonstrated women lawyers' concern over finding acceptance in the most public of legal arenas, the courtroom. Questions about whether women lawyers should even practice in the courtroom at all, and whether they should put their energy into charity and reform, also involved professional decisions that affected the public side of women lawyers' lives. At the same time, their professional decisions were shaped by the intimate details of their private lives. For nineteenth-century women lawyers, the burden of double consciousness not only affected their professional careers, it also permeated the inner sanctums of their personal lives, inextricably linking their public and private selves.

FOUR

"I *Think* I Haven't Neglected My Husband"

$\mathcal{I}$n 1889, Lelia Robinson asked women lawyers to consider a question she had been pondering for some time. "*Is* it practicable for a woman to successfully fulfill the duties of wife, mother and lawyer at the same time? Especially a young married woman?"[1] Once again, Robinson identified a pivotal issue for nineteenth-century women lawyers. Just as the question of the hat went to the heart of double consciousness in the public arena, the issue of marriage and career lay at the intersection of women lawyers' professional and personal lives. Women lawyers did not view marriage, motherhood, sexuality, and health simply as private concerns. They understood all too well that they would never be free to build their professional careers until the arrangements of their personal lives were well in order. They were not alone. Women in all professions, including medicine, academia, science, and social work, struggled with the question of how to balance marriage and a career.[2]

Nineteenth-century women lawyers were far from unanimous in their attitudes toward this important issue. Some held the separatist view that nineteenth-century women had to separate career and marriage by remaining single if they chose to follow a professional path. Others expressed the traditional notion that as soon as she married, a woman had to give up her career to devote herself exclusively to her domestic responsibilities. Still others expressed the integrated view that women, like men, could have both marriage and career.

Although nineteenth-century social observers often defined single women as spinsters who were undesirable marriage partners, unmarried women lawyers typically remained single by choice. Believing that they had to choose between marriage and career, they sacrificed marriage in the hope of establishing productive professional lives. Some single women lawyers believed that marriage imposed too many domestic obligations on women and was incompatible with a serious career. Marion Todd, a widow of eight years, spoke from experience when she explained that she would never remarry because the obligations of wifehood were "too great a responsibility."[3] Even single women were not necessarily free from household duties. Mary Greene, for example, lamented that she could not "practice just as a man does" because of her domestic responsibilities. "I have concluded that in the future I must sandwich law and housekeeping together as I have done in the past year."[4] Still, single women lawyers believed that they were freer than their married counterparts to devote time and energy to their careers. One woman lawyer explained that it appeared "that the majority of the practitioners who are sticking to their work and plodding on in the sure and safe way to win success are unmarried."[5]

Behind this idealized belief that single women lawyers enjoyed a unique freedom to work was the stark reality that they had to work simply to survive. Women lawyers, single or married, may have justified their careers with the moral assertion they would purify the profession and serve the special needs of women clients, but practicality, rather than high-minded principles, typically propelled single women into the law. Many had been teachers, for example, who had left education for the law in search of less arduous and more remunerative work.

Having made the decision to practice law, the very act of opening and maintaining an office highlighted the fact that a single woman's independence was often a matter of necessity rather than choice. The financial responsibilities were hers alone. "I opened my office alone, and wholly independent of others," explained Letitia Burlingame in 1889. With "no capital but courage and patience," she borrowed money to furnish her office and library and "faced the doubtful future."[6] Once in practice, most single women rejected the popular ideal that they would serve the special needs of women. Instead, they took any business they could find, especially when they were just starting out in practice. In 1888, Mary Greene planned to "open an office in the fall, in Boston . . .

[and] take whatever business comes, until I can afford to select—if that happy time ever arrives."[7] As a widow, Belva Lockwood approached her early years in law practice in precisely the same way, accepting "every case, no matter how difficult, occurring in civil, criminal, equitable and probate law."[8]

Similarly, Florence Cronise never turned a case away. In 1873 she and her sister, Nettie Cronise, opened an office together in Tiffin, Ohio. They had few clients at first. "We sat and waited," she explained, for the "occasional shadow [who] passed over the threshold and entered."[9] After Nettie married and entered into practice with her husband, Florence continued to practice alone. For the next fifteen years she handled a wide range of cases, including railroad suits; insurance, land, and labor claims; libel suits; suits against corporations; and divorce, alimony, and bastardy cases. Most of these cases had nothing to do with women's special needs or the uplifting of the legal profession. In short, for single or widowed women lawyers like Cronise, Greene, and Lockwood, the hard realities of life, not the romantic notions of ideal womanhood, determined the direction of their professional careers.

Marriage, of course, had the potential to alter radically the direction of a woman lawyer's professional life. By 1890, the census-takers found that 21 percent of practicing women lawyers were married and that another 14 percent were either widowed or divorced. At first glance, the census-takers would have concluded that marriage and law practice were incompatible. But marriage correlated with age, and the census-takers uncovered both young women who were single, but would eventually marry, as well as older women who were married, widowed, or divorced. In fact, many nineteenth-century women lawyers married at a remarkably high rate. Robinson found that 51 percent of the 120 women lawyers and law students she identified in 1890 were married. Similarly, over one-half of the members of the Equity Club, which included a more established cross-section of women lawyers, were married. Robinson concluded approvingly that the late-nineteenth-century woman lawyer "exists to quite a numerical degree in the married state as in that of single blessedness."[10] Compared with women doctors, who married at rates of 25 to 35 percent, some groups of women lawyers married at sharply higher rates as they became more settled in their professional lives. What is perhaps most important, however, are the similarities between the rates of marriage among women lawyers and women doctors. These similarities reveal shared qualities that enabled women in these two professions to balance career and marriage. Not only did they tend to have higher incomes than teachers or college professors; nineteenth-century women lawyers and doctors also had more professional autonomy. They practiced primarily in private offices, and set their own hours, working independently or with a husband, which permitted them to negotiate the demands of marriage and career.[11]

Some married women followed the path expected of nineteenth-century women and gave up their law work after they married. But even with their traditional marriages, they still valued their legal education, though not necessarily for professional reasons. Instead, they echoed the argument of women like Catherine Beecher and Emma Willard, who insisted that higher education would make women better wives and mothers. Rebecca May explained that a woman with legal education "will be a better woman, will make a more companionable wife, a mother better able to understand and direct her children—a *more intelligent citizen*."[12] Corinne Douglas shared a similar view. Although she believed that the first responsibility of a married woman, no matter how well educated, was always to her family, she still believed that professional training made a wife a better "helpmeet" to her husband.[13] Douglas's views mirrored her own experience. She studied law at the University of Michigan to help her husband who was a lawyer, not because of her own career aspirations, and she devoted her life to family responsibilities rather than to a legal career. Douglas's husband explained that his wife "finds her hands full in 'Domestic Relations,' so to speak, in taking care of her boy and other duties. She studied law for the purpose of helping me and not for the practice generally."[14]

Leona Lounsbury was another married woman who believed that legal study enhanced rather than detracted from feminine virtues. Her own legal education helped to confirm her belief in "the theory that true woman can think and act for herself independently yet modestly, at the same time advancing the virtues of womanhood."[15] Yet in Lounsbury's case, her lofty ideals about marriage and legal education for women contrasted sharply with the bleak and lonely reality of her daily life as a wife and mother.

Lounsbury met her husband while they were both law students at the University of Michigan. But the equality she enjoyed during her courtship disintegrated when she married and moved to Omaha, Nebraska, where her husband opened a law office and she stayed home and had a baby. The demands of housework and motherhood exhausted her physically and mentally. In addition, she felt isolated from the community of women lawyers to which she once, though briefly, belonged. "The complicated and inexhaustible duties of housewife have interfered materially with mental culture," she lamented. "I am much in need of correspondence with those who are more fearless than I." In an expression of deep despair over her inescapable loneliness she confessed: "I [am] in the home in which I have become, almost a voluntary prisoner."[16]

Although women lawyers like May, Douglas, and Lounsbury gave up their legal careers for women's traditional role in marriage, others rejected this self-sacrifice and adopted the view that a woman could be both a wife and lawyer. Ironically, one of the purest expressions of this integrated view was articulated by Emma Gillett, who never married. Speaking from the perspective of a single woman with a private law practice in real estate and pension law, she argued that single women had the best opportunity for professional success. She thought that married women could still have active legal careers if they rejected the traditional version of marriage with its sexual division of labor and carved out a marriage of autonomy and absolute equality. With this in mind, Gillett advised married women lawyers to follow closely the example of men lawyers by devoting their days to their legal work and their evenings to rest and leisure. "Men go home to their dinner, evening paper, a stroll down town," while women go home to "run a sewing machine" or to take on "domestic cares," she observed. "Self-sacrifice of this kind is absolutely wrong and unjust." Exposing the trap of the overburdened, married professional woman and anticipating the arguments of many twentieth-century women, Gillett advised that it was not enough for women simply to advance in their practices. They had to redefine their roles at home as well by modeling their behavior after men. "If we take up work that has been monopolized by men, we should study the manner in which they have accomplished the work and how they have spent the hours not occupied by their profession, and follow the general line of their experience."[17]

As a single woman, Gillett approached the question of marriage and career theoretically, envisioning an ideal marriage based on absolute equality between husband and wife. In contrast, married women lawyers approached the issue from experience and typically moved past images and ideals to organize their lives around the practical concerns of their daily lives. Those with active professional lives did not establish relationships of pure equality with their husbands as Gillett had envisioned. Instead, their marriages thrived on a spirit of equity, which emphasized fairness in their relationship rather than an even and precisely balanced allocation of responsibilities. Husbands and wives, individually and together, organized their lives to help each other and to accommodate each other's needs. In their pursuit of fairness to each other, they built relationships that sustained the integration of career and marriage in women's lives.

In contrast to the idealistic notion that women entered the law to help other women, most married women lawyers practiced law with the practical goal of helping their husbands. Ada Bittenbender studied law for two years under the tutelage of her husband before she joined him in practice. Emma Haddock entered law school ten years after her marriage and then joined her husband in his law practice. Laura LeValley met her husband when they were law students at the University of Michigan and then went into practice with him. Similarly, Margaret Wilcox, who met her husband when they were both teachers, went on to college and law school with him and then worked with him in his law practice.

For these women, the opportunity to work with their husbands made it possible to blend successfully marriage with a career in law. Although single women lawyers claimed greater freedom to devote their energy to their work, the reality was that in an era of strong prejudice against women in law, women lawyers who were married to lawyers had an advantage over single women lawyers. Single women typically had to confront on their own sexual discrimination and the difficult search for work. In contrast, women lawyers who were married to lawyers usually found that their husbands not only provided them with a secure and welcoming place to work, but also shielded them from public disapproval.

Given these advantages, women lawyers often viewed marriage to a lawyer as the ideal arrangement. Robinson believed that the "happiest thing, surely for a woman lawyer who marries is to marry into law rather than out of it." She singled out her friend, Margaret Wilcox, as an example: "Was there ever a more delightful romance than that of the husband and wife, who, having studied together in college and law school, graduate together to start . . . in practice together?"[18] Ironically, just two years later Robinson, already once married and divorced, married a man who was not a lawyer, thereby joining the small group of married women lawyers in the late nineteenth century whose husbands did not practice law. "Thus do we preach and not practice," she wrote to the Equity Club in the year of her marriage.[19] Privately, Robinson admitted to her friend, Catharine Waugh McCulloch, who had just married a lawyer, that she believed her own situation would be more difficult to manage. "I am braver than you, my dear, for I have made the hitherto untried experiment of marrying *out* of the profession, while you have safely married *into* it."[20]

McCulloch did not disagree with her friend. Referring to the newly married Robinson, she explained that "Mrs. [Robinson] Sawtelle writes me that she is braver than I in marrying a business man . . . Well perhaps if I should have fallen in love with a business man, I would have been willing to marry him, but I am thankful he happened to be a lawyer."[21] Nevertheless, Lelia Robinson Sawtelle was optimistic about her marriage and saw it as a crusade on behalf of expanding women lawyers' marital options. "I hope to prove that not only may a woman lawyer marry but she may marry any man she prefers, whatever his business, and it need not interfere with her practice."[22]

For the woman lawyer who was married to another lawyer, equity, not equality, typically characterized their professional relationship as well as their private relationship. Most lawyers in the 1880s were solo practitioners, although in cities several lawyers might have a partnership. Husband and wife may have shared such an office, but their daily working relationship did not reflect the pure equality Gillett had urged. Instead, it represented the expansion of the traditional marital relationship, with its sexual division of labor, beyond the home. The husband exercised ultimate power and authority, and the wife usually served as his assistant. The husband typically went to court where trial work was dominated by men. Meanwhile, the wife stayed in the office where she was welcomed and needed to prepare basic legal documents and to manage office business. These responsibilities reflected a wife's domestic role and demanded the same attention to detail, management, and compromise as did running a household and family. The married woman lawyer working with her lawyer husband was the ideal woman transposed into the safety of her husband's office—one who worked modestly and unobtrusively behind the scenes while he worked aggressively in the public eye.

Many married women lawyers seemed to accept this working relationship and even thrived on the organizational skills required in running a law office. Emma Haddock explained that she "preferred the preparation of a case to its argument," which she willingly left to her husband.[23] Similarly, Laura LeValley "never made an effort to take an active part in court." Instead, she was content to let her husband go to court while she stayed behind as a stenographer and office manager.[24]

Not all married women lawyers who practiced with their husbands restricted their legal work to the office. Ada Bittenbender shared a court practice with her husband and enjoyed court practice more than office work.[25] Nettie Cronise Lutes went to court while her "totally deaf" husband took care of most of the office responsibilities.[26] Anna Christy Fall of Massachusetts, also in law practice with her husband, did not let motherhood interfere with her active court practice, even when she was nursing a baby. Instead, her sister or a domestic servant brought the baby to court at a scheduled feeding time. The judge usually granted a recess at Fall's request, and she retreated into the witness room to nurse before resuming her position before the bench.[27] But Fall, Lutes, and Bittenbender were unique among married women lawyers in practice with their husbands. Most nineteenth-century wives willingly undertook the responsibilities of the office, grateful that their husbands handled the courtroom work.

For a nineteenth-century woman lawyer, the key to her ability to manage both a career and marriage was not establishing the right balance in the office; it was finding the right man. Newly married Catharine Waugh McCulloch made this clear when she explained that women lawyers need not fear marriage "but that it makes all the difference in the world who one marries."[28]

The right husband had several important qualities. First, he supported his wife's efforts to practice law. As McCulloch explained, he was "progressive enough to be proud that his wife was a lawyer."[29] Ada Kepley owed her very career to her husband who encouraged her to study law at a time when she lacked the confidence, though not the desire, to take on the challenge. "The customs of sex so bound me that I needed an impelling force, and I gratefully record this as due my 'partner' in law and life," she wrote.[30] Like Kepley, newly married Lelia Robinson Sawtelle benefited from her husband's support of her career. He willingly took time out from their honeymoon in Washington, D.C., so that Lelia could be admitted to the United States Supreme Court. Even though her husband was not a lawyer, Robinson believed that he would help her achieve her professional goals. "My husband is proud of my professional ambitions and does everything that a husband can do to encourage me in it," she explained. His wedding present was a "fine roll-top desk" for her office, and he barely complained when "every pair of socks is in need of mending." Despite his tolerance, Robinson felt uneasy about neglecting her husband's needs. "I sit down the same instant, usually, and have a pair ready in about three minutes."[31] Still, she felt that may not have been enough. "I *think* I haven't neglected my husband, but am not quite certain even of that," she confessed privately to McCulloch.[32]

In addition to supporting his wife's work, the so-called right husband had other qualities as well. McCulloch made a man's attitude toward woman suffrage a test of whether he would be a good husband. While in law school, she and her husband-to-be attended suffrage meetings together. Years later, she urged young women to follow her example. The best way to ensure future happiness, she argued, was to avoid marrying an anti-suffragist. Instead, she urged them to marry only a "suffrage husband" who would also accord "equality to his wife and other things though not forced by law."[33]

Women like McCulloch and Robinson recognized that marriage was not simply a private relationship but a distinctly political arrangement as well. With this keenly in mind, they deliberately sought husbands who shared their overall views on woman's role in society and who appreciated their own career aspirations. The task was not always easy. McCulloch acknowledged that many of the "good men" were already married, having been "snapped up like hot cakes. They are never bachelors except by choice," she explained.[34] Finally, the right husband was financially secure and willing to pay for the domestic servants needed to free his wife from domestic responsibilities, and thereby enable her to practice law. The McCulloch marriage, for one, relied on the services of a cook, a laundress, and a gardener.

With the few "good men" in high demand, not all women lawyers fared as well in marriage as did McCulloch, Robinson, or Kepley. The experience of Mary McHenry reveals just how destructive an unsupportive husband could be to a woman's career aspirations. The first woman to graduate from Hastings College of Law in 1882, McHenry was immediately admitted to the bar and opened a successful law practice. Her marriage to landscape artist William Keith, a widower with two children, abruptly ended what appeared to be a promising legal career. She moved with her husband and his children to Berkeley and gave up the law. In a letter to Robinson, she explained that although she hoped to resume her law practice some day, "her husband laughingly says, 'not much you will.'" In fact, McHenry never returned to the law. Instead, though she never had children of her own, she devoted her life to her family and even read to her husband nightly so "that he might save his eyes for his daily work."[35]

In contrast to McHenry, McCulloch's experience provides a closer look at the advantages marriage offered a woman lawyer if she married a supportive and financially secure husband. Young and single, McCulloch graduated from the Union College of Law and was admitted to the Illinois bar in 1886. Armed with impressive contacts and recommendations from judges and law school professors, she set out optimistically to find a job as a law clerk in Chicago. "Other classmates were doing the same already and why not I?" she explained.[36] But her enthusiasm soon gave way to despair. After answering every advertisement for a young lawyer, she finally gave up. "I dragged myself back collapsed with chagrin and failure," she recalled, for "it seemed as if there was no place on earth for a young woman just graduated from law school."[37]

Despite her social connections and premier educational training, McCulloch could not overcome the sexual prejudice against her among reputable lawyers in Chicago. But her sex was much less significant when she returned home to Rockford. There, among people who knew her, her social connections figured far more prominently and helped her to overcome the sexual discrimination she had experienced in Chicago. One of the deacons of her church gave her a desk in his real estate office and helped her to get started with a mortgage foreclosure case. Six months into her growing practice, she once again felt optimistic and enthusiastic about her prospects as a lawyer.[38]

Shortly after moving to Rockford, McCulloch resumed a courtship with a former law school classmate, Frank Hawthorn McCulloch. They married in 1890, and Catharine and her husband settled in Chicago. In doing so, Catharine Waugh McCulloch gave up her small, solo practice in Rockford and entered into her husband's larger, established practice in Chicago. In McCulloch's case, it was only through marriage that she finally gained entry into Chicago's legal establishment. Rather than impeding her legal career, marriage accelerated it considerably. Just months later, she shared that understanding with the Equity Club. "I believe now that instead of crippling my ability to be a lawyer that my prospects are much improved."[39] Meanwhile, her friends admired her husband for bringing her into his practice and waited to see if their working partnership would last. Robinson offered cautious congratulations: "I am proud of your husband, who after spending the usual years in establishing a practice, joyfully welcomes you to it as well as to him. I shall be interested extremely to know how it goes—whether your coming will help or hinder."[40]

From the very beginning, Frank brought his wife into his practice. They arrived together at their office every morning at nine, and they returned home at six each evening where dinner was waiting for them, prepared by a domestic servant. Catharine thrived on the arrangement: "I am more contented and yet more ambitious than ever before."[41] But although the McCullochs worked closely together, Catharine was never an equal participant with her husband. Frank was the unquestioned head of the firm of McCulloch and McCulloch. Initially, Catharine spent most of her time working on Frank's business. She gradually built up her own Chicago clientele, but her practice was never as busy as Frank's. Instead, Catharine devoted much of her energy to her woman suffrage work and her children. It was a daunting task to raise four children while working for woman suffrage and practicing law. Catharine managed it with remarkable success because she had the unquestioned support, both emotional and financial, of her husband in everything she did.

Frank, who had been an avid supporter of suffrage when he and Catharine met in law school, gave his wife unwavering support for her

Catharine Waugh McCulloch with baby at convention in Racine, 1901.

suffrage work, even though it often took her away from home. On one suffrage trip shortly after they married, Frank wrote Catharine a series of letters in which he reassured her about her decision to travel. Seeking to alleviate any financial concerns she might have, he repeatedly offered to send her money, explaining that he would "feel it a privilege to do something for the cause."[42] He also reassured Catharine that although he missed her tremendously, she did not need to worry about his well-being. "I am getting plenty to eat and all the clean clothes I want," he wrote.[43] He even joked with her about the domestic tasks he was doing in her absence. "Breakfast dishes are washed and the potatoes are pared for dinner . . . so you see my work is almost done for today."[44] His message to his wife was clear and constant: *"Don't worry about anything."*[45]

Frank steadfastly encouraged his wife's suffrage work, but he made his own contributions to the cause of woman's rights as well. He wrote several essays on behalf of woman's right to vote. He also championed the cause in other, less dramatic ways. In 1909, he and Catharine attended the alumni banquet for their law school. But the Chicago Athletic Association, the site of the dinner, would not admit Catharine because she was a woman. Frank persuaded the authorities to admit his wife, thereby weakening the strong tradition of sexual discrimination at the Chicago Athletic Association. In addition, he convinced the alumni officers to plan all future alumni activities in places that would permit the full participation of the women law graduates.[46]

Woman's rights leaders were quick to acknowledge Frank's importance to their cause. "I wish we had more of such men," a suffragist wrote to Catharine after receiving one of Frank's suffrage essays.[47] Ultimately, Frank's unbounded emotional and financial support made it possible for Catharine to remain at the center of Illinois suffrage activity and to continue her law work after she had children.

Even with the support and understanding of her husband, domestic responsibilities always intruded, making it impossible for Catharine to accomplish as much work as she would have liked. She recalled one day in 1901, the year she had taken off from work to be with her third baby. When Frank left in the morning, she optimistically announced that she needed only a few more hours to complete an article she was writing. The events of the day, however, made it impossible for her to accomplish even that limited task.[48]

McCulloch's description of the details of that particular day reveal that even the support of her husband could not help her escape the endless, small details of domestic life that have made it so difficult for generations of mothers to do serious work at home. Throughout the day, childcare responsibilities, household duties, and social obligations continually interrupted her. Although these obligations were part of women's work in late-nineteenth-century America, in McCulloch's case they assumed the particular character of her social class and professional status. As an upper-middle-class woman, McCulloch had the benefit of a handful of domestic servants, including a cook, a gardener, and a laundress. They performed most of the actual labor for the McCulloch household. Yet they did not provide the quiet, carefree environment McCulloch needed to accomplish serious work. In fact, the servants made their own demands on McCulloch's time, so that managing them filled most of the free moments that remained after she had tended to her children.

This particular day began at five in the morning when McCulloch awoke to nurse her baby. By seven both she and the baby were washed and dressed, and she was ready for breakfast with Frank and her two other children, aged nine and two. After Frank and her oldest child left, she tended to several household matters, conferred with the cook, and then nursed the baby again. At ten o'clock, she finally sat down at her desk, only to be interrupted twice by the laundress. McCulloch sat down again to write, but was interrupted by the gardener. When she returned to her desk, it was time to nurse her two-year-old. From noon until two she had lunch with her two oldest children, spoke with the gardener, and nursed the baby. In the afternoon, she wrote letters, mailed packages, made phone calls, and tended to her children. By the time she had paid the laundress and the gardener, it was almost five o'clock. She nursed the baby again, fed the two-year-old, and got all her children ready for bed. When Frank came home, they had a quiet dinner with the oldest child, and then all the children went to bed. By this time, it was nine o'clock. Frank edited what little she had written that day while she contemplated working until midnight to finish her article. But as she reflected on the schedule for the next day, with a committee meeting to attend and guests to entertain, she reluctantly decided to go to bed.

Given the nearly constant daily demands on McCulloch—even before the birth of her fourth child—it is remarkable how much she accomplished in her public life. In the very year in which she had such nonstop days, she drafted the bill that was passed by the Illinois legislature to give women equal guardianship rights with their husbands. Indeed, she accomplished a great deal during the busiest years of her childrearing: she drafted a bill that raised the legal age of consent for women in Illinois from fourteen to sixteen; she was legal adviser for the National American Woman Suffrage Association from 1904 through 1911; and she was twice elected justice of the peace for the Chicago suburb of Evanston. In fact, in her first campaign for justice of the peace, McCulloch turned her mothering responsibilities into an asset, claiming that as "the mother of little children," she would always be home or nearby and would therefore be easy to find by anyone needing her judicial services.[49]

McCulloch's full and productive life did not go unnoticed. Local newspapers featured her as an example of a woman who was "a good lawyer, a good justice of the peace, a good housekeeper, a good homemaker, and a most devoted mother."[50] Suffragist leaders happily claimed her as one of their own. The Reverend Anna Howard Shaw, who had married Catharine and Frank in 1890, deliberately hung a picture of the couple and their children in the Washington headquarters of the National American Woman Suffrage Association in 1910, "where everybody can see it." To Shaw, families like the McCulloch's helped prove to skeptics who "speak of us as a discontented lot" that suffragists could, in fact, be womanly: "We point to your group and to one or two other groups, with such pride."[51]

Women like McCulloch, as well as Robinson and Kepley, found that their professional careers benefited from marriage and the financial security it offered. Although the prevailing view in late-nineteenth-century America was that women must follow either the separatist approach and sacrifice marriage for career or the traditional approach and give up their career when they married, women like McCulloch were testimony to the fact that for this first generation of women lawyers the integrated view often prevailed; marriage could support and sustain, rather than hinder or destroy, a woman lawyer's public career.

Like marriage, the issue of women's health and sexuality forced nineteenth-century women lawyers to face the innermost sanctums of their private lives. Women's health was a highly charged subject in the late nineteenth century, one that women lawyers took very seriously. Their concerns over women's physical ability to endure the strains of law practice occurred within the context of the larger social debate over the nature of women's health, which was popularized in 1873 by Dr. Edward H. Clarke's *Sex in Education*.[52]

Thirteen years later, as the debate over the fragility of women's health still raged, Charles C. Moore, a lawyer in Litchfield, Connecticut, and a frequent contributor to popular law journals such as *Law Notes*, *Case and Comment*, and the *Green Bag*, applied Clarke's theories about the fragility of women's health specifically to women in law. In a short story entitled "The Woman Lawyer," written in 1886, Moore linked the concern for women's health with two other important issues, the question of marriage and the place of women in the courtroom.[53]

Moore told the tale of a young woman lawyer, Mary Padelford, who moved to the fictitious small town of Claremont, Connecticut, to set up a solo law practice. Single and alone, Padelford's vulnerability was accentuated by the fact that "her health had never been exceedingly rugged."[54] During her first year in Claremont, her health steadily declined as she spent long hours in her office and the courtroom to build up her law practice. Her acquaintances worried that she was overworked, and a close friend and colleague, Walter Perry, begged her to slow down.

By the spring, Padelford finally acknowledged that she needed a rest, and she planned a summer vacation "to recruit her failing strength."[55] But Padelford collapsed long before the summer arrived. During an appearance in court, she became so weak and tired that she fainted in her chair. The doctor pronounced her "seriously ill" and diagnosed her condition as "brain fever."[56] After four weeks of rest, Padelford finally recovered, renounced courtroom practice, and prepared to leave Claremont. But at the last moment, she married Walter Perry and entered into a law partnership with him. It was clear to the reader that the new Mrs. Perry would no longer have to risk her health in the courtroom. Under the protective eye of her loving husband, she would work cautiously in the office, taking care never to stress her health again.

"The Woman Lawyer" refocused the debate over the woman lawyer in the courtroom as an issue of women's health. More generally, Moore's short story popularized Clarke's medical arguments about women's health and raised questions about women's physical ability to practice law at all. Chicago lawyer Ellen Martin shared Clarke's concerns about the delicacy of the female reproductive system. "I refer to the close relation between the brain and the organs peculiar to women, and to the fact that any trouble with those organs (and a celebrated anatomist says they seem made to get out of order) seriously affects the brain and the nervous system."[57]

Martin spoke from experience. Her law partner and beloved friend, Mary Fredrika Perry, had died several years before from what Martin described as exhaustion and illness brought on by overwork. Perry was a young woman in her early thirties who had a reputation in Chicago for being a hardworking attorney who never lost a case. At the same time, she was well known for her kindhearted sympathy toward the needy and devoted much of her time to providing free legal services to poor women. Shortly before she became ill, she braved one of Chicago's coldest winter storms to bring warm clothing to the needy. To Martin, Perry's untimely death resulted from her rigorous work schedule and the imprudence of her charitable deeds. "Miss Perry's death was caused by overwork," she lamented, eerily echoing Clarke's own words.[58] As a result of Perry's death, Martin took careful steps not to overwork in her own law practice. She restricted herself to office work, avoided the stress of the courtroom, and gave money, rather than her time, to charity cases. But her views about the delicacy of female physiology represented a minority position among women lawyers.[59]

Emma Gillett acknowledged that she had a weak constitution, and she limited her practice to office work because of her delicate health. "I have never gone into jury cases and have done very little court work, but I deliberately chose this course at the beginning as I knew by experience that my nervous organism would break under the strain," she explained.[60] But Gillett was quick to point out that her weak constitution was unique to her, not a natural condition of womanhood. "This lack of nervous endurance I do not count as a feminine failing," she wrote.[61] Nor did she believe that her weak constitution was unchangeable. Instead, she explained that she had improved her health and strengthened her body through a steady regimen of exercise and a healthy diet.

Other women lawyers agreed that it was the material conditions of women's lives, rather than any weakness inherent in women's reproductive physiology, that caused their physical problems. They identified three components of women's lifestyle as being crucial to preserving women's health: a daily regimen of healthy food and exercise, meaningful work, and respectful sexual relations between husband and wife. Although Clarke's *Sex in Education* carried the weight of medical theory, the opinions of the women lawyers were supported by personal experiences.

McCulloch believed that the key to women's health was exercise, a nutritious diet, and sensible clothing. Echoing the wisdom of the health reformers in the early nineteenth century, she shared her personal health habits: "My creed includes no corsets, broad, low-heeled shoes, reform under garments, dresses in one piece hanging from the shoulders, no tea, little coffee or pork, few pies and cakes, much sleep, a little hoeing in the flower beds and a day in bed when occasion demands."[62] Moreover, McCulloch insisted that law was a particularly suitable profession for women, even more so than medicine, because the work schedule could be flexible. "We can be sick in comfort easier than in any other profession for the cases can be postponed till next week or next term while the doctor could not so easily shove aside a case of fever or a minister a marriage ceremony."[63]

Clarke warned women about the dangers of mental activity, but Letitia Burlingame learned from personal experience that meaningful work enhanced her physical and mental well-being. She had been sickly since childhood, and her health continued to deteriorate during twelve years of teaching. When she entered the law school at the University of Michigan, her friends feared that her health would decline even further. But she grew stronger and healthier in law school. "My health has steadily improved, so that I am now stronger than ever before," she insisted in 1887.[64] Two years later, at the end of her first year of practice, Burlingame believed that she was even healthier. "I am now stronger and able to endure more than at any other period of my life. Indeed I stand courtroom work better than many of the men."[65] Tragically, despite her claims of excellent health, Burlingame died a year and a half later from influenza, at the age of thirty-one. Burlingame was not the only young woman lawyer to suffer an untimely death. Almeda Hitchcock died in 1895 at the age of thirty-two, and Lelia Robinson died in 1891 at the age of forty. But their deaths did not justify Clarke's warnings, because neither woman died as a result of her work. Hitchcock succumbed to an illness she contracted while accompanying her physician husband to primitive parts of Hawaii, whereas Robinson died tragically from an accidental overdose of the drug belladonna.

Other women lawyers identified the sexual relations between husband and wife as central to preserving women's health. Unlike Clarke, who described the female reproductive system as naturally delicate and prone to illness, women lawyers defined female reproductive physiology as naturally healthy but sensitive to abuse. At a time when the only reliable method of birth control was abstinence, they embraced the prevalent medical wisdom that frequent sexual relations in marriage endangered a wife's health. To protect her health, nineteenth-century physicians strongly urged married couples to refrain from sexual intercourse, except when they wanted to reproduce. Many women took the matter further, understanding that it was also an important political issue between husband and wife. In an attempt to establish autonomy for a wife in marriage, they argued that it was up to the wife alone to determine when sexual relations should occur.[66]

Disputing the notion that the female reproductive organs were inherently delicate, women lawyers insisted that it was the abuse of these organs that caused women so much suffering. "Let us . . . put the blame for woman's diseases where it belongs—on the blind errors of our ancestors who in ages past abused the power that nature designed for the holiest uses," declared Martha Pearce.[67] Another woman lawyer confessed that although she had graduated with high standing from law school and had a promising legal career before she married, her husband's sexual demands had ruined her health and destroyed her chances for a professional life. Her friends believed that she had fallen victim to too much mental work. "The few who know of me would wisely nod their heads and quote the old story of 'over study,' " she wrote.[68] For a long time she listened quietly as they attributed her ills "to any cause but the true one."[69] Finally confessing the real source of her private torment, she lamented that "with all my study, I did not study woman in the marriage relation."[70]

Other women lawyers warned that sexual intercourse on demand carried with it the dangers of pregnancy and venereal diseases. Emma Gillett advised married women lawyers to insist upon "restraint" from their husbands.[71] Ada Bittenbender explained that she had openly discussed the issue with her husband: "I talked the matter over frankly with my husband as I do all other interests in life, and since have received his hearty consideration in this as in all efforts I make."[72] To solve the problem, Bittenbender recommended that married couples sleep apart. "I would recommend the occupying of separate beds, and also of bedchambers where convenient by married people."[73]

Bittenbender's sexual relationship with her husband added a new dimension to the profile of the right husband. In fact, McCulloch advised women not only to marry a "suffrage husband" but to find one who "also believes in the equal standard of purity for both sexes."[74] The willingness of Bittenbender and other women lawyers to discuss so openly marriage and sex reveals that they were keenly aware how connected were their professional lives and their most intimate personal lives.

In the late nineteenth century, women lawyers defined the professional challenges facing them as the modern legal profession took shape. Through their debates over issues such as court versus office practice, charity versus paying clients, professional versus political work, and marriage versus career, nineteenth-century women lawyers identified and worked to resolve the burden of double consciousness. Their diverse opinions on these questions of balancing gender and professional identity and of achieving sexual equality ensured that nineteenth-century women lawyers would find no simple solutions.

In 1890, the Equity Club's final year, Lelia Robinson published "Women Lawyers in the United States," a survey of the status of women lawyers in America.[75] Although she was well aware of the obstacles that women lawyers faced, Robinson focused on the inroads women had made into the legal profession. Her essay was a celebration of women lawyers' accomplishments and concluded with the optimistic claim that women would continue to enter the law in increasing numbers. Women lawyers in the early decades of the twentieth century did enjoy greater access to law schools and professional opportunities than had women lawyers in the late nineteenth century. But the tension between gender and professional identity remained a burden that challenged women lawyers to redefine the problem and create new solutions.

FIVE

"Some of Our Best Students Have Been Women"

*A*s the Equity Club came to an end in 1890, the law schools of New York University and Cornell University opened their doors to women.[1] Although the closing of the Equity Club symbolized the end of the era of the Victorian woman lawyer, the opening of these two major law schools to women signaled the beginning of a new era. Younger women lawyers stood at the threshold of the twentieth century with greater access to law schools than ever before. Over the next few decades, women's opportunities for legal education expanded as other law schools followed the examples of New York University and Cornell. In western New York, Buffalo Law School graduated its first two women law students in 1899.[2] The University of Chicago admitted women law students from its founding in 1901.[3] World War I accelerated the trend toward coeducation in law schools as male enrollments declined. In 1918, Yale Law School, whose doors women had tried to pry open for decades, finally admitted women as did the law school of Case Western Reserve University in Cleveland.[4] The phenomenon of sexual integration of American law schools was so widespread that by 1920, women had been admitted to 102 of 142 law schools.[5] This remarkable expansion of opportunities for law school education helped to build and define a new generation of women lawyers for the twentieth century.

The opening of law schools to women coincided with broad changes in the history of women's education in the late nineteenth and early twentieth centuries. In 1890, 63 percent of the 1,082 colleges in America were open to women, and 56,000 women attended college, where they made up 36 percent of the total college population.[6] The founding of large universities such as Johns Hopkins University, the University of Chicago, and Stanford University in the early 1890s increased women's opportunities for higher education in coeducational institutions. At the same time, new coordinate schools, such as Pembroke College at Brown University and Jackson at Tufts College, provided women with a higher education identical to, but separate from, that provided to men on campus.[7] Over the next few decades, the numbers of women attending college swelled so that by 1920, 283,000 college women, most from coeducational schools, represented 47 percent of the total population of students enrolled in institutions of higher learning.[8] The rush of women into colleges revealed how passionately they desired higher education and how little they feared the dangers of which Dr. Edward Clarke had once warned.

During this period, the number of law schools and law school students in the United States also grew dramatically. From 1870 to 1890, the number of law schools nearly doubled from thirty-one to sixty-one.[9] By 1910, the number had doubled again to 124.[10] By 1917, all but seven states had at least one law school. Moreover, several cities had more than one: Chicago had nine; Washington, D.C., had eight; New York had five; and St. Louis and San Francisco each had four.[11] By 1920, there were 142 law schools throughout the country. The increase in the number of law schools created a rapid growth in the law student population from 1,653 in 1870, to 4,518 in 1890, to 22,993 in 1916.[12]

These law schools varied in their schedules and standards for admission. The elite day schools, such as Harvard, Yale, and Columbia, had the strictest admission requirements and attracted the most privileged students—those whose socioeconomic position freed them from the need to earn money and enabled them to study law full-time. In contrast, the part-time law schools, which required fewer prerequisites, had a special appeal for less privileged students who had to work during the day and could only study law at night. Part-time law schools were first established in post–Civil War Washington, D.C., where Columbian College in 1865 and then Georgetown and National in 1870 enabled government employees to study law at night. During the next few decades, part-time law schools were founded in cities throughout the country, providing working-class and immigrant groups with an opportunity for upward mobility through a career in law.[13]

Together, the part-time law schools and the elite, full-time law schools composed a heterogeneous system of legal education that was the foundation of a rigidly stratified legal profession for the twentieth century. At the top of the professional hierarchy was the elite bar, a small group of wealthy and socially prominent lawyers who attended the prestigious, established full-time law schools. They dominated the profession through their control of corporate law firms, law schools, and the bar. At the bottom were the large numbers of less privileged lawyers of working-class origins and diverse ethnicities and races who attended the part-time evening law schools. Many of the elite members in the profession criticized the uneven professional standards created by the part-time schools. In contrast, Alfred Z. Reed, in his survey of legal education for the Carnegie Foundation in 1921, supported its diversity. Rather than recommending the closing of the part-time law schools, as many leaders in the legal profession had hoped, Reed sought to improve them. Reed urged the elite bar to acknowledge the two-tiered system of education in which full-time and part-time schools would coexist by reaching different segments of the population and by training lawyers for distinct positions in the professional hierarchy.[14] Women who studied law during this era took advantage of the range of law schools open to them, picking the law school that best suited their economic and personal needs. As a result, women lawyers became a diversely educated group who, upon graduation, entered an increasingly stratified legal profession.

More than any other law school at the turn of the century, New York University embraced Reed's vision of the diverse legal profession. Under the leadership of Clarence Ashley, dean of the law school, New York University offered lectures in the morning, afternoon, and evening so that students from different socioeconomic classes could study law. The morning session offered small classes and individual attention, attracting students who could afford to go to law school without working. The afternoon session was designed for students who had part-time jobs, and the evening school attracted students who had to work full-time to support their legal education. New York University Law School also admitted students of color. In 1922, two women, Anna Jones Robinson and Enid Foderingham, became the first two African-American women graduates.[15]

The commitment of New York University Law School to a heterogeneous student body distinguished it from the elite law schools of the day and aroused the concern of the Association of American Law Schools (AALS). The AALS was founded in 1900 by a group of prestigious law schools, including Harvard, Columbia, and Yale, in order to improve educational standards among all law schools. In their attempt to upgrade law school education, the AALS sought to discredit night schools such as the one at New York University. But Ashley was unwilling to sacrifice his commitment to working-class students, and he staunchly defended the university's evening law classes. New York University Law School paid a price for this commitment to democracy in legal education; in 1923, the AALS excluded it from its list of top-rated law schools.[16]

New York University Law School included women as well as working-class and minority students in its diverse student body. It first opened its doors to women in 1890, just four years after the state legislature passed a statute admitting women to the New York state bar. As soon as women had equal access with men to the state bar, the leaders at New York University believed that it was important to provide women with equal access to quality legal education as well. New York University Law School quickly emerged as one of the most popular law schools for women. By 1920, 303 women had graduated from the law school, and another 157 were enrolled.[17] Ultimately, the school played a central role in preparing women to practice law in the early twentieth century.

The university's commitment to providing legal education to women did not stop with the sexual integration of the law school. The same year that New York University opened its law school to women, it also established the Woman's Law Class, a separate law class for women.[18] With the opening of the law school to women and the founding of the Woman's Law Class in the same year, women in New York City had the unusual opportunity to choose between two distinct options. They could pursue the path taken by all other nineteenth-century women who had gone to law school by studying with men at a male-dominated law school such as Boston University or the University of Michigan, or they could follow a new avenue for women in law and study exclusively among other women in the Woman's Law Class.

The law school guaranteed women equal legal training with men and a law degree upon graduation, whereas the Woman's Law Class offered women the opportunity to study law in a friendly and supportive environment among other women, but without the promise of a law degree. As one graduate described it, the Woman's Law Class offered intelligent women "a 'trial spin,' a bird's eye view, a blazed path in the legal wilderness."[19]

The founders of the Woman's Law Class had three goals: to provide practical legal knowledge to women who needed either to protect their own personal affairs or to improve their positions in the workplace; to give leisured women the opportunity to expand their education and broaden their minds; and to prepare women who wished ultimately to enter a law school such as New York University.[20] These goals met the needs of women of different social classes and circumstances. Leisured women could find educational and cultural enrichment; stenographers, secretaries, and other working women could gain knowledge of the law for their jobs; and career-minded women could study law first in this safe, all-women's setting before entering a law school dominated by men. In addition, all women, particularly widows and single women, could learn their legal rights and how to manage and protect their property. The Woman's Law Class encouraged independence, self-improvement, and professional opportunity.

The Woman's Law Class was founded and run by some of New York City's most influential and socially prominent women. Its founder was Mrs. Leonard Weber, the wife of a well-known physician in the city. The accomplished physician Mary Putnam Jacobi was treasurer, and Helen Gould, the daughter of Jay Gould, the financier and railroad owner, was vice president. The Woman's Law Class also benefited from the support of such reform-minded men at New York University as Dean Ashley, Professor Isaac Franklin Russell of the law school, and Reverend Henry M. MacCracken, chancellor of the university.

Weber took a long and circuitous path before she began the Woman's Law Class. As the wife of a respected physician, she started her reform efforts by teaching poor, urban women the principles of health and hygiene. After five years, however, she concluded that many women were in greater need of legal counsel than medical advice. "To my amazement," she recalled, "I found that most mental suffering resulted from wrongs which needed legal advice."[21] As a result, Weber opened the Arbitration Society with her Swiss friend, Emily Kempin, who had graduated from the University of Zurich Law School and had come to New York City to practice and teach law. The Arbitration Society provided free legal services to the city's poor. Hundreds of poor men and women flocked to the society, seeking Kempin's legal advice. In fact, there was such an overwhelming demand for legal assistance that Kempin could not handle it all. Moreover, as a foreign citizen she could not be admitted to the New York bar, so she was unable to try cases in court. Although she could counsel women as well as research and prepare cases, she had to rely on male lawyers to take her cases to court. Some male lawyers offered their assistance to the Arbitration Society, but they did not stay long; they lost interest because of "the unremunerative character of the work."[22] Weber tried to attract women but could not find any in New York City who were sufficiently trained in law to be of help.

It was impossible for Weber and Kempin to sustain the work of the Arbitration Society until they found a way to train more women in law. They therefore redirected their efforts to this new goal. They disbanded the Arbitration Society and founded a new organization, the Woman's Legal Education Society, which was dedicated to providing women with legal education.[23] Its founding reflected a striking shift away from the goal of the Arbitration Society to serve the legal needs of the urban poor. Instead, the Woman's Legal Education Society reflected Weber's and Kempin's new focus on the professional and practical needs of middle- and upper-class women.[24] Kempin's new responsibilities mirrored this change. Whereas she had provided legal advice to poor men and women at the Arbitration Society, through the Woman's Legal Education Society she began to offer legal education to women who sought professional training, practical knowledge, or cultural enrichment. Still, Weber and Kempin remained sensitive to the plight of those in need; they offered scholarships to women who could not afford to pay the fees for Kempin's classes. Moreover, the training of women in the law represented more than an immediate concern to expand women's professional and educational opportunities. It reflected as well the long-range goal, first expressed in the Arbitration Society, to train women to provide legal charity to the poor.

In 1890, just as the New York University Law School became co-educational, the university agreed to sponsor Kempin's lectures to women only.[25] Men like MacCracken and Russell, loyal champions of educating women in law, were well aware of how isolated women felt as law students in male-run law schools. In the very process of approving the admission of women to the law school in the spring of 1890, the law school faculty articulated their keen sensitivity to the benefits to women of studying among other women. "It [is] highly important for any valuable result," they argued, "that enough women should unite in attendance to render one another aid and encouragement."[26] Concerned that women would not find such a community of women students at the law school, they were happy to endorse Weber's and Kempin's efforts to provide a separate series of lectures for women.

The agreement with the university gave the Woman's Legal Education Society institutional affiliation and legitimacy. Kempin received an official, but limited, appointment as a lecturer in law.[27] In addition, the university provided Kempin with a classroom and took over the responsibility of administering her courses, officially calling them the Woman's Law Class. In return, the Woman's Legal Education Society agreed to take full responsibility for Kempin's annual salary of $1,000 for the first four years and to cover the university's expenses in overseeing the Woman's Law Class. These financial responsibilities were not difficult for the directors of the Woman's Legal Education Society to meet. With their social connections and financial assets, they easily raised the funds for Kempin's salary as well as for eleven scholarships.

New York University announced the opening of the Woman's Law Class in its 1890–1891 catalogue, taking care to point out that although the lectures were administered by the university, they were not an official part of the law school.[28] Kempin offered a series of four courses: constitutional law, real estate, contracts, and domestic and probate law. Each course consisted of twelve lectures, and the fee was $5 per course. Daytime classes met Mondays, Wednesdays, and Fridays from 11 A.M. to noon. To accommodate the requests of working women, Kempin repeated her lectures in the evenings from 8 to 9 P.M. In addition, Kempin also taught a course on Roman law to the male students at the law school and gave a series of practical lectures to the members of the Woman's Legal Education Society on how to manage the legal aspects of business and family affairs. Similar to the presentations that nineteenth-century women doctors gave to women about health, hygiene, and female physiology, Kempin's lectures gave women practical information on how to manage the legal aspects of their business and family affairs.[29]

The first year of the Woman's Law Class under Kempin's tutelage was a remarkable success. Fifteen women enrolled, thirteen of whom completed the full course. Each of the thirteen graduates passed a formal exam and received a certificate, which, though it did not entitle its recipient to practice law, proved that she had satisfactorily completed the entire program. To celebrate and publicize the success of this first year of the Woman's Law Class, the directors of the Woman's Legal Education Society held a lavish graduation ceremony at Carnegie Hall on Seventh Avenue and Fifty-Seventh Street. The ceremony was attended by family and friends of the graduates, many of whom were prominent male lawyers who supported the Woman's Law Class.

The novelty of thirteen women graduating in law attracted the attention of the press. But despite the impressive accomplishments of the graduates, the *New York Times's* coverage of the event was influenced more by the femininity of the graduates than by their success. Under the heading "These Women Know Law: But They Don't Look at All Like Typical Lawyers," the *New York Times* reassured its readers that graduates of the Woman's Law Class would not compete with men lawyers because they "did not intend to enter the practice of the profession." Instead, the article reported that the graduates were the epitome of femininity and charm, not professional accomplishment. They "did not wear gowns suggestive of any desire to look like learned women lawyers." Rather, they sat before the audience in "pretty white dresses and looked as charming as the proverbial sweet girl graduate."[30] In fact, the *New York Times* never took the Woman's Law Class seriously. Over the years, its journalists continued to report on graduates with a paternalistic eye, emphasizing their femininity and diminishing their accomplishments. At the second graduation in April 1892, the newspaper once again reassured its readers that the graduates were still ladies. Undermining its own heading, "Women Learned in the Law," it reported that the male lawyers "sighed" as they viewed the graduates dressed in blue and white gowns. The study of "musty old law books" did nothing to diminish the women's "bright looks and pretty mannerisms."[31] Again, in 1894, the *New York Times* emphasized the graduates' appearances rather than their accomplishments: "Portias in pink and Portias in blue; Portias in light gowns and Portias in dark gowns; Portias with blue eyes and Portias with black eyes," the article's author exclaimed.[32] Not all newspapers were as condescending. An article in the *Brooklyn Standard Union* on the opening of the Woman's Law Class in the fall of 1897 offered instead a brief but respectable history of the class.[33] But for the most part, the Woman's Law Class never received the serious attention it deserved from the press. Over time, the early focus of the press on the femininity of the graduates subsided but was replaced by a fascination with their social class. With so many wives and daughters of wealthy and prominent citizens attending the Woman's Law Class, articles on the graduation ceremonies of the Woman's Law Class read like the New York social register. The *New York Times* set the tone by listing the names of women whom it identified as being "of considerable prominence in the social world."[34]

The Woman's Law Class ignored the patronizing tone of the press and continued its mission to educate women in the law. When Kempin returned to her family in Switzerland, the men at the law school came to the rescue. For ten years, Russell gave the morning lectures, and when he resigned in 1902, Ashley took over until 1916.[35] Ashley was the ideal person to bring the Woman's Law Class into the twentieth century. Not only was he familiar with women law students at his own university, but he had also taught a course in law in 1899 to the women at Bryn Mawr College.[36] Moreover, in 1900, his sister, Jesse Ashley, had entered the law school at New York University. His range of experience with women in legal education made him a dedicated supporter of the Woman's Law Class. Reflecting on the students in the Woman's Law Class in 1904, Ashley believed that "the average woman student is a better scholar than the average man."[37]

With Russell and then Ashley promising continuity and stability for the lectures, the Woman's Law Class thrived.[38] It raised substantial sums of money and by 1900 had a permanent endowment.[39] The reputation of the class grew as impressively as did its treasury. Mainstream law journals such as the *Albany Law Journal* acknowledged its success.[40] At the same time, such eminent educators as M. Carey Thomas, president of Bryn Mawr College; Julia Irvine, president of Wellesley College; and James M. Taylor, president of Vassar College, gave their hearty endorsements by speaking at commencements, dinners, or public events sponsored by the class.

During this era of growing public attention and financial growth, the numbers of students increased rapidly. In 1892, Russell's first year of lecturing to the Woman's Law Class, fifty-seven women were enrolled. Just four years later, in 1896, there were eighty women in the class, forty-seven of whom were to graduate.[41] By the end of Russell's ten years as professor of the Woman's Law Class, over seven hundred women had enrolled in the class since its founding, 460 of whom had graduated.[42]

The women who flocked to the Woman's Law Class were attracted by its unique features. Some sought knowledge of the law to manage their private legal affairs or simply for cultural enrichment. The Woman's Law Class provided them with an introduction to law that was unavailable from any other law school in New York City. Florence Sutro, who graduated from the class in its first year, had been denied admission to every law school in New York City (even though she was the wife of the Tax Commissioner of New York) before she was admitted into the Woman's Law Class. "I wrote to every law school of importance in the City of New York, requesting that I might be admitted as a student, not that I wanted to practice law, but because I thought it was nothing more than proper that a wife should be at least able to understand the rudiments of her husband's profession, and be able to somewhat understand the conversation of his colleagues," she explained in a letter to Chancellor MacCracken. "Unfortunately not one of these law schools could find a place for a woman," she continued. "You cannot know how thankful I was, and am, that the University of the City of New York was the first University to have courage enough to admit women as a class."[43]

Sutro's feelings were shared by many of the women who enrolled in the Woman's Law Class for cultural enrichment and self-improvement. Many of them were also the wives or daughters of some of New York City's wealthiest and most powerful men. Along with the desire for educational enrichment, they also shared an interest in learning how to manage and protect their sizable fortunes. Among this group of elite women were the wife of the editor of the Brooklyn *Eagle*, the daughter of the president of the Brooklyn Trust Company, the wife of Professor Russell, and Helen Gould.[44] In contrast, secretaries and stenographers entered the Woman's Law Class seeking upward mobility and higher salaries. With jobs that demanded their time during the day, they enrolled in the evening classes where scholarships were available to ease their financial burden.[45]

Though working women and women of wealth were drawn to the class for distinctly different reasons, they shared the belief that a general knowledge of the law would enhance their lives as women. Sutro expressed this view when she argued that the study of law for a woman was simply an extension of her proper role in society. "The study of law is to a woman a means of culture, linking all the special training of her education and experience."[46] Women like Sutro did not see themselves overstepping the boundaries of proper feminine behavior by studying law in the Woman's Law Class. Instead, they believed that their very participation reflected and embellished their womanly virtues and duties. The Woman's Law Class not only enabled women to avoid the competition and scorn awaiting them in a law school of predominantly men. It also, according to its supporters, preserved their femininity even as they studied law because with general legal knowledge all women made better wives, mothers, and citizens; working women were better able to support themselves; and women of means were able to manage their private legal matters.

The Woman's Law Class also attracted a third group of women— those who wished to become lawyers. The Woman's Law Class offered these aspiring women lawyers a number of advantages. First, it introduced them to the rudiments of law so that when they entered a formal law school program they were familiar with the material. Second, it offered them courses in a supportive, all-woman's setting. Graduates of the Woman's Law Class left feeling confident in their legal knowledge and their intellectual abilities. As a result, they felt prepared to confront the competitive, isolating, and often hostile experience at a male-dominated law school. Melle Stanleyetta Titus, who graduated from New York University Law School in 1893, understood well the benefits she received from her study with Kempin. In a discussion with Florence Sutro, she confessed that she never would have attempted to go to the law school if she had not been able to attend Kempin's law lectures first.[47]

The Woman's Law Class played such an influential part in its students' lives that several women returned as lecturers. Melle Stanleyetta Titus, Katherine Hogan, Anita Hetherington Haggerty, and Cornelia Hood all attended the first year of the Woman's Law Class, continued their studies at New York University Law School, and after graduation taught law to women. Titus, Hogan, and Haggerty lectured to the Woman's Law Class in the evening school, whereas Hood gave lectures modeled on the Woman's Law Class to women in Brooklyn. Hogan also offered a series of popular lectures on legal topics including "Woman in the Law," "Marriage and Divorce," and "Parent and Child."[48]

By the end of the nineteenth century, the Woman's Law Class had proven to be so successful that it became the model for the establishment of other women's law classes in cities around the country. By 1902, there were special law classes for women in Washington, D.C., Buffalo, San Francisco, Brooklyn, Chicago, and Philadelphia.[49] Francis A. Keay proposed the idea of organizing law lectures for women in Philadelphia during her second year of law school at the University of Pennsylvania. Her idea led to the founding in 1900 of the Civic and Legal Educational Society, which, under the leadership of prominent educators in Philadelphia including M. Carey Thomas of Bryn Mawr College and William Draper Lewis, dean of the law school of the University of Pennsylvania, sponsored lectures to women who wished to become acquainted with the practical side of the law.[50] Just two years later, the John Marshall Law School in Chicago began to offer a series of law lectures for women.[51] World War I created additional demand for women's law classes. In 1917, Jean Nelson-Penfield, a graduate of Brooklyn Law School, offered a series of women's law lectures to the "woman left behind" who needed basic legal knowledge to protect her property and family while she was on her own.[52]

But for all its success and its value to hundreds of women, the Woman's Law Class was not a substitute for a full legal education. The graduates of the Woman's Law Class attended lectures three times a week for four months, for a total of approximately forty-eight hours of study. In contrast, the students at the law school attended classes daily from the end of September through the beginning of June. When they graduated they had attended approximately one thousand hours of lectures over a two- or three-year period.[53] An article in the New York *Sun* on women's study of law at New York University summarized this difference. The women in the Woman's Law Class received only "a smattering of the law," explained the reporter. In contrast, "the real, serious work is done in the regular law classes."[54]

Aspiring women lawyers knew that the education they received through the Woman's Law Class could not substitute for a formal legal education. With professional goals in mind, they turned to the law school of New York University, where they could take a full course of legal study. In 1891, three graduates of the Woman's Law Class—Hogan, Hood, and Titus—enrolled in the law school.[55] Their training in the Woman's Law Class had prepared them well, and they graduated in 1893.[56] Moreover, Titus excelled among the more than one hundred male students in her class. In her senior year, she ranked among the top four students in her class and won the faculty prize of $100. Titus continued to excel after she graduated. In 1894, she was not only the first woman to be admitted to the New York State bar, but she also ranked fourth among the eighty-eight candidates who took the examination.[57]

Titus, Hood, and Hogan were the first of many aspiring women lawyers in New York City who attended the Woman's Law Class and subsequently enrolled at the law school. By 1901, nearly three-fourths of the thirty-two women who had earned the degree of LL.B. from New York University were graduates of the Woman's Law Class.[58] This close tie between the Woman's Law Class and the law school revealed the success of the class in achieving its goal of preparing career-minded women for law school.

Since it opened its doors to women in 1890, New York University had become one of the most popular, if not the most popular, law school for women in the country. But it still lived under the shadow of Columbia University Law School. Because of Columbia's excellent reputation, many women applied there first and turned to New York University only after Columbia had rejected them. Ruth Dick Hall of Illinois was one such woman. In the late 1890s she applied to the law school at Columbia but was rudely rejected. "I was informed that they would surrender their charter before they would admit a woman to their law department," she explained. After her abrupt refusal, Hall entered the law school at New York University.[59] In 1909, Inez Milholland followed

Hall's path. In her quest for what she defined as "the best training in the country," Milholland applied to Columbia as well as to Harvard. After both schools turned her down, she went to New York University and graduated in 1912. Columbia did not admit women for another decade. In 1911, Florence Allen, who ultimately achieved prominence in the 1930s as the first woman to be appointed to the United States Court of Appeals, also applied unsuccessfully to Columbia before she went to New York University, from which she graduated in 1913.[60] In 1913, Mary Bradford Peaks, a Ph.D. graduate from the University of Chicago and a professor of Greek and Latin at Vassar College, was also rejected from Columbia and then admitted to the law school at New York University; she graduated in 1916.[61]

With Columbia's doors closed to women, New York University became the law school of choice for women in New York. But even if New York University's law school was their second choice, the women who graduated typically professed a strong loyalty to the school. Florence Allen shared this deep appreciation. "I can never repay what I owe to New York University," Allen wrote in her autobiography.[62] Contrasting sharply her experience at New York University with the policy of exclusion she encountered at Columbia, she gratefully acknowledged New York University's commitment to educating women in law. "Unlike Columbia and many other law schools," she explained, "New York University constantly encouraged women law students."[63] In particular, Allen valued the self-confidence and feeling of competence that the law school instilled in its women students: "There we were in the Law School on equal terms with men, and we said to ourselves, if we pass our examinations and are admitted to the bar, no one can prevent us from practicing. This was the spirit given us by New York University Law School."[64]

Madeleine Zabriskie Doty, a graduate of the law school at New York University in 1902, found the same deep commitment to training women in law and thrived under the encouraging eye of Dean Ashley. She had entered law school uncertain about her ability to succeed. A friend from Smith College, whose brother had failed several law exams, had warned her upon their graduation that law school was "far too difficult" for women.[65] When Doty arrived at the law school, she found that many of her male classmates shared her friend's belief that women did not belong there. A group of male students even petitioned Dean Ashley to exclude the women students. But Ashley was loyal to the principle of sexual equality and firmly refused their request, suggesting that the men were afraid the women would surpass them. Their fear was sometimes justified. In 1907, Florence Bruning, one of only four women among ninety-six men, graduated with the highest honors in her class.[66]

Ashley did more than defend coeducation at New York University Law School. He gave the women special attention, drilling them rigorously in their studies. "The girls are called on continually," explained Doty. "The Dean makes me recite every day." Doty excelled under Ashley's close scrutiny and devoted attention, and she emerged from under his watchful eye confident that she was as competent as her male classmates. "I thought at first I should be afraid to recite before men," recalled Doty, "but I don't mind a bit, for they don't know any more law than I do." In her second year, when the work was harder—particularly her course in equity, which "threatens my destruction"—Doty's only consolation was that all the students in the class, men and women, were "in the same despair." And when she graduated, though she barely "squeezed through Equity," she had earned "several A's." Once she completed law school, Doty admitted that her experience at New York University had "not been strewn with the difficulties I anticipated." At her graduation, the significance of her accomplishment finally touched her. As she walked up to the platform to receive her diploma, "the women receiving a double share" of the enthusiastic applause, "little thrills of pleasure flowed over me," she recalled.[67]

The welcoming atmosphere at New York University Law School attracted many aspiring women lawyers. In barely a decade, from the entry of the first three women students in 1892 through 1901, thirty-two women had graduated from the law school. By contrast, at Boston University, only nineteen women had graduated from 1872 through 1900. Most striking, by 1920, 303 women had graduated from New York University Law School, whereas only ninety-four had graduated from Boston University and only twenty-nine had graduated from the University of Michigan.[68] Moreover, in the 1919–1920 academic year, another 157 women were enrolled at New York University Law School, making up 16 percent of the 979 students.[69]

By contrast, there were only six women among 372 male students in the law school at Michigan in 1919–1920[70] and eight women among ninety-seven men in the graduating class of the law school of Boston

University in 1920.[71] By the end of the first two decades of the twentieth century, it was clear that the law schools at Boston University and the University of Michigan, once havens for women seeking legal education, had fallen far behind New York University Law School in educating women lawyers. The support of Dean Ashley and the success of the Woman's Law Class created an atmosphere that welcomed and encouraged women and turned New York University into the premier university law school for women.

Although more women studied at New York University Law School than at any other coeducational law school, they were still a minority among their classmates. Fanny Carpenter, one of the earlier women graduates of the law school in 1896, recalled that she was one of only six women among several hundred men.[72] Similarly, Madeleine Doty recalled that when she entered in 1900, there were barely a dozen women among approximately two hundred men.[73] Clarice Baright attended with only "a very few" women and endured teasing from her male classmates because of her minority status. In one incident, she attended her class on property law on a winter day even though she was on the brink of contracting pneumonia. While she sat shivering and coughing in the front row of the classroom, she recalled that there were "a number of teasing boys making fun of me in the back."[74] The merriment of her male classmates took a more malicious turn when they opened the skylight in the classroom, permitting snow to fall on Baright's shivering body.

For the most part, life for the women at New York University Law School was shaped as much by their social class as it was by their minority position as women. Because of the availability of evening and afternoon classes and the university's strong commitment to a democratic law school, the students who attended reflected the ethnic, racial, and class diversity of New York City. Doty recalled the diversity among her classmates in the afternoon classes in 1900. "Among the students were two colored boys, a Chinaman, a policeman, a professional ball player, and several doctors." Doty did not have the tolerance toward her classmates that the law school encouraged. "Many of the men are shabbily dressed and not very clean, Russian or German Jews, such as one sees on the East side of N.Y.," she commented.[75] In fact, she found Jewish men particularly distasteful. A month into her first year of classes, she wrote that the women all sat in the front row of the classroom to keep their distance from the Jewish men in her class. "There is such a strong odor of garlic and dirt from the East-siders," she wrote. "It would be unendurable anywhere else."[76]

Doty was no less critical of her female classmates. She categorized them into three groups: "the flighty, illiterate stenographer, who comes to the law school to flirt, the hard working woman stenographer or book-keeper, who is trying to improve her position, and the woman, who has a little money and some brains, and doesn't know what to do with herself." Social class, rather than ethnicity, played the most important role in determining whom she befriended. Among a group of a dozen female classmates, Doty chose two wealthy, socially connected women. "They both have money and social position," she wrote. "One is a Christian; the other a Jewess." The "Christian" was Jessie Ashley, the daughter of a retired banker and former president of the Wabash railroad and the sister of Dean Ashley. The "Jewess" was Ida Rauh, a young woman from an overly protective, wealthy, Jewish family. Doty explained that Rauh's family made "a fuss when she is out after six without a maid, and she has to rush home from the law school."[77]

Moreover, although Dean Ashley encouraged an atmosphere of tolerance among the women at the law school, the women in Doty's class divided along class lines and deliberately antagonized each other. Doty was continually teased by the less fortunate women in her class. They tauntingly called her "Daughter" because her father visited the school so often and "Dr. Pankhurst" to berate her for her "narrow, saintly and collegiate view of life."[78] In addition, Doty was often the target of their practical jokes. In the fall of her first year, three of the "sporty looking women" in Doty's class invited her to lunch.[79] Flattered by their invitation, Doty easily fell victim to their plot, which was to escape before the lunch was over and leave her to pay the bill. On another occasion, these same women tormented her again. Aware of Doty's disdain for alcohol, one of them brought a cocktail to school, drank it flauntingly in her presence, and then tried to kiss her. "I got very angry and cried out at her and all of them," Doty wrote. "I told them they were materialists and I hated them. It was one of my Dr. Pa[n]khurst occasions which make me disliked," she admitted. Soon thereafter, Doty reported, one of them told her that she "was still a little prig and it would take years to get my college education out of me."[80]

Doty was not entirely blameless. She, Rauh, and Ashley were a formidable threesome. With their money, college education, and privileges of their social class, they enjoyed a lifestyle that was unattainable for most of the other women in the law school. "The trouble is we are envious because we can't be what you are," one of them admitted to Doty. But Doty and her group took little pity on them. To formalize their privilege, they organized a "fraternity" from which they ostracized those female classmates who did not meet their standards. "It is very exclusive," wrote Doty, "for there are so few nice women. I blackballed one of the candidates. I am sure she is an inveterate smoker because her fingers are all yellow."[81]

Doty was no less intolerant of her male classmates. "The librarian says several men have asked to be introduced, but I don't care to know them."[82] When she did find a boyfriend, she was careful to select "one of the few gentlemen in the Law School."[83] But even that relationship was brief, for Doty broke it off when he became too serious. Ida Rauh was equally uninterested in her male classmates, who were attracted to her "fine expressive face" and "stunning clothes."[84] Rauh simply ignored their stares.

The democratic ideals that were encouraged at New York University Law School eventually revealed to Doty, Rauh, and Ashley their intolerance and their hypocrisy in benefiting from the university's commitment to sexual equality in legal education while remaining insensitive to the working men and women in their classes. Sometime during their law school years, their condescension and intolerance gave way to compassion and idealism, and they came to appreciate the effect of social and economic conditions on one's life. Upon graduating, Doty acknowledged that she had changed during her years in law school. Referring to one of the women who had tormented her throughout the program, she confessed: "Two years ago I should have condemned her unheard as a woman who drank cocktails, a materialist without a soul and held myself superior. Now I realize the temerity of judging. What would I be like in the same environment?"[85]

Ironically, these same women who had been so intolerant of their less fortunate classmates in law school went on to become champions of the poor and oppressed after they graduated. For a while, Doty and Ashley were in partnership with another woman lawyer. The threesome was "the only all female law partnership in New York," claimed the *Woman's Journal.*[86] But their legal interests soon turned to radical causes.

Ashley devoted her legal knowledge to the cause of the labor movement and gave her services free to her poor clients. She joined the Socialist Party in 1908, helped found the Socialist newspaper, the *Call*, and was a loyal member of the International Workers of the World. In addition, she was a leader in the National American Woman Suffrage Association, where she worked to enlist the support of wealthy women and to win reforms for working-class women.[87]

Doty, who had been so relentlessly unsympathetic toward the less fortunate men and women in her law class, willingly gave up her prosperous law practice to become a leading advocate of prison reform. In 1912 she was appointed the first woman prison commissioner of New York State. After assuming the identity of a prisoner to investigate prison conditions, she wrote *Society's Misfits*, which called for the reform of prisons.[88] She and her friend Rauh were founding members of the Woman's Peace Party of New York. In addition, Rauh and Ashley became radical advocates of birth control and dispensed birth control literature in deliberate violation of the Comstock Laws.

These women rejected conventionalism in their private lives as well. Both Doty and Rauh married but retained their maiden names. And each of their husbands was a radical like themselves. Rauh married Max Eastman, editor of *The Masses* and founder of the Men's League for Woman Suffrage. Doty married Roger Nash Baldwin, a pacifist and founder of the American Civil Liberties Union.

While women of wealth obsessed about matters of social class in law school, women of modest means focused on the practical matters of fitting their law school obligations into a day filled with work and family responsibilities. For a woman in the evening classes, studying law while meeting financial and family obligations created a grueling schedule that left little time for musing about social frivolities. Clarice Baright could not afford to attend either the morning or afternoon sessions of the law school because her family depended on the financial assistance she provided from her full-time job as a clerk. Her very busy schedule was typical for a woman attending the night school. Six months after Baright began her law studies, she married and took on the added responsibilities of a wife.[89]

Mary Siegel, another night school student, began her day at six in the morning and did not stop until midnight. An immigrant from Russia in 1911, Siegel worked in a sweatshop from eight in the morning until she left to attend evening classes at New York University Law School. After classes, she went home to a crowded apartment where she studied a few hours before she went to sleep, only to get up again early the next morning to resume the same routine.[90]

Rose Weiss, a labor lawyer who graduated from the evening school in 1917, suffered under the same overload of responsibilities. "I survived it," she explained; "probably others can." Still, it was an exhausting task that she did not enthusiastically recommend. "I would not wish to repeat [my] experience of holding down a strenuous job and going to school every night for 3 years," she explained.[91] Despite the handicaps that outside obligations posed for evening students like Baright, Siegel, and Weiss, they were an extremely hard-working group of students who took their studies seriously. Ruth Lewison, who attended the morning, afternoon, and evening classes at different points during her student days, was particularly impressed with the women in the evening classes. They were "by far the most earnest," she explained. "They, I am convinced, will overcome any so-called obstacle and meet any requirements."[92]

Because New York University offered a range of options to women in search of legal education, it remained the school of choice among women law students in New York City, even though, by 1920, Brooklyn Law School, Fordham Law School, and the New Jersey Law School were also open to women. Moreover, in an era when the elite law schools in the Northeast—Columbia, Harvard, and Yale—were not open to women, New York University attracted women such as Allen, Milholland, and Doty, who went on to become prominent lawyers and reform leaders. Allen became the first woman to serve as a judge on a state supreme court and the first woman appointed as a judge to the federal court of appeals. Milholland became a militant suffragist, labor rights activist, pacifist, Socialist, and advocate of penal reform.[93] Another graduate, Elinor Byrns, became a suffrage activist, a leader in the Woman's Peace Party, and the first woman congressional candidate on the Socialist ticket in New York.[94] Crystal Eastman, sister of radical leader Max Eastman, was the first woman admitted to the New York City Bar Association. She became an avid supporter of suffrage, birth control, and equal employment opportunities for women, and she helped secure the passage of a workmen's compensation law in New York State. She was the first woman appointed to the commission of employers' liability and causes of industrial accidents in New York State.[95]

Women like Allen, Milholland, Byrns, and Eastman, along with Doty, Ashley, and Rauh, were part of a group of intelligent, politically astute, and privileged women who went on from New York University Law School to forge either successful professional careers or radical political and private lives. Had Columbia been open to women during their time, many, if not all of them, would have preferred to study law there. But the law school of New York University welcomed them warmly. Consequently, an entire generation of leaders in the New York feminist and radical community, in addition to hundreds of middle-class and working-class women, received their legal training at New York University and became part of the generation of young women lawyers in the early twentieth century.

Even as New York University Law School welcomed women, many women still tried to gain entrance into Harvard, Yale, and Columbia. Of all these law schools, Harvard was the most resistent to coeducation; administrators refused to admit women until 1950. It was also the most elite and restrictive law school in the country. As late as 1916, it was the only law school that required a college degree for admission. In an era when barely 20 percent of all Americans graduated from high school, Harvard Law School's requirement of a college degree eliminated all but a small, privileged group from even applying.[96]

Nevertheless, women seeking prestigious legal education often could not resist Harvard's allure. In June 1899, the same Francis A. Keay who initiated the idea of women's law lectures while she was a student at the University of Pennsylvania first applied for admission to Harvard Law School. As a graduate of Bryn Mawr College, Keay had the educational background necessary for admission, and many of the law school faculty were sympathetic to her desire to study law. At the same time, they could not accept the idea of admitting a woman to Harvard. Professor James B. Thayer, expressing the concerns shared by most of his colleagues, recognized Keay's inherent right to study law, but he did not want her or any woman in his classroom because he feared that a woman's presence would distract the male students.[97] Only former dean Christopher Langdell strongly opposed admitting Keay. Ultimately, they reached a compromise that everyone supported except Langdell. Under the proposed arrangement, Keay would not be admitted to the law school, but if she were accepted to Radcliffe College as a graduate student, the law school professors would admit her to their classes and give her the examinations. At the end of her study, however, she would not receive the Harvard degree of LL.B. because she was not officially a student at Harvard. Nevertheless, the law school faculty would strongly recommend her for the LL.B. from Radcliffe. The compromise preserved Harvard's all-male law school while permitting Keay to study law.[98]

James Barr Ames, dean of the law school, communicated the proposal to Agnes Irwin, dean of Radcliffe College.[99] Irwin and the Council of Radcliffe College supported it in full, and by the end of June 1899, it looked like Keay was on her way to studying law at Harvard. All that remained was the approval of the Fellows of Harvard College and the Board of Overseers of the University. But several weeks later the *Boston Herald* published a story, "Women in Harvard Law School," that revealed that the proposal was likely to be rejected by President Charles Eliot and the "conservative" overseers of the university.[100] In an interview with the newspaper at his summer home in Maine, Eliot had strongly opposed the proposition, charging that the law school faculty had no right to vote on the admission of women to Harvard. Moreover, he had argued that the university had no moral obligation to accept women into the law school because the state universities provided women with sufficient opportunities to study law. Years later, Keay surmised that Eliot had been influenced by the popular science literature of the day, which described women's intellectual abilities as inferior to men's.[101] Shortly after this article appeared, Eliot wrote a letter to the editor of the *Boston Herald* to clarify his opposition to coeducation at Harvard.[102]

Despite the obstacles before her, Keay, with the support of Dean Irwin, was optimistic that the proposal of the law school faculty would eventually win approval.[103] Meanwhile, Irwin began to receive information suggesting that Keay may not have been the ideal woman to break the sexual barrier at Harvard. M. Carey Thomas, president of Bryn Mawr, wrote to Irwin that she had serious reservations about Keay because Keay had displayed "a rather unusual anxiety to defer examinations and so on."[104] One of Keay's professors wrote a reserved letter of support. "I do not think her very strong intellectually but by no means weak," he wrote. But what Keay may have lacked in intellectual ability she made up for in her enthusiasm for the law. "What should count for much in recommending her," he went on, "is that she is really, genuinely interested in work along these lines."[105] Despite Keay's mediocre recommendations, the proposal to open Harvard Law School classes to Radcliffe students made its way up the administrative hierarchy.[106] Keay, though increasingly impatient, remained hopeful that "a favorable decision" would make "all the trouble to all concerned . . . seem worth while."[107] Sadly for Keay, President Eliot and the Fellows of Harvard College rejected the plan suggested by the law school faculty, thereby ending her hopes of studying law at Harvard.[108]

After Harvard rejected her, Keay immediately enrolled in the law school at the University of Pennsylvania. The university readily admitted Keay, but in her eyes the school did not measure up to Harvard. To Keay, Harvard had a "long tradition of culture and intellect" that the University of Pennsylvania lacked. She condescendingly described her classmates as "gentlemen at heart" but of "a different class of men" than those she met at Harvard. Keay hoped that her presence as a woman among so many uncultured young men would "help rub off the roughness" of the male students and give the school "a little higher culture."[109]

Keay suffered as one of only two woman at the law school. "I have felt like keeping in the background as much as possible," she confessed in a letter to Radcliffe's dean, Agnes Irwin.[110] In an effort to help Keay, Irwin wrote letters of introduction for her to several of her professors. William Draper Lewis, dean of the law school, reassured Irwin that he was completely satisfied with Keay's performance. "In my hour with the first year class, she sits in the front part of the room and I have already called on her twice. She did very well." Alluding to the prevailing notions about women's so-called delicate physical nature, Lewis went on to say that "if her health holds out [she] will stand well in her class."[111] Keay was grateful for Lewis's support and wrote to Irwin that she believed it was "greatly due to his influence that women are treated respectfully here."[112] A strong advocate of women's legal education, Lewis supported the women's law lectures that Keay organized in her second year of law school at Pennsylvania. He also encouraged Irwin to continue her struggle for coeducation at Harvard. "You must not give up the fight to get women into the professional schools at Harvard," he urged. "You are bound to succeed in the end." Speaking prophetically, he concluded that "once the change is made there will be no step backward."[113]

Though Harvard did not admit women for another half century, Keay's application initiated a debate that ensured that the question of coeducation at Harvard would never again be easily dismissed. Instead, the attempt by women to gain entry to Harvard Law School continued to torment fair-minded men, challenging them to find a solution to the conflict between their ideals about justice for women and their strong ties to single-sex education at Harvard Law School. The next opportunity for Harvard to face the issue of coeducation came a decade later when Inez Milholland applied to the law school in 1909. Milholland was a graduate of Vassar College who wanted to study law at a top-level law school. With that in mind, she first went in 1909 to England, where she tried unsuccessfully to gain admittance to the law schools of Oxford and Cambridge. She returned to New York in the fall of 1909 and applied to the law schools at both Harvard and Columbia. Her Harvard application rekindled the furor over the issue of coeducation at the law school. In a three-page letter, twenty-three-year-old Milholland challenged the dean and faculty of Harvard Law School to reject "the rose-colored world of sentimentality" associated with women and to embrace instead a "more rational" approach to the question of admitting women. Appealing to their belief in the new social scientific methodologies of the era, Milholland argued that her admission would enable Harvard to test objectively "the workability of the principle of co-education in the graduate schools and prove or disprove theories." At the same time, she made the very practical argument that she needed "the best training in the country" to help her overcome the sexual discrimination she knew she would encounter as a woman in the legal profession.[114]

Milholland's letter persuaded enough, though by no means all, of the law school faculty to vote to accept her application.[115] Several days after the vote, Milholland visited Henry Lee Higginson, a teaching fellow at the law school, and convinced him to support her candidacy as well. In fact, Higginson was so impressed with Milholland that he wrote a letter of support to A. Lawrence Lowell, president of Harvard. "If we are to begin at all with women," he wrote, "we certainly can do no better than with this young lady." In fact, Higginson believed that

Milholland was so extraordinary that he warned Lowell that she might surpass the men at Harvard. "It is, however, to be remembered that men are gradually being displaced by women," he cautioned, "and if they are all like this young lady, it would merely hasten our banishment."[116]

But Milholland did not persuade everyone. Several faculty members voted against the proposal to admit her.[117] Dean Ames expressed concern that if Harvard admitted Milholland, it could no longer "discriminate against other young women who applied."[118] Lowell dismissed Milholland's arguments, insisting that because women could go to other law schools it was not worth the risk of endangering what he called "the peculiar efficiency of our law school."[119] Lowell's decision found support beyond Harvard. An editorial in *Law Notes* applauded Lowell for rejecting Milholland. It also criticized Milholland for trying to "force herself" into Harvard and belittled her application as a frivolous and irresponsible quest for notoriety rather than a serious search for legal education.[120] Once again, Harvard Law School turned down an extremely able applicant simply because she was a woman.

Other elite law schools also resisted coeducation in the early years of the twentieth century but eventually admitted women. Yale Law School continued to exclude women for more than three decades after it had been embarrassed into admitting Alice Jordan in 1886. In 1918, Yale reversed its men-only policy when Isabelle Bridge applied for admission. Bridge had taken a law course with a Yale law professor teaching in a western state who had encouraged her to apply to Yale and had recommended her to his colleagues. With support from one of their own, the faculty voted to admit Bridge, and the administration accepted the recommendation, reversing the deeply rooted policy of single-sex education at Yale.[121]

Six women entered Yale Law School the following year, though Bridge became sick and was not among them. Among this first group of women at Yale was Matilda Fenberg, a teacher from Ohio who had always wanted to be a lawyer.[122] Though anxious about her first day on the unfamiliar campus, Fenberg was reassured by everyone she met. The dean's secretary advised her on courses to take and books to purchase. Several male students showed her around campus and helped her to find a place to live. A campus police officer offered her protection from any "wolves in sheep's clothing" she might encounter among her male classmates. One-time President of the United States William Howard

Taft, who taught constitutional law, made his office available as a lounge to her and the other female students. The admission of women to Yale did not go unnoticed. An editorial in the *New York Evening Post* hailed the decision at Yale as "a step of no small importance" and called on Columbia and Harvard, which still did not accept women, to follow Yale's example.[123]

Columbia University Law School vehemently resisted coeducation for almost another decade, and often turned women away with a remarkable lack of civility.[124] In 1922, Harlan Stone, dean of the law school, brusquely dismissed one female applicant's query about why Columbia did not admit women with the hostile retort: "We don't because we don't."[125] In 1910, Columbia made its first concession to women by opening up its newly created summer classes to them.[126] Yet the law school maintained its exclusionary policy in its regular courses, rejecting every woman who applied during the next few years. Among this group of unsuccessful applicants were Florence Allen and Mary Bradford Peaks, both of whom went on to New York University Law School. Even after she had graduated from New York University, Peaks still regretted that she had been unable to study at Columbia. "The law school of Columbia University, the best probably in the city, is not open to women," she lamented in 1920.[127]

In 1916, Columbia University Medical School opened its doors to women. This left the law school in the position of being the only department in the university that did not accept women on equal terms with men. Almost immediately this exclusionary policy began to attract public attention. In the fall of 1916, editorials appeared in a number of local newspapers and national periodicals, including the *Evening Post*, the *Tribune*, the *Nation*, and the *New Republic*.[128] The opinions were unanimous. They decried the law school's discrimination against women, belittled the hypocrisy of its open summer school policy, and called for an end to "masculinity as an entrance requirement."[129] The Women's City Club fueled the negative publicity by publishing the editorials in a pamphlet entitled *Shall Women Be Admitted to the Columbia Law School? Opinions of the Press and of Leading Lawyers*.[130] In addition, it listed the names of forty prominent male lawyers, including judges Learned Hand and Benjamin Cardozo, who had petitioned Columbia to open its law school to women.

Perhaps to silence the criticism, in the fall of 1917 Columbia appointed a woman, New York University Law School graduate Mabel E. Witte, as an instructor of law. Many applauded the appointment as an important step toward admitting women to the law school. The gesture was more apparent than real, however, because the appointment was in the department of extension classes, not in the regular law school. Much like the courses offered in the Woman's Law Class of New York University, the class was a noncredit course designed especially for women. Its major purpose was to offer women, particularly those left alone during World War I, practical knowledge of the law so that they could handle their own legal affairs.[131]

In 1920, the matter of coeducation at Columbia Law School resurfaced. With the passage of the Nineteenth Amendment giving women the right to vote, the faculty of Barnard College adopted a resolution declaring the law school's exclusionary policy "a 'very embarrassing' situation," and urged it to admit women. Although three members of the law school faculty supported the resolution, a majority of seven held firmly to the long-standing exclusion of women, claiming that women had the opportunity to study law elsewhere.[132] The matter reached the attention of leading woman's rights activists. In 1924 both the National League of Women Voters and the National Woman's Party entered the controversy, submitting a petition and a formal resolution to Columbia University requesting the admission of women to the law school. Again, the majority of the faculty resisted the pressure, claiming that coeducation was not in the best interests of the law school.[133]

Columbia's refusal to admit women appeared particularly unreasonable because it occurred at a time when most law schools were coeducational. Moreover, deans and faculty at law schools throughout the country had expressed satisfaction with the women students in their law schools. The dean at the University of Chicago Law School, which had accepted women since its opening in 1902, explained that "some of our best students have been women." Similarly, the dean at the law school at the University of Wisconsin explained that "in proportion to their numbers [the women students] attain a higher average than the men." The picture was the same at National University School of Law, where Belva Lockwood was forced to demand her degree from President Grant in 1871. "We are glad to have them," explained the dean of the women students. "They exert a desirable influence upon the men . . .

[and] have taken a very much larger percentage of honors than is proportionate to their numbers."[134] These schools were not alone in their approval. Other law schools, including those at the University of Texas, the University of Buffalo, Boston University, the University of Iowa, Kansas City School of Law, the University of Denver, the University of Cincinnati, and Hastings College of the Law, reported high achievement among their women students.

Against the backdrop of women's successful performance at so many law schools around the country and the mounting public pressure on Columbia to admit women, individual professors began to change their minds. In 1926, Professor Underhill Moore, one of the supporters of the Barnard resolution in 1920, made a formal proposal that the law school admit women. By this time, Dean Harlan Stone, who had been one of the strongest opponents of coeducation, had left Columbia to become a justice of the United States Supreme Court. One woman who had been rejected from the law school during Stone's deanship explained that "everyone knew that Harlan Stone promised women would be admitted to Columbia over his dead body. I wasn't surprised things changed soon after he left, but by then it was too late for me."[135] Stone's departure set the stage for reform, and the faculty, which overwhelmingly supported Moore's proposal, voted to accept women. Ellen Spencer Mussey hailed the opening of Columbia's law school to women and claimed that it was the result of "continuous pressure" from both men and women.[136]

Coeducation at Columbia University Law School was not without restrictions; initially, the law school was only open to graduates of Barnard College. But the first two women who applied revealed the inadequacy of this restriction. One was a graduate from Smith College with a master's and a Ph.D. from Columbia. The other was a graduate of Vassar with a master's degree from Columbia. As a result, the faculty loosened its restrictions to include women with graduate degrees from Columbia. Even that was not enough. Finally, in October 1928, the faculty abolished all restrictions against female candidates and admitted them to the law school on equal terms with men.[137]

Even though most law schools were open to women by the time Columbia admitted women, women remained a small, isolated minority among an overwhelming majority of male classmates. One answer to this problem was the founding of law school sororities, which offered women law students their own social and intellectual community. The first legal sorority in the country, Kappa Beta Pi, was founded in 1908 by ten women law students at Chicago-Kent College of Law. Just three years later, five women at the law school of the University of California at Los Angeles organized another legal sorority, Phi Delta Delta. Both sororities grew quickly beyond their local settings, reflecting the expansion of women into the male-dominated law schools in the 1910s. By 1923, there were twenty-three chapters of Kappa Beta Pi around the country, and by 1924, there were twenty chapters of Phi Delta Delta.[138] In 1949, Kappa Beta Pi had three thousand members and Phi Delta Delta had twenty-five hundred.[139]

The legal sororities met the unique needs of women law students. For example, they supported women's professional goals on campus. Kappa Beta Pi at the University of Texas, for one, held monthly meetings to help its members keep up to date on changing state laws.[140] The sororities also played a valuable social role by bringing women together in recreational ways such as rush teas. Local chapters helped to enhance social relations with male law students. At the University of California at Los Angeles, male law students played a major role in helping their female classmates to launch Phi Delta Delta. Drawing on their fraternity experience, they gave advice on founding the sorority and even helped to design the sorority pin.[141] On some campuses, the local chapters of the legal sororities also helped to alleviate tension created by the uneasy sexual integration of the law schools. At the University of Chicago, some of the male students had invited the women to attend the traditional "smoker" dinner party for the male law students, whereas others had urged them to stay away. Sensing the "frigid relations," the women law students declined to attend and organized through Kappa Beta Pi their own dinner instead. Modeled after the male smokers, the purpose of their dinner was to bring the new female students together with the other women law students and alumnae, away from the eye of their male classmates.[142] At the same time, the male students could enjoy their " 'smokes and jokes' in peace and freedom without feeling that they were sacrificing the good will of the young ladies."[143] Ultimately, legal sororities helped female culture to flourish in the male-dominated environment of the law schools.

The legal sororities also functioned in important ways on the national level through their respective journals, the *Kappa Beta Pi Quarterly* and the *Phi Delta Delta*. Within the pages of these publications, members shared both serious and lighthearted news, and a rich female culture among women in law emerged. The journals were important vehicles to forward professional ends. In 1925, the Kappa chapter of Kappa Beta Pi reported that it had organized a legal aid bureau in New Haven, Connecticut.[144] Individual members used the journals to announce office openings, address changes, and professional appointments and accomplishments. In 1924, the *Kappa Beta Pi* reprinted one of its member's essays, "Indian Country," because it was the first article written by a woman to be published in the *Journal of the American Bar Association*.[145] The *Phi Delta Delta* frequently published career sketches of its successful members.[146]

Just as important as the professional entries was the social, personal, and lighthearted news. It was here that the female culture of the sororities was most vivid. Marriages and births were proudly announced, sorority cheers and songs were printed, social events were reported, and woman's place in the field of law was staunchly defended. One notice in *Phi Delta Delta* announced the prize-winning cake of a sorority member in an Oregon baking contest, proclaiming this to be further evidence that women lawyers were as feminine as they were professional.[147] The women at Yale Law School used the *Kappa Beta Pi Quarterly* to invite their sisters in law from other chapters to transfer to Yale. Admitting lightheartedly that there were few romances among Yale law students, they pleaded with their "more skillful sisters [to] join us here at Yale and coach us in the gentler arts." But behind their lighthearted call was a serious desire for more women to join their small number at Yale.[148]

Although the legal sororities served an important role, both professionally and socially, for many women law students there was a darker side to them as well. Founded to give women law students a sense of community and female support, they did not welcome all women law students. Phi Delta Delta was restrictive on racial and religious lines. It was completely closed to women of color. Non-Christian women, although not totally excluded, could not be accepted through their local chapter but had to win unanimous consent of the National Executive Committee.[149] Florence Allen rejected the invitation to join the legal sorority at New York University precisely because of its discriminatory policies. When Allen's good friend Martha Gruening, the daughter of a renowned Jewish physician in New York City, was not invited to join, Allen declined the invitation. "When you ask Martha, I will consider it," she replied to their invitation. "They never asked Martha, and I never joined," she explained.[150]

In the long run, no legal sorority could counter the isolation that women felt when they studied law among so many men. At Boston University Law School, only 124 women graduated among 2,848 men from its opening in 1872 through the end of 1923.[151]

The situation was even more striking at the University of Michigan, where only 162 women, among 26,761 men, studied in the half century from 1870 through 1920.[152] Although the opening of most law schools to women by the 1920s enabled them to study on equal terms with men, women could not escape the hard reality that they were a very small minority in a setting dominated in all ways by men. A solution to that problem was for women to study law among themselves.

SIX

"Primarily for Women"

$\mathcal{T}$he opening of most male-run law schools to women by the 1920s made it possible for women to study law at practically any law school they chose. But even as law school became the standard for women's legal education, what was possible for women did not translate into true educational opportunity. Although educational choices increased for women in law, few women attended the male-run law schools, particularly the elite ones of the Northeast. It was during this era that law schools especially for women were founded. Women's law schools offered women the rare opportunity to study law together, apart from men. In this way they were not unlike the women's medical schools and hospitals that provided separate medical training for women only. But the women's medical institutions were founded decades earlier, some as early as the 1850s and 1860s, in an age of more rigid separation of the sexes. They began to close as coeducational opportunities expanded in medicine. In fact, fourteen women's medical schools closed before 1910.[1] In contrast, the women's law schools opened during this very era of expanding coeducation and sexual integration in the legal profession.

The two largest women's law schools were Washington College of Law, later part of American University Law School, in Washington D.C., and Portia Law School, later New England School of Law, in Boston. Both were part-time institutions with minimal admission requirements and low tuitions. They attracted women who worked by day as well as women from immigrant families. Their founding and early growth coincided with the increasing alarm among the elite bar—composed of white, American-born, Protestant men—over the growing number of ethnic, racial, and religious minorities who were entering the profession through the evening law schools. In contrast, the Cambridge Law School for Women in Cambridge, Massachusetts, was an exclusive full-time day school founded precisely for elite white women. But Cambridge was a small and short-lived venture, whereas Washington College and Portia trained more women lawyers in the early twentieth century than did any other law schools in the country, except for New York University. In doing so, they helped to spawn and nurture a new generation of women lawyers for the twentieth century. Yet as part-time institutions, they also assured that their graduates would enter the law at the bottom of the professional hierarchy.

The Washington College of Law was the first of these law schools founded especially for women.[2] Like the all-women's hospitals and medical schools, the Washington College of Law was built on a foundation of nineteenth-century feminism. Even though it admitted men, its founders, Ellen Spencer Mussey and one-time Equity Club member Emma Gillett, shared the goal of making professional opportunities available to women through legal education. Mussey and Gillett were the ideal women to undertake this unique educational venture for women. Both were tireless advocates of women's legal rights. Gillett campaigned for woman suffrage and later for the Equal Rights Amendment. Mussey fought to win equal guardianship rights for mothers and equal rights for women to sit on juries. Together they worked with Belva Lockwood to win married women's property and citizenship rights. The founding of the Washington College of Law represented their attempt to expand the cause of woman's rights beyond the law and into the legal profession. Built upon this foundation of nineteenth-century woman's rights, the Washington College of Law tried to bring the women lawyers movement into the early twentieth century.

Mussey and Gillett brought unique, individual strengths to the school. Mussey was the daughter of Platt T. Spencer, who had developed the Spencerian system of penmanship, the standard for script handwriting in the late nineteenth century.[3] He was also an abolitionist and temperance advocate who passed on his belief in reform to his daughter. Mussey first established her reputation in Washington, D.C., when she ran the ladies' department of the Spencerian Business College. Under her guidance, the ladies' department became a sought-out training ground for young women seeking government work. In 1871, she married a prominent Washington lawyer, Reuben Delavan Mussey, thereby freeing herself from the family penmanship business. After reading law with her husband, she began a lifelong commitment to practicing law with her husband and teaching law, especially to women.

Unlike Mussey, whose professional life was linked closely with her husband's, Emma Gillett turned to the law because she was a woman on her own, without parents or a husband.[4] Her father died when she was two, and Gillett worked as a young girl while she went to school in Wisconsin. She then became a teacher, but she quickly discovered that teaching was exhausting, unrewarding, and unremunerative. The difficulty she encountered settling her mother's estate inspired her to leave the work she hated and to study law. Gillett moved to Washington, D.C., hoping to follow Belva Lockwood into the law school of National University. By the time Gillett arrived, however, National had already closed its doors to women, so Gillett enrolled at Howard, the only law school open to women in the District of Columbia. After graduating in 1883, she found work in the law office of Watson J. Newton, an advocate of women lawyers, and worked with him, ultimately as his partner, until his death in 1913. As a practicing attorney, Gillett spoke out against the tendency of women lawyers to divert their energy into charity cases. Instead she proposed a model of sexual equality for women lawyers, urging them to work and rest in the same ways as men.

While Gillett and Mussey were working together on behalf of married women's property rights, Mussey received her first request from a young woman who wanted Mussey to teach her the law. Mussey initially resisted the request, but when the young woman returned with two other women, Mussey turned to Gillett, who agreed to help her teach law to the three young women. The following year four more women began to study with Mussey and Gillett. Word of their tutelage spread quickly among prospective women students, but Mussey and Gillett did not take lightly the prospect of teaching the law to women. They first tried to persuade Columbian College to admit the women. Only when Columbian refused did Mussey and Gillett proceed with their idea of opening a law school for women. In 1898, they founded the Washington College of Law, the only law school in the country "primarily for women."⁵ The Washington College of Law was unique among the law schools of its day for several reasons. First, it was the only law school in the country devoted especially to women. Although the Woman's Law Class of New York University was thriving by 1896, it did not grant degrees, which Washington College of Law did. Second, unlike any other law school in the country, Washington College of Law was run and taught primarily by women. Mussey taught constitutional law, and Gillett taught common law subjects. In addition, Mussey was the dean of the school, which meant that she was the first woman dean of any law school in the country. Gillett ran the school behind the scenes, doing most of the administrative work.

Washington College of Law was founded and run by women for women, but it was not exclusively a woman's institution. Mussey and Gillett accepted both male and female students, and they relied on men to help them run the school. In fact, the Washington College of Law probably would not have survived had Mussey and Gillett not had a group of extremely able and influential male lawyers willing to help them. Watson J. Newton, Gillett's law partner, was a member of the board of trustees as well as a willing instructor. In addition, Mussey and Gillett attracted a prestigious group of male lawyers in the nation's capital who were willing to give their time and experience to support a law school primarily for women. They included a dean of the law school of Catholic University, an associate justice of the Court of Appeals, a judge of the Court of Claims, and the chief justice of the District of Columbia Supreme Court. The influence and prestige of these eminent men in the Washington, D.C., legal establishment gave credibility to the Washington College of Law and underscored the power of sexual integration.

But the feminism at the Washington College of Law was tainted by the racism that prevailed in Washington, D.C., at the end of the nineteenth century. Women, as well as African Americans, were excluded from National Law School, Columbian Law School, Georgetown Law School, and Catholic University Law School. Only Howard University was open to all applicants, but it did not fully welcome women. Although Howard's antagonism toward female students made many women feel unwelcome, its commitment to the education of African Americans made it unacceptable to white women from the South. Even Gillett felt self-conscious at Howard among so many black students and found reassurance in the fact that her "professors were nearly all white and men of fine ability."[6] The combination of sexism at Howard and racism among white women in Washington, D.C., made Howard a last resort for white women seeking legal education in the nation's capital. Others chose to abandon their hopes of studying law rather than enroll in the racially integrated law school.

The racism that kept white women away from Howard propelled them to the Washington College of Law, where they were welcomed not only because they were women but also because they were white. Gillett and Mussey emphasized the racial purity of their school, unabashedly advertising it as a school for whites only.[7] In addition, the support from many powerful white men in Washington, D.C.'s legal establishment ensured that white women could study law apart from African Americans. The school's success revealed that white women in Washington, D.C., were no more open-minded than were their white brethren; they preferred to study law among those of their own race.

Mussey and Gillett did everything they could to make it possible for any woman who wished to study law to enroll at Washington College of Law, as long as she was white. Washington College was a part-time, evening law school with a nonrestrictive admissions policy. Although that placed it at the bottom of the law school hierarchy nationwide, it shared this status with every other law school in the city. Applicants simply had to be eighteen years of age, able to pass an exam in English, and "of good moral character."[8] Tuition was $40 per year, which was extremely low compared with the tuition at Harvard, which was $150, or tuition at other full-time day law schools such as Yale, Cornell, New York University, Boston University, and even Howard, all of which charged $100 annually.[9] These high tuitions were beyond the reach of all but the most economically comfortable and eliminated applicants from poor, ethnic, and nonwhite families.

With its flexible admissions policy and special commitment to women, Washington College of Law quickly found its intended niche in the law school marketplace. Although men in government service attended the city's all-male law schools at night to forward their careers, women who were secretaries, stenographers, or clerks enrolled to advance their employment situations. Twelve women enrolled during the school's first two years, and another ten women enrolled in 1898 along with the school's first male student. The school grew steadily in its first quarter century. By 1908, there were fifty-five students enrolled, and five years later the number had more than doubled to 128. But as enrollments increased at Washington College of Law, the proportion of female students gradually declined. In 1909, when the number of graduates reached a high point of sixteen, ten men graduated, surpassing for the first time the number of women graduates. The gradual decline in the proportion of women continued. In 1915, the enrollment of sixty-three women in the class represented barely 44 percent of the entire student body of 143, and in 1926, the seventeen women graduates were not even one-half of the class of fifty-three graduating students.[10]

This decline in the proportion of women at Washington College of Law coincided with the general opening of law schools to women both around the country and in Washington, D.C. In particular, two previously all-male law schools in the city, Columbian Law School and National University, began to admit women, although students were less than enthusiastic about this change. In 1903, several male students at Columbian refused to participate in commencement ceremonies because a woman was named to receive a doctorate of laws from the school. The faculty stood by the woman and threatened to revoke the male students' diplomas. With the faculty holding firm, all but one student, the president of the class, abandoned their threat. Still, the incident revealed the tension over coeducation that smoldered just below the surface at Columbian.[11]

Washington College of Law remained the only law school in the city to be truly hospitable to women, but by the 1910s the growing options for law school education had threatened the school's hold on women in the law school marketplace. Under pressure from both the Association of American Law Schools and the American Bar Association, many law schools chose to raise their educational standards. They increased tuition rates, tightened entrance requirements by demanding two years of prelaw college work, expanded the number of full-time faculty, and enlarged the size of their libraries. Mussey and Gillett took the opposite tack and resisted the trend to elevate standards. They kept tuition as low as possible, raising it only minimally and sporadically. By 1926, annual tuition was up to $100, but this was what other schools, including New York University and Howard, had charged more than thirty years earlier. In addition, although they raised admissions standards slightly in 1908 by requiring applicants to have a high school diploma, for the most part Washington College of Law held fast to its low admission criteria for the next three decades.

In 1924, in the midst of this nationwide trend to upgrade the standards of legal education, Emma Gillett resigned as dean of Washington College of Law. Her successor was Elizabeth Harris, the daughter of United States senator and Massachusetts probate judge Robert Orr Harris.[12] Harris began her legal education at Portia Law School in Boston, but transferred to Washington College of Law in hopes of finding a better school in the heart of Washington, D.C. Disappointed by what she found at her new school, she devoted the year of her deanship at Washington College to upgrading its standards. In particular, she proposed that the school require all incoming students to have at least one year of college, which was a modest requirement compared to the two-year requirement the Association of American Law Schools and the American Bar Association wanted law schools to adopt.

Harris's goals of educational reform met strong opposition from Gillett, who used her influence with the trustees to retain the school's tradition of minimal standards. Pointing to the deficit of $2,000 for 1924, Gillett argued that the school simply could not compete with the large university law schools unless there was "some advantage in requirements for admission." Lower tuition and smaller classes would not be "a sufficient inducement" to attract students if entrance requirements were stiffened beyond the requirement of a high school diploma.[13] Instead, Gillett argued that the new criteria proposed by Harris would impede the school's already difficult job of attracting students. Ultimately, the trustees decided to follow the advice of their old dean rather than adopt the views of their new one. As a result, Harris resigned and the school retained its minimal requirement of a high school diploma. Not until 1939 did the Washington College of Law finally fall in line with the trend to raise standards in law schools and accept the American Bar Association requirement of two years of college.[14]

The Washington College of Law was slow to upgrade its educational standards, but it remained a popular school among women seeking legal education. Though the numbers of men surpassed the numbers of women by 1908, the school continued to provide legal education to a large proportion of women nationwide who studied law in the first half of the twentieth century. For example, the sixty-three women who enrolled in Washington College of Law in 1915 alone represented approximately half of the 124 women graduates from Boston University Law School in the half century from 1872 to 1923.[15]

In addition, the Washington College of Law made its mark by graduating several women who became part of the inner circle of powerful women in Washington, D.C., in the 1920s and 1930s. Annabel Matthews graduated from the Washington College of Law in 1921 and became an expert on income tax and the first woman to serve on the United States Board of Tax Appeals. Alice Paul, one of the leading strategists in the militant wing of the woman suffrage movement and the founder of the National Woman's Party, graduated from the school in 1922 and went on to write and lead the campaign for the Equal Rights Amendment. Sue Shelton White, a leading suffragist from Tennessee, graduated in 1923 and became an advocate of the Equal Rights Amendment, which she helped draft, and an active participant in the New Deal—she worked in the National Recovery Administration, the National Emergency Council, and as the principal attorney for the Social Security Board.[16]

Of course, most graduates of the Washington College of Law did not lead the influential professional lives of a Matthews, Paul, or White. Most were drawn to the school with more modest career aspirations. One woman "had in mind advancement" from her position as a stenographer when she entered Washington College of Law.[17] Another explained that she entered the law school so that she could find work in the government as a law clerk.[18] Yet another attributed her appointment to head the Child Labor Tax Division of the Bureau of Internal Revenue to her studies at Washington College.[19] Still another, a clerk at the United States Census Bureau, became a law examiner in the Office of Indian Affairs after she graduated from Washington College of Law, and just a few years later she was promoted once again to the position of United States probate attorney to represent American Indian tribes in state courts.[20] Of course, not all of the women who graduated from the Washington College of Law achieved even their most modest career goals. One graduate gave up her hope of practicing law in the State Department "because as a woman I was refused admittance to the Solicitor's office"; instead she moved to New York where she was hired by a large private law firm.[21]

Still, the Washington College of Law did far more than enhance individual women's career opportunities in the law. Its unique mission to provide legal education to women attracted women from around the country and helped to make Washington, D.C., a city where women lawyers congregated. Moreover, with 148 women receiving their LL.B. and forty-seven earning their LL.M. during the school's first twenty years, Washington College of Law contributed significantly to building a new generation of women lawyers for the twentieth century.[22] At the same time, its policy of racial discrimination played a large role in determining that this new generation of women lawyers would be almost exclusively white. Finally, its rigid insistence on low entrance requirements and mediocre educational standards ensured that many in this new generation of women lawyers were poorly trained and unable to compete with men, or even the few women, who had graduated from the more rigorous law schools.

Although Washington College of Law was primarily a law school for women, true separatism in women's legal education did not occur until the 1908 founding of Portia Law School, the first and only all-woman's law school in the world.[23] As a women's institution in Boston, Portia joined the all-women's New England Hospital for Women and Children as an institution dedicated to promoting women's opportunities in male-dominated professions. Women in Boston had the opportunity to study either law or medicine in one of these all-women's settings. As an educational institution, Portia joined the ranks of the five other law schools in Boston: Harvard, Boston University, the newly founded Boston College Law School, Suffolk Law School, and the Boston YMCA Law School (later Northeastern). Together, these schools reflected the hierarchy in early twentieth-century legal education. Harvard, the symbol of excellence and exclusivity, took its place at the top. Just below it were the well-respected law schools at Boston University and Boston College. The YMCA Law School was close to the bottom of the hierarchy, and Suffolk was at the very bottom. Although both the YMCA school and Suffolk were part-time law schools that attracted the same student clientele—sons of poor New Englanders and working-class immigrants—the leaders of the Boston legal establishment viewed them very differently. From its founding, the YMCA school received the loyal support of leading lawyers in Boston, who believed that the school played the important social role of providing legal education to poor but deserving young men of Boston. Dean Ames of Harvard Law School supported the school from the start, and Louis Brandeis was one of many prominent lawyers who lectured there.[24]

In contrast, Suffolk Law School did not share the same ties to Boston's elite legal community. Its founder, Gleason Archer, was a graduate of Boston University Law School who detested the Harvard establishment for its exclusivity. The antagonism was mutual. The Harvard legal community viewed Suffolk Law School with a contemptuous and condescending eye because Archer shunned the reform-minded zeal that had inspired the creation of the YMCA Law School; he was motivated purely by profit. Both schools attracted the same class of students, but the elite legal establishment sharply distinguished between the two, declaring the students at Suffolk to be uneducated and unworthy, unlike the so-called respectable students at the YMCA. Harvard even tried to prevent Suffolk from receiving a state charter, but Archer prevailed.[25]

Portia took its place alongside Suffolk at the very bottom of the law school hierarchy in Boston. Its founder, Arthur Winfield MacLean, was Gleason Archer's classmate at Boston University Law School and his partner in law practice. MacLean shared Arthur's desire to profit from legal education and identified women as an untapped clientele in an increasingly competitive educational marketplace. He began Portia as a very modest venture, tutoring two young women in 1908. With ten women students the following year, it was clear that MacLean had correctly predicted that women would seize the opportunity to study the law.

In several ways, Portia was like any other part-time law school of the era. Classes were scheduled three evenings a week, from 6:00 to 7:30 P.M., to attract students who worked during the day.[26] The faculty were lawyers by day who were willing for a fee, to lecture on the practical aspects of the law in the evening. Tuition was low, a modest $75 that could be paid in installments. Admission requirements were also minimal. In the early years, a student could enroll at Portia without a high school degree. In 1914, the school upgraded its admissions criteria slightly: it required all of its students to have a high school diploma before they graduated, but permitted them to earn an equivalency degree while studying at Portia. In 1919, Portia received authority from the state to grant bachelor of laws degrees, and in 1920, it opened a day division; by 1926, the school began to offer a master's degree in law. Still, admissions standards remained low. Because students were only required to have some high school background before they entered Portia, they could earn high school equivalency degrees during the summer at the Portia Summer Preparatory Department, which opened in 1921.[27]

But although Portia fit the model of other part-time law schools of the day, it was unique because it was a law school for women only. Like Washington College of Law, Portia provided women with an educational setting where they could learn law together and escape the loneliness and alienation that other women endured at the predominantly male law schools. Yet there were important differences between the two schools. The founders of Washington College of Law were strong supporters of woman's rights and sexual equality. Situated in the heart of the nation's capital, the school attracted women who were often political activists, such as Alice Paul and Sue White, as well as those seeking opportunity and mobility in the seat of power in Washington, D.C. In contrast, MacLean was motivated by profit rather than politics. Though Portia was the only all-women's law school ever established in the United States, it was founded purely as a money-making venture. Moreover, although MacLean was a strong believer in women's abilities and a vocal defender of women in the law, his views were shaped more by the Victorian belief in women's uniqueness than by Mussey's and Gillett's belief in sexual equality. MacLean claimed that women would make excellent real estate lawyers because of their special attention to detail. He also asserted that they would make excellent divorce lawyers because they had a unique capacity to understand women's needs and a special desire for cooperation that would lead them to find amicable solutions out of court.[28]

MacLean's traditional views about women created an atmosphere at Portia that attracted a less activist group of students than those at Washington College of Law. Most were the daughters of Irish, Jewish, and Italian immigrants, and they took little interest in the politics of woman's rights or the fact that Portia was the only all-women's law school in the country.[29] To Mildred Salerno, the daughter of an Italian barber, Portia's uniqueness as an all-women's law school was irrelevant. Instead, with a $50 scholarship in hand and no idea of where to use it, she chose Portia impulsively when she learned that a friend was planning to enroll.[30]

With its emphasis on practicality rather than politics, Portia attracted other young women like Salerno who sought vocational training. In 1914, just six years after it opened, the school boasted an enrollment of forty women, more than the total number of women who had graduated from Boston University since 1870.[31] By the 1920s, Portia's new status as a degree-granting institution, its day classes, its high school program, and its master's program drew even more students to the school. Moreover, though Portia grew under the shadow of the other law schools in Boston, its graduates thrived. They performed impressively on the state bar exam, the only test that directly measured the competence of Portia graduates against those of all the other law schools in the state. At the top of the list were the graduates of both Harvard and Boston University. But throughout the 1920s, the women from Portia performed better on the state bar than men who had graduated from either Northeastern or Suffolk.[32] In less than two decades, MacLean's vision of a profitable, proprietary law school for women only had proven a remarkable success. In 1920 alone, there were over 170 women enrolled.[33] Measured by enrollment, it seemed that Portia had become almost overnight the most popular law school for women in the country. By 1929, 30 percent of all the women law students in the country were enrolled at Portia.[34]

Yet although Portia made a substantial contribution to opening the legal profession to women, there were limits to its commitment to an open bar. Portia welcomed young women from Irish, Italian, and Jewish families, but its tolerance for diversity did not always extend to minority women. Even so, its policies contrasted starkly with those of the Washington College of Law, which was restricted to white women only. Rather, Portia was more like the New England Hospital only several miles away; its commitment to women was at times challenged by its racism.[35]

Portia confronted the problem of race when Jama White, an African-American woman who enrolled at Portia in 1923, accused the school of racial intolerance.[36] From the beginning, MacLean and law professor Bessie Paige had made White feel unwelcome, apparently because they feared that her presence would provoke controversy and distract the students. Though the school tolerated her for two years, finally, in 1926, just as White was about to begin her final year at Portia, MacLean denied her admittance to the senior class. White sought an explanation from the trustees, but her request was rejected. With no other option available to her, she sued the school, claiming that she had been treated unfairly and expelled without reason or explanation. Arguing that the school had held itself up to be an institution "free from bias and prejudice," she charged that both MacClean and Paige had discriminated against her because of her color and that they had "maliciously concocted, schemed and devised false charges against her" to justify expelling her.[37] Nevertheless, the judge ruled with MacLean that White's presence endangered the proper learning environment at Portia.

The intolerance Jama White suffered at Portia contrasted sharply with the treatment of other minority women who followed her. In June 1931, the same year that White lost her case, another African-American woman, Dorothy R. Crockett, graduated from Portia. That same summer, Sui G. Woo became the first Chinese-American student admitted into the school.[38] Crockett and Woo were not the only women of color to be welcomed at Portia in the early 1930s. The school also treated Jackie Guild, a young middle-class African-American woman, with a kind of respect and sensitivity that Jama White never enjoyed. Guild's father, a successful Boston lawyer, inspired his daughter to study law. At first she enrolled in the day division at Portia, but when her family suffered serious financial losses, Guild had to find a daytime job and take classes in the evening. Rather than stand in her way as they had done to White, MacLean and Paige helped Guild finish her legal education. MacLean gave her a scholarship so that she could afford the evening classes, and Paige gave Guild a free bar review course. Although White's case stands as an accusation of racial prejudice at Portia, Guild's graduation in 1933, along with Crockett's in 1931 and Woo's in 1935, were testimony to the development of an atmosphere of racial tolerance at Portia in the early 1930s. This emerging racial tolerance may have been motivated in part by the decline in enrollment that the school suffered during the early years of the economic depression. Still, Guild believed that MacLean's and Paige's concern for her was genuine and that Paige had treated her so generously because she "truly cared for her students as people."[39]

Portia's enrollment continued to decline throughout the 1930s, threatening the survival of the school. Finally, in 1938, the same year that the similarly ailing Suffolk Law School made the financial decision to open its doors to women, Portia began to accept men. Its days as the country's only all-women's law school were over.

For a brief moment in 1915, women could attend another all-women's law school, the Cambridge Law School for Women. Its founding in Cambridge, Massachusetts, meant that for a short period of time, women in Boston actually had three law schools to choose from: Portia, Boston University, and the Cambridge Law School for Women. However, Cambridge Law School was not for every woman. Unlike both Portia and the Washington College of Law, Cambridge Law School was an elite institution founded to meet the needs of the most educationally privileged women. Its strict admission requirement of a bachelor's degree from a four-year college was equal to Harvard's and made it accessible only to women with the most prestigious undergraduate training.

The Cambridge Law School for Women was the product of yet another failed attempt to open Harvard Law School to women. In 1915, five years after Harvard had rejected Inez Milholland, a group of fifteen women petitioned Harvard to admit women to its law school.[40] Pointing to universities such as Massachusetts Institute of Technology and Johns Hopkins, which had successfully integrated women into their professional schools, the petition made the familiar argument that women deserved access to the very best legal education. At the same time, it echoed the nineteenth-century view about female uniqueness and insisted that women lawyers had a special role to play in charity law, settlement work, and the protection of female clients. Although these were familiar arguments, they came from the organized efforts of fifteen graduates of four of the most prestigious women's colleges in the country: Vassar, Barnard, Radcliffe, and Smith. Their educational credentials and collective voice were not easy to ignore.

The faculty of the Harvard Law School, whose positive response to Milholland's application had been rejected by President Lowell several years before, put off any formal action this time until they learned Lowell's opinion on the petition.[41] They were not the only ones who wanted to learn of Lowell's stand on the matter. In April 1915, Walter Lippman, editor of the *New Republic* and a supporter of the petition, wrote to Lowell to inquire about his view.[42] Lowell responded that Harvard had rejected the petition for several reasons. First, he argued that it was important to preserve Harvard's single-sex policy because Harvard was one of the few remaining law schools for men only. Second, he explained that he remained unconvinced that coeducation would improve the law school at Harvard; to the contrary, he believed that coeducation would "affect it injuriously."[43]

Although the petition's rejection ended the debate over coeducation at Harvard Law School, it inspired a new plan: the creation of a separate women's law class, which became the Cambridge Law School for Women. The leader of the new effort was Joseph Henry Beale, a professor at Harvard Law School and the father of one of the fifteen women who had signed the petition. When Harvard rejected the petition, Elizabeth Beale persuaded her father to help her find a way to study there. Beale was precisely the man to take on this challenge. He had long-established ties to the law school, beginning in the 1880s when he was a student there and had helped to found the *Harvard Law Review*. After graduating from Harvard Law School in 1887, Beale had practiced in Boston and returned to Harvard, where he had devoted his professional life to teaching law. He had been teaching law at Harvard for twenty-four years and held the prestigious title of Royal Professor of Law, the oldest chair in the law school, when his daughter enlisted his assistance.[44]

Beale agreed to help his daughter, but he did not throw his support behind the petition for coeducation. As a visiting dean in 1909 at the law school at the University of Chicago, he thought that there were limits to coeducation for women. In an interview with the *New York Times*, he explained that the women there were not treated by their teachers "in exactly the same way as the men," nor did they enjoy the same fellowship that the male students shared among themselves, particularly out of class.[45] Based on his experience at the University of Chicago, Beale supported Lowell's rejection of the women's petition to enter Harvard Law School, describing coeducation as "undesirable" for both Harvard as well as "the women themselves."[46] But although Beale rejected the notion of men and women learning law together, he strongly supported the idea of women studying law apart from men. His models for educating women in the law were the elite women's colleges in the Northeast. "Just as the experienced judgement of this part of the country has pronounced that separate colleges for women are wise, so it seems that separate law schools for women also are," he explained.[47] Yet as much as he wanted to provide the very best legal education to women, he was exclusionary as well, seeking only to make it available to the most educated women in the country. According to Beale, just as the law students at Harvard did not like to study with "men of less education," so too did the graduates of the elite women's colleges deserve a law school for women like themselves.[48]

Beale's plan was to provide young women with the same lectures from the same faculty who taught at Harvard Law School, but in a separate setting. The result would be an education that was separate from, but equal to, that available to men at Harvard. But from the very start, he encountered skepticism. Of all the administrators at Harvard, only Le Baron Russell Briggs, dean of Harvard College and president of Radcliffe College, was even guardedly supportive of the idea.[49] Others, including Lowell and Ezra Thayer, then dean of the law school, were initially against the idea for several reasons. First, they feared that a women's law class would place an undue burden on the law school faculty and "impair the efficiency" of their work at Harvard.[50] They also questioned the sincerity of Beale's commitment. Aware that his primary concern was to find a way for his daughter to study law, they were skeptical about his claim that he wanted to provide "scientific education" to Radcliffe students in subjects unavailable to them at Radcliffe.[51] Even the Radcliffe Council initially decided not to support Beale's plan because they believed there were not enough Radcliffe graduates who would be willing to undertake the work on Beale's terms—that is, to study law outside of Harvard Law School and without the promise of a law degree.[52]

In spite of the resistance from so many powerful individuals to his plan, Beale had the support of several of his law school colleagues who had agreed to participate in his school. Ultimately, with the help of Briggs, Beale overcame the reservations of Lowell and Thayer, and on September 30, 1915, he opened the Cambridge Law School for Women. Although they finally supported his endeavor, the leaders at Harvard demanded distance from it. Thus the name of the school revealed no relationship with Harvard. In addition, Radcliffe accepted no rent for the space it provided and took no responsibility for Beale's lectures.[53] Despite the formal independence of the Cambridge Law School from

Harvard University, the ties were undeniable. Radcliffe provided two rooms for the school and built bookcases to accommodate the school's "library"—Beale's personal collection of law books. Rather than hiding its actions, the Alumni Report of Radcliffe College proudly announced the "hospitality" that it was providing to the new school.[54]

The ties of Beale's school to Harvard Law School were also inescapable. At every turn Beale modeled his school after the law school at Harvard. Cambridge Law School had the same admission requirements as Harvard—a four-year college degree—which eliminated all but a small group of the most privileged women. Its professors taught the case method, which Langdell had introduced at Harvard and which Beale had helped to introduce at the University of Chicago, and there was a law club just like the moot court club at Harvard. Moreover, the entire teaching staff was composed of either Harvard law professors or graduate students, who taught the same courses to the women at the Cambridge Law School that they taught to the male law students at Harvard. Beale lectured on criminal law, torts, and principles of legal liability. Gustabus Hill Robinson, a graduate of Harvard Law School in 1909, gave the course on contracts. Chester Alden McLain, book editor of the *Harvard Law Review* in 1914, taught property. Whitney Hart Shepardson, a graduate of Oxford University Law School, taught procedure.[55]

The Cambridge Law School for Women got off to a good start and received attention from the local and national press. The *New York Times* hailed it as the first graduate law school exclusively for women in the country.[56] Yet, the title of the article, "First Women's Law School Opens This Fall," was both biased and inaccurate, for it ignored the existence of Portia Law School since 1906 and revealed the favoritism of the *New York Times* for the elite Cambridge Law School. About twenty-five women, all graduates of exclusive four-year colleges—including Radcliffe, Barnard, Bryn Mawr, Smith, and Vassar—applied to the Cambridge Law School in its first year, and nine women made up the first-year class.[57] Among this group of nine was Elizabeth Beale, who ironically married and raised five children but never practiced law.

Despite his daughter's lack of interest in practicing law, Beale still hoped to continue the law school in the fall of 1916.[58] Lectures were scheduled to begin in October, and a faculty meeting was planned to arrange teaching schedules. Yet in spite of Beale's best intentions, few

165

women sought admission, and it became clear by the end of the summer that the school would probably have to close. "We mayn't have a very large class," Beale wrote to one of the prospective faculty members in late August when only one woman was scheduled to begin classes in the fall.[59] As Beale's school floundered, Harvard's tolerance quickly evaporated, and by 1919, the university had completely given up any support for the endeavor. "There is no likelihood of its being started again," explained one administrator.[60] Still, Beale remained hopeful. He discussed with one of its graduates the possibility of reopening the school, and sent out a promotional letter announcing that the school might reopen "if a sufficient number of women want the education."[61] But the letter did not invite everyone. Entitled "What Are You Doing with Your AB Degree?" it spoke only to the female graduates of four-year colleges. Moreover, the letter made it clear that the school was not "a money making proposition," thereby deliberately distancing the Cambridge Law School from Portia Law School on the other side of the Charles River.

By the end of the 1910s, the women Beale wanted had their pick of most law schools in the country, and his school never reopened. Though it was a short-lived venture, the Cambridge Law School for Women helped to chip away at the mountain of resistance to coeducation at Harvard Law School. For years, individual professors had expressed sympathy for admitting women, but they had been unable to effect any change. Beale's stature at the university had enabled him to overcome the resistance of opponents to coeducation, and his proposal for a separate law school for women had been an intriguing innovation worthy of a try.

Yet the Cambridge Law School for Women never came close to achieving the potential Beale had envisioned for it. It stood at the opposite end of the educational spectrum from Portia and Washington College of Law, but it failed to attract the privileged women it had been founded to serve. In contrast, Portia Law School and Washington College of Law, with their deliberately democratic approaches, attracted hundreds of women and played a major role in accelerating the sexual integration of the legal profession. With New York University, they were most responsible for creating a new generation of women lawyers for the twentieth century. Their low entrance requirements, evening classes, and modest tuition rates ensured that this new generation of women lawyers would be economically and ethnically diverse.

But it cannot be forgotten that the racial discrimination at Washington College and the ambiguous policy at Portia also ensured that this generation of women lawyers would be predominantly white. In addition, the mediocre educational standards of Portia and Washington College of Law meant that the young women lawyers who graduated from them entered the legal profession ill-prepared to compete with the many male lawyers who were graduates of the full-time, university law schools that women could, but rarely did, attend. As Elizabeth Kemper Adams of the United States Employment Service astutely observed, "There is a danger of a supply of imperfectly trained women lawyers."[62]

SEVEN

"Woman's Position in the Profession"

with Douglas Lamar Jones

*D*uring the 1910s and 1920s, women lawyers moved beyond the goal of the nineteenth-century pioneers who had struggled to gain legal rights for women lawyers, and they sought to move into the mainstream by achieving the same level of success in law as did men. The idea that women lawyers could compete equally with men in the legal profession resonated throughout Beatrice Doerschuk's *Women in the Law,* a guide to legal training and opportunities in law for women published in 1920.[1] The publication of *Women in the Law* heralded the birth of the new woman lawyer in America by shifting the rationale for women in the legal profession from the politics of the nineteenth-century women lawyers movement to the idea that women were equally as capable as men in succeeding in law. Yet the reality of "woman's position in the profession," as Doerschuk described it, was less than encouraging. Women lawyers in the early twentieth century typically practiced law at the bottom of the professional ladder and lagged behind their men colleagues both economically and professionally. The signs of sexual discrimination were less obvious than in the nineteenth century, when men overtly excluded women from practice or law schools, but in law practice, women still had to find their place. Doerschuk and the Bureau of Vocational Information tried to redefine what it meant to be a woman lawyer in modern America.

The Bureau of Vocational Information, an all-women's organization founded in New York City in 1919 and run by women to help young, educated women make career choices, sponsored Doerschuk's *Women in the Law*. Using techniques of social scientific inquiry introduced in the early twentieth century, the bureau embraced the modern ideal of objectivity to evaluate the social progress of women lawyers. In its search for "a body of authenticated facts," the bureau employed survey questionnaires to describe in quantitative terms the educational and career possibilities for women lawyers.[2] As a result, the bureau minimized the personal experiences of the women lawyers it surveyed. Gathering information on a variety of professions and vocations, including agriculture, office work, and the law, the bureau published its studies for educators and guidance counselors.[3]

Doerschuk, assistant director of the bureau, described twentieth-century women lawyers in strictly professional terms. In her view, women lawyers were no longer activists engaged in a long struggle to gain the right to practice law.[4] She devoted only a page of her study to the entrance of women into the legal profession in the nineteenth century. Doerschuk viewed nineteenth-century women lawyers such as Myra Bradwell disdainfully as "pathfinders" whose primary accomplishment was their "militancy" because they spent all of their energy gaining the right to practice law rather than achieving success in the profession.[5] Once that path was cleared, to follow Doerschuk's frontier metaphor, the modern women of the twentieth century became the true pioneers who triumphed by pursuing their educations and careers. To Doerschuk, the doors of the profession were open to women, and their professional success was unrelated to woman's rights or feminism. They were professionals, just like male lawyers.

Doerschuk asserted that women could only achieve professional success through improved legal education. She complained of the "systemic disorganization of the legal profession," suggesting that the democratic tendencies in American society inevitably resulted in easy access to law practice by men and women alike.[6] Although Doerschuk credited the American Bar Association and the Association of American Law Schools with improving legal education, she maintained that those standards were inconsistently enforced.[7] Anticipating Alfred Z. Reed's 1921 critique of legal training in America, *Training for the Public Profession of the Law*,[8] Doerschuk concluded that women lawyers' "irregular record" in law training was the primary reason why they lacked distinction as practitioners.[9] The problem was not limited to the all-women's law schools, namely, Portia and Washington College of Law. According to Doerschuk, only 27 percent of the 102 coeducational law schools in 1920 required students to attend full-time and had high admission standards. Another 30 percent required full-time attendance but had low admission standards. The remaining 43 percent of the coeducational law schools were all deemed to be unsatisfactory because of part-time attendance requirements, which were combined in many cases with low entrance standards.

In 1921, Reed's report reiterated the conclusions of Doerschuk. Legal education in America was sharply stratified, with only about one-fifth of the law schools requiring full-time attendance and having high entrance standards.[10] Doerschuk and Reed both failed to appreciate the importance of the part-time law schools for women. Even if merit permitted women to gain admission to all law schools, many legal educators and practitioners continued to discriminate against women. Part-time law schools became a critical avenue through which women lawyers could enter an otherwise closed profession. The part-time law schools at least offered women lawyers the chance to compete in the local legal marketplace.

With access to the top law schools difficult and the part-time schools suited to the needs of many women, Doerschuk nevertheless presented a remedy for women in law that reflected the influence of Reed. (Reed not only reviewed *Women in the Law* prior to publication, but Doerschuk also interviewed him as part of her research.) The solution for women, according to Doerschuk, was to obtain the same training as men received at the best law schools: four-year college training, followed by a full-time law school education, and finally, an apprenticeship in a law office. In short, she advocated the elite, male model of legal education for women lawyers.[11] She referred explicitly to the "best law offices"— presumably those in New York City such as Cravath, Swain & Moore, the epitome of the emerging elite law firm—as drawing their new lawyers from few leading law schools.[12] Doerschuk wanted women lawyers to become part of the elite bar so that the doors of a successful career in law would open naturally. This vision of a profession governed by a meritocracy, in which the best lawyers rose to the top regardless of gender so long as they had equal training, permeated *Women in the Law*.[13]

Even though Doerschuk acknowledged that the legal profession was stratified and that women lawyers practiced in a "cross-section cut low across the smaller cases in each field," she asserted that women lawyers simply had not yet achieved success in "big business" law.[14] The emerging corporate law firm was Doerschuk's touchstone for success as she exhorted women lawyers to strive for true professional equality with men. Doerschuk also believed that women lawyers "arbitrarily" limited their practices to office work and avoided trial practice.[15] She recognized that many women still had an "antipathy . . . for court work . . . due to distaste, timidity, lack of confidence, and shrinking from the nervous strain it entails."[16] But she had little sympathy for women who avoided trial practice, no matter how difficult it was to them; instead, she urged women to pursue court work just like men. To support her view, she cited the dean of the University of Chicago Law School, who believed that women were more naturally suited to a court practice than an office practice.[17]

Doerschuk held women lawyers to the standards of the elite, male lawyers and was unrelenting in her belief that women lawyers could achieve professional equality. She simply dismissed many of the issues over which nineteenth-century women lawyers had agonized. She reported that she found "nothing in the fifty years of experience of women lawyers to indicate that they are, as women, better adapted to any one kind of legal work than to another."[18] Women, in her view, could specialize in any area of law they chose and, like men, would have access to wealth and power: it was merely a question of gaining the correct education and experience.[19] For Doerschuk, the women lawyers of 1920 were the true "pioneers," for she had no other way to explain their lack of success. They simply had not had enough time to have gained proper experience and training. To Doerschuk, the problem for women in law was not prejudice, nor was it the burden of double consciousness. It was the low educational standards of the law schools, which did not prepare women for competition with men. Women were the "newcomers" in law, so tradition was against them.[20]

Had Doerschuk understood more fully the history of women in law in nineteenth-century America, she might have been better able to reconcile the politics of women lawyers in the nineteenth century with the aspirations for equality of those of the twentieth century. In contrast, New York lawyer and bureau board member Dorothy Straus proposed the idea of a study of women lawyers precisely because of her experience in women's political movements. Straus, more clearly than Doerschuk, understood that "at the very center of all movements, radical and conservative alike . . . [was] the necessity of presenting to women who desire to share in those movements . . . all the facts available."[21] To Straus, the subject of women in law was an inherently political topic that warranted a study by the bureau. In the hands of Doerschuk, however, the political vision of women in law became channeled through the lens of professional equality and suggested that women lawyers of the early twentieth century were part of a redefinition of equality in the professions. By breaking from their nineteenth-century roots, both Doerschuk and Straus attempted to forge a new point of departure for women in law.

In the end, *Women in the Law* must be understood as an affirmation of the goal of women lawyers in the early twentieth century to define standards of professional achievement in objective ways for the purpose of securing greater access to professional advancement for women. Doerschuk's description of women lawyers in 1920 as "pioneers" revealed her own discomfort with the politically active women lawyers of the nineteenth century and obscured the historical development of women in the legal profession. If their legal training was equal to that for men, she proposed, women lawyers of the twentieth century would advance in an almost mechanistic fashion. Moreover, the ideal of the meritocracy in the profession would reward their efforts. *Women in the Law* represented a redefinition of success and optimism for women lawyers in the early twentieth century, one that was to be accomplished without an organized woman's rights movement. Instead, it posed an assimilationist vision that ignored the role of women's law schools, women's legal associations, and feminism in the training of women lawyers. The path to success for Doerschuk was the same one followed by elite, male lawyers. Although she understood that women lawyers were at the bottom of the ladder of success in the profession and reaching for its middle rungs, Doerschuk consistently ignored the gender stratification of the bar and presented a vision of training in law that emulated the male model of success.

Doerschuk observed that in the early twentieth century women lawyers broadened their effort to expand their "opportunities for preparation, application and advancement" in the legal profession.[22] Although the proportion of women lawyers to men lawyers in America in 1920 was small and remained so for another fifty years, the early twentieth century represented the first period of truly substantial growth in the actual number of women lawyers. Throughout all regions of America, but particularly in large cities such as New York, Chicago, Washington, D.C., Boston, and Los Angeles, women entered the legal profession in increasingly high numbers. Moreover, the patterns of growth of women in law were remarkable, given the discrimination that women faced as lawyers. Women's integration into the legal profession became all the more important because of the historic patterns of exclusion sanctioned by law and male attitudes toward the woman lawyer.

Given the rigid gender boundaries in the legal profession, the patterns of growth of women in the modern legal profession became firmly established. The United States Census, which enumerated women lawyers in practice at ten-year intervals, provides a useful indicator of the rate of growth of women lawyers. The problem with the census is that it obscures the absolute number of women trained to practice. Only five women lawyers appeared in the census in 1870. Although relatively few women lawyers appeared ten years later in 1880, and again in 1890, the rate of growth of women lawyers was astronomically high, increasing 1,400 percent between 1870 and 1880 (see Table 2). At first glance, this increase appears artificially high. But because women lawyers in the 1870s and 1880s were often excluded outright from practice, the fact that women lawyers entered the profession at all was remarkable.

By 1900, the census-takers found 1,010 women lawyers—more than ever before and a 385 percent increase over the number found in 1890. This sharp increase in the growth of women lawyers by 1900 marked the beginning of the new generation of women lawyers in the twentieth century. By 1920, the number had climbed to 1,738. In 1910, the census listed but 558 women lawyers, due most likely to undercounting. The underreporting of trained women lawyers in the census was chronic. Elizabeth Parsons of Omaha, Nebraska, for example, reported to the bureau in 1920 that although Nebraska had admitted thirty-three women to the bar, only two were in practice.[23] Moreover, many women lawyers preferred to work with their husbands or relatives, if they practiced at all, so they may have been missed by the census-takers.

Despite the anomalies in census data collection, the long-term trend reveals a remarkable growth rate of women lawyers from 1880 to 1930. Overall, rates of growth were naturally high in the nineteenth century as women first entered the all-male legal profession. Women entered law at consistently high rates in the early twentieth century, particularly when compared with their male counterparts. The growth of male lawyers from 1900 through the middle decades of the twentieth century was unusually low. Except for the decade 1920 to 1930, when the proportion of men entering the legal profession increased at a rate of 30 percent, the decennial growth rates for men never rose above 10 percent between 1900 and 1950. In contrast, the rate of growth of women in law between 1900 and 1950 never fell below 19 percent (excluding 1910) and typically exceeded it.

Still, women were the distinct minority in the legal profession in the early twentieth century, remaining but a small percentage of all lawyers: 1.1 percent in 1910, 1.4 percent in 1920, and 2.1 percent in 1930. Compared with other male-dominated professions such as medicine or science, in which, respectively, women composed only 5.0 and 4.7 percent in 1920, law was the most closed profession to women in the early and mid-twentieth century (see Table 3). Moreover, the legal profession was much more closed to women than were the female-dominated professions of teaching and social work, in which, respectively, women made up 86.0 and 66.0 percent in 1920. Yet the legal profession continued to attract women at rates of growth that far exceeded men throughout the early and mid-twentieth century.[24]

It was this small but steady stream of women into the legal profession that Doerschuk identified and defined as a cultural phenomenon worthy of study by the Bureau of Vocational Information. Confirming the growth in the number of women lawyers was a sharp, upward trend in the women listed in the *Martindale-Hubbell Law Directory* in 1939, the major directory of practicing lawyers in America. According to this directory, between 1910 and 1920 the numbers of women admitted to the bar more than doubled between 1910 and 1920, and tripled between 1920 and 1930 (see graph). Women lawyers in 1920 were more optimistic (58 percent) than pessimistic (29 percent) about law as "a vocation" for women. Only 13 percent expressed neutrality on the issue. At the same time, they understood clearly that as women in law they faced discrimination.[25]

The primary factor in the rapid expansion of women lawyers in the

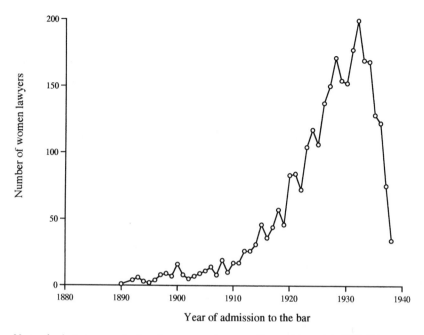

Year of admission to the bar for women lawyers. *Source: Martindale-Hubbell Law Dictionary, Seventy-First Annual Edition, 1939,* vol. 1 (New York: Martindale-Hubbell, 1939).

early twentieth century was the availability of law schools, particularly Portia, Washington College of Law, and New York University, which all welcomed women. As early as the 1870s, women saw law school as offering the best way to train for the practice of law. By the 1920s, this shift to formal legal education and away from the apprenticeship system, was common to both men and women. For women, in particular, a law school education provided the path to success on an equal level with men. *Women in the Law* reported that there were 606 women enrolled in law schools in America in the academic year 1914–15, and four years later, the number had increased to 1,068. Women entering law practice after 1900 consistently attended law school. Eighty-nine percent of the women listed in the 1939 *Martindale-Hubbell* graduated from a law school between 1900 and 1919, and another 86 percent graduated from law school between 1920 and 1939 (see Table 4). By 1949, the pattern of training of women lawyers was complete. Legal education was no longer a novelty; it had become an established fact in the life of the woman lawyer.

The enrollment of women in law schools in the 1920s underscored women's optimism about the profession, but the picture was more complex. With the numbers of women in all law schools rising from 1,166 in 1920 to 2,203 in 1930, women law students increased at all but the best law schools, those approved by groups such as the American Bar Association and the Association of American Law Schools. These schools, however, admitted only 381 women in 1920 and 523 in 1930. This difference revealed the sharp dichotomy between the approved law schools and those with lower standards, such as the part-time law schools.[26]

The growth of women in the legal profession in the early twentieth century occurred throughout all regions of the United States. New York, the District of Columbia, and Illinois, historically centers for women lawyers, continued to attract high proportions of women in the field (see Table 5). But women lawyers were not simply a phenomenon of the large cities of the East Coast or the Midwest. States such as Ohio, Texas, Oklahoma, and Nebraska trained women lawyers during this period of growth. No single state had an overwhelming number of women lawyers; rather, a few states with large cities and law schools that welcomed women accounted for about one-third of the women lawyers. Women surveyed by the bureau practiced or worked in 119 different cities and towns and the District of Columbia; by 1939, women lawyers practiced or worked in 375 cities and forty-seven states, the District of Columbia, and Hawaii; by 1949, women lawyers continued to disperse, working in 428 cities and towns, all forty-eight states, the District of Columbia, Alaska, Hawaii, Puerto Rico, and the Canal Zone.[27]

Although the expansion of women lawyers was a nationwide phenomenon, certain cities dominated during the period of the emergence of the new generation of women lawyers. Washington, D.C., New York City, Chicago, and Boston consistently attracted the highest proportion of women lawyers from 1920 to 1949 (see Table 6). Primarily due to the location of Portia in Boston and Washington College of Law in Washington, D.C., the openness of New York University to women, and the coeducational choices in Chicago, women in these cities thrived on the access both to legal education and to other women lawyers.

Women in rural areas like Texas or South Carolina experienced the isolation that many nineteenth-century women lawyers endured. Unlike their predecessors, however, isolated practitioners in the early twentieth

century could rely on national publications such as the *Women Lawyers'
Journal* and organizations such as the Women Lawyers' Association for
discussion of issues relating solely to women. Women lawyers in the
South frequently spoke to clubs on women's views of legal issues and
continually gave free advice in the hopes of gaining new clients.[28]
    The broad geographical dispersion of women lawyers in the twen-
tieth century reflected the nationwide popularity of law schools. The
women surveyed in 1920 attended sixty-one different law schools. By
1939, the women lawyers in the 1939 *Digest* attended 148 law schools;
by 1949, the number of law schools attended by the women in the
1949 *Digest* grew to 158 (see Table 7). New York University, Washington College of Law, and Portia ranked as the most popular law schools
among women lawyers in 1920, 1939, and 1949. With their histories
of institutional support for women in law, these three institutions were
central to the education of a new generation of women lawyers. Next
in importance were the large universities such as Michigan, Boston,
Chicago, Illinois, and Wisconsin, as well as Washington University in
St. Louis. Women, like men, typically attended law schools in their
home states. Women law students attended a broad spectrum of schools,
from the elite law schools to the evening and part-time schools.
    With broadened access to legal education also came isolation for
women lawyers. Many schools trained only one or two women per year.
In 1920, forty of the sixty-one schools attended by women surveyed
by the bureau trained two or fewer women lawyers. By 1939, seventy-
nine of 148 schools had two or fewer women graduates. This trend
finally began to change in 1949, when only fifty-seven of the 158 law
schools attended trained two or fewer women graduates. As more
women entered law school, women students were less isolated from
each other. Yet the fact remained that just as in the nineteenth century,
a woman attending a local law school might well train without another
woman in her class or in her school.[29]
    Unlike many nineteenth-century women lawyers who entered law
later in life, one of the unique characteristics of the new generation of
women lawyers was their relative youth. Over one-half of the women
lawyers listed in the 1939 *Digest* and in *Martindale-Hubbell* in 1939 were
in their twenties and thirties. About one-fourth of the women were in
their forties, and some 17 percent were over fifty years of age (see Table
8). Although the ages of the women surveyed by the Bureau of Voca-

tional Information are not available, the fact that most of them attended law school in the twenty years after 1900 suggests that the emergence of younger women lawyers began just after the turn of the century. Their youth undoubtedly affected their attitudes about law practice and their perspectives on both their success in law and their personal lives.

Youth was sometimes a liability for the women lawyers of the early twentieth century. Lawyers, as well as their clients, still tended to value age and experience rather than youth. Irene Hanks, a Chicago lawyer, had a pessimistic view: "[My] honest advice is *stay out* [of law]—especially very young women [because of the competition with men]."[30] Skepticism of young lawyers was natural in the hierarchical legal profession, which assumed that with experience came knowledge. Florence Weigle of New York City put it very plainly in 1920: men will hire women lawyers "if they don't have enough money to hire a man."[31] Yet there were advantages to youth. Olive Lapham of Chicago believed that the best years for women lawyers were their twenties and thirties because the sacrifices demanded of law practice were so high that younger women lawyers were better able to handle the "raw, sordid problems" of the law and to "battle for the dollar all the way."[32]

Gradually, by 1949, the age composition of women in law had become more balanced. Almost equal proportions of women lawyers were in their thirties as in their forties (31 percent each), and a substantial portion were in their fifties (21 percent) (see Table 8). The proportion of women in law who were in their twenties and thirties declined to 39 percent in 1949, down from 55 percent ten years earlier.

Marriage was always problematic for professional women of the late nineteenth and early twentieth centuries, primarily due to the difficulty of balancing family responsibilities with their careers. Because women lawyers of the early twentieth century were a young group, they had an unusual profile of family life among professional women in America. Their predecessors in groups like the Equity Club were as likely to be married as not (53 to 51 percent). In contrast, the census-takers in 1890 counted fewer women lawyers who were married: 21 percent, primarily because of distinctions between widowed or divorced women lawyers (see Table 9). The census-takers found more women lawyers who had yet to marry, but they likely undercounted married women lawyers who worked with their lawyer husbands. By 1920, 30 percent of the women lawyers surveyed by the bureau were married, and only 3 percent had been widowed or divorced. The high proportion of women lawyers who were single, 67 percent, suggests that many were young.

For many women lawyers, marriage remained outside of the practice of law as they sought to be independent professionals. Florence Allen, for example, advised in 1920 that women "should keep up their profession after marriage, staying home a larger portion of the time when the children are small."[33] But some women saw advantages to being single. "A single woman has a tremendous advantage over a married woman," observed Bertha Green in 1920, "as she can give her whole attention to her business, as a man does."[34] By 1939, the proportion of established women lawyers who were married increased to 43 percent, revealing again the natural aging of the women lawyers in the early twentieth century. By 1949, one-half of the women lawyers were married. More importantly, the proportion of women who were either widowed or divorced tripled from 1920 to 1949, suggesting that some women turned to law as a career in times of need, such as after the end of World War II (see Table 9).

The marital patterns of women lawyers were similar to those of women doctors. Women in both medicine and law married and continued to work in substantially higher proportions than did women in the so-called women's professions of teaching, nursing, and social work. According to the census, the proportions of married women lawyers and doctors in 1920, for example, were 34 percent and 33 percent, respectively. In contrast, married women represented only 10 percent of teachers, 8 percent of nurses, 11 percent of social workers, and 18 percent of women scientists. In part, the difference between women lawyers and doctors, on the one hand, and women teachers, scientists, nurses, and social workers, on the other, was the fact that the latter professionals had to find jobs in institutional settings; they could not work independently. Women teachers often resigned their positions upon marriage. But women lawyers and doctors, from the late-nineteenth to the mid-twentieth centuries, married and worked within their professions in strikingly similar patterns. In the late-nineteenth century women lawyers, both those in private practice and those in other careers, married at rates from 21 to 53 percent, whereas physicians married in more comparable proportions (25 to 35 percent). By the twentieth century, women lawyers and doctors married and worked in almost identical proportions: 29 to 44 percent for women lawyers, and 32 to 46 percent for women doctors.[35]

Married women lawyers limited the size of their families in order to accommodate their careers; only about a quarter of the women had even one or two children. Only 29 percent of the women in the 1939 *Who's Who* and only 29 percent of the women in the 1949 *Digest* even had children, despite the fact that nearly one-half of them were married (see Table 10).

That women lawyers would control their family sizes in order to achieve a career in law is consistent with their prior work histories. Work had been a vital part of the lives of the women surveyed by the Bureau of Vocational Information before they even became lawyers. A predominantly white, middle-class group of women, they had typically worked as teachers and principals (34 percent) or as stenographers and secretaries (27 and 8 percent, respectively) before entering the law (see Table 11). This pattern was common among women lawyers. Just as Emma Gillett and Almeda Hitchcock left teaching to enter the law in the nineteenth century, seeking better pay and more interesting work, Florence Allen left her jobs as a teacher and music critic to earn more money.[36] But women lawyers in the early twentieth century had not all worked as teachers and secretaries. Some had been exposed to the legal profession and the legal system through jobs as court stenographers, law clerks, government workers, title examiners, or assistants to lawyers. Overall, prospective women lawyers in 1920 were a salaried group of workers who either had some contact with the law or sought a better profession than teaching.

Twentieth-century women lawyers still faced the same problems as did nineteenth-century women lawyers: how to secure an independent practice in a male-dominated profession. Although they believed that they could succeed, women lawyers in the 1920s faced discrimination and limited opportunities in law practice. Despite these obstacles, women lawyers empowered themselves within the closed legal profession by carefully choosing their areas of practice, engaging in the general practice of law to enhance their ability to compete, and securing a niche in the world of the small practitioner. Although they did not succeed as spectacularly as Doerschuk might have hoped, a few early twentieth-century women lawyers attained significant success and most made modest gains within the closed legal profession. Others, of course, went on to seek career opportunities outside of the law.

Notwithstanding Doerschuk's assertion that a courtroom practice was ideal for women, women lawyers overwhelmingly believed that an office practice was the best choice. Whether located in New York City, Washington, D.C., or a southern or western city or town, women lawyers believed that an office practice gave women the best opportunities in law. Married and single women alike agreed that women lawyers were more likely to find professional opportunities outside of the courtroom. In particular, according to 45 percent of the women surveyed, probate work was thought to have been the single best specialization for women (see Table 12). A law practice in domestic relations ranked second, at 17 percent, among specialties that women in 1920 thought offered opportunities to women lawyers. Next in order were a general office practice and real estate law, ranking at 15 and 13 percent, respectively. Business law, trial work, and social welfare law rounded out the ideal preferences of women, at 3 to 4 percent.

In spite of their ideal specializations in law, women lawyers adapted their work to the realities of a legal profession dominated by men and male values. As they looked at their opportunities in law in 1920, they understood that power and access for women in the legal profession rested in an office practice. The major practice areas of women lawyers were probate law, wills, domestic relations, general office practice, and real estate law. These areas of the law all relied on qualities traditionally associated with femininity. Like many women lawyers in the nineteenth century, most women lawyers in 1920 saw themselves as negotiators, mediators, problem solvers, and drafters of legal documents to assist individuals and families. As they projected themselves into the predominantly male legal culture, they gravitated toward office practices rather than trial work. To Mary O'Toole of upstate New York, office work was "more profitable than trial work," which she saw as "exhausting and less profitable."[37] Most women did not see themselves as combatants in the fray of the male-dominated courtroom. Alfred Z. Reed shared this perception of the place of women in law, observing that "women will [not] be great jurists" because they were not "domineering and 'cruel' enough."[38] Some women lawyers agreed, acknowledging that "women's feelings are easily bruised . . . Men lawyers attack each other viciously for jury [e]ffect and walk out of court as friends; women cannot stand for that."[39] Sarah Buchanan of Mississippi noted that the average woman "shrinks from the shock of combat in legal forums."[40] A few women lawyers, such as Clara Foltz of California, saw opportunities in the courtroom, but in the early twentieth century, such women were unique.[41]

The reality of women lawyers' careers deviated from their ideals. Financial necessity encouraged them to engage in a broad range of specialties, broader even than what they believed to have been the ideal areas of specialization for women in law. Although women lawyers perceived that women's opportunities in law rested in specialties like probate law and domestic relations, most actually conducted general office practices (52 percent) (see Table 13). Only 20 percent of the women lawyers in 1920 specialized in probate law, the second highest specialty after a general office practice. They practiced law as it applied to real estate, domestic relations, criminal activity, trial work, banking and commercial relations, taxes, corporate transactions, bankruptcy, labor, and patents. The ideal of the specialized practice in probate law or domestic relations, specialties that women lawyers seemed to identify as uniquely female, gave way to the economic need to be as broad as possible and conduct an office practice that was both economically successful and personally satisfying. But there were limits to which women lawyers would expand their practices. They generally refused to accept collections cases, a form of legal work that easily supplemented a lawyer's income but required the attorney to appear frequently in court.

By 1939, the parameters of law practice for women were clear: two-thirds of women lawyers maintained general office practices. Women lawyers, not unlike their male counterparts, offered as wide a range of legal services as possible under the umbrella of the office practice. Most women lawyers settled into the world of the small practitioner, offering clients the general skills of the neighborhood law office.

In 1920, almost one-third of all women lawyers were solo practitioners—a proportion that increased slightly to 41 percent and 43 percent in 1939 and 1949, respectively (see Table 14). In 1939 there were a few more women lawyers in firms or associations than practicing alone, but a sharp decline occurred in 1949 as proportionally fewer women lawyers worked in law firms. What did change in 1949, however, was the proportion of women lawyers who worked outside of private practice, primarily in federal, state, and local government positions. The expansion of the federal bureaucracy during the New Deal and World War II, together with the fact that women gravitated towards salaried positions in corporations, began to shift the percentage of women lawyers in law firms by the 1940s.

Ironically, as all women joined the electorate for the first time in 1920, women lawyers became divided over the potential of suffrage to help them overcome sexual discrimination in the legal profession. As a political touchstone, suffrage had been the single most powerful issue for women for nearly eighty years. The Bureau of Vocational Information, acutely aware of the importance of suffrage, tried to assess its effects on women lawyers. Sixty-one percent of the women lawyers believed that suffrage helped women in law (see Table 15). Some among this optimistic majority focused on the intangible benefits of suffrage; they viewed the vote as empowering women lawyers and as therefore enhancing their status and respect (55 percent). Others saw the issue in more practical terms and tied suffrage to their desire to run for public office or to win appointments to positions in the courts (45 percent) (see Table 16).

Not all of the women in 1920 were so optimistic about the vote. About one-fourth were unsure of the effects of suffrage on them as lawyers, and 12 percent did not believe that suffrage would even help women in law. Eastern and midwestern women believed more strongly in the benefits of the vote than did southern and western women. In fact, women from the South and the West were four times as likely as women of the East and Midwest to reject the benefits of suffrage (see Table 15). Southern and western women defined suffrage as beneficial only in terms of status and respect, not for providing tangible work opportunities. Eastern and midwestern women had the opposite view; they saw access to work as the major benefit for women lawyers (see Table 16).

Similarly, women lawyers were divided over the benefits they had gained from World War I. Younger women lawyers, who graduated from law school between 1911 and 1920, were optimistic about their futures, believing that the social changes that had come with World

War I offered women unique opportunities in law. In contrast, older women who entered law practice before 1910 were less optimistic. They saw law opportunities as essentially unchanged, if not diminished, for women as a result of the war (see Table 17).

In the early twentieth century, the world of the small practitioner meant working alone or with one other lawyer. In 1920, about one-third of the practicing women lawyers worked as solo practitioners. This pattern of solo practice among women lawyers persisted in the 1930s and 1940s as women continued to find autonomy in the legal profession by creating independent law practices. Some women lawyers found that practicing law with their husbands, relatives, or friends was more to their liking and created partnerships or associations with law-yers in small firms.[42] These arrangements reflected the need of women lawyers to share the expenses of an office, a secretary, and a law library. In general, women lawyers in the early twentieth century who opened private practices of law ran their own offices. Remarkably, the nine-teenth-century ideal of the husband and wife firm persisted among the new generation of women lawyers, though it was never dominant. Women lawyers also practiced with relatives other than their husbands. The fact that women lawyers worked with husbands and relatives re-vealed that informal, social relationships continued to be important af-ter law school for some practicing women lawyers in the early twentieth century even as the idea of the meritocracy in the profession emerged as the ideal. These informal, family ties provided needed economic opportunities for some women lawyers, though the vast majority of women lawyers made their way independently.

The law firms in which women lawyers worked were small, number-ing usually no more than two lawyers. The existence of these firms contrasted sharply with the presence of large and growing corporate law firms in major American cities but was consistent with the law practices of men at the middle and lower levels of the profession. In 1939, *Martindale-Hubbell* captured this extreme emphasis on solo practice among women lawyers: it listed 78 percent of the women lawyers as solo practitioners or without a firm association, and only 22 percent as partners in a firm or associated with another attorney.[43]

Although most women lawyers worked in solo practice or with one other lawyer, they acknowledged that training for private practice re-quired a clerkship in a firm (see Table 18). Sixty percent of the women lawyers in 1920 viewed a clerkship as the preferred method to start a practice. But the best way to begin was probably the most difficult, because clerkships for women were scarce and often lasted for several years, impinging on women's ability to become independently successful. Some women lawyers flatly advised against clerkships because they lasted too long—they kept women in offices doing legal research, office work, and stenography, thereby preventing them from gaining experience in the courtroom.[44] For women who wanted trial practices, the clerkship proved to be the wrong avenue of professional training.

The closed nature of the legal profession kept newly trained women lawyers in clerkships for long periods of time because such jobs were often the only ones available to women. Helen Catterall, a graduate of the law school of Boston University, returned to law work after her husband died by working as a clerk responsible for legal research at the Boston firm of Hale and Dorr, a job she obtained through a friend from law school.[45] To move out of a clerkship, a woman needed either sufficient business to become self-supporting or family contacts to pave the way into practice. Still, women sought clerkships. Irene Hanks lamented her inability to break into the profession because she was a woman. The "men [lawyers] want a young man as clerk who can collect rents, act as office boy, [go] to court, etc."[46] Again, male lawyers' perceptions of the limitations of women lawyers impeded women's opportunities in law.

To build up their individual practices, many women lawyers in 1920 held onto the nineteenth-century belief that women composed a unique client base for women lawyers. The ease of talking with another woman, they thought, created a natural lawyer-client relationship.[47] Other women lawyers rejected this nineteenth-century notion, asserting that to become truly successful, women lawyers in the twentieth century needed to expand their lists of potential clients to include men.[48] In reality, the relationship of the woman client to the woman lawyer was a subtle one that involved a variety of issues such as social class, political sympathy, the costs and availability of legal services, and the complexity of the legal matter.[49]

Women clients made up a significant but not a dominant part of their law practices. Thirty-five percent of women lawyers in 1920 developed practices that were composed of more than one-half women clients. At the other extreme, 27 percent of the women practitioners maintained practices with less than one-third female clients. Thirty-eight percent had practices with 34 to 50 percent women as clients.[50] Women practitioners did not depend solely on women for their business, although clearly some women lawyers tailored their practices to mostly women. Although women in 1920 believed that women clients retained women lawyers more often than in the past, it is clear that women clients chose their lawyers for a variety of reasons.

Deriving an income from the practice of law was of central concern to women lawyers, who needed both to survive financially and to gain professional autonomy in the predominantly male legal profession. Women lawyers in the early twentieth century expressed their worries and frustrations over how to build a successful law practice just as nineteenth-century women lawyers had. They believed that there were many different reasons why it was difficult for women to succeed in law. Primary among these was the difficulty of wanting both to practice law and to have a family (34 percent) (see Table 19). Both married and single women lawyers identified balancing marriage and career as a problem, but more married women lawyers than single women lawyers pointed to marriage as interfering with success (45 percent married versus 29 percent single). In contrast, more single women than married women identified the problems of discrimination against women as an impediment to law practice (19 percent versus 9 percent).

Both married and single women lawyers (32 percent and 26 percent, respectively) agreed that it was difficult to become self-supporting in law practice, particularly compared with other fields of work for women. In comparison, more single women (10 percent) than married women (2 percent) denied that women had difficulties practicing. Women lawyers in 1920 firmly believed that lack of economic success in the practice of law was a factor in keeping women out of the legal profession, but they also asserted that it was by no means the primary explanation for why women were not practicing. Discrimination, balancing career and marriage, and a lack of interest in practice were equally important barriers for women.

Annual salary, the most objective measure of the financial success of a law practice, reveals that most women lawyers in 1920 made only modest achievements. Seventy percent of the women lawyers in 1920

earned annual incomes between $1,000 and $3,500. The highest income earned among them was only about $6,000.[51] These annual incomes reflect the localized law practices of the small practitioner, male and female alike. By 1939, the pattern was essentially the same, with 66 percent of the women in *Martindale-Hubbell* attaining a net worth of less than $5,000 per year. The major difference between 1920 and 1939 for women lawyers was that some women began to see more substantial gains in their incomes; some women lawyers achieved a substantial net worth of more than $20,000 per year, and in a few cases, more than $50,000 per year. Although the women who secured financial success were the exception and not the rule, they represented to women entering the profession the promise of professional success.[52]

Although women lawyers earned incomes that compared favorably with those of other professional women, male lawyers still surpassed them. In late-nineteenth-century Massachusetts, male lawyers earned an annual average of $2,000 to $3,000, and above-average incomes ranged from $5,000 to $10,000.[53] In New York City, two-thirds of the lawyers earned less than $3,000 in 1916, whereas a select few earned fees of $1,000,000.[54] The median annual income for all lawyers in the 1920s was $4,000, compared with Doerschuk's median income for women lawyers of $2,000.[55] The net worth of women lawyers reported in *Martindale-Hubbell* in 1939 confirms that women lawyers found modest financial success in law, with a few women far exceeding the average income levels of either men or women lawyers.

Women lawyers fared well when compared with women in other professions. Elizabeth Kemper Adams, in her 1921 study *Women Professional Workers*, singled out women doctors by reporting that "medical women as a group are earning more than women in other professions," but not by much. Women doctors in private practice earned annual salaries ranging from $1,200 to $5,100, with a median salary of $2,600. Salaried positions for physicians in hospitals, institutions, or social agencies ranged from $1,600 to $3,000.[56] Women teaching in colleges and universities in the 1920s generally earned less than their male counterparts who did the same work. At the best colleges and universities, salaries ranged from about $2,000 for instructors to $4,620 for full professors, whereas less prestigious schools paid their faculties between $1,600 and $2,860 per year. Women tended to cluster in the lower ranks of the academic ladder, where they struggled to advance.[57] Teachers ranked at the bottom of the pay scale in 1918, with salaries ranging from a median of $856 for elementary school teachers to a median of $1,224 for high school teachers. Although maximum salaries for teachers ranged from $2,200 to $3,000, such incomes were the exception, not the rule.[58] Thus women lawyers were as financially successful, if not more so, than women doctors and college professors. In addition, like all other professional women, women lawyers surpassed teachers financially.

Professional standing and stature were also important to women lawyers. As a service to its subscribers, *Martindale-Hubbell* ranked the lawyers whom it listed according to a three-tier estimate of legal ability. The publishers used several factors to compile this ranking, including the lawyer's place of practice, age, practical experience, and length of time in practice. They solicited the opinions of other lawyers to compile their "consensus of reliable opinion" on law practitioners. The highest ranking, an A, required that a lawyer have a minimum of ten years in practice plus a grade of "very high" from the outside references. The next rank, B, required no less than five years of practice plus a rank of "high" from the outside lawyers. The lowest category, other than no rank at all, was C, which required a grade of "fair" from the outside lawyers.[59]

Eighty-five percent of the women lawyers listed in *Martindale-Hubbell* in 1939 were not even ranked according to legal ability.[60] This exclusion was attributable, in part, to the fact that so many younger women lawyers had just entered the profession and were not yet qualified to be evaluated. In fact, 42 percent began to practice between 1930 and 1939, and another 40 percent entered practice between 1920 and 1929.[61] Yet the listing also included women from law schools with less stringent standards, making the possibility of a high ranking for such women remote. The chance of a fair evaluation for women was also undermined because the system relied on a network of predominantly male lawyers as outside reviewers.

Even so, 15 percent of the women listed in *Martindale-Hubbell* received rankings of A, B, or C—2 percent, 4 percent, and 9 percent, respectively. This fact, though modest, revealed a promise of success in the profession that was not merely financial. Beatrice Doerschuk's high standards of professional success did not reflect perfectly the professional expectations of twentieth-century women lawyers. Still, the seeds of her goal of a legal profession with equal opportunity for women and men had been planted.

As early as 1920, Doerschuk had discovered inadvertently the sobering fact that many women lawyers were not practicing law at all. She spent nearly thirty pages of *Women in the Law* outlining career alternatives that were also of interest to women.[62] Part of the mission of the Bureau of Vocational Information in sponsoring *Women in the Law* was to identify "vocational" opportunities for women with legal training. To that end, the bureau solicited information from both practicing women lawyers and those with an education in law who were in other lines of work—including state and federal government employees, women in business, social workers, law librarians, editors, teachers, educators, and stenographers.[63] Although most of the women surveyed by the bureau practiced law, Doerschuk included women who were not practicing law in order to sketch out the variety of options for women who did not elect to practice. Some women lawyers worked in law-related vocations or in business, where they typically chose fields traditionally held by women such as social work, stenography, education, and librarianship. Yet even these women lawyers who were not practicing law identified with the legal profession and defined themselves as lawyers.

The entrance of women into state and federal government represented perhaps the most significant alternative to law practice for women. As federal and state governments expanded in the 1930s and 1940s, women lawyers found a ready market for their skills, though not often in remunerative positions. By 1939, the proportion of women working for the federal government remained at 4 percent, but ten years later it had more than doubled to 9 percent. Most of the women in federal, state, and local government positions in 1949 worked in administrative law. Attorney General of the United States Thomas Clark singled out the contributions of women lawyers "in those agencies that function in the health, education and welfare fields."[64] Many fewer women lawyers worked as state and district attorney generals, though Clark also considered them worthy of mention. Working as a lawyer, whether in private practice or in the government, was more typical than working in business. Although women lawyers in business did not disappear, they declined substantially in 1939. They reappeared in 1949, but never at the same levels as in 1920.

Stenography, once a mainstay of vocational work for women with legal training, began to disappear as a career option for most women lawyers by 1949. Beginning in 1920 and continuing through the middle decades of the twentieth century, women lawyers sought to practice law or to work as lawyers or in a law-related field, not to work as stenographers. They surpassed the "vocational" training of *Women in the Law*, aspiring to professional goals within the legal profession. In this way, they slowly but surely gained a modicum of success either as private practitioners, in government positions, or in business.[65]

By the 1930s, women lawyers had generally achieved modest professional success, but primarily in areas of the law relating to an office practice. Only a small, elite group of women lawyers achieved both financial rewards from the law as well as professional stature, reflecting the ideals of Doerschuk. Although they set the standards of excellence and success for women in law, the vast majority strived to reach the same goals but never attained the same degree of financial security or professional stature.

Despite the limits of progress, however, the youthfulness of most of the women lawyers in the early twentieth century imbued in them a spirit of energy, optimism, and perhaps naïveté about their prospects in and out of the legal profession. Many sincerely believed that women would eventually compete in law on equal terms with men. They achieved modest economic success, expanded their areas of law practice, and carved out a niche in the local legal marketplace, thereby creating an encouraging picture of women lawyers attaining their goals.

EIGHT

"The Golden Age of Opportunity for Women"

$\mathcal{I}$n 1934, a group of women lawyers in California gathered to honor the accomplishments of women lawyers in the past.[1] Their celebration took the form of a dramatic pageant that recognized important women lawyers throughout the history of the western world. One by one, women lawyers crossed the stage, each representing an individual woman lawyer. The dramatization began with Deborah from the Old Testament, progressed to Afrenia of Rome and Portia of Shakespeare's *The Merchant of Venice*, and then reached the modern American era in the form of onetime Equity Club member Emma Haddock.[2]

To her audience in 1934, Haddock represented the best of the nineteenth-century woman lawyer. One of the first woman lawyers in Iowa, she was a pioneer who led a public life that conformed with the acceptable norms of behavior for women of her day. She devoted her legal career exclusively to helping her husband in his office practice. At the same time, she was an active club woman who generously donated her time to educating women on their legal rights. As one who sacrificed herself for the needs of others, Haddock's impersonator stood before this group of women lawyers in 1934 as the embodiment of nineteenth-century femininity in the law. "Remember always," she told her audience, "you will gain by being a lady as well as a lawyer."[3]

Once "Haddock" had retreated behind the curtain, a woman described as "the new woman lawyer" took center stage.[4] In contrast to

Haddock, who represented an era gone by, the new woman lawyer stood before her audience as the symbol of the modern woman lawyer for the twentieth century. Taking the torch from the women lawyers of the past, she symbolically preserved their legacy of courage, sympathy, and courtesy. But there were limits to this modern woman lawyer's debt to the past. Emma Haddock had selflessly devoted her legal expertise to the needs of others—that is, to her husband and the cause of women. In contrast, the new woman lawyer did not promise to sacrifice her professional career to charity, social reform, or woman's rights, or promise to put her husband and children before her career. Rather, with torch in hand, the new woman lawyer turned away from the path pursued by Emma Haddock and stood before her audience of women lawyers ready to blaze her own trail.

Some new women lawyers achieved noteworthy professional success, but they were a minority—the exceptional elite who captured the public's attention and set the standard for what was deemed possible for women lawyers in the early twentieth century. Inspired by the examples of this exceptional elite and reinforced by a climate of optimism and heightened expectations, the new women lawyers set out to reach great heights.

The optimism of new woman lawyers was enhanced by their newly cleared avenue to practice. They did not struggle for decades to gain admission to the bar as had dozens of women during the nineteenth century: every state bar was open to women; most law schools admitted women; enrollments in law schools soared; and by 1930 the number of women lawyers nationwide had increased dramatically to 3,385.[5] This progress was not limited to white women; African-American women benefited from this era of opportunity as well. A few African-American women graduated from some of the well-known law schools in the 1920s and early 1930s, including Boston University, John Marshall in Chicago, University of Pennsylvania, Fordham, and Yale. And they passed their state bars and practiced law in cities such as Chicago, Philadelphia, and New York. African-American women even gained a foothold in the South, practicing in Virginia, Texas, and Florida, and black lawyer Violette Neatly Anderson gained admission to practice before the United States Supreme Court.[6]

In this era, new women lawyers embodied the optimism, self-confidence, and dreams of young women in the 1910s and 1920s who sought to replace nineteenth-century views of womanhood with a new set of values.[7] Whereas the women of Emma Haddock's era had built their lives on the foundation of separate spheres, young women in the 1910s and 1920s sought to weaken, if not destroy, this bedrock of nineteenth-century women's lives. In their quest to blur the boundaries between men and women, they rejected the idea of sexual differences and embraced the belief in sexual equality with men. At the same time, they replaced the notion of a singular definition of womanhood with the claim that there was much that distinguished women from each other. This recognition of the differences among individual women reflected a growing reality in their lives. As they watched the immigration of Eastern European families to American cities and the migration of African-American families to the North, it was impossible to deny the fact that women were shaped by their race, social class, and ethnicity.

These new attitudes were part of a broad change in American values in which the absolute, moralistic ideals of Victorian-American culture were being substituted with the principles of science—objectivity, empiricism, and relativism. Best understood as the rise of a "science of society," the shift to empiricism touched all aspects of American life. The belief in a science of society helped to transform law from a fixed, absolute body of doctrines to a set of rules based on empiricism and the necessities of a particular historical era. Similarly, in medicine, the holistic view of health, which envisioned the patient in relation to the environment, gave way to a reductionist approach, which focused on a specific organ rather than the patient. In higher education, the sectarian colleges gave way to the secular university, and the social sciences surpassed religion in prestige. Within all the professions, an emphasis on merit as judged by rational, objective criteria began to replace the traditional subjective criteria of social class, race, ethnicity, and gender as the standards of excellence.[8]

The new vision of womanhood occurred within the context of these broad changes in American culture. Some women challenged traditional visions of womanhood within the walls of academe. As pioneers in the new social sciences, they sought to test scientifically the Victorian "truths" that women were intellectually and physically different from men. Professionally trained social workers took over from benevolent reformers the responsibility of unwed mothers. Other women rebelled in their private lives, rejecting the sexual code of their mothers and grandmothers and engaging freely in sex before marriage like men did. Still others moved into the public arena and fought for the Nineteenth Amendment, the ultimate symbol of women's political equality with men. This broad challenge to tradition was fueled by a commitment to change, a strong belief in women's as yet untapped potential, and an optimistic expectation that women would compete successfully with men in the meritocracy of twentieth-century American society.[9]

Professional women seized on meritocracy as the key to sexual integration. Women doctors, for example, put their faith in the many male-dominated medical schools and hospitals that had opened to women by the end of the century. Believing that women would be admitted to these institutions on the basis of merit, they optimistically turned away from the all-women's medical institutions that had enabled women to enter medicine in the second half of the nineteenth century. As women doctors willingly sought to compete on equal terms with men for admission to medical schools and positions at male-run hospitals, all-women's medical schools closed and the all-women's hospitals struggled to attract women doctors.[10]

This same belief in the advantages of the emerging meritocracy gave early twentieth-century women lawyers reason to be optimistic about their opportunities in the legal profession. Merit freed them from the traditional view of women as inherently unequal to men and gave them the opportunity to demonstrate their competence based on neutral, scientifically defined criteria. Merit also began to dismantle the women lawyers movement as it was constructed in the nineteenth century, with its emphasis on the legal disabilities and professional discrimination of women as a group. Instead, women lawyers in the early twentieth century redefined their goals to embrace the rhetoric of Beatrice Doerschuk, with her emphasis on the ability of each woman lawyer to compete on equal terms with men. Finally, the new focus on merit encouraged women to enter the law for personal autonomy. Women were well aware that the legal profession offered them avenues to independence—some intellectual, some financial, and others social. By choosing law, women envisioned for themselves a future of independence, financial reward, and prestige. In short, the new women lawyers adapted their feminist politics to the meritocratic ideals of professional advancement.

At the heart of the optimism and self-confidence of women lawyers in the early twentieth century was their belief in sexual equality. They relished competition with men and anticipated success on male terms. In the minds of these new women lawyers, their claim to sexual equality signaled the death of the double consciousness that had plagued nineteenth-century women lawyers. They triumphantly asserted that there was no longer any contradiction in women's lives between their gender and professional identity. As one woman lawyer explained, "The day has arrived when there are only *lawyers*, and not *men* and *women* lawyers."[11] Another echoed this view: "For my part, I want merely to be known as a 'lawyer' and not as a 'woman lawyer.'"[12]

To fully appreciate the energy, optimism, and professional commitment of this generation of new women lawyers, one had only to turn to Jane Thorndike, the heroine of *Portia Marries*, a novel written in 1926 by Jeannette Phillips Gibbs.[13] As author, lawyer, and wife, Gibbs was a model of the new woman of the day.[14] A graduate of Smith College, she followed in the footsteps of her father and grandfather, both of whom were prominent lawyers in Massachusetts, by earning her LL.B. in 1917 at Boston University Law School.[15] She was a member of the state bars of both Massachusetts and New York, though she never actively practiced law. Instead, she wrote novels about women. Her personal life mirrored the qualities of modern womanhood as well. She shared a companionate marriage with her husband, Hamilton Gibbs, who was also an author.

Portia Marries portrayed the new woman lawyer of the 1920s in striking contrast to the ways in which male authors had fictionalized women lawyers in the 1880s. Jane Thorndike, the leading character, embodied all the qualities of the successful new woman in law. She was a bright, independent woman who measured up to the most rigorous standards of merit while balancing her successful legal career with marriage and motherhood. At the start of the story, Jane was a young, attractive, single woman who, like many other women of her generation, found professional opportunities in law during World War I. Having built a successful office practice, she was content with what she referred to as her "full life" and its traditionally male characteristics of "competition, achievement, [and] ego."[16]

With such an active public life, Jane's personal life was limited, centering around her parents and sister. Her father, a successful doctor, was her intellectual and spiritual role model. She loved her fragile mother, but disapproved of her vapid life and her obsession with her nervous disorder, which Jane believed was only in her mother's mind. Jane disapproved of her sister, a traditional wife and mother. And she gave wise and practical business advice to her not-so-shrewd brother-in-law.

A visit to town from Thomas Kent, a former college boyfriend, ignited in Jane feelings of discontent about the emptiness of her personal life. "The urge to climb is one part of me but it isn't all," she confessed to her father, "and I want all the other parts too."[17] Jane began to date Tommy with the confidence of the women of her generation who believed that they could have both marriage and a career. Without a second thought, she easily slipped out of her blue wool suit, "her legal insignia,"[18] and into her green silk dress to hide her intellect and accentuate her femininity and youthfulness. With makeup on and cigarette in hand, she transformed herself from a hard-driving, no-nonsense lawyer into an alluring young woman.

Tommy fell in love. A sensitive and flexible new man of the era, he knew that Jane would never give up her career for the life of a traditional wife and mother, and he accepted her modern view of marriage. Jane's family, however, brought more traditional expectations to Jane's and Tommy's new marriage. Her parents, sister, brother-in-law, and even her law partner waited for the newly married Jane to settle down to the life of a traditional wife. With marriage, her sister explained, Jane finally "had a chance to be a woman instead of a lawyer."[19]

But Jane surprised them all: she and Tommy built a companionate marriage that made room for her legal career. In fact, their marriage pushed the contours of the companionate marriage beyond the boundaries of equality. Although wifely sacrifice was an outdated view, in Jane's and Tommy's particular arrangement sacrifice prevailed, though it was always Tommy who sacrificed his work or his personal desires to satisfy Jane. For her part, Jane placed her own self-interest first. She tried to keep her marriage a secret in public, kept her maiden name, and consistently put her career before her marriage. Even on her wedding day, Jane arrived late to the church, wearing her blue business suit and carrying her briefcase. Even though Tommy desperately wanted a two-week honeymoon, he settled for a Sunday afternoon with his new wife, who could not imagine leaving her work and her clients for even a day.

Jane continued to behave more like a traditional husband than a wife by sacrificing her marriage to the needs of her law practice. Eventually, she began to come home late from work, leaving Tommy to wait for her for dinner or eat alone. To make matters worse, she ignored Tommy's requests that she call him on the evenings when she was detained at the office. When Tommy expressed his discontent, the two began to quarrel. In the midst of this marital discord, Jane discovered that she was pregnant. But she kept the pregnancy a secret from Tommy and her law partner, Mr. Dwight, and continued her usual schedule at the office. In contrast to the traditional view that a pregnant woman suddenly became mentally and emotionally unstable and was unfit for rational judgement in the public arena, Jane continued to work as usual: "There was not a soul in the office who observed any change in her work. Mr. Dwight was absolutely unconscious of any mental disturbance in his partner."[20] The high point of her success occurred when her obstetrician, Dr. Thresher, who had gone to her law office in search of the absent Mr. Dwight, placed his legal affairs in her hands. Jane took over the situation with a directness and an air of self-confidence. "You are in my office now," she explained with a smile. "Any medical information you may have about your attorney is incompetent, immaterial and irrelevant here."[21] Awed by her control of the situation, Dr. Thresher "became a client and a meek one."[22] Totally satisfied with her legal counsel, he nevertheless left Jane's office completely disarmed about the relations between the sexes. As he walked out the door, he lamented: "Lawyer become patient, doctor become client, woman become man."[23]

Jane's success in her career was not duplicated at home, however. She and Tommy continued to quarrel as he grew increasingly dissatisfied with her absence in the evening and her refusal to reduce her work responsibilities. When Tommy planned a three-month business trip to Mexico, neither of them was able to express their unhappiness about being apart for so long. Tommy left thinking Jane did not care, and Jane, committed to their original promise to respect each other's independence, let him go without even sharing the secret of her pregnancy. In Tommy's absence, however, Jane realized how much she loved him and valued their relationship. In a letter, she finally revealed to him that she was pregnant and confessed how much she missed him. Tommy rushed home, and they began to rebuild their marriage.

While Jane and Tommy renewed their commitment to each other, Jane confounded others around her as she refused to give up her career. Even in the throes of childbirth, she never sacrificed her professional identity. At the hospital and under the influence of drugs to relieve her labor pains, her mind was still in the courtroom, and she groggily addressed her nurses and doctors as "Gentlemen of the Jury."[24] Moreover, Jane continued to practice law after the birth of her son. She worked in the morning, came home to spend time with her son in the afternoon, and returned to work in the evening.

The story ends seventeen years later. By this time, Jane had achieved fame as a lawyer, and Jane's son, Thomas, Jr., was eighteen and planning to study law and then practice with his mother. In the last scene of the book, Thomas met his father for lunch for a father-and-son talk about Jane. Thomas admitted that he had really wanted to dine with his mother but that she had been too busy for him when he appeared at her office at midday. His displeasure over the incident led him to complain further to his father about not having a traditional mother when he grew up. When Tommy responded by asking him if he would have preferred a traditional mother like his aunt, Mary, young Thomas responded with a resounding no and admitted that he appreciated his mother for her version of childrearing. The book closes with Jane at work and the two men in her life, Tommy and Thomas, sharing cigars over lunch as they praised Jane as wife, mother, and lawyer.

The message to the reader of *Portia Marries* was unmistakable: the day of the new woman lawyer had arrived. Unlike the fictitious Miss Padelford in the 1880s who was saved from the pressures of the courtroom by marriage, Jane Thorndike presented a new model of the woman lawyer for the twentieth century.[25] She was a self-confident and independent young woman who did not sacrifice or even slow down her career for marriage. Instead, she succeeded on her own in her law practice, built a companionate marriage with her husband, kept her maiden name professionally, and managed to balance the demands of her career with the responsibilities of motherhood. In stark contrast to Miss Padelford, whose feminine frailty prevented her from practicing law as an equal with men, Jane Thorndike achieved equality with men in her professional life and symbolized the quest for pure sexual equality that inspired the lives of so many young women in the 1910s and 1920s.

Although some reviewers criticized Gibbs for solving Jane Thorndike's problems too simply, they all praised her for presenting in a positive light the challenge of balancing marriage and career.[26] Moreover, even though Gibbs may have idealized her heroine's life, Jane Thorndike had goals and values similar to those of Gibbs's contemporaries. Like Jane, most women by 1920 were attracted to the law for personal reasons. The view put forward by nineteenth-century women lawyers that the law was a helping profession and that they would be its public servants did not appeal as strongly to this generation of new women. Instead, nearly two-thirds of women lawyers in 1920 said that they entered the law for personal gain and status, to develop their minds, or to be in what they saw as a dignified and studious line of work. Their perception of law as intellectually challenging and dignified reflected the upper-middle-class attitudes of women of their day. Law appealed to them because it was both appropriate to their social class and redeeming on an individual basis. Over 90 percent of the women surveyed viewed law as a profession for personal or financial gain.[27]

To many observers in the 1910s and 1920s, the fictionalized Jane Thorndike was a reality. Everywhere one turned, one could find examples of women who had achieved success within the new meritocracy of the legal profession. Women lawyers such as Helen Carloss, Emma Fall Schofield, and Edith Sampson were just a few of the many success stories. They stood as proof that individual women lawyers could compete as equals with men and excel in the most competitive of meritocracies. Helen Carloss was a young woman stifled in a small town who went to the city and found success.[28] Born in Yazoo City, Mississippi, Carloss yearned to escape the narrow life her elite southern upbringing offered her. Teaching was a profound disappointment. "I hated it. Simply hated it," she recalled.[29] When a friend received a government appointment in Washington, D.C., Carloss accompanied her in 1918, leaving the security of her hometown to find adventure and independence in a big city.

Carloss found a position as a clerk in the income tax division of the Internal Revenue Service. With an eye toward improving her job prospects, she enrolled in the law school at George Washington University, where she received her LL.B. in 1923. Her legal training enabled her to move up within her division at the Internal Revenue Service. She was a very successful lawyer and earned a reputation as being tough for her ability to collect taxes from delinquent payers. In fact, her opponents usually prepared for their cases against her by engaging a team of "the best men lawyers they can get."[30] In 1928, when she had been out of law school for only five years, Carloss replaced another woman attorney at the Department of Justice. Two years later, she became assistant to the attorney general in charge of the appellate work of the Justice Department's tax division. In just twelve years, Carloss had broken free from the constraints of her provincial southern upbringing and had fashioned for herself a fast-moving and successful professional life in the nation's capital.

Emma Fall Schofield was another accomplished new woman lawyer, but unlike Carloss, she followed her family traditions in forging her professional and private life.[31] Schofield grew up in a household of lawyers. Her mother, Anna Christy Fall, and father, George Howard Fall, shared a law practice in Boston in the late nineteenth century.[32] Schofield followed her mother's professional path. She graduated from Boston University Law School in 1908, married, had two children, and built a remarkable legal career. She was the first woman in Massachusetts to serve both as a commissioner on the Massachusetts Industrial Accident Board and as assistant attorney general. In addition, she was the first woman probation officer in the western part of the state, a dean of women at the Northeastern University Evening Law School, and a professor of constitutional law at Portia Law School. Schofield also balanced her legal career with marriage and motherhood. If Jane Thorndike symbolized the ideal new woman lawyer of the day, Emma Schofield stood as proof that this image could be a reality. True to the optimism of the times, Schofield viewed her success as typical rather than unique for her day; she declared her era "the golden age of opportunity for women."[33]

Edith Sampson's climb from poverty to professional success was proof that African-American women were part of this generation of new women lawyers.[34] Sampson grew up in a poor family in Pittsburgh. One of eight children, she worked in a fish market while her father worked in a cleaning shop and her mother made hat frames. As a child, she suffered racist taunts, but she grew into an adult who was comfortable with her race. "Color never bothered me very much," Sampson recalled. "I know what I am, and a blonde I am not."[35]

Sampson got her break at eighteen when Associated Charities in Pittsburgh sent her to New York City to attend the New York School of Social Work. Her instructor in a law course, George W. Kirckwey, a Columbia University law professor and former law dean, was so impressed by her abilities that he encouraged her to go to law school. Sampson moved to Chicago, where she worked during the day to pay for evening classes at John Marshall Law School. She received her LL.B. in 1925 and was admitted to the state bar in 1927. This was the beginning of her remarkable climb up the professional ladder. She became the first African-American woman to earn an LL.M. from Loyola University in 1927. In the 1930s, Sampson worked in private practice while she was a referee of the Cook County Juvenile Court. In 1947, she became the first African-American woman in Illinois to be appointed assistant state's attorney.

One had only to turn to the popular lawyers' magazine *Case and Comment* to see that other women lawyers had also achieved this level of professional success.[36] The male editorial board of this journal devoted its entire October 1914 issue to the topic of women lawyers. They invited eleven accomplished women lawyers to contribute articles, which together left no doubt that women had succeeded in the meritocracy of the legal profession. The lead article, "The Twentieth Century Portia," by New York attorney Isabel Giles, conveyed the point that this was a special issue devoted to a discussion of the woman lawyer for modern times.[37] Giles's essay touted the advances women had made in the legal profession and optimistically claimed that women lawyers had "come to stay."[38] Moreover, she shared with the new women lawyers of the day a belief in the possibility of achieving sexual equality in the legal profession. Articulating their optimism—and political naïveté— Giles claimed: "Before the half-way milestone is passed (and the year 1950 now sounds a great many centuries off), there will probably be little discrimination in the public mind between men and women lawyers."[39]

Other articles in this women's issue of *Case and Comment* reinforced Giles's message of sexual equality among twentieth-century lawyers. New York attorney Edith Griswold wrote about patent law, revealing her keen grasp of the legal, intellectual, and economic issues involved in this specialty. In her article, she claimed it was an ideal area of legal practice for women.[40] Griswold's message was clear: women in the early twentieth century were ready and able to master the arena of practical science and the laws of invention. Refuting the notion that only men belonged in the "fighting profession," Marion Weston Cottle of Washington, D.C., claimed the courtroom for women lawyers.[41] "The ability to try and argue cases is, where men are concerned, largely a matter of individual fitness; and the same is true of women. It is manifestly unfair to indulge in generalities when speaking of women, which no one would think of using in referring to men."[42] Lawyer Jean Norris demonstrated the extent of women lawyers' successes, listing over twenty of the most successful women lawyers in the country.[43] Whereas Norris created a general impression of women lawyers' active professional involvement, Chicago attorney Nellie Carlin provided an in-depth example of one woman lawyer's work as public guardian of Cook County, Illinois.[44]

The overall message of the women's issue of *Case and Comment* was that by 1914 active, intelligent women had entered the legal profession and were forging ahead with productive careers in all areas of the law. Confident about their position and optimistic about what lay ahead, these new women lawyers were the successful elite among women lawyers of the day. Still, they represented the possibility of a future where all women would assume their position as equals with men in the legal meritocracy.[45]

Although *Case and Comment* demonstrated the success of women lawyers to a primarily white, professional, male audience, popular magazines enhanced this growing impression. In 1915, the widely read women's magazine *Good Housekeeping* gave its white, middle-class, female readers essentially the same message about the success of women in law. An article entitled "Your Daughter's Career, If She Wants to Be a Lawyer," advised mothers on the advantages and disadvantages of their daughters' entering the law in the 1910s.[46] Painting a rosy picture of women's new position in the profession, the article made the familiar argument that women in the 1910s no longer faced institutional barriers to law schools and bar associations, and it reinforced the image of the successful woman lawyer. Echoing Cottle in *Case and Comment*, the article quoted Edith Griswold, onetime president of the Women Lawyers' Association: "As for specialized fields, I find no general difference between men and women that would fit one sex for one line and one for another. There is as much variety in women's inclinations as in men's."[47]

As if to legitimate the optimistic claims of these women lawyers, the *Good Housekeeping* article turned to longtime male supporters of women in law such as Clarence D. Ashley, dean of the New York University Law School. He commented, "After many years' observation, I find *no difference* between men and women as to legal aptitude. The day has passed when it can be maintained successfully that women's minds are not so well adapted to the study of law as are men's."[48] Finally, the article identified successful individual women lawyers who practiced in a wide range of legal specialties, including corporate and criminal law and legal aid.

Other women's magazines reinforced this optimistic picture of the new woman lawyer. In 1920, *Green Book Magazine* published the testimonials of two successful women lawyers who enthusiastically embraced sexual equality in the legal profession. In "The Law Is Long—But It's Worth It!" Helen Christine Bennett described the experiences and philosophy of a woman lawyer, Harriet H.[49] The daughter of a southern judge, Harriet decided as a young girl to follow in her father's footsteps. From the beginning of her professional career, she proved that she was a woman lawyer for the twentieth century. She had an active solo practice with both men and women clients, and she represented them in both her office and in court. Her general philosophy in all her professional dealings was to emphasize her professional identity over her femininity. "I would never deny my sex or try to apologize for it; but neither was I going to defend it nor flaunt it," she explained.[50] Yet she tried to hide the fact that she was a woman by using her initial, H., rather than her first name, in her business dealings. In addition, Harriet professed no special allegiance to women clients, whom she claimed were often temperamental and unreliable in paying their bills. She admitted, instead, that she preferred to represent men, who were "far more businesslike."[51]

Harriet also embraced sexual equality in her private life. She had a companionate marriage and shared with her husband an agreement that neither would bring their work home at night. Moreover, like the new women of the day who flocked to makeup counters in department stores, she worked hard in her personal life to preserve and accentuate her attractiveness. Without a shred of self-consciousness, she publicly admitted that she dyed her hair red and moisturized her face every evening "as carefully . . . [as] any actress."[52] Harriet H. firmly believed that women lawyers could have it all; they no longer had to choose between a life of books and a life of beauty. Law did not make women "less feminine," she argued. In fact, one had only to "take a look" to see that women lawyers were among "the prettiest, smartest, finest girls" around.[53]

Just half a year later, *Green Book Magazine* portrayed once again the new woman in the law. The cover of the magazine pictured a courtroom in which a young woman lawyer stood confidently before her male client and addressed a male judge.[54] An article entitled "A Woman and the Law" focused on Rosalie Janoer, a Polish immigrant who became a lawyer in New York City.[55] Janoer's journey in life from being a fifteen-year-old millinery worker to a successful attorney was testimony to the opportunities open to a young immigrant woman who was willing to work hard, believed in the possibilities of individual effort, and embraced the values of the new woman lawyer.

Alone in New York City and forced to support herself, Janoer quickly progressed from being a millinery worker, to a translator in a hospital, to an office employee. Hoping ultimately to practice law, she enrolled in the evening division of New York University Law School. As a law student, Janoer sacrificed a social life as well as sleep—she studied law by night and supported herself with her office job during the day. After graduating, she established what ultimately became a very lucrative legal career and embraced the new values of sexual equality. In doing so, she sought to redefine what it meant to be a woman lawyer in the twentieth century.

At the heart of Janoer's professional philosophy was her belief in the meritocracy. Her goal was to compete on equal terms with men and to become as financially successful as the most renowned male attorney. In an era when a small but elite group of male lawyers earned enormous sums of money and wielded power serving the interests of corporations, Janoer believed that commercial success was the key to equality for women in the legal profession. She wrote: "It seems to me women have been lawyers long enough to be just lawyers, not women lawyers; but to demonstrate this thoroughly, I think women owe it to themselves to make not only a reputation but a big commercial success. It is the last thing they need, the thing which will really put them on a level with men . . . I believe it is essential to equality with men in the profession."[56] From the point of view of business success, Janoer admitted that her own legal career had gotten off to the wrong start. During the early years of her practice, she had willingly offered pro bono counsel to those who could not afford to pay. She discovered, however, that although her philanthropic efforts gave her "moral satisfaction," they brought her "no business" and in fact obstructed the growth of her practice.[57] To put herself back on the path to financial success, Janoer rejected one of the nineteenth-century tenets for women lawyers: that charity law was a natural obligation of women. Consequently, she turned down all charity cases and accepted only paying clients. Instead, she met her social obligations in a traditionally masculine way by donating money rather than time. This, she said, was the efficient, rather than the sentimental, method of charity: "Charity work is the biggest stumbling block in the path of women lawyers . . . For myself and all my sex I determined to put a stop to that. When some one asked me to take a case for charity, I got out my check-book and offered to start a fund to employ a lawyer. That," she asserted, "is the rational way to give help."[58]

Other women lawyers shared Janoer's unsentimental approach. By 1920, Clara Foltz, who had forced Hastings law school to open to women students in the late nineteenth century, warned that charity and reform consumed too much time and energy and destroyed a woman lawyer's chances for professional success. If a woman lawyer "prefers to engage in child welfare work, takes up legal-aid work, runs here, there and everywhere at the whim of every ambitious clubwoman, omitting to charge for her services," Foltz remarked, "she cannot hope to win while her eyes are bright."[59]

Annette Abbott Adams was another new woman lawyer who built her professional career on what she called "the neuter conception of work."[60] Adams, who had been a teacher in California, turned to law in order to help her widowed mother in her business. But after she graduated from the law school of the University of California in 1912, she made law her life's work and opened an office with Marguerite Ogden, the daughter of a judge from Oakland. Adams's general practice often brought her into the courtroom, and she quickly earned a reputation for her skill and force. In 1914, she was appointed assistant United States attorney for the northern district of California and became the first woman lawyer to receive an appointment as a federal prosecutor. In 1920 she blazed another trail as the first woman lawyer to become an assistant attorney general in Washington, D.C. At a time when many women lawyers struggled to support themselves, Adams stood out as a model of the successful new woman lawyer of the 1910s and 1920s. Like Janoer, Adams was true to the new vision of womanhood for the early twentieth century: she demanded to be judged on her merits and refused to accept any work that did not pay her what a man would receive.

Adams was only one of a small group of women lawyers who broke the barriers to women in the courtroom. In 1921, President Warren G. Harding appointed Mabel Walker Willebrandt to replace Adams as assistant attorney general.[61] The appointment made Willebrandt the highest ranking woman in the federal government and one of the most powerful women lawyers in the country. She was responsible for important matters involving prohibition as well as tax and prison law. Although Willebrandt had not been a prohibitionist before her appointment, she was a rigorous defender of the law. At the same time, her work in prisons led to reforms and innovations, including the creation of the first federal prison for women.

Violette Neatly Anderson's appointment to the position of assistant prosecuting attorney in Chicago in 1922 was particularly noteworthy because she was African American.[62] Her success demonstrated that the neutral standards of the merit system made room for some talented women of color. As a courtroom reporter for fifteen years, Anderson had learned the ways of the courtroom well before she entered professional practice. After graduating from Chicago Law School in 1920, she moved with ease into litigation and willingly accepted criminal cases. In 1922, she successfully defended a woman accused of killing her common-law husband.[63] The victory led to her appointment as the first black assistant prosecuting attorney in Chicago.

Whereas some women lawyers entered the courtroom as litigators, others, like Florence Allen and Jane Bolin, proved that with hard work and impressive skills women could make their way to the bench as well. Graduating second in her law class at New York University in 1913, Allen looked for a position in a law firm in Cleveland, but even family connections could not help her to find work.[64] Eventually she opened her own office practice, volunteered for the Cleveland Legal Aid Society, and worked for woman suffrage. In less than a decade, Allen had advanced in the Ohio court system from assistant county prosecutor of Cuyahoga County to common pleas court judge. She eventually became the first woman judge on the Ohio Supreme Court, but her reputation extended well beyond the state. In 1934, President Franklin D. Roosevelt appointed her judge of the Sixth U.S. Circuit Court of Appeals, making her the first woman judge on the United States Court of Appeals.

Although Jane Bolin did not reach the same judicial heights as did Allen, her appointment to the domestic relations court of New York City in 1939 was noteworthy because, like Anderson, she was African American.[65] Born in 1908 in Poughkeepsie, New York, Bolin enjoyed a privileged life for a woman of any race. Her father was a lawyer who sent his daughter to Wellesley, where she graduated in 1928. Bolin then entered Yale Law School and in 1931 became the first African-American woman to earn an LL.B. from that elite institution. She practiced law for several years with her husband who was also a lawyer, and in 1939 Mayor Fiorello La Guardia appointed her to the bench of the Domestic Relations Court of New York City, making her the first African-American woman judge in the country.

Women such as Carloss, Allen, Willebrandt, and Bolin reached the upper levels of the male-dominated court system, an accomplishment that even the very best male lawyers rarely attained. And they did so because of their professional abilities, not because they were women. One male lawyer insisted that Allen did not receive her appointment "because she was a woman. All we did was to see that she was not rejected because she was a woman."[66] Similarly, Carloss claimed that men never gave her special consideration because she was a woman: "They have never shown me any favors; they have treated me as an equal. That is the way it should be."[67]

Willebrandt, Allen, and Bolin, whose professional work brought them into the courtroom, helped introduce a new etiquette of sexual equality into this once male preserve. The goal of this new etiquette was to minimize women lawyers' gender identity and to highlight their professional identity instead. "Never let a single juror get the impression that it is a man against a woman battle," advised one woman lawyer.[68] A few male lawyers echoed this call. Urging women lawyers to spend time in the courtroom to get an "at home" feeling in what would otherwise be a "strange environment," Judge Frederick Hoffman of Cincinnati advised: "Remember to be a lawyer . . . Women must adopt that professional point of view."[69]

In their quest for neutral standards in the courtroom, women lawyers in the 1910s and 1920s rejected the titles of "Miss" and "Madam" used for addressing nineteenth-century women lawyers in court. They saw these titles as symbols of male condescension and hostility toward women in the courtroom, even as subtle weapons in the hands of the judge and opposing counsel to call attention to women lawyers' femininity and to belittle them in court. Mary Siegel encountered this hostility in her early years as a lawyer in New York in the 1920s. "There were many times when a judge would reveal either his resentment or his condescending tolerance of my professional status by asking if I preferred to be addressed as 'Madam' or 'Lady,' " she recalled. On one such occasion, the judge, upon discovering that Siegel was the attorney and not the stenographer he had originally assumed her to be, remarked in astonishment: "My God! What do I call you? Do you prefer 'she' lawyer, 'woman' lawyer or 'female' lawyer?" Siegel responded simply that "counselor" would be the appropriate address.[70]

Siegel was not alone in her desire for the adoption of a gender neutral title to be shared by all lawyers. Claiming that a "trained legal mind has no sex," Katherine Kilpatrick Makielski called for the use of the appellation "attorney."[71] At the annual meeting of the National Association of Women Lawyers, a group of young women lawyers expressed this desire to camouflage their sex and obliterate their differences with their male colleagues. "DO NOT CALL US PORTIAS," they demanded.[72]

The new courtroom etiquette influenced more than the civilities women lawyers demanded of male attorneys. It also produced a new fashion code for women lawyers in the courtroom that emphasized their equality with men. By the 1910s, women lawyers for the most part had rejected the hat as a vestige of Victorian ladydom and had agreed that they should remove their hats in the courtroom just as men did. The *Women Lawyers' Journal* consistently supported this position; it never deviated from the message that a hat was inappropriate attire for the woman lawyer in court. An article published in 1912 entitled "Appropriate Attire for the Woman Court Lawyer" declared that women's hats should "be tabooed" in the court.[73] The article took aim at three women lawyers who had worn hats in court, ridiculing them for their poor judgment and unprofessional behavior and portraying them as eccentric and out of step with the majority of women lawyers of the day. Two years later, the *Women Lawyers' Journal* once again took up the issue of the hat. An editorial entitled "The Question of Cap and Gown" supported the view that women lawyers, like men, should appear "before the bench with heads uncovered."[74] It was during this era that the *Ladies' Home Journal* began to advise business women on appropriate dress.[75]

Mary Siegel learned the new rules of courtroom attire during her very first visit to court. She entered the courtroom following the old rules, wearing her hat, which she referred to as "the symbol of gentility." But the order to remove it initiated her quickly into the new customs of the day, leaving her confused but intrigued by the change. "I remember the strange feeling of being both insulted and exhilarated by the experience," she recalled.[76] Whereas Siegel learned the lesson of courtroom fashion the hard way, Tiera Farrow, a successful lawyer in Kansas City, deliberately used her hat as a device to put the principle of sexual equality into practice every time she entered a courtroom. "I learned to do what was customary and never anything different or unusual that might call attention to myself, and even to my presence. I would, upon entering the courtroom, remove my hat, place it among the men's hats on the hat rack, and looking neither to the left nor right, take a seat in the lawyers' enclosure."[77] Other women lawyers took the same tack. Mabel Van Dyke Bell of Kentucky wore a white tailored blouse, a black skirt, "and no hat" in the courtroom, and African-American Ruth Whitehead Whaley explained that "I never speak in court with my hat on."[78]

Given their intense desire to achieve professional equality with men in the courtroom, women lawyers in the 1910s and 1920s did more than reject the tradition of the hat. They understood all too well that a woman lawyer would never be viewed equally with her male colleagues in court as long as she wore a dress rather than pants. With this in mind, women lawyers in the 1910s sought to apply the principle of pure equality to the entire costume of both men and women lawyers.

But they did not urge women to adopt the male custom of wearing trousers. Rather, women lawyers sought a sexually neutral standard of attire by urging all lawyers, men and women, to wear a robe in court. Women lawyers were not alone in their advocacy of the robe as the standard outfit for all lawyers. They found support for their call from no less than former president William Howard Taft, who believed that lawyers would command more professional respect if, as lawyers did in England, they wore robes rather than street clothes.[79]

Women lawyers agreed with Taft's argument that the robe would increase popular respect for all lawyers. But they had additional reasons for advocating its use. First, they argued that the robe was a simpler uniform than a dress or suit. Tiera Farrow, who thought she could minimize her sex by hanging her hat on the coat rack like men, found that her dresses detracted from her professional presence by drawing attention to the fact that she was a woman. On one occasion she endured the smirks of male lawyers when she entered the courtroom with her corset strings hanging down below her dress. On another occasion she endured their ridicule when she appeared in court with her skirt on inside out. "What a laugh [the men lawyers] and maybe the judge, too, must have had at my expense!" she mused years later.[80] Such embarrassing mistakes would have been hidden under the loose folds of a robe.

Women lawyers were keenly aware that the robe had other advantages that transcended the tangible categories of comfort and practicality. Unlike the hat, which had served to highlight a nineteenth-century woman lawyer's differences from a man, the robe conveyed the idea of equality between the sexes. It offered a single standard of dress, a sexually neutral outfit that would erase "sex-consciousness" in the courtroom.[81]

Despite the rhetoric about achieving pure equality through courtroom attire, individual women lawyers continued to find ways to preserve some symbol of their femininity. Isabella M. Pettus of New York City visibly placed her purse and handkerchief next to her legal papers in court.[82] Both Edith Sampson of Chicago and Judge Jean Norris of New York City wore pearls. These feminine touches made it easier for a tradition-bound public to accept the presence of women lawyers in the courtroom. One reporter captured the femininity of Judge Norris in his description of her presence in the courtroom: "True, the Judge wears a robe. But within the robe there is a woman."[83]

Although many new women lawyers focused on achieving equality with men in the most public of forums, the courtroom, others sought to find sexual equality in their private lives. This was possible because of the emergence of the companionate marriage, which represented an important break from the conventional marriages of nineteenth-century America. Whereas a wife in a traditional marriage led a life defined by dependency, obligation, and obedience, the ideal companionate marriage was built on friendship, mutuality, and equality. As Elizabeth Kemper Adams observed: "It is no longer taken as a matter of course that women will entirely give up their professional work when they marry, and hence cannot expect to receive serious professional consideration. A growing number of professional married couples—most of them young—are working out the problem together, and making a genuine contribution to social adjustment."[84] Crystal Eastman typified the new view about work and marriage. She wrote: "I grew up confidently expecting to have a profession and earn my own living, and also confidently expecting to be married and have children. It was fifty-fifty with me. I was just as passionately determined to have children as I was to have a career."[85]

To make possible their vision of a full life, new women lawyers deconstructed traditional views of domesticity and reconstructed them for a new era of sexual equality. Many women of this generation rejected the nineteenth-century view that domestic chores were the natural duties of women and argued instead that domestic responsibilities were simple tasks that anyone could perform. But modern women lawyers took their attack on nineteenth-century conventions beyond their assault on housework. They also debunked the traditional notion that motherhood was the sacred, quintessential state of womanhood. Instead, they insisted that childrearing was not an all-encompassing task for the young mother, and that she did not need to sacrifice a career to raise her children.

These were lofty claims, but women lawyers were undaunted. Many believed that women could both marry and practice law. "A woman can be a whole woman and still be good in her vocation," explained one woman lawyer in 1920.[86] Two elements provided them with the ability to balance a career with their traditional roles of wife and mother. First, they relied on the privileges of their social class and urged women lawyers to hire domestic servants. One woman lawyer explained that the married woman lawyer need only to hire someone to relieve her of the "burden of household responsibilities and permit her to return to work."[87] Florence Allen, who never married, nevertheless believed that a married woman lawyer had the right to use her income from her law practice to hire domestic help. "If she earns a living wage, she can afford to pay a living wage to have the burden of the house lifted from her."[88]

Like household duties, the responsibilities of childcare could also be performed by others. Rejecting the nineteenth-century romanticization of motherhood, one woman lawyer sought to bring a level of objectivity to the responsibility of childrearing: "Children do not need a mother's whole attention—they are often better off with others."[89] Women lawyers in the early decades of the twentieth century found that they could manage their careers and their homes as long as they hired someone else to do the domestic work.

Still, most women lawyers recognized the limits of domestic servants for solving the demands of their careers. Even the most loyal and efficient servant could not provide all the assistance a woman lawyer needed if her husband did not approve of her career. From this point of view, little had changed in the past half century. Like nineteenth-century women lawyers, new women lawyers understood all too well that above all else, the key to maintaining a happy marriage and a successful career was, still, to marry the "right man."[90] "Choose the broader-minded man, who has risen above expecting that his wife should be his housekeeper," advised one woman lawyer.[91] Some warned young women to make sure that a potential husband understand clearly her intentions to pursue a career after marriage. One woman lawyer explained that a young woman should not marry a man unless "he is willing for her to follow her vocation. She would not be happy with a selfish man."[92] Another echoed this view, explaining that a woman should have an "agreement before marriage that she may continue to be a person and a personality separate from her husband!"[93]

Emma Fall Schofield spoke from personal experience on this matter. Balancing her busy professional career with the demands of family life

would have been impossible without the help of her supportive husband, and she urged young women to choose "a cooperative husband"
for a marriage partner. Echoing the nineteenth-century advice of Catharine Waugh McCulloch to marry the "right husband," Schofield explained that a "girl must be very sure that her husband is sympathetic
with her ideals and what she hopes to attain and will be willing to let
her do the things she wants to do."[94]
     For a few, this marital freedom included the right to retain their
maiden name after they married. A woman should "keep [her] maiden
name in the business world," advised one woman lawyer in 1920.[95] Edith
Sampson and Jane Bolin, both of whom were married to lawyers, carried
on their own law practices under their maiden names.[96] Ella Graubert,
however, had to fight for the right to use her maiden name in her law
practice. With the support of the Lucy Stone League she won that right
in 1927 and became the first married woman to practice law under her
maiden name in Pennsylvania.[97]
     But for most women lawyers, the "right man" did far more than permit
his wife to keep her maiden name. Rather, he accepted a division of
labor in marriage that reflected his commitment to the ideals of sexual
equality and woman's independence. For a while, Madeleine Zabriskie
Doty found such a husband in Roger Nash Baldwin, the civil liberties
activist and director of the American Civil Liberties Union. From the
beginning, Baldwin was attracted to Doty as much for her strength as
for her beauty.[98] Their marriage had all the elements of the ideal companionate marriage. With the support of her husband, Doty retained
her maiden name, had an active public career, supported herself financially, and hired a domestic servant to do the household chores.[99] The
contours of Doty's marriage to Baldwin revealed the new standard of
sexual equality as it applied to marriage in the early twentieth century.
     The standard of equality between husband and wife also created a
new model for the ideal sexual relationship in the modern marriage of
the twentieth century. The discovery of female sexuality in the early
twentieth century redefined what should ideally occur in the marital
bedroom. Sexual fulfillment for the wife suddenly became one of the
most important elements of the new marriage. Marriage manuals advised young couples that sexual pleasure was healthy for their marriages
and that they should communicate their most intimate needs with each
other and work together to achieve sexual satisfaction. The new em-

phasis on female sexuality seemed to promise women equal fulfillment with men in bed. At the same time, the accessibility of the diaphragm to white, urban, middle-class women in the 1910s and 1920s enabled women to be sexually active without the fear of pregnancy. All of this combined to enable many women in the 1910s and 1920s to discover the depth of their own sexual passion.

Inez Milholland Boissevain reveled in her sexual desires and enjoyed a passionate sexual relationship with her husband, a prominent Dutch businessman who supported his wife's public career. At times she was coy and seductive as she expressed her desires. "I am getting tired of calling you little boy and baby," she wrote her husband just three months into their marriage. "Henceforward you shall be my big strong man—whom I need, and whom I can depend on. That is what I prefer. Or anyway, it is what I prefer tonight."[100] The following evening she was in a very different mood and gleefully shared her sexual desire with her equally passionate husband. "Do you know I wanted to say 69 to you tonight? And was that what you were telling me to shut up about? Well, I'm glad you understood what I was saying—but then you would!!! With your dirty mind."[101]

In both their personal and professional lives, it was clear that some women lawyers had truly benefited from the new meritocracy in the law. The objective standards of excellence had enabled them to enter into all areas of the legal profession. Some worked in the courtroom as equals with their male colleagues, and a few even reached the very top of the professional hierarchy and held positions of enormous prestige and power. In their private lives, they not only balanced marriage with career, but were also equal partners with their husbands. These women, however, were the exceptional elite. They set the standard and nourished the image of the successful new woman lawyer.

Both the popular press and the professional journals paraded the successes of individual women lawyers before their readers, and Beatrice Doerschuk urged young women-lawyers-to-be to achieve grand goals within the meritocracy of the legal profession. Little did they realize the enormity of the task.

NINE

"Girl Lawyer Has Small Chance for Success"

*A*s early as 1912, Boston attorney Alice Parker Lesser exposed the hard reality behind the belief that meritocracy would lead to sexual equality in the legal profession. In an interview with the Boston *Saturday Evening Traveller*, she confessed: "I realize that for years I and other women lawyers have lied when we said that we were on an equal basis with men in our profession. It is not so, and I am going to tell the real truth about the situation now. The field of law is no better today for girls than it was 20 years ago when they entered it." Women had more opportunities than ever before to study law, she explained, but they still lacked the opportunity to practice it. "Of course, she has all the book learning any lawyer can have . . . But practice of law tells another tale." The title of the article, "Girl Lawyer Has Small Chance for Success," summed up Lesser's gloomy picture.[1]

Although the new women lawyers began the century believing in the promises of sexual equality and meritocracy for women in the legal profession, by the end of the 1920s they had come to understand that their optimism had been misplaced. Despite the remarkable success of some individual women lawyers, most women lawyers never came close to achieving the professional prestige, autonomy, or financial security of women like Florence Allen and Mabel Walker Willebrandt, who reached the top of the professional hierarchy. The accomplishments of the successful elite had inflated both the expectations and the standards of achievement for all women in law, when in fact most women lawyers made much more modest gains.

Women doctors and professors shared a similar fate.[2] Having broken the barriers into medicine and higher education, they remained at the lower rungs of their professional ladders. By the 1920s, women doctors, who had begun the century optimistic about their professional opportunities, also recognized that they were far from achieving equality with men in the medical profession. Although most medical schools and hospitals were open to women, few women gained admission. In fact, the numbers of women doctors began to decline in the decade of the 1910s. In addition, even though women doctors began to specialize, they congregated in the least prestigious areas, such as public health and children's diseases and made little headway into the prestigious laboratory and surgical specialties, which men dominated. Women in higher education faced similar discrimination. Many found teaching positions, but they rarely taught at the well-known universities and colleges. Instead, they ended up in small schools with little prestige, where they taught courses such as home economics and rarely advanced beyond the lowest rungs of the academic ladder.

In 1920, in the midst of the heady days of the suffrage success, many women lawyers acknowledged that there were limits to their accomplishments in the law. In 1920, New York lawyer Anna Parrons complained to the Bureau of Vocational Information that women had no opportunities for lucrative corporate work: "Big corporations will never give their work to women, and unless one can get big business the chances of financial success are small."[3] But whereas some women lawyers deplored the dearth of opportunities for women in the elite corporate law firms, others lamented an even more serious problem—the near impossibility of finding even a modest clerkship or office position.[4]

Gertrude Smith, a graduate of New York University Law School, encountered relentless sexual discrimination in her search for a clerkship in New York City. In a letter to lawyer Inez Milholland, Smith explained that she had answered every advertisement for a legal position and was willing to accept a small weekly salary of only $5 to cover the costs of carfare and lunch. Despite her law degree from New York University and her desperate willingness to accept any position, she was always turned down. "They inform me very politely that I must not forget I am a woman and therefore would not be of any service to them," she wrote. With little money to spare and no prospect of work in sight, she asked: "My dear Miss Milholland, are there no men in this city [who] have enough to give a woman lawyer a chance to show her worth . . . ?" Nearly broken by the relentless discrimination she encountered from male lawyers in New York, Smith confessed to Milholland: "I have lost all my ambition and courage."[5]

Anna Moscowitz Kross, a Jewish immigrant from Russia and a graduate of New York University Law School, had the double burden of gender and ethnicity. Law firms continually rejected her with the brazen claim: "We want a man." She finally found work in the office of a friend where she gained experience but earned no money. Anne Schieber, a graduate of National University Law School in Washington, D.C., worked at the Internal Revenue Service as an auditor for nineteen years without ever receiving a promotion. Shieber had no illusions about the neutrality of the meritocracy. With her excellent performance record, she blamed her lack of advancement on the discrimination against her because she was a woman and a Jew.[6]

Sexual discrimination was not unique to New York City. In Chicago, Irene Hanks reported that she had "been denied openings on the sole objection of sex."[7] Alice Greenacre explained that not only had she failed to find a clerkship in Chicago, but other women lawyers had also informed her "that no woman had ever had a law clerkship in a law office in Chicago."[8] In addition, according to another woman lawyer in the city, the Chicago Bar Association was "not cordial in its treatment of its women members."[9]

Women lawyers endured the same prejudice and hardships in other cities throughout the country. Lawyer N. L. Riley of Tacoma, Washington, echoed Parrons's complaint that corporate law positions were closed to women who only found opportunities in the "least remunerative branches" of law.[10] Bertha Green of Mountain Home, Idaho, reported that in her "part of the country a woman can hardly get a position in a law office, as 'there ain't no sich animile.' "[11] Elizabeth Parsons reported an even bleaker situation in Omaha, Nebraska. "In this city, the legal firms won't have a woman lawyer around except as a stenographer or clerk."[12] Four or five women had tried to set up law practices in Omaha, but all of them gave up because they could not make a living. The state of Nebraska was no more hospitable to women lawyers than was the city of Omaha. Of thirty-three women who had successfully passed the Nebraska bar, only Parsons and one other woman were in active practice.[13]

The same Tiera Farrow who hung her hat with the men's in the court-room could not find one male attorney in Kansas City, Missouri, to hire her. As a result, she opened an office with another woman at a greater financial expense than either of them could afford. Their office was a very modest venture. They shared one room with two desks, four chairs, a bookcase of law books, and a typewriter. Despite their efforts to economize, business was so meager that both women were forced to find other jobs just to survive. They were insulted or ignored by male lawyers and judges, and after two years of working together, they had made no money. Farrow's partner became so discouraged that she quit the law and went to New York City to become a secretary. Farrow moved to an even smaller office, tried to live even more modestly, and settled into a solo practice that barely allowed her to make ends meet.[14]

Women lawyers in the South encountered particularly strong resistance. In Baltimore, the city bar association refused to admit women as late as 1931. This policy effectively locked the women lawyers of Baltimore out of both the Maryland state bar and the American Bar Association because both associations required members to belong to their local bar association.[15] The situation for women lawyers in Georgia was even worse because the Georgia bar did not open to women until 1916 and then only after a bitter struggle. The debate began in 1911 when Minnie Anderson Hale, a graduate of the Atlanta Law School, applied for, but was denied, admission to the bar. Several weeks later, the Georgia legislature defeated a bill that would have made women eligible for the bar. But it could not escape the issue.

The following year, Georgia McIntire-Weaver, onetime dressmaker, stenographer, and honors graduate of Atlanta Law School, forced the Georgia legislature to reconsider reforming the law that prohibited women's admission to the bar. Despite the support of eminent male attorneys and judges, the legislature again refused to pass the reform. But even the Georgia legislature could not stop Georgia McIntire-Weaver. In a letter to Catharine Waugh McCulloch, she explained: "I intend to practice law in Ga., if the effort causes me to serve the rest of my life in jail. I shall at least have the pleasure of making the *chivalrous* gentlemen of the South support me there."[16] She relocated to West Virginia, which had admitted women lawyers since 1896, passed the bar, and set up practice. Having passed the bar in another state, Mc-Intire-Weaver became eligible to return to Georgia to practice.

The situation in Georgia was closely monitored by the press, including professional journals such as *Law Notes* and the *Women Lawyers' Journal* as well as the popular women's magazine *Good Housekeeping*. In its article, "Your Daughter's Career," *Good Housekeeping* used the example of McIntire-Weaver in Georgia to warn its female readership of the obstacles awaiting the aspiring woman lawyer.[17] In 1916, the supreme court of Georgia again denied a woman admission to the bar, but for the last time. Within months, the Georgia legislature had passed an act to permit women to practice law, and on August 19, 1916, Georgia had joined the ranks of the other forty-five states or territories that had already admitted women to the bar on equal terms with men.[18]

Two women lawyers, Mary Johnson and Betty Reynolds Cobb, immediately gained admission to the Georgia bar in 1916, but women lawyers in Georgia still had an uphill fight. They numbered only twenty-five in the entire state by 1920. Compared with states such as Massachusetts, which had over one hundred women lawyers, and California, which had almost 350, the women lawyers of Georgia were a very small group. Representing barely 1 percent of the practicing attorneys in the state, they made their careers alone under conditions strikingly similar to those encountered by the pioneer women lawyers half a century earlier. Cobb admitted that even though she had what she described as a "pleasant and reasonably remunerative" office practice, Georgia was still reluctant to welcome women lawyers. "I do not think our section of the country is ready, quite yet, to make 'easy sailing' for a woman lawyer," she wrote. Moreover, Cobb linked what she perceived to be the deep hostility against women lawyers in Georgia to the woman suffrage movement and the advancement of women in general. In a blunt warning to women not to try to establish a legal career in the South, she explained: "To put it in a nutshell, I would not advise any young woman to study law with a view to practicing it below the 'Mason and Dixon Line' for the next generation at least. We haven't the vote yet; and if we ever get it, it will be when it is forced upon our law makers by a Federal Amendment and will not come as a State Law. Can I say anything more illuminating on the attitude of our men toward women?"[19]

The difficulties encountered by women lawyers in Georgia, New

York, Chicago, Baltimore, Nebraska, and Washington, D.C., indicate that there was a national pattern of discrimination against women in the legal profession. Frances R. Calloway, office manager and registrar at DePaul University Law School in Chicago, attested to the pervasiveness of this sexual discrimination. "Out of hundreds of requests for law clerks . . . I have never received one request for a young woman, nor have I been able to place one unless through influence, as the daughter of a lawyer."[20]

African-American women suffered even deeper discrimination as race combined with sex to yield even more difficult obstacles. Although a few were able to overcome the hardships of economic struggle and racism to succeed in the legal profession, for the most part, black women who became lawyers, like Jane Bolin, were part of the African-American social elite. Sadie Mossell Alexander's father was the first African American to graduate from the University of Pennsylvania Law School, and her husband was a graduate of Harvard Law School. Inez Fields of Hampton, Virginia, was the daughter of a lawyer and the wife of a professor of industrial education. Sallie White was the wife of the dean of faculty at the all-black Central Law School in Kentucky.[21]

For women such as Alexander, White, and Bolin, marriage to a lawyer eased their way into the legal profession. Both Alexander and Bolin shared an office practice with their husbands. Yet even these most privileged of African-American women faced obstacles that white women lawyers never knew. Racial discrimination was a harsh reality that left women like Sadie Alexander with little patience for the problems of white women lawyers. "When I hear white women lawyers complaining about their lot it amuses me. It is the same problem I have been facing all my life."[22] Yet even African-American women lawyers identified gender as the more insurmountable obstacle. An article in *Ebony* in 1947 explained that "most colored Portias agree that their sex is a far greater barrier than color to successful law careers."[23]

In the end, no degree of social privilege could fully shelter an African-American woman lawyer from the dual prejudices of racism and sexism. The paltry number of African-American women lawyers was testimony to that fact. Although three black women lawyers practiced law in Virginia in the 1920s, they remained the only African-American women to practice law there until after World War II.[24] Black women lawyers fared even worse in other southern states. None practiced law in Mississippi, Louisiana, Kentucky, or Arkansas before 1945.[25] Nor did they do much better in other regions of the country. In 1930, there were only four African-American women lawyers in the District of Columbia, three in New York State, and none in Massachusetts.[26] By 1940, there were only thirty-nine African-American women lawyers scattered throughout the country. These thirty-nine stood in stark contrast to the 1,013 black male lawyers and in even starker contrast to the 4,146 white women lawyers in the country during this year. Together, black and white women lawyers were a small group when compared with the 172,329 white, male lawyers in 1940.[27]

The bleakness of the situation did not escape women lawyers in 1920. Although Beatrice Doerschuk urged women to believe in the promise of a meritocracy, the very women she surveyed were realists who understood that they sought careers in a closed profession. In short, they knew that the meritocracy in the legal profession was not working for them and that discrimination was a central aspect of their careers in law. Two-thirds of them believed that sexual discrimination or prejudice in some form was the single most important limitation to a law career for women (see Table 20). Some said that men received the best jobs; others said that the profession was overcrowded with men; and still others said it was hard and lonely to be a pioneer in a profession run by men. Unmarried women lawyers, out on their own, were much more conscious of discrimination than were married women lawyers (73 percent versus 51 percent).

One-fourth of women lawyers linked gender concerns with the economics of law practice. Some believed that it was difficult to attract clients; others thought that it was too difficult for women to begin a law practice; and still others lamented that they had to practice law full-time. For these women, sexual discrimination and the economics of law practice overlapped. But a few women, 9 percent, viewed the practice of law for women differently. They criticized it as inherently uninteresting, dry, mentally unchallenging, and even undignified. Married women believed that the inherent limitations of a legal career were more of a problem than did single women (17 percent versus 5 percent). But even these women were in the minority.

Women lawyers in 1920 understood that men had a better chance to succeed in law than did women. Regardless of marital status or place of residence, 73 percent of women lawyers in 1920 explicitly stated that men had a better chance to succeed in law, whereas only 12 percent of the women thought that their chances of success were equal with men (see Table 21). Some women were more hopeful; 9 percent believed that the chances for women's success in law had increased, and another 7 percent thought that success was up to each individual woman. Inescapably, women lawyers in 1920 faced the fact that discrimination defined their place in the legal profession. Most of them understood the stark reality that prejudice against women prevented them from succeeding as equals with men.

Continued discrimination against women was easiest to see in the courtroom, where men were welcome and women were not. Male lawyers in the early twentieth century shared the fear of their predecessors in the late nineteenth century that women had a special power to manipulate a judge and jury. In an article aptly titled, "Is the Conviction of a Beautiful Woman an Impossibility?" the *American Lawyer* charged in 1904 that it was practically impossible for a male prosecutor, regardless of his skill and experience as a litigator, to persuade a jury to convict a woman.[28] According to the article, male lawyers were defenseless against the vast array of feminine ammunition—beauty, charm, sensuality, and feigned helplessness—that a woman brought with her into the courtroom. "Is there no way in which such a condition may be remedied; by which the woman who is guilty of a crime shall be punished for it, without regard for her personality, her beauty, or her wiles?" mused one lawyer in the article. The answer was a resounding no.

In 1917, a judge in New York City echoed the concerns of male lawyers about the flirtatiousness of women in the courtroom. In a poem entitled "It Can't Be Done," he evoked the familiar images of the provocative, alluring woman whose very presence in court threatened the justice system. Although he directed his assault at the female plaintiff, his words mocked all womanhood and could as easily apply to the woman lawyer:

> For women have flirted with juries
> Since judges and law courts began,
> And there's never a chance
> that she'll cut out the glance
> That makes a mere boob of mere man.

Though judges commit and mandamus,
And use all the arts of their game,
The Lady may sigh,
but that look in her eye
Will linger along just the same.[29]

Despite men's fears of a female invasion of the courtroom, most women lawyers in this era avoided trial work. Some admitted that litigation was a physical and emotional strain on women. Others acknowledged that competing against men with experience in the courtroom placed them at an undue disadvantage. "It takes years of practice and familiarity with court routine to acquire the ease of manner and sureness of action that the man lawyer seems to have naturally in the courtroom," explained one woman lawyer in 1920.[30] Although a few women lawyers achieved success as trial lawyers or judges, for the most part courtroom work remained closed to the new woman lawyer. At the same time, there were few opportunities for women in lucrative office practices because the new field of corporate law was closed to ethnic and racial minorities, as well as to women.

In fact, by the 1920s and 1930s, the late-nineteenth-century patterns of discrimination against women lawyers in the courtroom were reinforced rather than altered. Only 6 percent of women lawyers in 1920 specialized in trial work and criminal law (see Table 13). Women lawyers understood that their best opportunities were not in litigation, but in office practice. In their quest for independence and power, they followed the trend toward professional specialization, but had to gravitate toward opportunities outside of the courtroom, corporations, and financial institutions. Although most women lawyers had general office practices (52 percent in 1920 and 66 percent in 1939), the leading specialty among women was probate law, followed by real estate law.

On the one hand, the women lawyers in 1920 broke the feminine stereotype in that few sought opportunities in the "helping" side of law, such as social welfare, juvenile work, or legal aid. Yet they did not totally reject the notion of helping through the law. Rather, they redirected it from public law to family law. Wills and estates, domestic relations, a general practice, and real estate law shared an important feature: they represented the legal side of the caring quality in women. Women lawyers envisioned themselves as employing their feminine strengths by acting as counselors of law, negotiators, mediators, and drafters of legal documents for the family.

Although many women lawyers in the 1910s and 1920s joined the chorus of women hailing sexual equality in the public arena, most actually built their professional lives on the old, familiar refrain of sexual differences. At the same time that women lawyers argued that each woman's individual temperament determined her own approach to the law, they also argued the opposite—that women lawyers, as a group, often approached the law differently than did men.[31] In deliberately emphasizing what one woman lawyer termed "the eternal feminine," women lawyers in the 1910s and 1920s contradicted their very claims to sexual equality in the legal profession.[32] They believed that their femininity, not the neutral, objective criteria of the meritocracy, was their key to professional success. When asked what qualities a woman needed to succeed in law, one woman lawyer in 1920 advised women to "cultivate and maintain a woman's natural sweetness and femininity. It helps not only to secure clients but to hold them."[33] Another yearned for the feminine privileges women lawyers had enjoyed before the rise of the meritocracy. "Women have gained rights but they have lost privileges. They receive no more courtesy and chivalry," she lamented. "Personally, I'm rather tired of rights. I'd love to have a few privileges."[34] Male lawyers, when they were sympathetic to women lawyers, typically echoed these views. "Do not let yourself become unfeminine," warned one male lawyer in a speech to women lawyers in 1918. "If you do, then much of your power and usefulness in your chosen profession will have departed."[35]

Like nineteenth-century women lawyers who thrived on their sexual differences from men, modern women lawyers understood that they could use their femininity to claim their niche in the legal profession. Some women lawyers believed that they could serve male and female clients equally. Yet many expressed the more traditional view that they, rather than men, were especially suited to women clients because women would find it easier to discuss personal legal matters with them rather than with a man. In fact, the experiences of the women lawyers surveyed in 1920 reveal that some relied heavily on women clients. Women lawyers emphasized the virtues of their femininity in other ways as well. They argued that their "flair for detail" made them valuable partners in male law firms. "In my opinion," explained one woman lawyer, "the ideal firm of attorneys is one consisting of both men and women working as a complement to each other."[36] Expressing the optimism of many women lawyers of her day, she predicted that sexually integrated law firms would be "quite universal in the next decade."[37]

At the same time that women lawyers relied on their unique female qualities to serve their professional interests, they also argued that the legal profession would benefit from their feminine virtues. Echoing the themes of the nineteenth century, they claimed that their womanly sympathies, morality, and domestic nature would complement the competitive and aggressive qualities that men brought to the law. Women would uplift the profession, preserve the humane point of view, and protect the legal needs of women and children. Moreover, women lawyers would replace the combative approach of men with their own conciliatory style. Employing a medical metaphor that revealed a similar sexual division of labor in medicine, one woman lawyer explained that women lawyers were especially skilled at "the social hygiene of law as opposed to legal surgery."[38]

By the early twentieth century, women lawyers' emphasis on conciliation rather than confrontation had gained them greater respect throughout the legal profession. The catalyst for this new view was the growth of corporations and business trusts, which had brought the legal profession into closer relations with business during the last quarter of the nineteenth century and the early decades of the twentieth. By the turn of the century, business law had emerged as a specialty dominated almost exclusively by wealthy and powerful male lawyers. With prestige and money behind them, these new corporate lawyers became the leaders of the profession for the twentieth century. With the power to define its goals and values, they linked the interests of big business, patriotism, and the legal profession. The new legal profession evolved hand in hand with American capitalism.[39]

The drive for profit motivated corporate lawyers to give up the masculine model of aggressiveness and confrontation that had dominated the courtroom and to adopt the restraint and mediation skills that women tended to bring to the law. As early as 1901, William P. Rogers of Indiana University Law School identified this conciliatory approach with women lawyers. In an article entitled "Is Law a Field for Woman's Work?" he defended women in the legal profession by describing the advantages of compromise and conciliation to his male colleagues. Specifically, he advised them to reject their contentious, flamboyant approach; to adopt a more moderate and even-tempered style; and to rely on the skills of negotiation and compromise that women used in office practice rather than on expensive court battles. Rogers wrote: "The business world is seeking more and more to steer clear of [the trial lawyer's] domain by consulting in advance his less pretentious but more valuable associate. The shrewd business man knows of how much more worth it is to be kept out of a law suit than to win one. The aim of the true lawyer is not and should not be to promote litigation. To the contrary, it should be to avoid it."[40]

At the same time that corporate lawyers began to adopt women lawyers' conciliatory style, a few women lawyers began publicly to critique the passive acceptance by most women lawyers of the new corporate values in the legal profession. Rejecting the view that financial success was the route to professional equality with men, these female critics called on women lawyers to mount a crusade to reform the legal profession. Jesse Ashley issued this challenge to women lawyers in 1912. In an essay in the *Women Lawyers' Journal*, she launched a bitter critique of women's efforts to pursue equality in the legal profession by blindly following the lead of men. "With pathetic eagerness to conform to all traditions and to be like men lawyers they bow to custom, conform to theory and go on uncomplaining in their brother's footsteps."[41] Sexual equality on male terms, according to Ashley, meant that women lawyers had to passively accept a legal system that protected property before people. Ashley called on women lawyers to reject this model of sexual equality and to resurrect women's traditional commitment to reform in an all-out attempt to redefine the values and goals of the American legal system.

This was a bold call, but Ashley was no blind idealist. She recognized the enormity of her request and understood that most women, as much as they might wish to reform the law, were engaged in a professional struggle simply to survive. As a result, they were in no position to take up her challenge. To do so, she acknowledged, "would lead to professional suicide. It is hard enough for women lawyers to earn their bread in practice of the law under the most favorable conditions, and to be known as 'crank' lawyers seeking to 'reform the world' would make starvation certain." Torn between their ideals and their desire for professional acceptance, women lawyers, according to Ashley, were tormented by the question, "Shall we reverence the law?"[42]

Several years later, another New York lawyer, Elinor Byrns, echoed Ashley's themes. In an essay in the *New Republic* entitled "The Woman Lawyer," Byrns elaborated on the problems women lawyers faced when they tried to reject the male model of success in the legal profession.[43] Byrns defined three distinct groups of women lawyers in the 1910s. The first group was male-identified and included women lawyers who had achieved sexual equality in the legal profession by emulating men. "Their creed is that by proving their ability to do, in the same way that men do, some of the things men lawyers are doing, they will establish their fitness for the practice of law and will gradually be given greater opportunities," Byrns explained.[44]

The second group of women lawyers had become disillusioned by the gap between their personal ideals and the actual practice of the law. As a result, they had abandoned the legal profession to become active in social reform, where they could put their principles into action. The third group of women lawyers wished to stay in the law, but rejected the male model of success. "They do not want success if it means they must do what the successful men lawyers are doing," Byrns wrote.[45] Like Ashley, Byrns accused male lawyers of allying with the "rich and powerful" in a relationship where male lawyers and big business colluded to protect property and profit at the expense of human welfare. It was the role of male lawyers in this relationship to find ways to circumvent the law whenever it threatened to impede the interests of big business.

Byrns developed her critique of corporate law practice firsthand while she worked in one of the corporate law firms in New York City. Over the course of her two years as a file clerk, she evolved from a young lawyer aspiring to be as good as the men in the office to their sharpest critic, accusing them of using their "knowledge of the law . . . to help big business."[46] In a piercing attack, she charged that the firm's prestige and power came from its ability to protect the "dignity and security" of its clients as it helped them "conduct their business as they pleased."[47] Disgusted with these policies, Byrns left the law firm—rejecting the men who turned law into what she called a "game" for the rich and powerful—and established her own solo practice.

Byrns called on other women lawyers to join her crusade to transform the practice of the law. But she understood all too well the conservative position that entrapped most women seeking to make their livelihood as lawyers. The only hope for change, in her view, lay among a few "revolutionists at heart," that is, those women lawyers who were part of the early twentieth-century women's rights movement. "The suffrage campaign and our struggles for feminism have developed our fighting spirit," she explained. But even with the backing of a vibrant women's movement, Byrns remained bewildered about how she and other women lawyers could affect social revolution. Unable to offer a plan of action, she acknowledged the dilemma of her position. Echoing Ashley's query, "Shall we reverence the law?" Byrns could do no more than pose the haunting question: "What are we to do?"[48]

A minority of privileged women lawyers had the financial resources to devote their public lives to the needs of women and the poor. Others found their answers to Byrns's and Ashley's questions in the women's legal institutions and the social welfare institutions that had reinvigorated and redirected the women lawyers movement. Institutions such as legal aid societies, women's courts, and children's courts were the product of the combined efforts of feminists, male social reformers, and liberal male lawyers who rejected the values of the new corporate law firms and wished to make the law accessible to the needs of the poor and dependent.

Moreover, these institutions brought professionalism and reform together by paying lawyers to protect those who could not afford to protect themselves. As a result, these institutions changed the terms of the long-standing debate over the place of philanthropy and reform in women lawyers' professional lives. They were one answer to Ashley's and Bryns's calls for action because they provided women lawyers with a way to earn their livelihood in the male-dominated profession of law while they devoted their careers to the traditionally womanly task of helping others. Women lawyers in the 1910s proudly claimed that their work for the poor and dependent placed them in the vanguard of the scientific reform of society. "Everywhere the women lawyers are serving the public not through amateurish and sentimental meddling, but through planned application of trained intelligence to social problems," reported one woman.[49] Anna Moscowitz Kross, a labor lawyer in New York City, expressed a similar view in calling for the appointment of women judges to special night courts for women. Women lawyers, she argued, would bring both "sympathetic hearts" and a "scientific system" to the sensitive problem of prostitution.[50] In their new positions of legal authority, women judges helped to reform the judicial system so that it would be more responsive to the needs of women.

As a measure of the integration of women lawyers into the legal profession, the appointment or election of women lawyers as judges cannot be underestimated. Judges in twentieth-century American society were the repository of legal knowledge, as well as a model of temperament and respect among other lawyers and the public at large. Historically, there were but a handful of women judges in nineteenth-century America. For the most part, these women worked in the territories or had been appointed by courts to serve in special capacities such as a master in chancery or a United States commissioner to assist judges in the fact-finding process. By the turn of the century, some women became justices of the peace, a local office that had little involvement in dispute resolution.

By the 1920s and 1930s, new opportunities for women lawyers to become judges had emerged, but they clustered at the very bottom of the judicial hierarchy. In cases representing several areas of law—probate courts, women's courts, juvenile courts, and courts of domestic relations—women lawyers appeared more frequently in state courts that were tied to progressive and feminist reforms and for which women were deemed uniquely suited as judges (see Table 22). Because women lawyers specialized in these areas, they naturally brought to the courtroom their years of experience in practice. Only a few women judges in the 1920s and 1930s were able to enter more traditional courtrooms: Florence Allen in the court of common pleas in 1921; Edith Atkinson in the circuit court of Florida in 1924; and Emma F. Schofield of the district court in Massachusetts in 1930.

Women lawyers found some of their first opportunities for judgeships in the juvenile courts, which were founded at the height of progressivism in the first decade of the twentieth century. Women such as Mary Bartelme of Chicago and Luella North of Herkimer County in upstate New York benefited from the cultural assumption that women judges could best understand the legal needs of children. The rise of the juvenile courts had been the product of an alliance between several groups: club women, especially the National Congress of Mothers; social workers and leaders in the settlement house movement; and liberal male attorneys. Influenced by the psychological theories of G. Stanley Hall, these groups believed that juveniles had unique needs that required a system of justice separate from that which served adults. Ideally, the juvenile court would shield young offenders in a number of ways. It would protect them from incarceration with adult criminals. In addition, the judge could bypass the uniform and arbitrary system of laws in the adult courts and treat young offenders on an individual basis. Through a punishment or probation that fit the unique circumstances, the juvenile court was designed to enable the legal system to rescue the young before they became hardened criminals.

The nation's first juvenile court opened in Chicago in 1899. It represented the joint efforts of Jane Addams and Julia Lathrop of Hull House, the Chicago Woman's Club, and the Chicago Bar Association. The idea caught on quickly. Within five years, ten states had organized juvenile courts, and by 1920, all but three states had a juvenile court. The rapid acceptance of the juvenile court system revealed the popularity of the idea of institutionalizing into the American courts the principle of state protection of children, which was also the core of early twentieth century protective labor legislation.[51]

Of course, the juvenile court was not an ideal system. Its goal of protecting American youth meant that it was especially designed to reach the children of immigrant and poor families. In New York City alone, 71 percent of all the children who were brought to the juvenile court in 1925 were the children of immigrant parents.[52] From this perspective, the juvenile courts were part of the network of progressive institutions that were founded to preserve social stability when cities were increasingly burdened by growing numbers of immigrant and poor families. At the same time, the juvenile court system was vulnerable to the charge of judicial bias. In its attempt to create an alternative model of justice to the adult court, the juvenile court system bypassed the uniform rules of law, particularly due process, which had protected the defendant in adult court. Instead, it gave the juvenile court judge practically unbridled authority to determine the handling of each case. From the point of view of the child, this could be advantageous or disadvantageous, depending on the bias of the judge.

Ideally, the juvenile court judge assumed the role of a parent. A male judge was expected to act like a benevolent but authoritative father. Women lawyers, however, could make an even higher claim to the bench of the juvenile court: they could serve as judicial mothers. They argued that their traditional feminine virtues made them especially suited for the juvenile courts, where sympathy and understanding were so highly valued. Unlike the adult courts, where many women lawyers felt that they had to deemphasize their femininity, the juvenile courts gave them a place to nurture it. When a young girl entered Orfa Jean Shontz's juvenile courtroom in Los Angeles, for example, she saw "pictures on the walls, curtains, not bars, at the windows, and a big vase of roses, fresh from the garden."[53] Women lawyers argued that a woman judge in juvenile court gave the firm but gentle direction best given to a child by a mother at home. "Here women of gentle, yet firm, strong character, trained in the law, yet with the mother heart . . . may find a field for labor which is truly feminine. Surely this is woman's own department," wrote one woman lawyer who argued that no male lawyer, regardless of his professional experience, could match women lawyers' understanding of childhood and domestic matters in the courtroom.[54] "It seems to me," echoed another woman lawyer on behalf of women judges in juvenile courts, "that the child feels a higher regard for promises made to mother, teacher or woman than to man and that woman inspires the child to worthier and nobler achievements than men."[55] In 1918, Woodrow Wilson put his presidential authority behind this cultural assumption that women lawyers were the ideal judges to sit on the benches of the juvenile courts by appointing a woman lawyer, Kathryn Sellers, to the position of judge of the juvenile court of the District of Columbia. His action won strong praise from both women and men in the profession. An editorial in the legal journal *Law Notes* expressed the prevailing view: "The judge of the juvenile court is a parent more than a judge and the President has done well to provide a judicial mother for the delinquent children of Washington."[56]

In the 1910s and 1920s, cities such as Los Angeles, Chicago, and New York took the idea of women lawyers' special, protective role in the judiciary system a step beyond juvenile courts and established separate courts for women. Drawing on the principles of protective labor legislation and the model of the juvenile courts, the women's courts rested on the belief that women, like children, needed special protections before the law. Many advocates argued that the harsh treatment and stiff punishments dealt to male offenders in the criminal courts were inappropriate to female offenders. Instead, women needed an alternative criminal court system that emphasized understanding and rehabilitation. Within the privacy of the women's court, female offenders would encounter a wise and sympathetic woman judge who would understand their unique needs and help them to reform.

Judge Georgia Bullock of the Los Angeles Woman's Court, the first such court in the country, brought her womanly sensibilities to the bench. Her vision of the court was that it should administer social welfare as much as justice. With this in mind, Bullock did not hesitate to incarcerate women, but her sentences were intended to be restorative rather than punitive. Motivated by her keen understanding of the harsh realities of poor women's lives, she often sent women to jail, but for a rest, not for a punishment. "In my court these girls and women are sent to jail—not because I want to punish them, but because I want to help them, if possible. If they are arrested and fined today, they return tomorrow to the same path. But, if we give them a jail sentence, they rest and receive medical treatment. Thirty or sixty days later they come out refreshed, with brighter eyes and a gain in weight—at least a little better equipped to attempt to come-back to health and respectability, if they are so inclined." Not all women prisoners appreciated Bullock's approach to sentencing; one objected to the maximum sentence of 180 days that she had received as a drug user.[57]

Together with the juvenile courts, the women's courts made up a separate women's legal system apart from, but supported by, the male-dominated mainstream of the legal profession. Many male lawyers encouraged the view that women lawyers, rather than men, could best interpret the law for women and children and protect their legal rights. Women lawyers defended this claim. They were quick to argue that in the women's courts they could provide women with the justice unavailable to them from male lawyers. They claimed that although male lawyers understood the needs of men before the law, they could never fully comprehend the legal needs of women and therefore could not offer women full justice.

Women lawyers charged that male judges were guilty of bias when it came to prostitutes and victims of sexual abuse. Washington, D.C., lawyer Grace Rohleder explained that they could not receive fair treatment in the traditional, male-run courtroom: "Men sympathize with men and make allowances for them, and in a courtroom filled with men, with a male judge upon the bench and male officials in every department, the unfortunate victim of male-self-indulgence will find no sympathy and very little justice." The only answer to the problem, Rohleder insisted, was the appointment of women to the bench to oversee women's cases.[58] Farrow used her position as municipal court judge in Kansas City to redirect the focus away from the prostitutes who came to her court and onto the men who patronized them. "The law is directed solely against you women," she told prostitutes in her court, and she instructed police officers to arrest the men who sought the services of prostitutes as well as the women themselves.[59] Even in divorce cases, which were beyond the reach of the women's courts, women lawyers claimed that male judges tended to view divorce through the eye of the husband.

Women lawyers appreciated the professional advantages offered by the separate women's and children's courts. Here they could be both women and lawyers, bringing what many of them still argued were their uniquely feminine qualities of nurturing, sensitivity, and understanding to cases dealing specifically with women and children. But the courts did more than ideologically support women lawyers' claims to the courtroom. From a practical point of view, they provided women lawyers with their best, if not only, opportunity to find positions as judges. Along with Georgia Bullock in Los Angeles, women such as Mary Bartelme of Chicago, Reah Whitehead of Seattle, Kathryn Sellers of the District of Columbia, Luella North of upstate New York, and Jean Norris of New York City all gained positions on the bench in juvenile, family, and women's courts in the early twentieth century. These courts for women and children became so admired during this period that popular magazines such as *Good Housekeeping* enthusiastically supported them.[60]

The idea of a separate women's legal system was not new. It had been popularized in 1888 in Edward Bellamy's utopian novel, *Looking Backward*, in which Bellamy described his vision of the ideal judicial system for the year 2000. In Bellamy's legal system, only women judges heard cases involving women, and men judges heard cases involving men. In 1915, Charlotte Perkins Gilman also portrayed the virtues of an all-woman's judicial system in her feminist utopia, *Herland*.[61] But Bellamy's and Gilman's vision for the future never evolved. Whereas the juvenile courts of the Progressive era became an integral part of the legal system, the women's courts were short-lived—they fell victim to women lawyers' desire for professional integration and male lawyers' insistence that women should compete as equals with men for court positions. Still, for a brief time in the 1910s and 1920s, women lawyers successfully staked out a territory for themselves in both the women's courts and the juvenile courts. Ironically, in this era of the new woman and sexual equality, women lawyers found their greatest opportunities for judgeships and courtroom work in the separate women's courts designed to perpetuate the Victorian emphasis on woman's inherent domesticity and need for special care and protection. Moreover, these courts were outside of the established court system, lacking the prestige, power, and permanence of the mainstream courts, which were dominated by men.

It was also in this era that women lawyers further identified themselves as separate from their male colleagues by establishing their own all-women's professional organizations. In 1899, the Women Lawyers' Club of New York was founded. Others followed shortly thereafter, including the Massachusetts Association of Women Lawyers in 1904, the Women's Bar Association of Illinois in 1914, the Women's Bar Association of the District of Columbia in 1917, and the Portia Club of Milwaukee in 1920. Throughout the last quarter of the nineteenth century and the early decades of the twentieth, local and state bar associations grew in number and size, gradually bringing structure, hierarchy, and formality to the legal profession. Thus the founding of women's legal associations placed women lawyers squarely within the mainstream of their profession.[62]

At the same time, the founding of women lawyers' separate professional groups revealed just how far outside the mainstream of the legal profession women lawyers really were. In fact, in establishing their own bar associations, women were motivated as much by sexual discrimination as by professional identification. Many of the male-run bar associations—including those of New York City, Boston, and the District of Columbia, as well as the American Bar Association—did not admit women.

Together, the women lawyers' organizations became the institutional vehicles for the women lawyers movement as it evolved in the early twentieth century. The founding of the Women Lawyers' Club in New York City in 1899, for example, reflected the familiar themes of earlier women's organizations. On the one hand, it was borne out of discrimination. The underlying reason for its organization was the fact that women were excluded from the bar association of New York City. At the same time, the Women Lawyers' Club provided women lawyers with the unique opportunity to come together for social as well as professional interaction. In 1900, it institutionalized its ties to the woman's rights movement by joining the General Federation of Women's Clubs.[63] Twenty years later, women lawyers in the nation's capital founded their own professional organization because they were excluded from the bar association of the District of Columbia. Established in 1917 at the height of the woman suffrage movement, the Women's Bar Association of the District of Columbia had close ties to woman's rights leaders. At its first annual dinner, its members honored a number of these leaders, including Anna Howard Shaw, onetime president of the National American Woman Suffrage Association, and Julia Lathrop, a social worker and advocate of a juvenile court system.[64]

The founding of the *Women Lawyers' Journal* in 1911 helped expand the women's bar associations beyond their local regions. Established by the Women Lawyers' Club in New York as a way to attract new members, it achieved its goal almost immediately. Membership in the Women Lawyers' Club grew from twenty in 1911 to seventy-six in just two years, and by 1914, the ranks had swelled to about 130 members. Members came not only from New York, but also from fifteen states as well as Canada and France. Moreover, they included some of the most distinguished women lawyers: Washington, D.C., attorneys Emma Gillett and Ellen Spencer Mussey, Chicago lawyer Catharine Waugh McCulloch, and San Francisco attorney Annette Adams. The new members broadened the scope and character of the Women Lawyers' Club, and in 1913 the name of the club was officially changed to the Women Lawyers' Association to convey its national focus.[65]

The *Women Lawyers' Journal* became the major vehicle for women lawyers to share a range of concerns. Its editors kept close track of professional matters such as which bar associations remained closed and which had been opened to women. It invited its readers to share their views on practical matters such as how to start a practice and how to attract clients. It enabled women lawyers to discuss and monitor the progress of legal reforms, including custody rights, protective labor legislation, the establishment of women's and children's courts, and suffrage. It also provided a way for individual women lawyers to announce changes and achievements in their careers. The opening of an office, the passing of a bar, the winning of a case, or the appointment to a judgeship all became newsworthy items to share.

The success of the *Journal* helped to build a national network of women lawyers. Just as the Equity Club letters had brought women lawyers together in the late 1880s, the *Journal* made it possible for women lawyers around the country to communicate with each other. To be sure, the *Journal* was a larger, more formal, and more structured endeavor than the Equity Club annual ever was. It reached more women and persisted through the twentieth century. Still, it was fueled by the same blend of professional and womanly concerns that had inspired the Equity Club. The age-old quest of nineteenth-century women lawyers for professional community and sisterly support was unmistakable within the pages of the *Women Lawyers' Journal*. Even in this era of new women, it muted the call for individual success and sexual equality with its strong spirit of sisterhood.

The national influence of the *Women Lawyers' Journal* placed women lawyers of New York at the center of the growing network of women lawyers. As early as 1919, the Women's Bar Association of the District of Columbia began to urge the Women Lawyers' Association to look beyond its metropolitan roots and to formalize its growing national influence. In 1923, the Women Lawyers' Association thus reorganized and became the National Association of Women Lawyers.[66] By this time, many women lawyers were already members of the American Bar Association, which had opened its doors to women in 1918. Although membership in the American Bar Association was an important step toward professional integration and equality for women lawyers, the leaders of the Women Lawyers' Association went forward with its reorganization into a national association, insisting that women lawyers still needed their own national organization. In this way, women lawyers were not unlike women doctors, who founded their American Medical Women's Association in 1915, the same year that they were first admitted into the American Medical Association.

Not all women lawyers agreed with the need for a separate professional organization for women. Some criticized those organizations, championing instead the virtues of the meritocracy and sexual integration in law. Alice Birdsall of Phoenix, Arizona, was one lawyer who believed that where sexual equality existed, "organized effort . . . should not be limited along sex lines." The spirit of equality that she claimed prevailed in her state enabled women lawyers to practice "without thought of sex lines." Thus, there was "no need of separate organizations" for women lawyers in Arizona.[67] Lawyer L. H. Shoemaker of Jacksonville, Florida, agreed with Birdsall that the achievement of equality with men eradicated women lawyers' need for their own professional organizations. She called for a unification of the profession, urging all lawyers, men and women, to join one national organization, the American Bar Association. "There is need for and in fact should be but one National Lawyers' Association, and that [should be] the American Bar Association," she argued.[68]

The leaders of the National Association of Women Lawyers disagreed. They claimed that their organization would supplement, rather than duplicate, the services of the American Bar Association, thereby providing women lawyers with social and professional advantages that were unavailable to them in the male-run organizations. Throughout the 1920s, the leaders of the National Association of Women Lawyers continued to remind women lawyers that sexual discrimination still permeated the legal profession and that collective action, rather than individual effort, was the only way to overcome the problem. In the 1930s, this call for solidarity took on a more poignant ring. With the economic depression threatening to dismantle the inroads women had made into the legal profession, women lawyers increasingly called on each other to sacrifice individual gain for the good of the community of women lawyers.[69] In 1935, Burnita Shelton Matthews, president of the National Association of Women Lawyers, reminded women lawyers that even though the American Bar Association had been opened to women, other bar associations remained closed. In addition, she pointed out that sexually integrated bar associations rarely gave women committee appointments or leadership positions. In the few cases where women attained positions of stature, they owed them to the collective efforts of the women's bar associations, which pressured the male-run associations to give women lawyers a chance. Matthews preached the hard truth that despite women lawyers' claims of progress and optimism for professional success in the 1910s and 1920s, in the 1930s women lawyers still had not reached their goal of sexual equality with their male colleagues: "Although the dawn is in the sky, the day of equal opportunity for women lawyers has not yet come."[70]

In order to hasten that day of equal opportunity, Matthews and others in the National Association of Women Lawyers called on women lawyers to put aside personal goals and work for the interests of women lawyers as a group. Lillian Rock, chair of the membership committee in 1930, emphasized the importance of creating a community of women in the law: "No one of us, no individual standing alone, isolated, is so powerful as to be beyond the need of kindred support either in adversity or success."[71]

Bullock, for one, benefited from the collective support of other women. Her rise to the bench was the product of her own efforts combined with the organized efforts of women to secure the appointment of women as judges. Motivated by "a secret ambition . . . to do judicial work," Bullock's bid for judge of the police court in 1923 relied on the rhetoric of the women's movement: "Keep a Woman Judge in a Woman's Court."[72] Her message gained credence from the organized efforts of other women who urged her appointment because "now is the opportune time to have a woman judge appointed."[73] Over the years, as Bullock moved up the judicial ladder from the women's court to the municipal court and eventually to the superior court, she continued to ally herself with women's issues, appealing "to the cause of women generally."[74] Professional women rallied to her side. Phi Delta Delta endorsed Bullock in 1928 for superior court judge, the first such endorsement by the local chapter.[75] Ultimately, Bullock's judicial career found success because she publicly identified herself with women and used them for personal gain.

But Bullock did not only rely on women's support. Her relentless ambition to climb up the judicial hierarchy had few boundaries. She warmly thanked the Knights of the Ku Klux Klan for their endorsement in her 1929 campaign.[76] Moreover, when it came to her private practice, Bullock placed her own self-interest before the concerns of other women lawyers. As noble as Rock's call for "kindred support" may have been, Bullock showed no concern for the community of women lawyers when she found herself caught between the interests of a woman lawyer in New York City and a male lawyer in Los Angeles. Bullock received a collection case from lawyer Olive Scott Gabriel of New York City which Bullock then referred to a male lawyer, J. M. Fursee of Los Angeles. Fursee collected the debt, retained his 25 percent fee, and gave Bullock a one-third referral fee. Gabriel also expected a one-third referral fee from Fursee, but she received nothing. Criticizing Bullock for even using a male lawyer in the case, the one-time president of the National Association of Women Lawyers wrote to Bullock: "I urge all out of town claims to be given to our women lawyers." Unknown to Gabriel, however, Bullock often split fees with male lawyers to augment her income and even hired them to manage her cases while she vacationed in New York City and Maine. In this incident, Bullock rejected Gabriel's appeal to women's solidarity and instead promoted her own financial interests.[77]

Rock's plea to women lawyers to use the power of the women's legal community for more than personal gain had a particular appeal in the depression era of economic suffering and human pain. In her words, "We will refuse to believe that you are content merely with the study and practice of that law; rather, we are convinced that you will want and eventually must have a part in the making and blending of that law." Rock envisioned the National Association of Women Lawyers as the ideal vehicle to bring about this legal reform and social change. She called on women lawyers to move past "personal success" and join in this united effort to do "something more encompassing, more humane and less personal."[78]

Burnita Shelton Matthews was one woman who built her legal career on this model of sisterhood and social concern. She worked in a law firm with two other women, Laura Berrien and Rebecca Greathouse, who shared her deep commitment to advancing women's legal rights. As a president of both the Women's Bar Association of the District of Columbia and the National Association of Women Lawyers, Matthews was a leader in efforts to promote women lawyers' professional interests. In addition, she was a driving force in the reform of women's legal rights. Her strong belief in the importance of women's equality before the law led her to join the Woman's Party. As chair of its lawyers' council, she directed extensive research into the laws of the United States as they related to women. She was a strong supporter of an equal rights amendment as well as an advocate of women's property rights and the rights of women to be jurors. She drafted the women juror law for the District of Columbia and revised the inheritance statutes of New York in 1923 so that they would no longer discriminate against women.[79]

Other women lawyers, such as Sue Shelton White and Lucy Somerville Howorth, found opportunities to link their legal careers with their politics in the new government agencies of the 1930s.[80] But these premier government positions were difficult for women to obtain. Although many women lawyers and law students looked to Washington for job opportunities given the activist government of the Roosevelt administration and its sympathy for minorities and the poor, few jobs were made available to women lawyers. Only a small group of women lawyers who had political ties received the coveted government appointments.

In 1932, Mary Connor Myers, a Washington, D.C., lawyer, surveyed the federal positions held by women lawyers. She found that women lawyers held only a small minority of federal jobs. Moreover, most of their positions were classified as clerical, administrative, or fiscal jobs, all of which required no legal training and paid a lower salary than jobs classified as professional positions. The War Department and the Department of Agriculture employed seven women lawyers each, but none in a legal position. There were nineteen women lawyers in the Interior Department, but only one held the status of attorney. Seventeen others performed legal work, but held lower classifications and received smaller salaries. The Treasury Department employed thirteen women lawyers to do highly technical tax law, but it gave them less desirable assignments and paid them lower salaries than men in similar positions. Five women lawyers held strictly legal positions in the Department of Justice, but one was demoted after she married and was given an annual salary that was $1,000 less than that received by the only other attorney, a man who did precisely the same work. The Department of Labor, which housed the Naturalization Bureau, the Children's Bureau, and the Women's Bureau, was the only department that escaped complaints about sexual discrimination. Yet even here, only a dozen or so women held professional positions. Even the Women's Bureau employed only three women lawyers, and although their work included studies of labor legislation and court decisions relative to the employment of women, they were hired as social economists rather than as attorneys.

The bleak conclusion was hard to avoid. Women lawyers who went to Washington to find positions in the federal government found sexual discrimination rather than job opportunities. "There is no doubt," wrote Myers, "despite protests to the contrary by most administrative officers, that there exists an intention, if only subconscious, to admit professional women only to inferior positions on an equal basis with men."[81] Myers called on women lawyers to work together to pressure the government to open more positions for women lawyers. Echoing Rock's critique of individualism, Myers claimed that "the Horatio Alger days are over, if they ever existed." The best way for women lawyers to advance their cause, she argued, was to "throw aside their individualistic attitude and proceed to accomplishment through cooperation."[82]

Despite the call for collective action, most women lawyers in the 1910s through the 1930s worked alone. They looked for employment in law offices, tried their hands at solo practice or found positions in the business world of banks, real estate offices, and insurance agencies. Some considered themselves lucky if they found a job as a stenographer or law clerk; others were unable to find legal work at all. For these women, law practice was a job they performed for financial support—an occupation detached from sexual politics and the world of ideals.

Like their professional lives, the personal lives of the new women lawyers fell short of their expectations. Companionate marriage, the hope and promise for the new woman, proved to be frustrating as well as fulfilling. Ideally, the companionate marriage offered women hope by emphasizing friendship and mutuality between husband and wife, rather than the dependency, obligation, and obedience that characterized the traditional wife. Husband and wife were to be close companions who discussed household matters together, made joint decisions about financial and domestic concerns, shared their leisure time, and enjoyed a mutually fulfilling sexual relationship.

But the emphasis of the companionate marriage on empowering women in their homes ignored the importance of their public lives. Many older feminists, including Charlotte Perkins Gilman and Jane Addams, lashed out at this new emphasis on women's domestic bliss and were particularly skeptical about the sudden strident call for husband and wife to focus so much attention on the wife's sexual needs. Their skepticism revealed a major flaw in the modern marriage of the 1910s and 1920s. The new emphasis on companionship between husband and wife was meant for the privacy of the home and stopped at the doorway to the world beyond. The career wife rarely received the respect and support for her work from her husband that she was expected to give to him.

Given the limitations of the new companionate marriage, many women lawyers in the 1910s and 1920s were dubious about the possibility of married women competing as equals with men in the legal profession. Tiera Farrow's experience was typical. She became engaged to one of her law school classmates, who persuaded her that they would "make a good team in a law office." Farrow was horrified, however, when she discovered that her fiancé's vision of marital partnership would keep her in the office as a stenographer and clerk while he went off to court. Her strong desire for sexual equality and her fiancé's distinctly different vision of the nature of a companionate marriage made the contemplation of marriage impossible, and she broke off her engagement.[83]

Mabel Walker Willebrandt also discovered that a modern marriage was incompatible with her career aspirations.[84] Just two years after she married, both she and her husband, Arthur, set their sights on studying law at the University of Southern California. They agreed that first Arthur would attend law school full-time for a year while Mabel studied part-time at night and worked full-time to support them. Then, in the second year, Arthur would work so that Mabel could study law full-time. But their agreement never worked out the way they had planned. For three years, Mabel worked full-time as a teacher and principal of a school to pay for both her husband's tuition as well as her own. At the same time, she assumed full responsibility for the domestic demands of cooking, cleaning, and other household chores. Remarkably, she found the time and energy to take evening and early morning law classes. With Mabel's support, Arthur graduated from law school in 1915. But Mabel was still teaching and taking law classes part-time and had yet another year of study before her. The disintegration of their agreement, combined with the burden of assuming all the domestic responsibilities, doomed the young marriage to failure. Faced with the choice between her marriage or a career in law, Willebrandt left her husband in 1916.

Although Willebrandt's attempt at a companionate marriage failed, her divorce freed her from the encumbrances of marriage and she began a remarkably quick rise up the professional ladder. She began her professional ascent in 1916 working as a public defender for women's cases while building a private practice. In addition, she immersed herself in professional activities and women's organizations, making a name for herself throughout California. In 1921, only five years after her divorce, she received her appointment as assistant attorney general. Willebrandt's struggle to study law while holding a job and caring for her husband had revealed the inequality at the heart of a supposedly companionate marriage. In contrast, her meteoric climb from public defender in Los Angeles to assistant attorney general in only five years was testimony to the personal freedom and professional opportunity she derived from leaving her husband in 1916.

Years after her divorce, Willebrandt advised younger couples on how to avoid the mistakes of her marriage. In an article entitled "Give Women a Fighting Chance," she reinterpreted companionate marriage to meet women's needs. In Willebrandt's reconception of the ideal marriage, the wife did not submerge her needs to those of her husband. Failing to achieve this in her own marriage, she emphasized the importance of creating a relationship of "mutual understanding" that respected and nurtured the wife's intellectual, emotional, and economic independence. The lesson Willebrandt had learned from her own marital failure was that in a healthy marital partnership the husband made "necessary adjustments" so that the wife could "have both a 'child' and a 'job' if she wants both."[85]

Even feminist Madeleine Doty could not save her companionate marriage to Roger Nash Baldwin. As Baldwin described it, their relationship had all the elements of the modern marriage of the day: "We were both busily at work, but we shared expenses on a 50–50 basis, since we both agreed on our independence, and Madeleine was a staunch feminist. She never took my name nor did we have joint accounts save to divide 50–50 the rent and housekeeping. A maid came in by the hour, cleaned up and cooked when required, though I did most of it, since Madeleine neither could cook a dinner nor wanted to learn."[86]

Unfortunately, neither the equality of their relationship nor Doty's independence and freedom guaranteed them happiness. In fact, she and her husband had different notions of the very meaning of freedom in their lives. Doty wanted freedom in the intellectual and spiritual parts of her life. But she wanted structure, not freedom, in the daily pattern of her marriage. "To me . . . daily life was like the red and green lights of traffic. Without them there was confusion," she explained.[87] Baldwin, on the other hand, wanted a broader, open-ended freedom that resisted any marital responsibility. Their conflicting interpretations of marital freedom doomed the relationship from the start. When Doty wanted her husband to stay home in the evenings, Baldwin resisted. "I was too obstinate to yield my presumed freedom to marriage obligations," he admitted years later.[88] Tragically, the love that Doty and Baldwin shared and their attempts at compromise could not save their marriage; they divorced in 1935.

Farrow's, Willebrandt's, and Doty's failed attempts at marriage revealed the difficulties many women encountered as they contemplated marriage and a legal career. In this era, 44 percent of women lawyers in 1920 believed that companionate marriage and sexual equality between husband and wife represented the new ideals for a modern age. In contrast, 47 percent questioned these new values, believing that marriage and a career for women lawyers were incompatible.[89] "Either is a full size job if properly filled. One must choose," explained one woman lawyer.[90] "If they want to practice law, eliminate the word *matrimony* from their vocabulary and vice versa," echoed another.[91] Once married, a woman lawyer assumed a host of domestic responsibilities that made it impossible for her to compete as an equal with men in the legal profession. "A single woman has a tremendous advantage over a married woman, as she can give her whole attention to her business as a man does. No married woman's opportunity can compare with that of a man, married or single," wrote Bertha Green, a lawyer from Nebraska who was the wife of a lawyer and the mother of three children. Acknowledging that she barely practiced law and only did so "to show my family that I could support myself if I had to," she confessed that she could never figure out how to make a husband and wife equal in their professional lives. "I have never yet been able to figure out a way that would make a married woman as free in mind and body to follow her chosen business as a married man is."[92]

On the surface, the views of women lawyers such as Green sounded strikingly similar to those of nineteenth-century women lawyers, who had expressed the separatist view that women could not have both a marriage and a career. But this group of modern women lawyers was different. They rejected the notion that marriage and career were inherently incompatible for women. Rather, they believed that it was the only pragmatic response to the reality of women's lives. In taking this view, women lawyers linked their separatist stand to their sharp critique of men, who, they believed, left women no other practical choice. One woman lawyer explained that men simply did not like to marry professional women: "Men do not care to marry women with set ways, independent character, who are able to care for themselves. They admire the type, but love never. They may make excellent mothers but men want wives who are more dependent upon them and look up to them."[93] Green explained that married men simply did not intend to make the same sacrifices for their families that they expected of their wives: "A woman with a husband and children cannot make a great success of the law without neglecting them. If little Jim has the diphtheria, the father takes a room at the hotel and goes right on with his practice. The mother lawyer is quarantined with Jim."[94]

Because this group of modern women lawyers laid the blame on men, the solution was that men change by giving up their tradition-bound views of womanhood and treating women as truly equal partners. Then, claimed many women lawyers, the need for the separatist approach would disappear. As one woman lawyer explained, women would finally be able to balance marriage and career as equals with men when "a new and different generation of men arrives who will be trained to regard women as equals in all respects."[95]

Although some women lawyers took the separatist approach to marriage, more than three times as many expressed the traditional view that marriage must take priority over career in the life of a married woman lawyer. "A woman should give up her profession when she marries," explained one woman lawyer.[96] "I believe woman's true sphere is in the home," echoed another. "A true woman gladly fills her place in the home when true love comes."[97] But women in 1920 understood the traditional approach as a practical response to the realities of a woman's life—not as an absolute, immutable condition. Personal sacrifice was not a universal reality for all married women. Again, it depended on the type of man a woman married. Embedded in the advice to follow the husband's lead was the unspoken message that a woman could, in fact, combine marriage and law if she married a man who treated her fairly.

Nor did children require absolute sacrifice on the part of the mother. Women lawyers in 1920 believed that motherhood necessitated only a temporary sacrifice when children were young and at home. "If there are children," explained one woman, "there seems to be no other way than to drop out of the profession for a few years."[98] Another, Sarah Shulkjobe of Hope, Arkansas, advised women to marry a lawyer, miss a few years when their children were young, and then "get right back into work."[99] Hortense Ward, the first woman to be admitted to the Texas bar, followed this model. She "was the usual married woman with three small children" before she joined her husband, also a lawyer, in practice.[100]

To these women lawyers, it was motherhood, not marriage, that required the sacrifice of their legal careers, and even this sacrifice was short-lived. "Unless there are children, there should be no conflict," explained one.[101] Another echoed this outlook: when "no children bless the union . . . it would be unthinkable to engage in no profitable or worthwhile business. The world needs workers too badly for women to sit idle."[102] Florence Allen expressed the same views. "I believe that the time of the average housewife is taken up more with the *house* than with the *family* except when the children are small," she explained.[103]

Although women lawyers in 1920 may have viewed marriage and career in a more progressive way, their views were a far cry from the self-assured claim to companionate marriage that seemed to propel so many new women into matrimony. In fact, many women lawyers in 1920 had serious doubts about how a woman lawyer could actually organize her life to balance marriage and career. Throwing their hands up in the air, some left that task to each individual woman. In doing so, they freed women from the prescribed behavior expected of Victorian women and embraced, instead, the new emphasis on individuality and diversity among women. But with this freedom came little guidance. Some (8 percent) admitted that they had no idea about how to resolve the paradox. "If a professional woman marries and has children," wrote one woman, "whether she continues her chosen vocation is too personal for me to undertake: I can't dictate what her course shall be."[104] Another woman echoed her sentiment: "If a woman marries, she should solve her own problems. Any woman capable of passing a bar examination has mentality enough to map out her own life."[105] Single women felt especially unqualified to offer advice. "I'm a spinster," explained one woman lawyer, and "my theories of marriage are so without practical experience in the subject that I have no judgment in the matter."[106]

Another reiterated her views: "'Tis not for a very contented old maid to rush in where angels fear to tread."[107] Simply put, to many new women lawyers who advocated an integrated view of marriage and career, the question of how to balance the two successfully was "a matter of individual taste."[108]

But this tendency to place the problem of balancing marriage and career in the hands of each individual woman lawyer revealed a darker side as well. Despite the optimistic claims about the hope of a future where women lawyers could balance marriage and career just as men did, the call was more rhetoric than reality. By the mid-1920s, many women lawyers discovered firsthand how difficult it was to balance their careers with marriage. Some, like Doty and Willebrandt, grew tired of the struggle and gave up their marriages. Others took the more traditional route and sacrificed their careers to stay with their husbands. Some women lawyers in 1920 counseled younger women to give up their career aspirations if their husbands did not want them to work. "If your husband objects to your pursuing your profession, give it up," explained one woman.[109] "If the man objects," echoed another, "for the happiness of all concerned, give it up."[110]

Lucy R. Tunis, of Boston, followed this advice. Though she was a successful lawyer, she abandoned her active career for her husband. In an article entitled "I Gave Up My Law Books for a Cook Book," she admitted to the readers of *American Magazine* that she had failed in her attempt to have both a marriage and a career. When she faced a choice between her own professional needs and those of her husband, she willingly abandoned her law practice in Boston and moved with her husband to New York City. But according to Tunis, her sacrifice brought its own rich rewards of domestic fulfillment in the sanctuary of her home. "And what was I to get in return? I would find happiness in the home that I knew I could create, the home that was to be an inspiration for my husband. I would gain satisfaction in being perfect at one job at least, in conquering the problem of housework that had baffled me, and in striving to make the husband I loved happy."[111]

In reality, there was no single, simple answer. Despite all the optimistic claims about equality for women in marriage and the possibility of balancing family and career, the truth was that most women lawyers in the early decades of the twentieth century still faced the wrenching choice between building a career and nurturing a family. Sue Shelton

White captured the difficult situation: "Marriage is too much of a compromise; it lops off a woman's life as an individual. Yet the renunciation too is a lopping off. We choose between the frying-pan and the fire—both very uncomfortable."[112]

Looking at the 1930s from the perspective of 1869 when Myra Bradwell first sought entry into the legal profession, how did women lawyers fare? The decades from 1869 to 1899 marked the period when women lawyers first broke into the engendered, closed legal profession. There was no doubt that they had made significant advances. Though few in number, women were practicing law in almost every state of the union and had established themselves as permanent members of the legal profession for the twentieth century. They worked in a wide range of situations, including solo practice, law firms, business offices, government agencies, and courts. These accomplishments had fueled the optimism that many women lawyers had shared at the beginning of the twentieth century.

But there was another side to the story. The period from 1900 to the 1930s marked an era when optimism about the possibilities for women in the law was tempered by a growing pessimism about the realities of women lawyers' professional achievements. The legal profession remained in many ways engendered and closed to women. As women lawyers continued to encounter sexual discrimination, their high hopes for the future gave way to a more realistic acceptance of their current situation. The prediction in the 1920s of sexually integrated law firms in the 1930s looked increasingly naïve and unattainable. Moreover, women lawyers continued to face the burden of double consciousness—the tension between their gender and professional identity which the Equity Club members identified in the 1880s. Gradually they recognized the hard fact that women lawyers were far from achieving their goal of professional equality with men.

Mary Lathrop, the first woman to integrate the American Bar Association in 1918, captured this harsh truth: "The law is a man's field and will remain so. It will always be a battle for women."[113] Five years later, Burnita Matthews echoed Lathrop's lament. "We live as yet in a man's world instead of a world for ALL human beings," she wrote.[114] Moreover, even as women lawyers as a group traded in their optimism for a more realistic assessment of the task before them, they reached no consensus on how best to achieve their goal. Some women lawyers held on to the traditional feminine ways by reinterpreting for the twentieth century the notion of sexual differences and woman's unique virtues. Others turned their back on these nineteenth-century values and pushed forward on their professional road, claiming the virtues of universal equality between men and women. By the mid-twentieth century, women lawyers were far from reaching their goal of equality. Instead, the task of balancing gender and professional identity was still a challenge and remains a legacy for women lawyers today.

Appendix 1
Tables

Table 1. Dates of first admission of women to practice law, 1869–1923

Date of statute	Date of admission	Juris-diction	Name	Type of admission
1870	1869	Iowa	Arabelle Mansfield	Admission by a court; 2 *Chicago Legal News* 146 (1870). 1870: Act of Mar. 8, 1870, ch. 21, 1870 Iowa Acts 21.
	1870	Mo.	Lemma Barkaloo	Admission by a court.
	1871	Mich.	Sarah Kilgore	Admission by a court.
	1872	Utah	Phoebe W. Couzins	Admission by a court.
	1872	D.C.	Charlotte E. Ray	Admission by a court.
1899	1872	Maine	Clara H. Nash	Admission by a court; 1899 Acts and Resolves, ch. 98.
	1873	Ohio	Nettie C. Lutes	Admission by a court.
1874	1873	Ill.	Alta M. Hulett	1874: Revised statutes of State of Illinois, ch. 13, July 6, 1874.
1878	1875	Wis.	Elsi B. Botensak	1878: Revised Statutes subd. 5, sec. 2586, 1878.
1877	1877	Minn.	Martha Dorsett	1877: Act of Feb. 28, 1877, ch. 123, 1877 Minn. Laws 220.
	1878	N.C.	Tabitha A. Holton	Admission by a court.
1878	1878	Calif.	Clara S. Foltz	1878: Act of April 1878, ch. 154, 88 Cal. Acts 96.
1879	1879	U.S.	Belva Lockwood	1879: 20 U.S.C. sec. 292 (1879).
	1881	Kan.	J.M. Kellogg	Admission by a court.
	1881	Nebr.	Ada Bittenbender	Admission by a court.

Table 1. (continued)

Date of statute	Date of admission	Juris-diction	Name	Type of admission
1882	1882	Mass.	Lelia J. Robinson	1882: Mass. Gen. L., ch. 139 (1882).
1882	1882	Conn.	Mary Hall	1882: *In re* Hall, 50 Conn. 131 (1882).
1883	1883	Pa.	Carrie Kilgore	1883: *In re* Kilgore, 18 *Am. L. Rev.* 478 (1884).
1890	1885	Wash.	Mary Leonard	1890: State of Washington Act of Mar. 28, 1890, 1889–90 Wash. Laws 519.
1885	1886	Oreg.	Mary Leonard	1885: Act of Nov. 20, 1885, 1885 Or. Laws 5.
1886	1886	N.Y.	Kate Stoneman	1886: Act of May 19, 1886, ch. 425, 1886 N.Y. Laws 668.
	1888	Hawaii	Almeda E. Hitchcock	1888: Unpub. Order of Sup. Ct. of Hawaiian Kingdom.
	1890	N.H.	Marilla M. Ricker	1890: Ricker's Petition, 66 N.H. 207 (1890).
	1890	Mont.	Ella J. Knowles	Admission by a court.
1891	1891	Colo.	Mary S. Thomas	1891: *In re* Thomas, 16 Colo. 441 (1891). 1897: Act of April 17, 1897, ch. 29, 1897 Colo. Laws 114.
1893	1893	Nev.	Laura Ray Tilden	1893: Act of Jan. 31, 1893, ch. 3, 1893 Nev. Laws 12.
1893	1893	Ind.	Atty. Leach	1893: *In re* Leach, 134 Ind. 665 (1893).
1893	1893	S.Dak.	Nellie A. Douglass	1893: Act of Feb. 16, 1893, ch. 21, 1893 S. Dak. Laws 41.
	1894	Va.	Belva Lockwood	Admission by a court.
1899	1895	Idaho	Helen L. Young	1899: Act of Feb. 18, 1899. 1899 Idaho Laws 421.
1895	1895	N.J.	Mary Philbrook	Act of March 20, 1895, ch. 190, 1895 N.J. Acts 366.
	1896	W.Va.	Agnes J. Morrison	Admission by a court.
	1898	La.	Betty Runnels	Admission by a court.
	1898	Fla.	Louise R. Pinnell	Admission by a court.
	1898	Okla.	Laura Lykins	Admission by a court.
	1899	Wyo.	Grace Hebard	Admission by a court.
1902	1902	Md.	Etta H. Maddox	1902: Act of April 8, 1902, ch. 399, 1902 Md. Laws 566.
	1903	Ariz.	Beatrice Hopson; Vivian Hopson	Admission by a court.
	1905	N.Dak.	Helen Hamilton	Admission by a court.
	1907	Ala.	Luelle L. Allen	Admission by a court.

Table 1. (continued)

Date of statute	Date of admission	Juris- diction	Name	Type of admission
1907	1907	Tenn.	Marion S. Griffin	1907: Act of Feb. 13, 1907, ch. 69, 1907 Tenn. Laws 188.
	1910	Tex.	Hortense Ward	Admission by a court.
	1912	Ky.	Ruby J. Gordon	Admission by a court.
	1914	Vt.	Ellen M. M. Hoar	Admission by a court.
	1914	Miss.	L. H. Greaves	Admission by a court.
1915	1950	Alaska	Mildred Herman	1915: Act of April 28, 1915, ch. 38, 1915 Alaska Laws 82.
1916	1916	Ga.	Mary C. Johnson	1916: Act of Aug. 19, 1916, no. 471, 1916 Ga. Acts 76.
	1917	N.Mex.	Catherine Mabry	Admission by a court.
1918	1918	S.C.	Claudia J. Sullivan	1918: Act of Feb. 14, 1918, no. 441, 1917 S.C. Laws 779.
	1918	Ark.	Sarah Jobe	Admission by a court.
	1920	R.I.	Ada L. Sawyer	Admission by a court.
Con. Am.	1923	Del.	Sybil Ward; Evangelyn Barsky	1923: Constitutional Amendment (33 Del. Laws, ch. 3).

Sources: The statutory information was compiled by the author. The names of women lawyers and dates of admission are from lists prepared by Larry Berkson, "Women on The Bench: A Brief History," *Judicature* 65 (1982): 290, Table 1; and Karen Berger Morello, *The Invisible Bar: The Woman Lawyer in America, 1638 to the Present* (New York: Random House, 1986), pp. 37–38.

Table 2. Decennial growth of women and men lawyers, 1870–1960

	Women lawyers		Men lawyers	
Year	N	% change	N	% change
1870	(5)	—	(40,731)	—
1880	(75)	1400	(64,062)	57
1890	(208)	177	(89,422)	40
1900	(1,010)	385	(113,693)	27
1910	(558)	−45	(114,146)	0.4
1920	(1,738)	212	(120,781)	6
1930	(3,385)	95	(157,220)	30
1940	(4,187)	24	(173,456)	10
1950	(6,348)	52	(176,063)	2
1960	(7,543)	19	(205,515)	17

Sources: Calculated from U.S. Bureau of the Census, *Ninth Census,* vol. 1, pp. 674, 686; *Tenth Census,* vol. 1, p. 744; *Eleventh Census,* vol. 1, pt. 2, p. ci; *Twelfth Census,* vol. 2, pt. 2, p. 505; *Thirteenth Census,* vol. 4, p. 93; *Fourteenth Census,* vol. 4, p. 42; *Fifteenth Census,* vol. 4, p. 14; *Sixteenth Census,* vol. 3, p. 75; *Seventeenth Census,* vol. 2, pt. 1, pp. 1–261; *Eighteenth Census,* vol. 1, pt. 1, pp. 1–522.

Table 3. Women as a percentage of male- and female-dominated professions, compared, 1910–1940

	Year			
Profession	1910	1920	1930	1940
Male-dominated professions				
Lawyers	1.1	1.4	2.1	2.4
Doctors	6.0	5.0	4.4	4.6
Scientists	n.a.	4.7	5.8	7.0
Female-dominated professions				
Schoolteachers	n.a.	86.0	81.0	75.7
Social workers	56.0	66.0	80.0	65.0

Source: Adapted from Nancy F. Cott, *The Grounding of Modern Feminism* (New Haven: Yale University Press, 1987), p. 219, Table 7.1.

Table 4. Cohorts of women lawyers by date of graduation from law school

	1920		1939		1949	
Law school cohorts	%	N	%	N	%	N
1860–79	1	(1)	—	—	—	—
1880–99	9	(12)	1	(3)	1	(2)
1900–19	89	(118)	14	(85)	8	(26)
1920–39	2	(2)	86	(534)	58	(198)
1940+	—	—	—	—	34	(118)
Total N		(133)		(622)		(344)

Sources: BVI questionnaires; Fiona Hale Cook, ed., *Who's Who Among Women Lawyers, 1939* (Boston: Fiona Hale Cook, 1939) (hereinafter 1939 *Who's Who*); and Laura Miller Derry, ed., *Digest of Women Lawyers and Judges: Biographical Sketches and Data of Women Lawyers and Judges of the United States and its Possessions, 1949* (U.S.A.: Laura Miller Derry, 1949) (hereinafter 1949 *Digest*).
Note: Percentages may not add to 100 due to rounding.

Table 5. Rank order of top ten states of current practice of women lawyers, 1920, 1939, and 1949

1920		1939		1949	
State	%	State	%	State	%
Illinois	12.7	New York	14.2	New York	11.7
New York	10.0	D.C.	10.7	D.C.	10.4
California	8.1	Massachusetts	9.4	Illinois	8.4
D.C.	5.9	Illinois	7.3	Massachusetts	5.7
Massachusetts	5.4	Ohio	6.0	Ohio	5.2
Ohio	4.1	California	5.7	Texas	5.2
Oklahoma	4.1	New Jersey	3.6	California	4.6
Washington	4.1	Pennsylvania	3.3	Michigan	3.2
Nebraska	3.2	Texas	2.7	Georgia	2.8
New Jersey	2.7	Michigan	2.1	Washington	2.6

Sources: BVI questionnaires; 1939 *Who's Who,* and 1949 *Digest.*

Table 6. Rank order of top ten cities of current practice of women lawyers, 1920, 1939, and 1949

1920		1939		1949	
City	%	City	%	City	%
Chicago	9.5	Washington, D.C.	10.7	Washington, D.C.	10.4
New York	7.2	New York	8.2	New York	6.6
Washington, D.C.	5.9	Boston	5.8	Chicago	5.6
Boston	3.6	Chicago	5.1	Boston	2.2
Los Angeles	2.7	Los Angeles	2.4	Atlanta	2.0
Seattle	2.3	Cleveland	1.8	Dallas	1.8
Oklahoma City	1.8	Buffalo	1.5	Los Angeles	1.7
Oakland	1.4	Seattle	1.4	Brooklyn	1.4
Omaha	1.4	Philadelphia	1.3	Indianapolis	1.3
Cleveland	1.4	Brooklyn	1.2	Detroit	1.2

Sources: BVI questionnaires; 1939 *Who's Who;* and 1949 *Digest.*

Table 7. Rank order of top ten law schools attended by women, 1920, 1939, and 1949

1920	N	1939	N	1949	N
New York Univ.	14	New York Univ.	55	New York Univ.	37
Washington College		Portia	49	George Washington	35
of Law	13	Washington College		Washington College	
Univ. of Chicago	10	of Law	45	of Law	31
Univ. of Michigan	8	George Washington	32	Portia	31
Boston Univ.	7	Boston Univ.	31	National Univ.	29
Washington Univ.	7	New Jersey School		John Marshall	26
Univ. of Illinois	5	of Law	22	Washington Univ.	24
Univ. of Wisconsin	4	Univ. of Chicago	20	Univ. of Chicago	22
Univ. of California	4	National Univ.	19	Boston Univ.	21
Ohio State Univ.	4	Brooklyn Law School	19	De Paul Univ.	21
Chicago-Kent	4	Washington Univ.	18	Yale	20
Univ. of Nebraska	4	Northeastern	16	Univ. of Texas	20
		Univ. of Michigan	15	Indiana Univ.	20
		Northwestern	15	Brooklyn Law School	19
		USC	14	Northeastern	17
Total schools	61		148		158

Sources: BVI questionnaires; 1939 Who's Who; and 1949 Digest.
Note: This table contains full-time and part-time law schools.

Table 8. Ages of women lawyers, 1939 and 1949

	Who's Who 1939		Martindale-Hubbell 1939		Digest 1949	
Ages	%	N	%	N	%	N
20–29	12	(87)	13	(299)	8	(70)
30–39	43	(315)	42	(968)	31	(263)
40–49	28	(203)	27	(615)	31	(268)
50–59	11	(84)	12	(286)	21	(177)
60–69	5	(36)	6	(127)	7	(56)
70–79	1	(9)	1	(28)	2	(18)
80–89	—	—	—	—	1	(8)
Total N		(734)		(2,323)		(860)

Sources: 1939 Who's Who; Martindale-Hubbell Law Directory, 1939; and 1949 Digest.
Note: Unknowns are excluded. Percentages may not add to 100 due to rounding.

Table 9. Marital status of women lawyers, 1887–1949

Status	1887–90	1890	1890	1920	1939	1939	1949
Married	53%	51%	21%	30%	44%	43%	50%
Unmarried	47%	49%	65%	67%	50%	57%	41%
Widowed/ divorced	—	—	14%	3%	6%	—	9%
Total *N*	(30)	(117)	(208)	(205)	(906)	(1,380)	(1,084)

Sources: For 1887–90, calculated from the letters of the Equity Club members printed in Virginia G. Drachman, *Women Lawyers and the Origins of Professional Identity in America, 1887–1890* (Ann Arbor: The University of Michigan Press, 1993); for 1890, calculated from Lelia J. Robinson, "Women Lawyers in the United States," 2 *Green Bag* 10 (1890); for 1890, U.S. Bureau of the Census, *Eleventh Census*, vol. I, p. ci; p. 414; for 1920, BVI questionnaires; for 1939, 1939 *Who's Who*; for 1949, 1949 *Digest*.

Table 10. Proportions of women lawyers by number of children in 1939 and 1949

No. of children	1939 %	1939 N	1949 %	1949 N
0	76	(721)	70	(811)
1	13	(122)	14	(171)
2	8	(77)	9	(108)
3	2	(18)	4	(47)
4	1	(7)	1	(13)
5	—	(1)	1	(6)
6	—	(2)	—	(1)
Total *N*		(948)		(1,157)

Sources: For 1939, 1939 *Who's Who*; for 1949, 1949 *Digest*.
Note: Unknowns are excluded. Percentages may not add to 100 due to rounding.

Table 11. First or only work experience of women lawyers prior to law career, 1920

Occupation	%	N
Teacher; school principal	34	(54)
Stenographer	27	(43)
Secretary	8	(12)
Law clerk	7	(11)
Government job/civil service	4	(7)
Lawyer	4	(7)
Bookkeeper	3	(5)
Editor	2	(3)
Legal aid society	1	(2)
Court reporter	1	(2)
Assistant to lawyer	1	(2)
Social service	1	(2)
Chautauqua	0.6	(1)
Title examiner	0.6	(1)
Writer	0.6	(1)
Housewife	0.6	(1)
Law librarian	0.6	(1)
Deputy clerk	0.6	(1)
None	1	(2)
Total N		(158)

Source: BVI questionnaires.
Note: Unknowns are excluded. Percentages may not add to 100 due to rounding.

Table 12. Best opportunities for women in law, 1920

Specialization	%	N
Probate/wills	45	(66)
Domestic relations	17	(25)
Office, general practice	15	(22)
Real estate	13	(19)
Social welfare law	4	(6)
Business law	3	(5)
Trial work	3	(5)
Total N		(148)

Source: BVI questionnaires.
Note: Unknowns are excluded. Percentages may not add to 100 due to rounding.

Table 13. Primary specializations in law among women lawyers, 1920, 1939, and 1949

Specialization	1920 %	1920 N	1939 %	1939 N	1949 %	1949 N
General practice; office	52	(81)	66	(221)	68	(79)
Wills and estates	20	(31)	13	(44)	11	(13)
Real estate	6	(10)	7	(22)	8	(9)
Domestic relations	5	(7)	2	(6)	3	(3)
Criminal law	3	(5)	1	(4)	1	(2)
Trial work	3	(5)	1	(4)	1	(2)
Commercial/banking	2	(3)	2	(8)	—	(0)
Tax	2	(3)	2	(5)	3	(3)
Corporate	2	(3)	3	(10)	1	(1)
Bankruptcy	2	(3)	1	(2)	—	(0)
Labor	1	(2)	—	(0)	1	(1)
Patent law	3	(4)	3	(10)	3	(3)
Total N		(157)		(336)		(116)

Sources: BVI questionnaires; 1939 Who's Who; and 1949 Digest.
Note: Unknowns are excluded. Percentages may not add to 100 due to rounding.

Table 14. Primary positions in law by practicing and non-practicing women lawyers, 1920, 1939, and 1949

Primary position	1920 %	1920 N	1939 %	1939 N	1949 %	1949 N
Private practitioners						
Solo law practice	32	(58)	41	(345)	43	(473)
Partner of law firm or associated with firm	19	(34)	45	(378)	22	(245)
Not currently in practice						
Law clerk	3	(6)	0.8	(7)	2	(16)
Federal judge	1	(1)	0.4	(3)	1	(12)
State and local judge	1	(1)	0.4	(3)	2	(26)
Lawyer for federal government	4	(7)	4	(36)	9	(96)
Lawyer for state or local government or agency	6	(11)	5	(39)	5	(57)
Lawyer for business or bank	10	(18)	1	(11)	7	(78)

Table 14. (continued)

Primary position	1920 %	1920 N	1939 %	1939 N	1949 %	1949 N
Stenographer	4	(8)	—	(0)	—	(0)
Legal secretary	4	(8)	0.5	(4)	2	(18)
Retired/inactive	1	(2)	0.1	(1)	5	(50)
Education	5	(9)	1	(10)	2	(19)
Unemployed	4	(8)	2	(13)	1	(15)
Housewife	6	(10)	—	(0)	0.09	(1)
Total N		(181)		(850)		(1,106)

Sources: BVI questionnaires; 1939 *Who's Who,* and 1949 *Digest.*
Note: Unknowns are excluded. Percentages may not add to 100 due to rounding.

Table 15. Importance of Suffrage Amendment to women lawyers, by region, 1920

Response	East	Midwest	South	West	Total
Yes	70%	63%	47%	55%	61%
	(38)	(39)	(16)	(22)	(115)
No	6%	5%	21%	25%	12%
	(3)	(3)	(7)	(10)	(23)
Unsure	24%	32%	33%	20%	27%
	(13)	(20)	(11)	(8)	(52)
Total	28%	33%	18%	21%	100%
	(54)	(62)	(34)	(40)	(190)

Source: BVI questionnaires.
Chi square 0.013.

Table 16. Reasons that suffrage helped women in law, by region, 1920

Reasons	East	Midwest	South	West	Total
Respect for women	43%	51%	77%	68%	55%
	(16)	(18)	(10)	(15)	(59)
Access to work	57%	49%	23%	32%	45%
	(21)	(17)	(3)	(7)	(48)
Total	35%	33%	12%	21%	100%
	(37)	(35)	(13)	(22)	(107)

Source: BVI questionnaires.
Chi square 0.097.

Table 17. Effect of World War I on women in law, by law school cohort, 1920

Effect	Law school cohort		Total
	Pre-1910	1911–20	
More opportunity	38%	65%	60%
	(13)	(97)	(110)
Same opportunity	47%	29%	32%
	(16)	(43)	(59)
Less opportunity	15%	6%	8%
	(5)	(9)	(14)
Total	19%	81%	100%
	(34)	(149)	(183)

Source: BVI questionnaires.
Chi square 0.012.

Table 18. How to get started in law, 1920

Opportunity	%	N
Clerk or firm	60	(127)
Stenographer	2	(5)
Own office	9	(19)
Contacts	4	(8)
Social welfare	2	(4)
Other	23	(49)
Total N		(212)

Source: BVI questionnaires.

Table 19. Reasons that women lawyers were not practicing, by marital status, 1920

	Marital status					
Reason	Married		Unmarried		Total	
Discrimination	9%	(5)	19%	(25)	16%	(30)
Marriage	45%	(25)	29%	(39)	34%	(64)
Economic	32%	(18)	26%	(35)	28%	(53)
No interest in law	13%	(7)	17%	(23)	16%	(30)
Not true	2%	(1)	10%	(13)	8%	(14)
Total	29%	(56)	71%	(135)		(191)

Source: BVI questionnaires.
Note: Unknowns are excluded. Percentages may not add to 100 due to rounding.
Chi square 0.047.

Table 20. Women lawyers' views about the limitations of their profession, by marital status, 1920

	Marital status					
Limitation	Married		Unmarried		Total	
Concern about discrimination	51%	(21)	73%	(63)	66%	(84)
Economic concerns about practice of law	32%	(13)	22%	(19)	25%	(32)
Profession of law limited in appeal	17%	(7)	5%	(4)	9%	(11)
Total	32%	(41)	68%	(86)	100%	(127)

Source: BVI questionnaires.
Chi square 0.018.

Table 21. Chances for men versus women in law, 1920

Chances	%	N
Better chance for men	73	(140)
Equal chances	12	(23)
Chances for women increasing	9	(17)
Up to individual	7	(13)
Total N		(193)

Source: BVI questionnaires.
Note: Percentages may not add to 100 due to rounding.

Table 22. First women judges in America, 1870–1979, by date of first appointment

Date	Woman judge	Jurisdiction and court
1870	Esther Morris	Wyoming Territory: Justice of the Peace
1884	Marilla Ricker	District of Columbia: U.S. Commissioner
1886	Carrie Kilgore	Pennsylvania: Master in Chancery
1907	Catharine McCulloch	Illinois: Justice of the Peace
1914	Reah Whitehead	Washington: Justice Court
1915	Georgia Bullock	California: Women's Court (Police Court)
1915	Frances Hopkins	Missouri: Temporary Probate
1921	Camille Kelley	Tennessee: Juvenile Court
1921	Florence Allen	Ohio: Common Pleas
1923	Virginia H. Mayfield	Alabama: Domestic Relations
1924	Edith Atkinson	Florida: Circuit Court
1927	Aldona E. Appleton	New Jersey: Juvenile and Domestic Relations
1928	Mary H. Adams	Vermont: Probate Court
1930	Emma F. Scofield	Massachusetts: District Court
	Sadie Shulman	Massachusetts: Municipal Court
1930	Grace Miles	Kansas: Probate Court
1934	Carrie H. Buck	Hawaii: District Court
1935	Idella Jeness	New Hampshire: Municipal Court
1935	Rosalie Whitney	New York: Domestic Relations
1935	Sarah T. Hughes	Texas: District Court
1935	Reva B. Bosone	Utah: City Court
1938	Irene S. Ingham	Colorado: District Court
1940	Anna J. V. Levy	Louisiana: Juvenile Court
1940	M. Eleanor Nolan	Minnesota: Municipal Court

Table 22.   (continued)

Date	Woman judge	Jurisdiction and court
1941	Lilia N. Neuenfelt	Michigan: General Jurisdiction
1942	Ruth O. Williams	Virginia: County Court
1944	Louise B. Taylor	South Carolina: Magistrate Court
1946	Matilda Pollard	Nevada: Justice of the Peace
1947	Ruth F. Hale	Arkansas: Chancery Court
1949	Susie Sharp	North Carolina: Superior Court
1950	Lorna E. Lockwood	Arizona: Superior Court
1951	Helen E. Brown	Maryland: Housing Court
1954	Jean C. Lewis	Oregon: Circuit Court
1956	Florence K. Murray	Rhode Island: Superior Court
1957	Stella Atkins	Georgia: Municipal Court
1959	Elizabeth D. Hallanan	West Virginia: Juvenile Court
1960	Margaret Driscoll	Connecticut: Juvenile Court
1964	V. Sue Shields	Indiana: Superior Court
1967	Mary A. Miller	Alaska: District Court
1970	Olga Bennett	Wisconsin: County Court
1971	Roxanna Arsht	Delaware: Family Court
1971	Lenore L. Prather	Mississippi: Chancery Court
1971	Elizabeth D. Pitman	Nebraska: Municipal Court
1971	Mary C. Walters	New Mexico: District Court
1973	Lynn E. Brady	Iowa: Municipal Court
1973	Harriet P. Henry	Maine: District Court
1974	Mildred Ramynke	South Dakota: Circuit Court
1978	Diana Barz	Montana: District Court
1979	Ann C. Mahoney	North Dakota: County Court

Source: Recalculated by the author from Larry Berkson, "Women on the Bench: A Brief History," *Judicature* 65 (1982): 290, Table 1. Georgia Bullock was the first woman judge in several different California courts; see Georgia P. Bullock to Selina Solomons, Dec. 30, 1915, Bullock Papers; and Georgia P. Bullock, "Her Record," box 14, folder on Elections, Bullock Papers.

Note: Oklahoma and Idaho were not available.

Appendix 2
Sources and Methods

with Douglas Lamar Jones

This book relies, in part, on the quantitative analysis of four separate sources of data on women lawyers: the survey questionnaires of women lawyers collected by the Bureau of Vocational Information in 1920 (Arthur and Elizabeth Schlesinger Library, Radcliffe College, Cambridge, Mass.); the 1939 *Martindale-Hubbell Law Directory*, vol. 1 (New York: Martindale-Hubbell, 1939); *Who's Who Among Women Lawyers*, edited by Fiona Hale Cook (Boston: Fiona Hale Cook, 1939); and a 1949 *Digest of Women Lawyers and Judges*, edited by Laura Miller Derry (U.S.A.: Laura Miller Derry, 1949). Although the data given in each of the four sources was not identical, the bureau's 1920 data, the 1939 *Who's Who*, and the 1949 *Digest* were coded identically in order to create as much comparative information as possible. The 1939 *Martindale-Hubbell* data was more discrete, so it required a separate codebook for its analysis. In addition, the bureau's 1920 data contained information that does not appear in any of the other three sources, so it, too, required an additional codebook. A few words about each of these sources are in order.

The data from the bureau was gathered by Beatrice Doerschuk, assistant director of the Bureau of Vocational Information and author of the bureau's study, *Women in the Law: An Analysis of Training, Practice, and Salaried Positions* (New York: Bureau of Vocational Information, Bulletin no. 3, 1920). Doerschuk initially identified approximately 1,700 women graduates of law school and practitioners, almost the exact number found by the census-takers in 1920. From this group, Doerschuk selected 827 women who received questionnaires, yielding 297 responses. In actuality, the bureau sent two different questionnaires. The first, dated February 1918, was a narrowly drawn instrument that focused almost exclusively on traditional questions on vocational training and education. The second, a revised and expanded questionnaire, was completed by most respondents in March or April 1920. Only the 1920 questionnaire appeared in the appendix of Women in the Law.

The bureau's 1920 questionnaire asked broad questions about the attitudes of women lawyers toward the practice of law: its advantages and disadvantages; the effects of suffrage; the importance of World War I; the chances for women to succeed in law; and the nature of women's legal practice. For our purposes, the biographical information was of mixed quality. Age data was insufficient, but education, place of residence, work experience, and year of graduation from law school were useful. The evidence on attitudes of women lawyers was very good but not detailed.

The survival of 221 of the bureau's 1920 questionnaires permitted a second look at women in law in 1920. Not every one of the women lawyers surveyed by the bureau answered all of the questions posed, primarily because the questionnaire frequently asked for narrative answers. The total numbers of women lawyers shown in the tables for 1920 in this book, therefore, vary when compared with the tables that Doerschuk included in her text. Her tables frequently included all 297 of the respondents, whereas this study relied only on the 221 surviving 1920 questionnaires, 62 percent of which came from women in private law practice. To the extent possible, this book asked different questions than those posed originally by Doerschuk. It used control variables, defined generational cohorts, analyzed central tendencies, and employed measures of statistical significance. Although the small number of responses to some questions made extensive statistical analysis difficult, the results of this study reveal more complex attitudes among women lawyers in 1920 than those portrayed in Women in the Law.

In order to find a general, inclusive list of women lawyers in the early twentieth century, this book examined a sample of women lawyers listed in the 1939 edition of the Martindale-Hubbell Law Directory. One year of Martindale-Hubbell was selected that overlapped with the 1939 Who's Who to provide a measure of comparability. The book employed a one in five sample of all women listed in all geographic areas (urban and rural), which resulted in a total sample of 3,461 women lawyers from forty-eight states, the District of Columbia, and Hawaii. The sample provided information on age, marital status, law practice, income, and status within the profession for a broad cross-section of women lawyers.

Two published digests of women lawyers in America appeared in the 1930s and 1940s, the 1939 *Who's Who* and the 1949 *Digest*. All of the entries in both were analyzed. Unlike the bureau's 1920 survey, compilers of the 1939 *Who's Who* celebrated the arrival of women in law. It contained 948 entries, whereas the 1949 *Digest* had 1,157. The 1939 *Who's Who* was more selective than the bureau's sample or that of *Martindale-Hubbell*. For example, 753 of the 3,461 women in *Martindale-Hubbell* also appeared in the 1939 *Who's Who*. The editors of the 1939 *Who's Who* self-consciously sought to include "prominent" women lawyers. To some degree then, *Who's Who* revealed a slight bias toward professional accomplishment, but less so than one might think. The *Martindale-Hubbell* sample proved to be remarkably similar to the 1939 *Who's Who*. Specializations in law, education, age, marital status, and other biographical data were remarkably similar among all of the sources studied.

In order to obtain a sketch of the attributes of women lawyers as they matured in the profession, the book investigates the 1949 *Digest*. Similar to *Martindale-Hubbell*, the 1949 *Digest* was more inclusive of women lawyers, regardless of "prominence." By 1949, women lawyers had attained more status and recognition, so that the 1949 *Digest* summarized a different point on the professional path than the earlier surveys.

To some degree, all of the quantitative sources reflected some bias, which in turn must be evaluated and balanced. The bureau's 1920 questionnaires lacked a systematic pool of respondents, and some responses were narrative rather than nominal. But these questionnaires, when compared with both census data and other sources, held up well. Moreover, as the first survey of women lawyers in the twentieth century, it was an invaluable source. *Martindale-Hubbell*, in contrast, was a model of order and consistency; it provided a very inclusive list of women lawyers in 1939. With its age, economic, and professional data, it too provided valuable information, but it lacked the attitudinal survey of the bureau's 1920 questionnaires. The 1939 *Who's Who*, because it was designed to reflect "prominent" women lawyers, may be slightly biased toward successful and older women lawyers. Yet when compared with other sources, the data proved remarkably consistent. Finally, the 1949 *Digest* also must be seen as somewhat biased toward successful women in law because by 1949, women were, as a group, more successful than they had been earlier in the twentieth century.

Abbreviations

A. Matthews Papers	Annabel Matthews Papers, The Arthur and Elizabeth Schlesinger Library, Radcliffe College, Cambridge, Massachusetts
B. Matthews Papers	Burnita Shelton Matthews Papers, The Arthur and Elizabeth Schlesinger Library, Radcliffe College, Cambridge, Massachusetts
Briggs Papers	Le Baron Russell Briggs Papers, Radcliffe College Archives, The Arthur and Elizabeth Schlesinger Library, Radcliffe College, Cambridge, Massachusetts
Bullock Papers	Georgia Phillips (Morgan) Bullock Papers, Department of Special Collections, University Research Library, University of California at Los Angeles
BVI Records	Bureau of Vocational Information Records, The Arthur and Elizabeth Schlesinger Library, Radcliffe College, Cambridge, Massachusetts
Cooley Collection	Thomas Cooley Collection, Bentley Historical Library, University of Michigan, Ann Arbor, Michigan
Dennett Papers	Mary Ware Dennett Papers, The Arthur and Elizabeth Schlesinger Library, Radcliffe College, Cambridge, Massachusetts
Dillon Collection	Mary Earhart Dillon Collection, The Arthur and Elizabeth Schlesinger Library, Radcliffe College, Cambridge, Massachusetts

Doty Papers	Madeleine Zabriskie Doty Papers, Sophia Smith Collection, Smith College, Northampton, Massachusetts
Harvard Archives	Harvard University Archives, Pusey Library, Harvard University, Cambridge, Massachusetts
HLSL	Harvard Law School Library, Harvard University, Cambridge, Massachusetts
HWS	*History of Woman Suffrage*, ed. Elizabeth Cady Stanton, Susan B. Anthony, and Matilda Joslyn Gage (Rochester, N.Y.: Susan B. Anthony, ca. 1881, 1887)
Lockwood Papers	Belva Lockwood Papers, Syracuse University Archives, Syracuse, New York
Lowell Presidential Papers	A. Lawrence Lowell Presidential Papers, Harvard University Archives, Pusey Library, Harvard University, Cambridge, Massachusetts
McCulloch Papers	Catharine Waugh McCulloch Papers, The Arthur and Elizabeth Schlesinger Library, Radcliffe College, Cambridge, Massachusetts
Milholland Papers	Inez Milholland Papers, The Arthur and Elizabeth Schlesinger Library, Radcliffe College, Cambridge, Massachusetts
NYUA	New York University Archives, Elmer Holmes Bobst Library, Office of University Archives, New York
PLSA	Portia Law School and Calvin Coolidge College Archives, New England School of Law, Boston, Massachusetts
RCA	Radcliffe College Archives, The Arthur and Elizabeth Schlesinger Library, Radcliffe College, Cambridge, Massachusetts
SL	The Arthur and Elizabeth Schlesinger Library, Radcliffe College, Cambridge, Massachusetts
Smith Collection	Sophia Smith Collection, Smith College, Northampton, Massachusetts
Tompkins Scrapbook	Leslie J. Tompkins Scrapbook, New York University Archives, Elmer Holmes Bobst Library, Office of University Archives, New York University, New York
WCLA	Washington College of Law Archives, Office of Institutional Advancement, American University, Washington, D.C.

WLC   Records of the Woman's Law Class and Woman's Legal Education Society, New York University Archives, Elmer Holmes Bobst Library, Office of University Archives, New York University, New York

Notes

Introduction

1. Jane M. Slocum to "Dear Sisters in Law" [1887], in Virginia G. Drachman, *Women Lawyers and the Origins of Professional Identity in America: The Letters of the Equity Club, 1887 to 1890* (Ann Arbor: University of Michigan Press, 1993), pp. 67–70, quotation from p. 67.

2. See Alme E. Hitchcock to "Dear Sisters-in-Law," May 8, 1889, in Drachman, *Women Lawyers*, pp. 166–167; Rebecca May to the Ladies of the Equity Club, May 1, 1887, in ibid., pp. 61–62; and Laura de F. Gordon to "My Dear Sisters-in-Law," Apr. 26, 1887, in ibid., pp. 50–51.

3. Although it was not unheard of for a woman in colonial America to serve as an attorney, this book concerns itself with the origins of women lawyers in modern American history. On the changing numbers of women lawyers since 1960, see Cynthia Fuchs Epstein, *Women in Law* (New York: Basic Books, 1981), pp. 4–5, and Kermit L. Hall, *The Magic Mirror: Law in American History* (New York: Oxford University Press, 1989), p. 288.

4. Michael Grossberg, "Institutionalizing Masculinity: The Law as a Masculine Profession," in Mark C. Carnes and Clyde Griffen, eds., *Meanings for Manhood: Constructions of Manhood in Victorian America* (Chicago: University of Chicago Press, 1990), pp. 133–151.

5. See Table 4.

6. Mary Roth Walsh, *"Doctors Wanted: No Women Need Apply": Sexual Barriers in the Medical Profession, 1835–1975* (New Haven: Yale University Press, 1977); Virginia G. Drachman, *Hospital with a Heart: Women Doctors and the Paradox of Separatism at the New England Hospital, 1862–1969* (Ithaca, N.Y.: Cornell University Press, 1984); Regina Markell Morantz-Sanchez, *Sympathy and Science: Women*

Physicians in American Medicine (New York: Oxford University Press, 1985), pp. 64–89; and Gloria Melnik Moldow, *Women Doctors in Gilded-Age Washington: Race, Gender, and Professionalization* (Champaign: Illinois University Press, 1987), pp. 75–93.

7. Ellen Carol DuBois, *Feminism and Suffrage: The Emergence of an Independent Women's Movement in America, 1848–1869* (Ithaca, N.Y.: Cornell University Press, 1978).

8. Martha K. Pearce to Equity Club [1887], in Drachman, *Women Lawyers,* pp. 62–63, quotation from p. 63.

9. On women lawyers' managing marriage and career, see Virginia G. Drachman, " 'My "Partner" in Law and Life': Marriage in the Lives of Women Lawyers in Late Nineteenth- and Early Twentieth-Century America," 14 *Law and Social Inquiry* 221–250 (1989). On women doctors' balancing of marriage and career, see Virginia G. Drachman, "The Limits of Progress: The Professional Lives of Women Doctors, 1881–1926," *Bulletin of the History of Medicine* 60 (1986): 58–72, esp. 61–63, 69; Morantz-Sanchez, *Sympathy and Science,* esp. pp. 134–142, and Morantz-Sanchez, "The Many Faces of Intimacy: Professional Options and Personal Choices among Nineteenth- and Twentieth-Century Women Physicians," in Penina G. Abir-Am and Dorinda Outram, eds., *Uneasy Careers and Intimate Lives: Women in Science, 1789–1979* (New Brunswick, N.J.: Rutgers University Press, 1987), pp. 45–59. For an analysis of nineteenth-century feminists' views on marriage and career, see William Leach, *True Love and Perfect Union: The Feminist Reform of Sex and Society* (New York: Basic Books, 1980), pp. 195–201. Nancy F. Cott analyzes early twentieth-century advocates of women pursuing both career and marriage in her *Grounding of Modern Feminism* (New Haven: Yale University Press, 1993), pp. 179–211. For the relationship between marriage and the state in late-nineteenth-century America, see Cott, "Giving Character to Our Whole Civil Polity: Marriage and the Public Order in the Late Nineteenth Century," in Linda A. Kerber, Alice Kessler Harris, and Kathryn Kish Sklar, eds., *U.S. History as Women's History: New Feminist Essays* (Chapel Hill: University of North Carolina Press, 1995), pp. 107–121. See also generally Elaine Tyler May, *Great Expectations: Marriage and Divorce in Post-Victorian America* (Chicago: University of Chicago Press, 1980).

10. See, for example, Karen Blair, *The Clubwoman as Feminist: True Womanhood Redefined, 1868–1914* (New York: Holmes and Meier, 1980); Ruth Borden, *Women and Temperance: The Quest for Power and Liberty, 1873–1920* (Philadelphia: Temple University Press, 1981); Mari Jo Buhle, *Women and American Socialism, 1870–1920* (Chicago: University of Illinois Press, 1983); Drachman, *Hospital with a Heart;* Blanche Weisen Cook, "Female Support Networks and Political Activism: Lillian Wald, Crystal Eastman, Emma Goldman," *Chrysalis* 3 (1977): 43–61; Nancy F. Cott, *The Bonds of Womanhood: "Women's Sphere" in New England, 1780–1835* (New Haven, Conn.: Yale University Press, 1977); Estelle Freedman, "Separatism as Strategy: Female Institution Building and American Feminism, 1870–1930," *Feminist Studies* 5 (1979): 512–529; Nancy A. Hewitt, *Women's Ac-*

tivism and Social Change: Rochester, New York, 1822–1872 (Ithaca, N.Y.: Cornell University Press, 1984); Anne Firor Scott, *Natural Allies: Women's Associations in American History* (Chicago: University of Illinois Press, 1993); and Kathryn Kish Sklar, *Florence Kelley and the Nation's Work: The Rise of Women's Political Culture, 1830–1900* (New Haven, Conn.: Yale University Press, 1995).

11. The historiography of women's entry in the professions includes Walsh, *"Doctors Wanted"*; Drachman, *Hospital with a Heart*; Morantz-Sanchez, *Sympathy and Science*; and Moldow, *Women Doctors in Gilded-Age Washington.* Women scientists are discussed in Margaret W. Rossiter, *Women Scientists in America: Struggles and Strategies to 1940* (Baltimore, Md.: Johns Hopkins University Press, 1982). For the social sciences, see Rosalind Rosenberg, *Beyond Separate Spheres: Intellectual Roots of Feminism* (New Haven, Conn.: Yale University Press, 1982). See also Penina Migdal Glazer and Miriam Slater, *Unequal Colleagues: The Entrance of Women into the Professions, 1890–1940* (New Brunswick, N.J.: Rutgers University Press, 1987); Stephanie J. Shaw, *What a Woman Ought to Be and to Do: Black Professional Women Workers during the Jim Crow Era* (Chicago: University of Chicago Press, 1996); Ellen Fitzpatrick, *Endless Crusade: Women Social Scientists and Progressive Reform* (New York: Oxford University Press, 1990); Barbara Melosh, *"The Physician's Hand": Work Culture and Conflict in American Nursing* (Philadelphia: Temple University Press, 1982); Susan M. Reverby, *Ordered to Care: The Dilemma of American Nursing, 1850–1945* (New York: Cambridge University Press, 1987); Darlene Clark Hine, *Black Women in White: Racial Conflict and Cooperation in the Nursing Profession, 1890–1950* (Bloomington: University of Indiana Press, 1989); and Regina G. Kunzel, *Fallen Women, Problem Girls: Unmarried Mothers and the Professionalization of Social Work, 1890–1945* (New Haven, Conn.: Yale University Press, 1993). See also Joan Jacobs Brumberg and Nancy Tomes, "Women in the Professions: A Research Agenda for American Historians," *Reviews in American History* 10 (1982): 275–296.

A few women's historians include women lawyers in their broader historical studies. Cott's *Grounding of Modern Feminism* was particularly valuable in this study. See also Joan Hoff, *Law, Gender, and Injustice: A Legal History of U.S. Women* (New York: New York University Press, 1991); Patricia M. Hummer, *The Decade of Elusive Promise: Professional Women in the United States, 1920–1930* (Ann Arbor: MRI Press, 1979); Barbara J. Harris, *Beyond Her Sphere: Women and the Professions in American History* (Westport, Conn.: Greenwood, 1978); Rosalind Rosenberg, *Divided Lives: American Women in the Twentieth Century* (New York: Hill and Wang, 1992); J. Stanley Lemons, *The Woman Citizen: Social Feminism in the 1920s* (Urbana: University of Illinois Press, 1973); and Joyce Antler, *The Educated Woman and Professionalization: The Struggle for a New Feminine Identity, 1890–1920* (New York: Garland, 1987).

There is a sparse and highly selective historiography of women lawyers in modern American history. See Dorothy M. Brown, *Mabel Walker Willebrandt: A Study of Power, Loyalty, and Law* (Knoxville: University of Tennessee Press, 1984); Elizabeth Perry, *Belle Moskowitz: Feminine Politics and the Exercise of Power in the Age of Alfred E. Smith* (New York: Routledge, 1992); Jane M. Friedman, *America's First Woman Lawyer: The Biography of Myra Bradwell* (Buffalo, N.Y.: Prometheus Books, 1993); Ted Berkman, *The Lady and the Law: The Remarkable Life of Fanny Holtzmann* (Boston: Little, Brown, 1976); Karen Berger Morello, *The Invisible Bar: The Woman Lawyer in America, 1638 to the Present* (Boston: Beacon, 1986); and Jeanette E. Tuve, *First Lady of the Law: Florence Ellinwood Allen* (New York: University Press of America, 1984). See also Ronald Chester, *Unequal Access: Women Lawyers in a Changing America* (South Hadley, Mass.: Bergin and Garvey, 1985); D. Kelly Weisberg, "Barred from the Bar: Women and Legal Education in the United States, 1870–1890," 28 *Journal of Legal Education* 485–507 (1977); Kermit L. Hall, ed., *The Legal Profession: Major Historical Interpretations* (New York: Garland, 1987); and Douglas Lamar Jones, "Lelia J. Robinson's Case and the Entry of Women into the Legal Profession in Massachusetts," in Russell K. Osgood, ed., *The History of the Law in Massachusetts: The Supreme Judicial Court, 1692–1992* (Charlottesville: The University of Virginia Press, 1992), pp. 241–274. See Epstein's *Women in Law* for women lawyers in the 1960s and 1970s. My earlier works on women lawyers began to fill the void in the literature on the history of women lawyers. See *Women Lawyers;* "The New Woman Lawyer and the Challenge of Sexual Equality in Early Twentieth-Century America," 28 *Indiana Law Review* 227–258 (1995); "Women Lawyers and the Quest for Professional Identity in Late Nineteenth-Century America," 88 *Michigan Law Review* 2414–2443 (1990); " 'My "Partner" in Law and Life' "; and "Entering the Male Domain: Women Lawyers in the Courtroom in Modern American History," 77 *Massachusetts Law Review* 44–50 (1992).

12. See Jerold S. Auerbach, *Unequal Justice: Lawyers and Social Change in Modern America* (New York: Oxford University Press, 1976), and Lawrence M. Friedman, *A History of American Law* (New York: Simon and Schuster, 1985). See also Stephen Botein, "Professional History Reconsidered," 21 *American Journal of Legal History* 125–156 (1977); and Burton Bledstein, *The Culture of Professionalism: The Middle Class and the Development of Higher Education in America* (New York: Norton, 1976). There is a brief discussion of women's legal education in Robert Stevens, *Law School: Legal Education in America from the 1850s to the 1980s* (Chapel Hill: University of North Carolina Press, 1983). African-American women lawyers are included in J. Clay Smith, Jr., *Emancipation: The Making of the Black Lawyer, 1844–1944* (Philadelphia: University of Pennsylvania, 1993). For a perceptive analysis of the male dominance of the legal profession, see Grossberg, "Institutionalizing Masculinity."

13. Bradwell v. State of Illinois, 83 U.S. (16 Wall.) 442 (1873). For the emphasis on Bradwell, see Eleanor Flexner, *Century of Struggle: The Woman's Rights Movement in the United States* (New York: Atheneum, 1968), p. 12. See also William E. Nelson, *The Fourteenth Amendment: From Political Principle to Judicial Doctrine* (Cambridge, Mass.: Harvard University Press, 1988), pp. 151–181; Hoff, *Law, Gender, and Injustice,* pp. 151–191; Hall, *Magic Mirror,* pp. 216–218; Frances Olsen, "From False Paternalism to False Equality: Judicial Assaults on Female Com-

munity, Illinois, 1869–1895," 84 *Michigan Law Review* 1518 (1986); and Carol Ellen DuBois, "Outgrowing the Compact of the Fathers: Equal Rights, Woman Suffrage, and the United States Constitution, 1820–1878," *Journal of American History* 74 (1987): 836–862. It was not until 1971 that the United States Supreme Court ruled in favor of a woman's constitutional right to equal protection under the law in Reed v. Reed, 404 U.S. 71 (1971). The history of woman's rights is briefly but cogently summarized by Justice Ruth Bader Ginsburg in United States v. Virginia, nos. 94–1941 and 94–2107, slip op. at 26 (U.S., June 26, 1996), the decision that integrated Virginia Military Institute. She explicitly refers to the discrimination against nineteenth-century women seeking to practice law or to attend law school.

1. "A Sphere with an Infinite and Indeterminable Radius"

1. For a contemporary discussion, see "Some Judicial Views of Woman's Sphere," 15 *Law Notes* 103 (1911).

2. Motion to Admit Miss Lavinia Goodell to the Bar of this Court, 39 Wisc. 232, quotations at 242 and 244–245 (1875).

3. Ibid., 242.

4. *In re* Kilgore, 18 *American Law Review* 478, quotations at 478–479 (1884).

5. See *In re* Bradwell, 55 Ill. 535 (1869); Bradwell v. State of Illinois, 83 U.S. (16 Wall.) 442 (1873); *In re* Mrs. Belva Lockwood, 8 Ct. Cl. 346 (1873); Motion to Admit Miss Lavinia Goodell to the Bar of this Court, 39 Wisc. 232 (1875); In the Matter of the Application of Martha Angle Dorsett to be Admitted to Practice as an Attorney and Counselor at Law in said Court, 1 *Syllabi* 5 (1876); Lelia J. Robinson's Case, 131 Mass. 376 (1881); *In re* Leonard, 12 Or. 93 (1885); *In re* Kate Stoneman, 40 Hun. 638 (1886); Notes of Cases, 33 *Albany Law Journal* 402 (1886); *In re* Belva A. Lockwood, 154 U.S. 116 (1894); Attorney General v. Abbott, 121 Mich. 540 (1899); *Ex parte* Griffin, 71 S.W. 746 (Sup. Ct. Tenn., 1901); *In re* Etta H. Maddox, 93 Md. 727 (1901).

6. See *In re* Hall, 50 Conn. 131 (1882); *In re* Kilgore, 18 *American Law Review* 478 (1884); *In re* Ricker, 66 N.H. 207 (1890); *In re* Thomas 16 Colo. 441 (1891); and *In re* Leach, 134 Ind. 665 (1893).

7. Michael Grossberg, "Institutionalizing Masculinity: The Law as a Masculine Profession," in Mark C. Carnes and Clyde Griffen, eds., *Meanings for Manhood: Constructions of Manhood in Victorian America* (Chicago: University of Chicago Press, 1990), pp. 133–155. One gets a good sense of the frontier, male courtroom from Daniel H. Calhoun, *Professional Lives in America: Structure and Aspiration, 1750–1850* (Cambridge, Mass.: Harvard University Press, 1965), pp. 59–87, and David Herbert Donald, *Lincoln* (New York: Simon and Schuster, 1995), pp. 70–74, 96–106, and 142–157. For background on the urban bar, see Douglas Lamar Jones et al., *Discovering the Public Interest: A History of the Boston Bar Association* (Canoga Park, Calif.: CCA Publications, 1993), pp. 31–47; 50–53.

8. See Table 1.

9. 20 U.S.C. sec. 292 (1879).

10. Gerda Lerner, *The Grimké Sisters from South Carolina: Pioneers for Woman's Rights and Abolition* (New York: Schocken, 1971), p. 28; and Elizabeth Cady Stanton, *Eighty Years and More: Reminiscences, 1815–1897* (1898; reprint, New York: Schocken, 1971), pp. 31–32.

11. For the emergence of the woman's rights movement, see Ellen Carol DuBois, *Feminism and Suffrage: The Emergence of an Independent Women's Movement in America, 1848–1869* (Ithaca, N.Y.: Cornell University Press, 1978); and Eleanor Flexner, *Century of Struggle: The Woman's Rights Movement in the United States* (New York: Atheneum, 1968), pp. 105–178.

12. Catherine B. Cleary, "Lavinia Goodell, First Woman Lawyer in Wisconsin," *Wisconsin Magazine of History* 74 (1991), p. 245.

13. Elizabeth Jones, Address to the Tenth National Woman's Rights Convention, New York City, May 10–11, 1860, in Mari Jo Buhle and Paul Buhle, eds., *The Concise History of Woman Suffrage: Selections from the Classic Work of Stanton, Anthony, Gage, and Harper* (Urbana: University of Illinois Press, 1978), pp. 164–169, quotation from p. 165.

14. DuBois, *Feminism and Suffrage*, provides the essential contextual background for understanding the beginnings of the nineteenth-century woman's rights movement. For a thoughtful analysis of the constitutional issues of citizenship, equal rights, and suffrage in nineteenth-century America, see Carol Ellen DuBois, "Outgrowing the Compact of the Fathers: Equal Rights, Woman Suffrage, and the United States Constitution, 1820–1878," *Journal of American History* 74 (1987): 836–862, and Ellen Carol DuBois, "Taking the Law into Our Own Hands: *Bradwell, Minor,* and Suffrage Militance in the 1870s," in Nancy Hewitt and Susanne Lebsock, eds., *Visible Women: New Essays in American Activism* (Champaign: University of Illinois Press, 1993), pp. 19–40.

15. *HWS*, vol. 2, p. 586.

16. Flexner, *Century of Struggle*, pp. 168–169. William E. Nelson, in his *Fourteenth Amendment: From Political Principle to Judicial Doctrine* (Cambridge, Mass.: Harvard University Press, 1988), provides a recent legal historical analysis of the creation of the Fourteenth Amendment.

17. *HWS*, vol. 2, pp. 586–601, 626–627.

18. *HWS*, vol. 2, pp. 627–698. See also Joan Hoff, *Law, Gender and Injustice: A Legal History of U.S. Women* (New York: New York University Press, 1991), p. 160; and DuBois, "Outgrowing the Compact of the Fathers," pp. 859–860.

19. For a general background on these three women, see Jane M. Friedman, *America's First Woman Lawyer: The Biography of Myra Bradwell* (Buffalo, N.Y.: Prometheus, 1993); Edward T. James, ed., *Notable American Women, 1607–1950* (Cambridge, Mass.: Harvard University Press, 1971), pp. 413–416; and Cleary, "Lavinia Goodell."

20. See, for example, Flexner, *Century of Struggle*, pp. 120–121; Hoff, *Law, Gender, and Injustice,* pp. 165–170; and Friedman, *America's First Woman Lawyer,*

p. 28. For another perspective on the *Bradwell* decisions, see Frances Olsen, "From False Paternalism to False Equality: Judicial Assaults on Female Community, Illinois, 1869–1895," 84 *Michigan Law Review* 1518 (1986).

21. See, for example, Lockwood, 8 Ct. Cl., at 346; and Goodell, 39 Wisc., at 232.

22. Friedman, *America's First Woman Lawyer*, pp. 18, 29.

23. The briefs of women lawyers such as Bradwell and Lelia Robinson routinely cited the *Chicago Legal News* as a source for decisions on women in the law.

24. In the Matter of the Application of Myra Bradwell for License to Practice Law, Supreme Court of Illinois, September Term, 1869 (hereinafter Handwritten Brief, pp. 1–2.

25. Ibid., p. 2.

26. Ibid., p. 3.

27. Ibid., pp. 4–5.

28. Ibid., pp. 7–8; *Chicago Legal News*, 1870, p. 146; Act of Mar. 8, 1870, ch. 21, 1870, Iowa Acts 21.

29. See *HWS*, vol. 2, p. 603, where the clerk's letter is reprinted.

30. In the Matter of the Application of Myra Bradwell to Obtain a License to Practice as an Attorney at Law, Supreme Court of Illinois, September Term, 1869 (hereinafter Additional Brief).

31. Joseph Story, *Commentaries on the Law of Agency as a Branch of Commercial and Maritime Jurisprudence, with Occasional Illustrations from the Civil and Foreign Law* (Boston: C. C. Little and J. Brown, 1839).

32. Additional Brief, pp. 2–4.

33. Ibid., pp. 4–6.

34. Ibid., p. 7.

35. Ibid., p. 8.

36. DuBois, *Feminism and Suffrage*, pp. 180–181; *HWS*, vol. 2, pp. 369, 371.

37. The amended Additional Brief appears in Myra Bradwell Plaintiff in Error v. The State of Illinois, Supreme Court of the United States, no. 487, pp. 8–9. The amended Additional Brief was not in the files of the Supreme Court of Illinois.

38. Amended Additional Brief, p. 9. Bradwell probably referred either to the Civil Rights Act of 1866 (14 Stat. 27) or the Enforcement Act of 1870 (16 Stat. 141), which was a partial reenactment of the Civil Rights Bill of 1866, when she referred to the "civil rights bill." Because these acts were part of the congressional effort to enforce the Fourteenth Amendment, it made sense for Bradwell to cite them in her amended Additional Brief. See Lawrence H. Tribe, *American Constitutional Law* (Mineola, N.Y.: Foundation Press, 1988), p. 330, n. 2.

39. *In re* Bradwell, 55 Ill., at 537.

40. Ibid., at 537–538.

41. Ibid., at 539.

42. Ibid.

43. Ibid.
44. Ibid.
45. Goodell, 39 Wisc., at 245.
46. Ibid.
47. Ibid.
48. Bradwell, 83 U.S., at 141.
49. Ibid., at 142.
50. *In re* Lockwood, 8 Ct. Cl., at 355.
51. Goodell, 39 Wisc., at 245.
52. Ibid., at 245–246.
53. Ibid., at 246.
54. In the Matter of the Application of Martha Angle Dorsett, 1 *Syllabi*, at 5.
55. Ibid., at 6.
56. Ibid.
57. Ibid. Dorsett gained admission to practice law in Minnesota in 1877, after the legislature enacted a law permitting women to do so.
58. *In re* Bradwell, 55 Ill., at 539; *In re* Lockwood, 8 Ct. Cl., at 352.
59. Goodell, 39 Wisc., at 244.
60. *In re* Lockwood, 8 Ct. Cl., at 352; Bradwell, 83 U.S., at 446.
61. *In re* Bradwell, 55 Ill., at 535–536; Bradwell v. State, 83 U.S., at 446.
62. *In re* Bradwell, at 535–536; *In re* Lockwood, Ct. Cl., at 352–353.
63. *In re* Lockwood, 8 Ct. Cl., at 353, quotation at 349.
64. *In re* Bradwell, 83 U.S., at 446.
65. For example, see *In re* Bradwell, 55 Ill., at 541; *In re* Lockwood, 8 Ct. Cl., at 353; and Goodell, 39 Wisc., at 242. See Table 1 on the dates of admission to practice for women lawyers. This issue of legitimacy and order is discussed in Duncan Kennedy, "Toward an Historical Understanding of Legal Consciousness: The Case of Classical Legal Thought in America," 3 *Research in Law and Sociology* 3 (1980); and Morton J. Horwitz, *The Transformation of American Law, 1780–1860* (Cambridge, Mass.: Harvard University Press, 1977), pp. 9–31.
66. Goodell, 39 Wisc., at 242.
67. *In re* Bradwell, 55 Ill., at 539.
68. Ibid.; for Justice Nott, see *In re* Lockwood, 8 Ct. Cl., at 355.
69. Bradwell v. State of Illinois, 83 U.S. (16 Wall.) 442 (1873).
70. Slaughterhouse Cases, 38 U.S. (16 Wall.) 36 (1873).
71. Ibid., at 408.
72. Morton J. Horwitz, *The Transformation of American Law, 1870–1960: The Crisis of Legal Orthodoxy* (Cambridge, Mass.: Harvard University Press 1992), p. 24. See also Nelson, *The Fourteenth Amendment;* Charles Fairman, *Reconstruction and Reunion, 1864–1888* (New York: MacMillan, 1971), pp. 1320–1363; and Tribe, *American Constitutional Law*, pp. 548–558.
73. Bradwell v. State of Illinois, 83 U.S. (16 Wall.), at 445.

74. Myra Bradwell, Plaintiff in Error vs. The State of Illinois. Argument for Plaintiff in Error. Sup. Ct. of the United States, December term, 1871, no. 67, at 6.

75. Bradwell, 83 U.S. (16 Wall.), at 446.

76. Ibid.

77. Horwitz, *Transformation of American Law, 1870–1960*, pp. 27–30.

78. Bradwell, 83 U.S. (16 Wall.), at 446. Apparently Chief Justice Chase prepared but did not publish an opinion in which he concluded that the majority decision applied only to Bradwell's status as a citizen of a state, not to the right of women to practice law. 5 *New Jersey Law Journal* 188 (1882).

79. Bradwell, 83 U.S. (16 Wall.), at 445.

80. Minor v. Happersett, 83 U.S. (21 Wall.) 162 (1874).

81. Ibid., at 176.

82. Ibid., at 183. For background on Minor's legal strategy, see Flexner, *Century of Struggle*, pp. 168–170.

83. National Woman Suffrage Association, Appeal and Petition for a Sixteenth Amendment, Nov. 10, 1876, in Buhle and Buhle, *Concise History of Woman Suffrage*, pp. 304–306.

84. Gouger v. Timberlake et al., 148 Ind. 38, at 39–40 (1896).

85. Opinion of the Justices, 107 Mass. 607 (1871).

86. State, *ex rel.*, v. Davidson, 92 Tenn. 531, at 533–534 (1893).

87. Harris v. Burr, 32 Or. 348 (1898).

88. Opinion of the Justices, 150 Mass. 387, at 389 (1890).

89. Russell v. Guptill, 13 Wash. 360 (1896).

90. Attorney General v. Abbott, 121 Mich. 540 (1899).

91. Opinion of the Justices, 107 Mass. 607.

92. Opinion of the Justices, 150 Mass. 586.

93. See Nathaniel C. Moak, "Are Women Legally Eligible in New York as Notaries Public?" 41 *Albany Law Journal* 244 (1890), in which the author concludes that women were eligible to be notaries. See also State, *ex rel.*, v. Davidson, 92 Tenn. 531.

94. Opinion of the Justices, 150 Mass. 586, at 591–592 (1890). By 1896, the Massachusetts state legislature had sought and received approval from the supreme judicial court to pass a statute permitting women to serve as notaries. *In re* Opinion of the Justices, 165 Mass. 599 (1896).

95. State, *ex rel.*, v. Davidson, 92 Tenn. 531.

96. See Table 1.

97. Revised Statutes of State of Illinois, ch. 13, July 6, 1874; [Wisconsin] Revised Statutes subd. 5, sec. 2586, 1878; and 20 U.S.C. sec. 292 (1879).

98. The unpublished bench decision is reprinted in Fairman, *Reconstruction and Reunion*, pp. 1366–1367.

99. For the legislative debates, see 6 Cong. Rec. 240 (1877); 7 Cong. Rec. 1235, 1821, 2704–2705, 3558–3559 (1878); and 8 Cong. Rec. 1082–1084, 1221, 1413 (1879).

100. Lelia J. Robinson's Case, 131 Mass. 376 (1881). See also Douglas Lamar Jones, "Lelia J. Robinson's Case and the Entry of Women into the Legal Profession in Massachusetts," in Russell K. Osgood, ed., *The History of the Law in Massachusetts: The Supreme Judicial Court, 1692–1992* (Charlottesville: University of Virginia Press, 1992), pp. 241–274.

101. Robinson, 131 Mass., at 379, 381–382.

102. Flexner, *Century of Struggle*, pp. 217–218.

103. Jones, "Lelia J. Robinson's Case," p. 246.

104. Petitioner's Brief in Support [of Admission to the Bar], Lelia J. Robinson's Case, 131 Mass. 376 (1881) (no. 3650), at 1–2.

105. Ibid., at 3–8, quotation at 7–8.

106. *Amici Curae* Brief in Opposition [to Admission to the Bar], Lelia J. Robinson's Case, 131 Mass., (no. 3650).

107. Ibid., at 1–2.

108. Ibid., at 5.

109. Ibid., at 9.

110. Ibid., at 10.

111. Petitioner's Supplemental Brief, in Support [of Admission to the Bar], Lelia J. Robinson's Case, 131 Mass. (no. 3650) [hereinafter Supplemental Brief], at 3.

112. Ibid., at 1–3.

113. Ada H. Kepley, *A Farm Philosopher: A Love Story* (Teutopolis, Ill.: Woman's Printery, 1912), p. 55.

114. Supplemental Brief, at 3.

115. Ibid.

116. Ibid., at 4.

117. Ibid., at 4–5.

118. Ibid., at 5.

119. Mass. Gen. L., ch. 139 (1882); Lelia J. Robinson to Martha Pearce, April 9, 1887, in Virginia G. Drachman, *Women Lawyers and the Origins of Professional Identity in America: The Letters of the Equity Club, 1887–1890* (Ann Arbor: University of Michigan Press, 1993), pp. 64–67; unpublished records of the Boston Bar Association, Boston, Mass.

120. *In re* Leonard, 12 Or. 93, at 94 (1885); Notes of Cases, 33 *Albany Law Journal* 402 (1886); and In the matter of the Application of Kate Stoneman, 40 Hun. 638 (1886). The *Stoneman* case was not officially reported because just after the court's decision the New York legislature voted to admit women to practice law.

121. *In re* Hall, 50 Conn. 131 (1882).

122. See ibid.; *In re* Kilgore, 18 *American Law Review* 478 (1884); *In Re* Ricker, 66 N.H. 207 (1890); *In re* Thomas 16 Colo. 441 (1891); and *In re* Leach, 134 Ind. 665 (1893).

123. In the Matter of the Application of Miss Mary Hall for Admission to the Bar, *In re* Hall, 50 Conn. 131 (1882), Brief for Plaintiff, p. 9.

124. Ibid., Brief for Defendant, pp. 1–4.

125. *In re* Hall, 50 Conn. 131, at 135.

126. Ibid., at 137.

127. Ibid., at 138.

128. Justice Whitefield Pardee dissented from the majority decision in *Hall*, citing the absence of women lawyers at common law and the need for the legislature, rather than the court, to act. Ibid., at 138–139.

129. Ibid., at 137.

130. Ibid., at 132.

131. *In re* Kilgore, 18 *American Law Review* 478 (1884).

132. Ibid., at 478.

133. Ibid., at 478–479. Kilgore gained admission to the bar of the supreme court of Pennsylvania in 1886. *In re* Application of Kilgore, 5 A. 872 (1886).

134. For the decline in the Boston Bar, see Jones, *Discovering the Public Interest*, pp. 49–91.

135. *HWS*, vol. 2, pp. 586–587; In the Matter of the Petition of Marilla M. Ricker for Admission to the Bar, Brief in Support, pp. 1–3. 66 N.H. 207 (1890).

136. In the Matter of the Petition of Marilla M. Ricker for Admission to the Bar, Supplemental Brief in Support, 66 N.H. 207 (1890).

137. In the Matter of the Petition of Marilla M. Ricker, 66 N.H. 207, at 250.

138. Ibid., at 250–251.

139. Ibid., at 255.

140. On Charles Doe, see Morton Keller, *Affairs of State: Public Life in Late-Nineteenth-Century America* (Cambridge, Mass.: Harvard University Press, 1977), pp. 364–365; Lelia J. Robinson to [Catharine Waugh McCulloch], Sept. 5, 1890, box 2, folder 36, Grace H. Harte Papers, ser. 2, Dillon Collection.

141. *In re* Thomas, 16 Colo. 441 (1891).

142. Ibid., at 443–444.

143. Ibid., at 444–445.

144. Ibid., at 446.

145. *In re* Petition of Leach, 134 Ind. 665 (1893).

146. Ibid., at 668–669.

147. Ibid., at 670.

148. See Table 1.

149. Mary Putnam Jacobi, *"Common Sense" Applied to Woman Suffrage* (New York: G. P. Putnam's Sons, 1915), pp. 55–56.

2. "I Was the Only Woman in a Large School of Men"

1. In 1870, Ada Kepley graduated from the Union College of Law in Chicago to become the first woman in the United States to earn a law degree. Sara Kilgore Wertman graduated from the University of Michigan in 1871, and Phoebe Couzins and Mary Hickey graduated from Washington University and the State University of Iowa, respectively, in 1873.

2. On the history of women and higher education, see Barbara Miller

Solomon, *In the Company of Educated Women: A History of Women and Higher Education in America* (New Haven, Conn.: Yale University Press, 1985); Lynn D. Gordon, *Gender and Higher Education in the Progressive Era* (New Haven, Conn.: Yale University Press, 1990); Patricia Ann Palmieri, *In Adamless Eden: The Community of Women at Wellesley* (New Haven, Conn.: Yale University Press, 1995); Helen Lefkowitz Horowitz, *Alma Mater: Design and Experience in the Women's Colleges from Their Nineteenth-Century Beginnings to the 1930s* (New York: Alfred A. Knopf, 1984); and Patricia Albjerg Graham, "Expansion and Exclusion: A History of Women in American Higher Education," *Signs* 3 (1978): 759–773. Earlier studies include Mabel Newcomer, *A Century of Higher Education for American Women* (New York: Harper, 1959); and Thomas Woody, *A History of Women's Education in the United States*, 2 vols. (New York: Science Press, 1929).

3. Solomon, *In the Company of Educated Women*, p. 44.

4. See, for example, Carroll Smith-Rosenberg and Charles Rosenberg, "The Female Animal: Medical and Biological Views of Woman and Her Role in Nineteenth-Century America," *Journal of American History* 60 (1973): 332–356; and Martha H. Verbrugge, *Able-Bodied Womanhood: Personal Health and Social Change in Nineteenth-Century Boston* (New York: Oxford University Press, 1988), esp. pp. 97–138.

5. As quoted in Karen Berger Morello, *The Invisible Bar: The Woman Lawyer in America, 1638 to the Present* (New York: Random House, 1986), p. 46.

6. Edward H. Clarke, *Sex in Education; or, A Fair Chance for the Girls* (Boston: James R. Osgood, 1873). For an insightful analysis of Clarke, see Rosalind Rosenberg, *Beyond Separate Spheres: Intellectual Roots of Modern Feminism* (New Haven, Conn.: Yale University Press, 1982), esp. pp. 5–27.

7. Four books challenging Clarke appeared in 1874, the year after *Sex in Education* was originally published: Anna C. Brackett, ed., *The Education of American Girls Considered in a Series of Essays* (New York: G. P. Putnam, 1874); Julia Ward Howe, ed., *Sex in Education: A Reply to Dr. E. H. Clarke's "Sex in Education"* (Boston: Roberts, 1874); George Fisk Comfort and A. M. Comfort, *Woman's Education and Woman's Health: Chiefly in Reply to "Sex in Education"* (Syracuse, N.Y.: Thomas W. Durston, 1874); and Eliza Bisbee Duffey, *No Sex in Education; or, An Equal Chance for Both Boys and Girls* (Philadelphia: J. M. Stoddart, 1874). Several years later, Dr. Mary Putnam Jacobi wrote her celebrated attack on Clarke, which won her the prestigious Boylston Medical Prize at Harvard Medical School. See Mary Putnam Jacobi, *The Question of Rest for Women during Menstruation* (New York: G. P. Putnam's Sons, 1877).

8. M. Carey Thomas, "Present Tendencies in Women's Colleges and University Education," *Education Review* 25 (1908): 68.

9. Olive San Louie Anderson, *An American Girl and Her Four Years in a Boys' College* (New York: D. Appleton, 1878). On Anderson's novel, see Dorothy Gies McGuigan, *A Dangerous Experiment: One Hundred Years of Women at the University of Michigan* (Ann Arbor: University of Michigan Press, 1970), pp. 47–52.

10. Robert Stevens, *Law School: Legal Education in America from the 1850s to the*

1980s (Chapel Hill: University of North Carolina Press, 1983), p. 4; and Lawrence M. Friedman, *A History of American Law* (New York: Simon & Schuster, 1985), pp. 318–322.

11. Stevens, *Law School,* p. 8.

12. This discussion is based primarily on ibid., esp. pp. 3–50. See also Jerold Auerbach, *Unequal Justice: Lawyers and Social Change in Modern America* (New York: Oxford University Press, 1976), pp. 14–39; and Friedman, *A History of American Law,* pp. 606–610.

13. Stevens, *Law School,* pp. 25, 36.

14. For an analysis of the effects of an all-women's medical institution on women doctors, see Virginia G. Drachman, *Hospital with a Heart: Women Doctors and the Paradox of Separatism at the New England Hospital, 1862 to 1969* (Ithaca, N.Y.: Cornell University Press, 1984). More generally, see Mary Roth Walsh, *"Doctors Wanted: No Women Need Apply": Sexual Barriers in the Medical Profession, 1835–1975* (New Haven, Conn.: Yale University Press, 1977); Regina Markell Morantz-Sanchez, *Sympathy and Science: Women Physicians in American Medicine* (New York: Oxford University Press, 1985); and Gloria Melnik Moldow, *Women Doctors in Gilded-Age Washington: Race, Gender, and Professionalization* (Champaign: Illinois University Press, 1987).

15. "Concerning Women," *Woman's Journal* 1 (1870): 114; and *Woman's Journal* 33 (1902): 68.

16. Allan Nevins and Milton Halsey Thomas, eds., *The Diary of George Templeton Strong: Post-War Years, 1865–1875* (New York: Macmillan, 1952), p. 256.

17. M. C. Klingelsmith, "A Pioneer Woman Lawyer of Pennsylvania," 9 *Women Lawyers' Journal* 18 (1920).

18. "News and Notes," *Woman's Journal* 2 (1871): 349. See also Arthur E. Sutherland, *The Law at Harvard: A History of Ideas and Men, 1817–1967* (Cambridge, Mass.: Harvard University Press, 1967), pp. 319–320.

19. Mary Greene, "Women in the Law," *Woman's Journal* 22 (1891): 56.

20. Anthony Chase, "The Birth of the Modern Law School," 23 *American Journal of Legal History* 329–348 (1979).

21. Frederick C. Hicks, *Yale Law School: 1869–1894, Including the County Court House Period* (New Haven, Conn.: Yale University Press, 1937), p. 72.

22. Belva A. Lockwood, "My Efforts to Become a Lawyer," *Lippincott's Monthly Magazine* (Jan.–June 1888): 215–229, quotation from p. 222. Also on Lockwood see Madeleine Stern, *We the Women: Career Firsts of Nineteenth-Century America* (New York: Schult, 1963), pp. 205–234; Edward T. James, ed., *Notable American Women, 1607–1950: A Biographical Dictionary* (Cambridge, Mass.: Harvard University Press, 1971), pp. 413–416; and Julia Davis, "A Feisty Schoolmarm Made the Lawyers Sit Up and Take Notice," *Smithsonian* (Mar. 1981): 133–150. Various newspapers, including the *New York Times* and the *Chicago Legal News,* followed Lockwood's attempts to gain admission to practice law. See, for example, "Women as Attorneys," *New York Times,* May 12, 1874, p. 1; "Women Lawyers," *New York Times,* Oct. 19, 1878, p. 3; "The United States Supreme Court," *New*

York Times, Mar. 3, 1879, p. 5; "Mrs. Lockwood in Maryland," *New York Times,* May 11, 1881, p. 1; Belva A. Lockwood, "Shall Women Be Admitted to the Bar?" *Chicago Legal News,* Mar. 30, 1878, pp. 224–225; B. A. Lockwood, "Mrs. Lockwood's Case," *Chicago Legal News,* Nov. 16, 1878, pp. 70–71; and "Admission of Women to the Bar," *Chicago Legal News,* Feb. 15, 1879, p. 179. See Lockwood Papers and the Peace Collection of Swarthmore College, Swarthmore, Pennsylvania.

23. Lockwood, "My Efforts to Become a Lawyer," p. 224.

24. See Belva A. McNall Lockwood to Frank Smalley, Dean of College of Liberal Arts, National University, Feb. 16, 1906, Lockwood Papers.

25. On the history of Howard University Law School, see Walter Dyson, *Howard University: The Capstone of Negro Education, A History: 1867–1940* (Washington, D.C.: Howard University Press, 1941), pp. 219–238. On John Mercer Langston, see Maxwell Bloomfield, *American Lawyers in a Changing Society, 1776–1876* (Cambridge, Mass.: Harvard University Press, 1976), pp. 302–339.

26. Moldow, *Women Doctors in Gilded-Age Washington,* pp. 37–47.

27. Lelia J. Robinson, "Women Lawyers in the United States," 2 *Green Bag* 28 (1890). Years later, Mary Ann Shadd Cary enrolled again at Howard and received her diploma in 1883. Also on Cary, see Shirley J. Yee, *Black Women Abolitionists: A Study in Activism, 1828–1860* (Knoxville: University of Tennessee Press, 1992).

28. On Charlotte Ray, see Darlene Clark Hine, ed., *Black Women in America: An Historical Encyclopedia,* vol. 2 (Brooklyn, N.Y.: Carlson, 1993), pp. 965–966; *Notable American Women,* pp. 121–122; Robinson, "Women Lawyers," p. 28; Phebe A. Hanaford, *Daughters of America; or Women of the Century* (Augusta, Ga.: True and Company, 1882), p. 649; "Concerning Women," *Women's Journal* 3 (1872): 97; "The Legal World Moves," *Chicago Legal News,* Mar. 23, 1872, p. 186; and Morello, *Invisible Bar,* pp. 145–148.

29. *President's Report,* Howard University, 1870, as quoted in *Notable American Women,* p. 121.

30. Hanaford, *Daughters of America,* p. 649.

31. Calculated from the list of women graduates of the law school, 1872 to 1940 in Dyson, *Howard University,* pp. 237–238.

32. Lelia Robinson made this observation in her "Women Lawyers," p. 13.

33. Emlin McClain, "Law Department of the State University of Iowa," 1 *Green Bag* 374–394, quotation from 377 (1889).

34. Morello, *Invisible Bar,* p. 46.

35. Elizabeth Gaspar Brown, *Legal Education at Michigan, 1859–1959* (Ann Arbor: University of Michigan Law School, 1959); Stevens, *Law School;* and Henry Wade Rogers, "Law School of the University of Michigan," 1 *Green Bag* 189–208 (1889).

36. See Eleanor Rust Collier, "The Boston University School of Law, 1872–1900," unpublished manuscript in Boston University Law School Archives, Pappas Law Library, Boston University Law School; "Decades of Progress: The

Beginning Years, 1872–1900," *Brief* (fall 1977): pp. 18–24; George R. Swasey, "Boston University Law School," 1 *Green Bag* 54 (1889); and Stevens, *Law School*, p. 82.

37. Mortimer D. Schwartz, Susan L. Brandt, and Patience Milrod, "Clara Shortridge Foltz: Pioneer in the Law," 27 *Hastings Law Review* 545–564 (1976); Barbara Allen Babcock, "Clara Shortridge Foltz: 'First Woman,'" 30 *Arizona Law Review* 673–717 (1988); Barbara Allen Babcock, "Reconstructing the Person: The Case of Clara Shortridge Foltz," *Biography* 12 (1989): 5–16; Barbara Allen Babcock, "Clara Shortridge Foltz: Constitution-Maker," 66 *Indiana Law Journal* 849–940 (1991); and *Notable American Women*, pp. 641–643. See also "In Memoriam," 21 *Women Lawyers' Journal* 52–53 (1934); and Oscar T. Shuck, *History of the Bench and Bar of California: History, Anecdotes, Reminiscences* (San Francisco: Occident Printing House, 1889), pp. 828–832.

38. Foltz v. Hoge, 54 Cal. 28 (1879). On the case that Foltz and Gordon brought against Hastings College of Law, see Babcock, "Clara Shortridge Foltz: Constitution-Maker"; Charles W. Slack, "Hastings College of the Law," 12 *Green Bag* 518–526 (1889); and Thomas Garden Barnes, *Hastings College of the Law: The First Century* (San Francisco: University of California, Hastings College of the Law Press, 1978), pp. 47–61.

39. Babcock, "Clara Shortridge Foltz: 'First Woman'," p. 712.

40. In 1882, Mary McHenry became the first woman to graduate from Hastings College of Law.

41. Stevens, *Law School*, p. 83.

42. Robinson, "Women Lawyers," 12–13; Greene, "Women in the Law," 56; Hicks, *Yale Law School*, pp. 73–75; and "The First Woman Student at Yale," *Chicago Legal News*, Oct. 1885, p. 59.

43. Hicks, *Yale Law School*, p. 73.

44. "The First Woman Student at Yale."

45. Hicks, *Yale Law School*, pp. 74–75.

46. Greene, "Women in the Law."

47. On Carrie Burnham Kilgore, see Margaret C. Klingelsmith, "A Pioneer Woman Lawyer of Pennsylvania"; Klingelsmith, "Women Lawyers in Pennsylvania," 5 *Women Lawyers' Journal* 22 (1915); "Application of a Woman for Admission to the Philadelphia Bar," *Chicago Legal News*, Jan. 1875, p. 135; and *Notable American Women*, pp. 329–330.

48. Klingelsmith, "Pioneer Woman Lawyer of Pennsylvania."

49. The Equity Club letters have been reprinted in Virginia G. Drachman, *Women Lawyers and the Origins of Professional Identity in America: The Letters of the Equity Club, 1887 to 1890* (Ann Arbor: University of Michigan, 1993). See Emma M. Gillett to Equity Club, Apr. 18, 1888, at p. 96. The original letters are in the Lelia Josephine Robinson Papers, ser. 9, Dillon Collection.

50. Almeda E. Hitchcock to Equity Club, Apr. 30, 1888, in Drachman, *Women Lawyers*, p. 103. On Hitchcock, see Drachman, *Women Lawyers*, pp. 233–235, and Suzanne Espennet Case, "Almeda Eliza Hitchcock (Moore)," in Mari

J. Matsuda, ed., *Called from Within: Early Women Lawyers of Hawaii* (Honolulu: University of Hawaii Press, 1992), pp. 17–36.

51. Letitia L. Burlingame to Equity Club, Apr. 23, 1887, in Drachman, *Women Lawyers*, pp. 45–47, quotation from p. 45.

52. Margaret Lyons Wilcox to Equity Club, May 2, 1887, in ibid., pp. 70–72, quotation from p. 70.

53. Jane M. Slocum to Equity Club, [1887], in ibid., pp. 67–70, in particular p. 69. Jane Slocum was unique because she studied law at the University of Michigan to improve her teaching.

54. From undated and unidentified materials in the Phoebe Couzins Collection, Missouri Historical Society, St. Louis, as quoted in Morello, *Invisible Bar*, p. 46.

55. Mary A. Greene to Equity Club, Apr. 27, 1887, in Drachman, *Women Lawyers*, pp. 51–53, quotation from p. 53.

56. Douglas Lamar Jones, "Lelia J. Robinson's Case and the Entry of Women into the Legal Profession in Massachusetts," in Russell K. Osgood, ed., *The History of the Law in Massachusetts: The Supreme Judicial Court, 1692–1992* (Charlottesville: University of Virginia Press, 1992), pp. 241–274.

57. Clara Shortridge Foltz, "Struggles and Triumphs of a Woman Lawyer," *New American Woman* (Nov. 1916): 12, as quoted in Schwartz et al., "Clara Shortridge Foltz: Pioneer in the Law," p. 551.

58. Klingelsmith, "A Pioneer Woman Lawyer of Pennsylvania," p. 18.

59. "Miss Alice Jordan Makes Her Debut in a Moot Court at Law," *Chicago Legal News*, May 8, 1886, p. 293.

60. Dyson, *Howard University*, p. 231.

61. Howard University, *President's Report, 1870*, as quoted in *Notable American Women*, p. 121, and Morello, *Invisible Bar*, p. 146.

62. Robinson, "Women Lawyers," p. 28.

63. Undated and unidentified materials from the Phoebe Couzins Collection of the Missouri Historical Society, St. Louis, as quoted in Morello, *Invisible Bar*, pp. 46–47.

64. Emma Haddock to Equity Club, May 12, 1888, Iowa City, in Drachman, *Women Lawyers*, pp. 100–102, quotation from p. 101. On Haddock, see ibid., pp. 231–233; Hanaford, *Daughters of America*, pp. 641–642; and Robinson, "Women Lawyers," p. 22.

65. Tiera Farrow, *Lawyer in Petticoats* (New York: Vantage, 1953), pp. 22–23. Farrow was referring to William Blackstone, *Commentaries on the Laws of England*. See Bernard C. Gavit, ed., *Blackstone's Commentaries on the Law* (Washington, D.C.: Washington Law Book Co., 1941).

66. See Lelia Josephine Robinson to Equity Club, Apr. 7, 1888, in Drachman, *Women Lawyers*, pp. 126–127, quotation from p. 127; and Lelia Robinson Sawtelle's letter to the editor, *Woman's Journal*, Mar. 17, 1891, printed in *Woman's Journal* 22 (1891): 90. See also Jones, "Lelia J. Robinson's Case."

67. Jessie E. Wright to Equity Club, Apr. 23, 1888, in Drachman, *Women*

Lawyers, pp. 141–145, quotation from p. 141. On Jessie Wright Whitcomb, see Drachman, *Women Lawyers*, pp. 273–275; Whitcomb's memoir, "Reminiscences," in the Kansas State Historical Society, Topeka, Kansas; and Robinson, "Women Lawyers," 30.

68. Mary A. Greene to Equity Club, Apr. 5, 1888, in Drachman, *Women Lawyers*, pp. 97–99, quotation from p. 97.

69. Mary A. Greene to Equity Club, Apr. 27, 1887, in ibid., pp. 51–53, in particular p. 52.

70. Robinson, "Women Lawyers," 30; and *A Catalogue of the Graduates of the Boston University Law School, 1873–1905* (Boston: Boston University, 1905), pp. 79–80.

71. Catharine Waugh McCulloch, "1903 Class Day on Evanston Campus," unpublished paper in box 3, folder 39, Catharine Waugh McCulloch Papers, ser. 6, Dillon Collection.

72. Ibid.

73. Ibid.

74. Ibid.

75. On women medical students at the University of Michigan, see "Women in the Medical School," *Chronicle* 1 (1869–1870): 216. See also McGuigan, *A Dangerous Experiment*, pp. 31–37.

76. Jane M. Slocum to Equity Club, [1887], in Drachman, *Women Lawyers*, pp. 67–70, quotation from p. 68.

77. O. C. Burlingame, ed., *Lettie Lavilla Burlingame: Her Life Pages, Stories, Poems and Essays* (Joliet, Ill.: J. E. Williams, 1895), p. 318.

78. Almeda E. Hitchcock to Equity Club, Apr. 30, 1888, in Drachman, *Women Lawyers*, pp. 103–104, quotation from p. 104.

79. Martha K. Pearce, Report of the Corresponding Secretary, 1888, in ibid., pp. 75–87, quotation from p. 79.

80. "Women at Ann Arbor," *Woman's Journal* 4 (1873): 315.

81. Thomas McIntyre Cooley was best known for *A Treatise on the Constitutional Limitations Which Rest upon the Legislative Power of the States of the American Union* (Boston: Little, Brown, 1868). Slocum's quotations are from her letter to the Equity Club, [1887], in Drachman, *Women Lawyers*, p. 68.

82. Cora A. Benneson to Equity Club, Dec. 12, 1887, in ibid., pp. 43–45, quotation from p. 43.

83. Robinson, "Women Lawyers," 16.

84. Lettie L. Burlingame to Equity Club, May 17, 1888, in Drachman, *Women Lawyers*, pp. 91–93, in particular p. 92.

85. Thomas Cooley to A. D. White, June 5, 1871, Cooley Collection.

86. Ibid.

87. Jane M. Slocum to Judge Cooley, June 17, 18[73], Ann Arbor, box 1, Cooley Collection.

88. Cora Agnes Benneson, "Life of Women at Michigan University," *Woman's Journal* 21 (Aug. 3, 1889).

89. Brown, *Legal Education at Michigan*, pp. 700–702.

90. Thomas Cooley to A. D. White, June 5, 1871, Cooley Collection.

91. Burlingame, *Lettie Lavilla Burlingame*, pp. 98–99.

92. Ibid., p. 316.

93. Ibid., p. 323.

94. Ibid., p. 326.

95. Ibid., pp. 323–324. See also Pearce, Report of the Corresponding Secretary, 1888, pp. 76–77.

96. Martha K. Pearce to Equity Club, [1887], in Drachman, *Women Lawyers*, pp. 62–63.

97. Laura de F. Gordon to Equity Club, Apr. 26, 1887, in ibid., pp. 50–51, quotation from p. 50.

98. Stevens, *Law School*, p. 76.

99. Hitchcock to Equity Club, Apr. 30, 1888, in Drachman, *Women Lawyers*, pp. 103–104.

100. Stevens, *Law School*, p. 76.

3. "Sweeter Manners, Purer Laws"

1. Lelia J. Robinson to Equity Club, Apr. 9, 1887, in Virginia G. Drachman, *Women Lawyers and the Origins of Professional Identity in America: The Letters of the Equity Club, 1887 to 1890* (Ann Arbor: University of Michigan Press, 1993), pp. 64–67, quotation from p. 66; also quoted in Nancy F. Cott, *The Grounding of Modern Feminism* (New Haven, Conn.: Yale University Press, 1987), p. 232.

2. Sara K. Wertman to Equity Club, May 7, 1888, in Drachman, *Women Lawyers*, p. 138.

3. Martha K. Pearce to Equity Club, [1887], in ibid., pp. 62–63, quotation from p. 63; also quoted in Cott, *Grounding of Modern Feminism*, p. 232. In 1903, W. E. B. DuBois identified a similar tension for African Americans between race and national identity. See W. E. Barghardt Du Bois, *The Souls of Black Folk* (New York: New American Library, 1969), pp. 45–47. This task of balancing gender and professional identity still faced women lawyers in the 1960s and 1970s. See Cynthia Fuchs Epstein's *Women in Law* (New York: Basic Books, 1981). More recently, Martha Minow confronted the problem of difference for women as they are treated under the law in her *Making All the Difference: Inclusion, Exclusion, and American Law* (Ithaca, N.Y.: Cornell University Press, 1990).

4. Michael Grossberg, "Institutionalizing Masculinity: The Law as a Masculine Profession," in Mark C. Carnes and Clyde Griffen, eds., *Meanings for Manhood: Constructions of Manhood in Victorian America* (Chicago: University of Chicago Press, 1990), pp. 133–151, and Daniel H. Calhoun, *Professional Lives in America: Structure and Aspiration, 1750–1850* (Cambridge, Mass.: Harvard University Press, 1965), pp. 59–87.

5. On the influence of the gender-role conflict on all women in nineteenth-century America, see William Leach, *True Love and Perfect Union: The Femi-*

nist Reform of Sex and Society (New York: Basic Books, 1980); and Carroll Smith-Rosenberg, "Beauty, the Beast, and the Militant Woman: A Case Study in Sex Roles and Social Stress in Jacksonian America," in Smith-Rosenberg, *Disorderly Conduct: Visions of Gender in Victorian America* (New York: Oxford University Press, 1985) pp. 109–128. For background on how the conflict between gender and professional identity affected nineteenth-century women doctors, see Virginia G. Drachman, *Hospital with a Heart: Women Doctors and the Paradox of Separatism at the New England Hospital, 1862–1969* (Ithaca, N.Y.: University of Cornell Press, 1984), pp. 103–177; and Regina Markell Morantz-Sanchez, *Sympathy and Science: Women Physicians in American Medicine* (New York: Oxford University Press, 1985), pp. 184–203. On the conflict's effect on nineteenth-century women in science, see Margaret W. Rossiter, *Women Scientists in America: Struggles and Strategies to 1940* (Baltimore, Md.: Johns Hopkins University Press, 1982), pp. 51–99. On women in the social sciences, see Rosalind Rosenberg, *Beyond Separate Spheres: Intellectual Roots of Feminism* (New Haven, Conn.: Yale University Press, 1982). See also Lori D. Ginzberg, *Women and the Work of Benevolence: Morality, Politics, and Class in the Nineteenth-Century United States* (New Haven, Conn.: Yale University Press, 1990).

6. On the rise of the women's club movement in the nineteenth century, see Karen J. Blair, *The Club Woman as Feminist: True Womanhood Redefined, 1868–1914* (New York: Holmes and Meier, 1980).

7. See Table 2. The following discussion of the Equity Club is drawn from Drachman, *Women Lawyers.*

8. Martha Pearce, Report of the Corresponding Secretary of the Equity Club, 1888, in Drachman, *Women Lawyers,* pp. 75–87, quotation from p. 79.

9. William Shakespeare, *The Merchant of Venice,* ed. Brents Stirling (New York: Penguin, 1987), pp. 100–101. Male lawyers were aware of the power of Shakespeare's Portia as a symbol of women in the law. See untitled note in 6 *Albany Law Journal* 184 (1873). I would like to thank David Chambers for suggesting to me the interpretive meaning of equity for the Equity Club. On the history of the equity courts, see Stanley N. Katz, "The Politics of Law in Colonial America: Controversies over Chancery Courts and Equity Law in the Eighteenth Century," in Donald Fleming and Bernard Bailyn, eds., *Perspectives in American History: Law in American History* (Cambridge, Mass.: Harvard University Press, 1971), pp. 257–284; Arthur R. Hogue, *Origins of the Common Law* (Bloomington: Indiana University Press, 1966), pp. 157, 165–167, 177–178; and Bernard C. Gavit, ed., *Blackstone's Commentaries on the Law* (Washington, D.C.: Washington Law Book Co., 1941). For the standard treatise on equity law, see John Norton Pomeroy, LL.D., *A Treatise on Equity Jurisprudence as Administered in the United States of America,* 3 vols. (San Francisco: A. L. Bancroft, 1881). On the effect of equity jurisprudence on women's legal status, see Linda K. Kerber, *Women of the Republic: Intellect and Ideology in Revolutionary America* (New York: W. W. Norton, 1980), pp. 139–155; and Joan Hoff, *Law, Gender, and Injustice: A Legal History of U.S. Women* (New York: New York University Press, 1991).

10. O. C. Burlingame, ed., *Lettie Lavilla Burlingame: Her Life Pages. Stories, Poems, and Essays* (Joliet, Ill.: H. E. Williams, 1895), p. 322.

11. Pearce, Report of the Corresponding Secretary, 1888, p. 78.

12. Martha K. Pearce, Report of the Corresponding Secretary, 1889, in Drachman, *Women Lawyers*, pp. 150–151, quotation from p. 150.

13. On Waite, see ibid., pp. 268–271; Edward T. James, ed., *Notable American Women, 1607–1950: A Biographical Dictionary* (Cambridge, Mass.: Harvard University Press, 1971), pp. 523–525; and James Grant Wilson and John Fiske, eds., *Appleton's Cyclopedia of American Biography*, vol. 6 (New York: D. Appleton, 1889), p. 317. Catharine Waugh McCulloch wrote a biographical sketch of Waite, "Catharine Van Valkenburg Waite, Lawyer," typewritten sketch, n.d., in box 4, folder 87, McCulloch Papers, ser. 6, Dillon Collection. An obituary is in *Chicago Legal News*, Nov. 15, 1913, p. 117.

14. Burlingame, *Lettie Lavilla Burlingame*, p. 325.

15. *Annual Report of the New England Hospital*, 1867, p. 12. See Drachman, *Hospital with a Heart*, esp. pp. 44–70; Walsh, *"Doctors Wanted,"* pp. 76–105; and Morantz-Sanchez, *Sympathy and Science*, pp. 144–202.

16. "Modern Portias in Practice," *New York Times*, Mar. 11, 1894, p. 16.

17. Corinne Williams Douglas to Equity Club, May 7, 1887, in Drachman, *Women Lawyers*, pp. 48–50, quotation from pp. 48–49.

18. Mary A. Greene to Equity Club, Apr. 5, 1888, in ibid., pp. 97–99, quotation from p. 97.

19. Greene to Equity Club, Apr. 27, 1887, in ibid., pp. 51–53, quotation from p. 52.

20. Emma Haddock to Equity Club, May 12, 1888, in ibid., pp. 100–102, quotation from p. 102.

21. Greene to Equity Club, Apr. 27, 1887, in ibid., quotation from p. 52.

22. Tiera Farrow, *Lawyer in Petticoats* (New York: Vantage, 1953), p. 24.

23. Laura de F. Gordon to Equity Club, Apr. 26, 1887, in Drachman, *Women Lawyers*, pp. 50–51, quotation from p. 51.

24. Margaret L. Wilcox to Equity Club, Apr. 20, 1888, in ibid., pp. 138–141, quotation from p. 139.

25. Martha Strickland, "Woman and the Forum," 3 *Green Bag* 240–243, quotation from 242 (1891). For a response by male lawyers to Strickland's article, see "Current Topics," 43 *Albany Law Journal* 406 (1891).

26. Strickland, "Woman and the Forum," p. 240.

27. Ibid.

28. Ibid., p. 242.

29. Ibid., p. 241.

30. Ibid., pp. 241–242.

31. Ibid., p. 243.

32. Ada H. Kepley to Equity Club, July 3, 1888, in Drachman, *Women Lawyers*, pp. 106–108, quotation from p. 108.

33. Wertman to Equity Club, May 7, 1888, in ibid., p. 138.

34. Ibid.

35. James P. Root quoted in "M. Fredrika Perry," *Chicago Legal News,* June 30, 1883, pp. 825–826, quotation from p. 825.

36. Ibid., p. 826.

37. Robinson to Equity Club, Apr. 9, 1887 in Drachman, *Women Lawyers,* p. 66.

38. Florence Cronise to Equity Club, [1889], in ibid., pp. 157–159, all quotations from p. 158.

39. See Ginzberg, *Women and the Work of Benevolence;* and Angel Kwolek-Folland, *Engendering Business: Men and Women in the Corporate Office, 1870–1930* (Baltimore, Md.: Johns Hopkins University Press, 1994).

40. Thomas Wharton, "The Lady Lawyer's First Client," pt. 1, *Lippincott's Magazine* (Oct. 1885): 334–347, and pt. 2 (Nov. 1885): 429–439.

41. Ibid., p. 434.

42. Ibid.

43. Ibid., p. 436.

44. Ibid., p. 434.

45. Lelia Josephine Robinson to Equity Club, Apr. 7, 1888, in Drachman, *Women Lawyers,* pp. 117–127, quotation from p. 117–118.

46. Ellen A. Martin to Equity Club, May 25, 1888, in ibid., pp. 112–116, quotation from p. 115.

47. Emma M. Gillett to Equity Club, Apr. 18, 1888, in ibid., pp. 96–97, quotation from pp. 96–97.

48. Florence Cronise to Equity Club, [1889], in ibid., pp. 157–159, quotation from p. 158.

49. Emma M. Gillett to Equity Club, Apr. 27, 1889 in ibid., pp. 159–162, quotation from p. 161.

50. Ibid., p. 161.

51. Ibid.

52. Marion Todd to Equity Club, Apr. 4, 1888, in ibid., pp. 128–132, quotation from p. 130.

53. Mortimer D. Schwartz, Susan L. Brandt, and Patience Milrod, "Clara Shortridge Foltz," 27 *Hastings Law Journal* 545–564, quotation from 555 (1976).

54. Advertisement of Lelia Robinson Sawtelle in *Woman's Journal* 22 (1891): 35, and Sarah Deutsch, "Learning to Talk More Like a Man: Boston's Women's Class-Bridging Organizations, 1870–1940," 97 *American Historical Review* (1992): 379, 394.

55. Lelia Josephine Robinson, *Law Made Easy: A Book for the People* (Chicago: Sanitary Publishing, 1886), and *The Law of Husband and Wife* (Boston: Lee and Shepard, 1889).

56. On Lelia Robinson, see Douglas Lamar Jones, "Lelia J. Robinson's Case and the Entry of Women into the Legal Profession in Massachusetts," in Russell K. Osgood, ed., *The History of the Law in Massachusetts: The Supreme Judicial Court,*

1692–1992 (Charlottesville: University of Virginia Press, 1992), pp. 241–274; and Drachman, *Women Lawyers*, pp. 257–262. See also Mary A. Greene, "Mrs. Lelia Robinson Sawtelle—First Woman Lawyer of Massachusetts," in 7 *Woman Lawyers' Journal* 51 (1890); and "Miss Lelia Josephine Robinson," *Chicago Legal News*, Jan. 4, 1890, p. 147.

57. Catharine G. Waugh to Equity Club, Apr. 26, 1889, in Drachman, *Women Lawyers*, pp. 173–177, quotation from p. 174.

58. Ibid., p. 174.

59. Ibid.

60. Florence Cronise to Equity Club, May 23, 1888, in ibid., pp. 94–95, quotation from p. 95.

61. Kepley to Equity Club, July 3, 1888, in ibid., p. 108.

62. Ada M. Bittenbender to Equity Club, May 10, 1889, in ibid., pp. 151–154, quotation from p. 153.

63. Ada M. Bittenbender to Equity Club, Apr. 27, 1887, in ibid., pp. 90–91, quotation from p. 90.

64. See, for example, William P. Rogers, "Is Law a Field for Women's Work?" 24 *American Bar Association Reports* 548, 561–562 (1884), and Daniel H. Calhoun, *Professional Lives in America: Structure and Aspiration, 1750–1850* (Cambridge, Mass.: Harvard University Press, 1965), pp. 59–87.

65. *In re* Motion to Admit Miss Lavinia Goodell to the Bar of This Court, 39 Wisc. 232, 246 (1875). For the views of other male judges and attorneys on women lawyers, see "Our Learned Brother: Interviewed as to His Attitude Toward His Sister in Law," *New York Times*, June 16, 1895, p. 26.

66. "Paper of A. H. Davis," in "Symposium on Women at the Georgia Bar," 11 *Georgia Bar Association Reports* 548, quotation from 561 (1884).

67. Marcus Reed, "Is Portia Possible?" *MacMillan's Magazine* (Mar. 1906): 375–382, quotations from pp. 375, 377.

68. The cartoon appeared as the frontispiece to the Equity Club Annual, 1888, on file in Robinson Papers, ser. 9, folder 346, Dillon Collection. For another discussion of the dangers posed by pretty women lawyers, see "Beauty as an Asset for Women Lawyers," 12 *Law Notes* 165 (1908).

69. "Woman—What She Is and What She Is Not, in the Opinion of Judge Grosscup," *New York Times*, Nov. 7, 1909, sec. 5, p. 4. For similar views, see "Current Topics," 43 *Albany Law Journal* 405 (1891).

70. Thomas Wharton, "The Lady Lawyer's First Client," p. 434.

71. "A Lady among the Lawyers," *Chicago Legal News*, Oct. 29, 1870, p. 36.

72. Douglas to Equity Club, May 7, 1887, in Drachman, *Women Lawyers*, p. 49.

73. Robinson, "Women Lawyers," 15.

74. Gillett to Equity Club, Apr. 18, 1888, in Drachman, *Women Lawyers*, p. 96.

75. On Hall see Robinson, "Women Lawyers," 29.

76. See Robinson to Equity Club, Apr. 9, 1887 in Drachman, *Women Lawyers*,

pp. 64–67; Cronise to Equity Club, May 23, 1888, in Drachman, *Women Lawyers*, pp. 94–95; and Lettie L. Burlingame to Equity Club, Apr. 22, 1889, in Drachman, *Women Lawyers*, pp. 154–157.

77. Burlingame to Equity Club, Apr. 22, 1889, in Drachman, *Women Lawyers*, p. 155.

78. Martin to Equity Club, May 25, 1888, in ibid., p. 113.

79. Robinson to Equity Club, Apr. 9, 1887, in ibid., p. 65.

80. Robinson to Equity Club, Apr. 7, 1888, in ibid., p. 125.

81. Emma M. Gillett to Equity Club, Apr. 27, 1889, in ibid., pp. 159–162, in particular p. 159.

82. Gillett to Equity Club, July 30, 1890, in ibid., pp. 184–185.

83. Catharine G. Waugh to Equity Club, Apr. 26, 1889, in ibid., pp. 173–177, quotation from p. 174.

84. Martin to Equity Club, May 25, 1888, in ibid., p. 113.

85. Ibid. See also " 'Girl Lawyer Has Small Chance for Success,' Says Mrs. Lesser," *Saturday Evening Traveller* (Boston), June 8, 1912.

86. Ada M. Bittenbender to Equity Club, Apr. 27, 1888, in Drachman, *Women Lawyers*, pp. 90–91.

87. Cronise to Equity Club, May 23, 1888, in ibid., p. 95.

88. Lettie L. Burlingame to Equity Club, May 17, 1888, in ibid., pp. 91–93, quotation from p. 92.

89. Burlingame to Equity Club, Apr. 22, 1889, in ibid., p. 155.

90. Almeda E. Hitchcock to Equity Club, Aug. 28, 1890, in ibid., pp. 188–189, quotation from p. 188.

91. Robinson to Equity Club, Apr. 7, 1888, in ibid., p. 121.

92. Ibid.

93. Ibid., pp. 121–125.

94. Waugh to Equity Club, Apr. 26, 1889, in ibid., pp. 175–176.

95. "Milwaukee's Woman Lawyer," *New York Times*, Apr. 22, 1883, p. 1; see also "Miss Kane Again in Jail," *New York Times*, May 1, 1883, p. 1.

96. See "Milwaukee's Woman Lawyer"; and "Miss Kane's Revenge," *New York Times*, Apr. 23, 1883, p. 4.

97. All quotes are from "Miss Kane's Revenge."

98. Kane moved to Chicago in 1883 where she was a successful criminal defense lawyer. Also on Kane see "Miss Kate Kane," *Chicago Legal News*, June 28, 1890, p. 359; and [Catharine Waugh McCulloch], "Kate Kane Rossi," typewritten sketch, n.d., in box 12, folder 36, McCulloch Papers.

99. Claudia B. Kidwell, *Cutting a Fashionable Fit: Dressmakers' Drafting Systems in the United States* (Washington, D.C.: Smithsonian Institution Press, 1979), pp. 93–94.

100. Florence Hartley, *The Ladies' Book of Etiquette and Manual of Politeness* (Boston: DeWolfe, Fiske, 1873), pp. 21–33; and Mme. Gertrude G. de Aguirre, *Women in the Business World or Hints and Helps to Prosperity* (Boston: Arena, 1894), pp. 98–104.

101. Catharine G. Waugh to Equity Club, May 2, 1888, in Drachman, *Women Lawyers*, pp. 133–137, quotation from p. 135.

102. "Mrs. Belva Lockwood Breaks a Tradition," *Washington D.C. Star*, Feb. 7, 1954; and Julia Davis, "A Feisty Schoolmarm Made the Lawyers Sit Up and Take Notice," *Smithsonian* (Mar. 1981): 133–150, esp. p. 138.

103. *San Francisco Chronicle*, Feb. 25, 1879, p. 1, cited in Barbara Allen Babcock, "Clara Shortridge Foltz: 'First Woman,' " 30 *Arizona Law Review* 673–717, quotation from 709 (1988).

104. Ibid., p. 709.

105. Joan Nunn, *Fashion in Costume, 1200–1980* (New York: Schocken, 1984); Elizabeth Ewing, *History of Twentieth-Century Fashion* (Totowa, N.J.: Barnes and Noble, 1974); Lois W. Banner, *American Beauty* (New York: Alfred A. Knopf, 1983); and Mrs. Burton Harrison, *The Well-Bred Girl in Society* (New York: McClure, 1898), pp. 27–28, 44–45.

106. Robinson to Equity Club, Apr. 7, 1888, in Drachman, *Women Lawyers*, p. 127.

107. Ibid.

108. Ibid.

109. Waugh to Equity Club, May 2, 1888, in ibid., p. 134.

110. *San Francisco Call*, Feb. 25, 1879, cited in Babcock, "Clara Shortridge Foltz," 709.

111. "Should a Woman Lawyer Wear Her Hat in Court?" *Chicago Legal News*, Mar. 25, 1876, p. 530.

112. Wharton, "Lady Lawyer's First Client," pp. 337–338.

113. Burlingame to Equity Club, May 17, 1888, in Drachman, *Women Lawyers*, p. 92.

114. Ibid.

115. Margaret L. Wilcox to Equity Club, June 1, 1889, in ibid., pp. 177–178, quotation from pp. 177–178.

4. "I *Think* I Haven't Neglected My Husband"

1. Lelia J. Robinson to Equity Club, May 22, 1889, in Virginia G. Drachman, *Women Lawyers and the Origins of Professional Identity in America: The Letters of the Equity Club, 1887–1890* (Ann Arbor: University of Michigan Press, 1993), pp. 168–171, quotation from p. 171.

2. On marriage in the lives of nineteenth-century women doctors, see Regina Markell Morantz-Sanchez, *Sympathy and Science: Women Physicians in American Medicine* (New York: Oxford University Press, 1985), pp. 129–143; Regina Markell Morantz-Sanchez, "The Many Faces of Intimacy: Professional Options and Personal Choices Among Nineteenth- and Twentieth-Century Women Physicians," in Penina G. Abir-Am and Dorinda Outram, eds., *Uneasy Careers and Intimate Lives: Women in Science, 1789–1979* (New Brunswick, N.J.: Rutgers University Press, 1987); and Virginia G. Drachman, "The Limits of Pro-

gress: Women Doctors' Professional Lives, 1881–1926," *Bulletin of the History of Medicine* 60 (1986): 58–72. On nineteenth-century women scientists, see Nancy G. Slack, "Nineteenth-Century American Women Botanists: Wives, Widows, and Work," in Abir-Am and Outram, *Uneasy Careers and Intimate Lives*, pp. 77–103. On the problem of balancing marriage and career more generally in this era, see William Leach, *True Love and Perfect Union* (New York: Basic Books, 1980), esp. pp. 158–212. For an analysis of marriage as a public institution and its relationship to the state, see Nancy F. Cott, "Giving Character to Our Whole Civil Polity: Marriage and the Public Order in the Late Nineteenth Century," in Linda K. Kerber, Alice Kessler-Harris, and Kathryn Kish Sklar, eds., *U.S. History as Women's History: New Feminist Essays* (Chapel Hill: University of North Carolina Press, 1995), pp. 107–121. See also generally Elaine Tyler May, *Great Expectations: Marriage and Divorce in Post-Victorian America* (Chicago: University of Chicago Press, 1980), pp. 1–72.

3. Marion Todd to Equity Club, Apr. 4, 1888, in Drachman, *Women Lawyers*, pp. 128–132, quotation from p. 130.

4. Mary A. Greene to Equity Club, May 14, 1890, in ibid., pp. 186–187, quotation from p. 187.

5. Emma M. Gillett to Equity Club, Apr. 27, 1889, in ibid., pp. 159–162, quotation from p. 162.

6. Lettie L. Burlingame to Equity Club, Apr. 22, 1889, in ibid., pp. 154–157, quotation from p. 155.

7. Mary A. Greene to Equity Club, Apr. 5, 1888, in ibid., pp. 97–99, quotation from p. 98.

8. Belva A. Lockwood to Equity Club, Apr. 30, 1887, in ibid., pp. 56–59, quotation from p. 58.

9. Florence Cronise to Equity Club, May 23, 1888, in ibid., pp. 94–95, quotation from p. 94.

10. Lelia J. Robinson, "Women Lawyers in the United States," 2 *Green Bag* 10–31, quotation from 11 (1890). The Equity Club members were not a precise mirror of practicing women lawyers because the club included some women who were not currently in practice. The census-takers, counting only practicing women lawyers in 1890, found that 21 percent were married and that 14 percent had been married, widowed, or divorced. As an older, mature group of women, the Equity Club members naturally had a somewhat higher rate of marriage than did the women lawyers found by the census-takers, many of whom were young and as yet unmarried. See Table 9.

11. On women doctors, see Morantz-Sanchez, *Sympathy and Science*, pp. 136–137.

12. Rebecca May to Equity Club, May 1, 1887, in Drachman, *Women Lawyers*, pp. 61–62, quotation from p. 62.

13. Corinne Williams Douglas to Equity Club, May 7, 1887, in ibid., pp. 48–50, quotation from p. 49.

14. Robinson, "Women Lawyers," p. 19.

15. Leona T. Lounsbury to Equity Club, Apr. 27, 1887, in Drachman, *Women Lawyers*, pp. 59–60, quotation from p. 60.

16. Ibid., p. 60.

17. Emma M. Gillett to Equity Club, Apr. 27, 1889, in ibid., p. 159–162, quotation from p. 161.

18. Lelia Josephine Robinson to Equity Club, Apr. 7, 1888, in ibid., pp. 117–127, quotation from p. 118.

19. Lelia Robinson Sawtelle to Equity Club, Sept. 18, 1890, in ibid., pp. 200–201, quotation from p. 200.

20. Lelia Robinson Sawtelle to "My dear little Kitty Waugh," Sept. 5, 1890, Boston, box 2, folder 36, Grace H. Harte Papers, ser. 2, Dillon Collection.

21. Catharine Waugh McCulloch to Equity Club, Nov. 8, 1890, in Drachman, *Women Lawyers*, pp. 191–192, quotation from p. 192.

22. Sawtelle to "Kitty Waugh."

23. Emma Haddock to Equity Club, May 12, 1888, in Drachman, *Women Lawyers*, pp. 100–102, quotation from p. 101.

24. Laura A. W. LeValley to Equity Club, Apr. 20, 1888, in ibid., pp. 109–110, quotation from p. 109.

25. Ada M. Bittenbender to Equity Club, Apr. 27, 1888, in ibid., pp. 90–91, in particular p. 90.

26. Robinson, "Women Lawyers," p. 23.

27. Alice Parker Hutchins, "Anna Christy Fall," 18 *Women Lawyers' Journal* 36–37 (1930); and Emma Fall Schofield, *Anna Christy Fall: My Remarkable Mother, April 23, 1855–January 13, 1930* (Malden, Mass.: n.p., 1978).

28. Catharine Waugh McCulloch to Equity Club, Nov. 8, 1890 in Drachman, *Women Lawyers*, pp. 191–192, quotation from p. 192.

29. Ibid.

30. Ada H. Kepley to Equity Club, July 3, 1888, in ibid., pp. 106–108, quotation from p. 107.

31. Lelia Robinson Sawtelle to Equity Club, in ibid., pp. 200–201, quotation from pp. 200–201.

32. Sawtelle to "Kitty Waugh."

33. Catharine Waugh McCulloch, "Commends Pledge Not to Wed Anti-Suffragists," letter to the editor, *Chicago Record Herald* [1908?], in box 4, folder 121, McCulloch Papers, sec. 6, Dillon Collection.

34. Ibid.

35. Robinson, "Women Lawyers," p. 26. Annegret Ogden, "Love and Marriage: Five California Couples," *The Californians* (July–Aug. 1987): 8–19, esp. pp. 12–13.

36. Catharine G. Waugh, "Women as Law Clerks," handwritten reminiscence, 1888, box 4, McCulloch Papers, ser. 6, Dillon Collection.

37. Ibid.

38. "Author of Suffrage Bill," *Boston Globe*, Aug. 11, 1913, box 13, folder 70, McCulloch Papers, ser. 6, Dillon Collection.

39. McCulloch to Equity Club, Nov. 8, 1890, in Drachman, *Women Lawyers*, pp. 191–192, quotation from p. 192.

40. Sawtelle to "Kitty Waugh."

41. McCulloch to Equity Club, Nov. 8, 1890, in Drachman, *Women Lawyers*, p. 192.

42. Frank McCulloch to "My dear, dear Girl," Jan. 14, 1891, box 1, folder 14, McCulloch Papers. Frank also offered money to Catharine in a letter to "My darling Wife," Jan. 8, 1891, box 1, folder 14, McCulloch Papers, and in a letter to "My dear Catharine," Sept. 27, 1895, box 1, folder 13, McCulloch Papers.

43. McCulloch to "My dear, dear Girl."

44. Frank McCulloch to "My dear Catharine," Jan. 25, 1891, box 1, folder 14, McCulloch Papers.

45. McCulloch to "My dear, dear Girl."

46. Handwritten note attached to the program of the annual banquet of the alumni association of the Northwestern University Law School, 1908–1909, box 3, folder 67, McCulloch Papers, ser. 6, Dillon Collection.

47. Iva G. Wooden to Mrs. [Catharine Waugh] McCulloch, Dec. 21, 1912, box 10, folder 265, McCulloch Papers, ser. 6, Dillon Collection. See also Frank H. McCulloch's suffrage essay, "Some Questions for Woman Suffragists from a Mere Man," n.d., Chicago, box 12, folder 298, McCulloch Papers, ser. 6, Dillon Collection.

48. The following description of Catharine McCulloch's day as well as all quotes come from "1901 in the Summer," handwritten account by Catharine G. Waugh McCulloch of a day at home, 1901, box 6, folder 192, McCulloch Papers, ser. 6, Dillon Collection.

49. "Catharine W. McCulloch: A Character Sketch," *Evanston Press*, Mar. 30, 1907, box 3, folder 67, McCulloch Papers, ser. 6, Dillon Collection.

50. "Chicago Suffragettes at Home," *Sunday Record-Herald* (Chicago), Nov. 28, 1909, box 3, folder 67, McCulloch Papers, ser. 6, Dillon Collection.

51. Anna Howard Shaw to Mrs. [Catharine Waugh] McCulloch, Dec. 29, 1910, New York, box 10, folder 255, McCulloch Papers, ser. 6, Dillon Collection.

52. Edward H. Clarke, *Sex in Education; or, A Fair Chance for the Girls* (Boston: James R. Osgood, 1873).

53. Charles C. Moore, "The Woman Lawyer," 26 *Green Bag* 525–531 (1914), first published in *Daily Times* (Hartford, Conn.), May 17, 1886.

54. Ibid. p. 527.

55. Ibid., p. 529.

56. Ibid., pp. 530–531.

57. Ellen A. Martin to Equity Club, May 25, 1888, in Drachman, *Women Lawyers*, pp. 112–116, quotation from p. 114.

58. Ibid., p. 114. On M. Fredrika Perry, see "Chicago Women," *Chicago Legal News*, Sept. 4, 1880, p. 434; and "M. Fredrika Perry," *Chicago Legal News*, June 30, 1883, pp. 825–826.

59. As secretary of the Equity Club, Martha Pearce encouraged a debate on Martin's views. See Martha Pearce, Report of the Corresponding Secretary, [1888], in Drachman, *Women Lawyers,* pp. 75–87, quotation from p. 84.

60. Gillett to Equity Club, Apr. 27, 1889, in ibid., p. 159.

61. Ibid.

62. Catharine G. Waugh to Equity Club, Apr. 26, 1889, in ibid., pp. 173–177, quotation from p. 175.

63. Ibid.

64. Letitia L. Burlingame to Equity Club, Apr. 23, 1887, in ibid., pp. 45–47, quotation from p. 45.

65. Lettie L. Burlingame to Equity Club, Apr. 22, 1889, in ibid., pp. 154–157, quotation from p. 156.

66. Linda Gordon, *Woman's Body, Woman's Right: A Social History of Birth Control in America* (New York: Grossman, 1976), and James W. Reed, *From Private Vice to Public Virtue: The Birth Control Movement and American Society since 1830* (New York: Basic Books, 1978).

67. Pearce, Report of the Corresponding Secretary, p. 85.

68. Ibid.

69. Ibid., p. 86.

70. Ibid.

71. Gillett to Equity Club, Apr. 27, 1889, in ibid., p. 162.

72. Bittenbender to Equity Club, May 10, 1889, in ibid., p. 152.

73. Ibid., pp. 152–153.

74. McCulloch, "Commends Pledge."

75. Robinson, "Women Lawyers."

5. "Some of Our Best Students Have Been Women"

1. On women at Cornell University, see Charlotte Conable, *Women at Cornell: The Myth of Equal Education* (Ithaca, N.Y.: Cornell University Press, 1970). On women at New York University Law School, see Phyllis Eckhaus, "Restless Women: The Pioneering Alumnae of New York University Law School," unpublished paper in NYUA; Phyllis A. Klein, "'I Taught Them a Woman Could Be a Lawyer': Women Law Students and New Women Lawyers in New York City, 1919–1929," unpublished paper in NYUA; Karen Sotiropoulos, "Women in Law at NYU, 1890–1920," unpublished paper in NYUA; *One Hundred Years of Women, NYU School of Law: 1892–1992* (New York: New York University, 1992); and Leslie Jay Tompkins, "The University Law School: A Reminiscence," 4 *New York University Law Review* 35–50 (1927).

2. Gilbert J. Pedersen, *Buffalo Law School: A History, 1887–1962* (Buffalo: University of Buffalo Alumni Association, 1962), pp. 50–51.

3. Frank L. Ellsworth, *Law on the Midway: The Founding of the University of Chicago Law School* (Chicago: University of Chicago Press, 1977), p. 127.

4. Five women enrolled in 1918 when Case Western Reserve University

opened its law school to women. See C. H. Cramer, *The Law School at Case Western Reserve University: A History, 1892–1977*, (Cleveland, Ohio: The Law School, Case Western Reserve University, 1977), p. 47.

5. Beatrice Doerschuk, *Women in the Law*, bulletin no. 3, Bureau of Vocational Information (New York, 1920), table 2, pp. 114–124; and Alfred Zantzinger Reed, *Training for the Public Profession of the Law: Historical Development and Principal Contemporary Problems of Legal Education in the United States with Some Account of Conditions in England and Canada*, bulletin no. 15, Carnegie Foundation for the Advancement of Teaching (New York: 1921), appendix, p. 441.

6. Barbara Miller Solomon, *In the Company of Educated Women* (New Haven, Conn.: Yale University Press, 1985), pp. 44, 63. See also Lynn D. Gordon, *Gender and Higher Education in the Progressive Era* (New Haven, Conn.: Yale University Press, 1990); Conable, *Women at Cornell*; Helen Lefkowitz Horowitz, *Alma Mater: Design and Experience in the Women's Colleges from Their Nineteenth-Century Beginnings to the 1930s* (New York: Alfred A. Knopf, 1984); Patricia Ann Palmieri, *In Adamless Eden: The Community of Women Faculty at Wellesley* (New Haven, Conn.: Yale University Press, 1995); Mabel Newcomer, *A Century of Higher Education for American Women* (New York: Harper, 1959); and Thomas Woody, *A History of Women's Education in the United States*, 2 vols. (New York: Science Press, 1929).

7. On Jackson College, see Russell Miller, *Light on the Hill: A History of Tufts College, 1852–1952* (Boston: Beacon, 1966).

8. Solomon, *In the Company of Educated Women*, p. 63.

9. Reed, *Training for the Public Profession of the Law*, p. 442.

10. Ibid.

11. Robert Stevens, *Law School: Legal Education in America from the 1850s to the 1980s* (Chapel Hill: University of North Carolina Press, 1983), p. 76.

12. Reed, *Training for the Public Profession of the Law*, pp. 442, 443.

13. On part-time law schools, see Stevens, *Law School*, esp. pp. 73–111; and Jerold S. Auerbach, *Unequal Justice: Lawyers and Social Change in Modern America* (New York: Oxford University Press, 1976), esp. pp. 74–101.

14. Reed, *Training for the Public Profession of the Law*, pp. 398–402, 415–416. On Reed see Stevens, *Law School*, pp. 112–117, 128–129, and Auerbach, *Unequal Justice*, pp. 110–112.

15. See "The University Law School," 4 *New York University Law Review* 35–50 (1927); and *University Law School Preliminary Circular of Information, 1907–1908*, (New York City), p. 7 in box 3, Tompkins Scrapbook. On African-American women at New York University Law School, see J. Clay Smith, Jr., *Emancipation: The Making of the Black Lawyer, 1844–1944* (Philadelphia: University of Pennsylvania Press, 1993), p. 405.

16. "The University Law School." See also "Night Classes, Low Rating," 1923, clipping from unidentified newspaper, box 4, folder 5, Tompkins Scrapbook.

17. Doerschuk, *Women in the Law*, table 2, pp. 114–124, esp. p. 120; See also Bureau of Vocational Information, interview with Clara Lehring, Secretary,

New York University Law School, Jan. 30, 1920, box 9, folder 132, BVI Records; and Clara Lehring to Beatrice Doerschuk, Feb. 9, 1920, box 10, folder 145, BVI Records. On women at New York University Law School, see generally Eckhaus, "Restless Women"; Klein, " 'I Taught Them a Woman Could Be a Lawyer' "; Sotiropoulos, "Women in Law at NYU"; and *One Hundred Years of Women, NYU School of Law.*

18. The papers of the Woman's Law Class of New York University are available in NYUA. On the Woman's Law Class, see *"For the Better Protection of Their Rights": A History of the First Fifty Years of the Woman's Legal Education Society and the Woman's Law Class at New York University* (New York: New York University Press, 1940) in box 2, folder 20, WLC. See also "Women Lawyers: Opening of the New York University Classes for 1897–98," *Brooklyn Standard Union,* Oct. 2, 1897, in box 2, folder 18, WLC; Isabella Mary Pettus, "The Work of the Woman's Law Class, New York University," 1 *Women Lawyers' Journal* 20–22 (1911); and Pettus, "The Legal Education of Women," *Journal of Social Science* 38 (1900): 234–244, esp. p. 242.

19. Pettus, "Work of the Woman's Law Class, New York University," pp. 21–22, quotation from p. 22.

20. "The Woman's Law Class, Announcements for the Eighteenth Year, 1908–09," 8 *New York University Bulletin* 3 (1908).

21. *"For the Better Protection of Their Rights,"* p. 10.

22. Ibid., p. 11.

23. See *Articles of Incorporation, and By-Laws of the Woman's Legal Education Society* (New York: Styles and Cash, 1897), box 1, folder 3, WLC; and "A Law School for Women," *New York Times,* Aug. 6, 1889, p. 8.

24. *Articles of Incorporation.*

25. "A Law School for Women," *New York Times,* Aug. 6, 1889, p. 8; and "Law School for Women," *New York Times,* Oct. 5, 1889, p. 2. See also Faculty Minutes, May 5, 1890, box 1, folder 5, WLC.

26. Faculty Minutes, May 5, 1890.

27. *Chancellor's Report,* New York University, 1890, in box 1, folder 5, WLC.

28. *The University of the City of New York Catalogue and Announcements* (1890–1891), pp. 174–175, box 1, folder 5, WLC.

29. On the nineteenth-century female physiological societies, see Martha H. Verbrugge, *Able-Bodied Womanhood: Personal Health and Social Change in Nineteenth-Century Boston* (New York: Oxford University Press, 1988).

30. The above quotations are from "These Women Know Law: But They Don't Look at All Like Typical Lawyers," *New York Times,* Apr. 11, 1891, p. 4.

31. "Women Learned in the Law," *New York Times,* Apr. 30, 1892, p. 8.

32. "Portias Young and Fair," *New York Times,* Apr. 6, 1894, p. 5. See also "Woman's Study of the Law," *Sun* (New York), Feb. 7, 1904, box 2, folder 18, WLC.

33. "Women Lawyers," *Brooklyn Standard Union,* Oct. 20, 1897.

34. "Woman's Law Class Opens," *New York Times,* Oct. 25, 1898, p. 9. See

also "Young Women Law Students," *New York Times*, Apr. 5, 1895, p. 3; "The Woman's Law Class," *New York Times*, Mar. 31, 1899, p. 7; and "Women Graduate in Law," *New York Times*, Mar. 30, 1900, p. 2.

35. Prior to Russell and Ashley, Professor Christopher J. Tiedeman volunteered to take Kempin's place for a year. *Chancellor's Report*, New York University, 1890, p. 11.

36. *"For the Better Protection of Their Rights,"* p. 50.

37. "Woman's Study of the Law."

38. Clarence D. Ashley to Chancellor Henry M. MacCracken, May 5, 1902, box 1, folder 1, WLC.

39. "Law Class Alumnae," *New York Times*, Apr. 22, 1900, p. 11. Also typed text of speech to Mr. Chancellor [MacCracken]: Ladies and Gentlemen, [1901], box 1, folder 14, WLC.

40. "Women Receive Law Certificates," 61 *Albany Law Journal* 218–230 (1900).

41. "Women Lawyers," *Brooklyn Standard Union*, Oct. 20, 1897, box 2, folder 18, WLC.

42. Typed text of speech to Chancellor [MacCracken].

43. Florence Sutro to Rev. Dr. MacCracken, June 15, 1895, box 1, folder 7, WLC.

44. "With Women Lawyers," *Woman's Journal* 30 (1899): 109.

45. Pettus, "The Work of the Woman's Law Class, New York University." On the availability of scholarships, see "The Woman's Law Class, Announcements of the Eighteenth Year," *New York University Bulletin*, June 20, 1908, pp. 5–6, box 3, Tompkins Scrapbook.

46. Mrs. Theodore Sutro, "Why Women Study Law," *Chicago Legal News*, Oct. 18, 1902, pp. 77–78, quotation from p. 77.

47. Florence Sutro to Rev. Dr. MacCracken.

48. *"For the Better Protection of Their Rights,"* p. 30.

49. "The Study of Law by Women," *Chicago Legal News*, Nov. 12, 1902, p. 110.

50. "Will Not Depend on Men for Law," *New York Herald*, Nov. 4, 1900, box 2, folder 18, WLC.

51. "Day Law Class for Women," *Chicago Legal News*, Oct. 27, 1906, p. 143.

52. "The Woman Left Behind," 7 *Women Lawyers' Journal* 14 (1917).

53. *University Law School, Preliminary Circular of Information, 1907–08.*

54. "Woman's Study of Law."

55. Theodore Francis Jones, ed., *New York University, 1832–1932* (New York: New York University Press, 1933), p. 273.

56. The first female graduates of New York University Law School were Julia Amanda Wilson, Rose Otliffe Levere, and Agnes Kennedy Mulligan, all of whom graduated in 1892. See *One Hundred Years of Women, NYU School of Law, 1892–1992*, p. 3.

57. "The Law and the Lady," 60 *Albany Law Journal* 91 (1899).

58. Typed text of speech to Chancellor [MacCracken].

59. "Miss Ruth Dick Hall," *Chicago Legal News*, June 16, 1900, p. 361.

60. Florence Ellinwood Allen, *To Do Justly* (Cleveland, Ohio: Case Western Reserve University Press, 1965), p. 25. See also handwritten questionnaire to Bureau of Vocational Information, no. 6, Mar. 12, 1920, BVI Records.

61. BVI questionnaire no. 4, Mar. 15, 1920, BVI Records.

62. Allen, *To Do Justly*, p. 25. For another example, see "Encourages Young Women," *New York University Alumnus*, Feb. 1928, p. 11, in box 4, folder 6, Tompkins Scrapbook.

63. Ibid., p. 25.

64. Ibid., p. 28.

65. The following discussion of Madeleine Doty is from *A Tap on the Shoulder*, chap. 2:"The Law School," unpublished autobiography in box 2, folder 23, Doty Papers.

66. "Women Lawyers," *Woman's Journal* 38 (1907): 93.

67. Doty, *Tap on the Shoulder*, p. 6.

68. Doerschuk, *Women in the Law*, table 2, pp. 114–124. On the University of Michigan, see Elizabeth Gaspar Brown, *Legal Education at Michigan, 1859–1959* (Ann Arbor: University of Michigan Press, 1959), pp. 700–701. On New York University, see Clara Lehring to Beatrice Doerschuk. On Boston University, see *Alumni Directory of Boston University* (Boston: Alumni Bureau of Boston University, 1924), pp. 137–181. Seventy-seven graduates were reported by Florence White, Secretary to the Dean, to Beatrice Doerschuk, Oct. 28, 1919, box 10, folder 145, BVI Records.

69. Interview with Miss Clara Lehring, secretary at New York University Law School, Jan. 30, 1920, box 9, folder 132, BVI Records.

70. Brown, *Legal Education at Michigan*, p. 701.

71. *Annual Directory of Boston University*, pp. 175–176.

72. BVI questionnaire no. 55, Mar. 5, 1920, BVI Records.

73. Doty, *Tap on the Shoulder*, p. 1.

74. "Encourages Young Women," *New York University Alumnus*, Feb. 1928, p. 11, box 4, folder 6, Tompkins Scrapbook.

75. Doty, *Tap on the Shoulder*, p. 1.

76. Ibid., p. 2.

77. Ibid.

78. Ibid., p. 1. In calling Doty "Dr. Pankhurst," her classmates were derisively referring to Emmeline Pankhurst, the militant woman's suffragist in England.

79. Ibid., p. 2.

80. Ibid., p. 4.

81. Ibid., p. 3.

82. Ibid.

83. Ibid., p. 4.

84. Ibid., p. 2.

85. Ibid., p. 6.

86. "Women Lawyers," 36 *Woman's Journal* 181 (1905). Also see Peggy Lamson, *Roger Baldwin: Founder of the American Civil Liberties Union* (Boston: Houghton Mifflin, 1976); and "A Memo on Madeleine Zabriskie Doty," typewritten document in box 1, folder 4, Doty Papers.

87. On Ashley see "Jessie Ashley: A Victim of Pneumonia," *Call* (New York), Jan. 21, 1919, and "Friends Pay Tribute to Miss Ashley's Memory," *Call* (n.d.), both newsclippings in box 2, folder 30, Dennett Collection. See also Mari Jo Buhle, *Women and American Socialism, 1870–1920* (Chicago: University of Illinois Press, 1983), pp. 258, 276, 278.

88. Madeleine Zabriskie Doty, *Society's Misfits* (New York: Century, 1916).

89. On Baright, see "Encourages Young Women."

90. Mary G. Siegel, " 'Crossing the Bar': A 'She' Lawyer in 1917," 7 *Women's Rights Law Reporter* 357–363 (1982).

91. BVI questionnaire no. 118, Mar. 4, 1920, BVI Records.

92. "Legal Education: Ruth Lewison, New York Lawyer and Educator, Appears at Hearing before N.Y. Court of Appeals," 15 *Women Lawyers' Journal* 9 (1927).

93. On Florence Allen, see Barbara Sicherman and Carol Hurd Green, eds., *Notable American Women: The Modern Period* (Cambridge, Mass.: Harvard University Press, 1980), pp. 11–13; and Jeannette Tuve, *First Lady of the Law: Florence Ellinwood Allen* (New York: University Press of America, 1984). See also Allen's autobiography, *To Do Justly.* On Inez Milholland, see James, *Notable American Women, 1607–1950,* pp. 188–190. Milholland's papers are at SL.

94. On Byrns, see her papers in Dennett Papers, and "The Woman Lawyer," *New Republic,* Jan. 8, 1916, pp. 246–247.

95. On Eastman, see Sicherman and Green, *Notable American Women, The Modern Period,* pp. 543–545; and Blanche Wiesen Cook, ed., *Crystal Eastman on Women and Revolution* (New York: Oxford University Press, 1978).

96. Auerbach, *Unequal Justice,* pp. 28–29. On Harvard Law School, see "The Harvard Idea: You Must Have an A.B. or You Can't Enter as a Law Student—Without It You Are Not Fit to Practice Law," *Chicago Legal News,* Oct. 21, 1893, p. 62; and "The Harvard Departure," *Chicago Legal News,* Oct. 21, 1893, p. 82. On discrimination against women at Harvard generally, see Marcia Graham Synnott, *The Half-Opened Door: Discrimination and Admissions at Harvard, Yale, and Princeton, 1900–1970* (Westport, Conn.: Greenwood, 1979).

97. See Stevens, *Law School,* p. 83.

98. Meeting of Law Faculty of Harvard University, June 24, 1899, in Minutes of Faculty Meetings, p. 163, Harvard Law School, Sept. 1870–June 1928, HLSL.

99. James Barr Ames to Miss Agnes Irwin, June 27, 1899, Correspondence and Papers of the Council (hereinafter Correspondence), RCA.

100. "Women in Harvard Law School: The Faculty Favors Admission of Radcliffe Graduate Students, But May be Overruled by the Overseers," *Boston Herald* [1899], Correspondence.

101. Interview of Mrs. Frances Keay Ballard, Mar. 18, 1920, box 9, folder 132, BVI Records.

102. "President Eliot on Coeducation at Harvard," *Boston Herald* [July or Aug.] 1899, Correspondence.

103. Frances Keay to Miss [Agnes] Irwin, Sept. 9, 1899, Correspondence.

104. M. Carey Thomas to Miss [Agnes] Irwin, Aug. 21, 1899, Correspondence.

105. [?] Keasbey to Miss [M. Carey] Thomas, Aug. 2, 1899, Correspondence.

106. Meeting of the President and Fellows of Harvard College, Sept. 26, 1899, pp. 262, 263, President and Fellows ser. 2, Reports to the Overseers, vol. 8, Harvard Archives; see also Overseers Records, vol. 13, Sept. 29, 1899, p. 442, also in President and Fellows ser. 2, Reports to the Overseers, vol. 8, Harvard Archives.

107. Frances Keay to Miss [Agnes] Irwin, Oct. 8, 1899, Correspondence.

108. Meeting of the President and Fellows of Harvard College, Oct. 16, 1899, President and Fellows ser. 2, Report of the Overseers, p. 266, Harvard Archives; see also Overseers Records, vol. 13, Sept. 29, 1899, p. 442, and Nov. 22, 1899, pp. 445–446.

109. Frances Keay to Miss [Agnes] Irwin, Nov. 5, 1899, Correspondence.

110. Frances Keay to Miss [Agnes] Irwin, Oct. 29, 1899, Correspondence.

111. W[illiam Draper] Lewis to Miss [Agnes] Irwin, Nov. 3, 1899, Correspondence.

112. Keay to Irwin, Nov. 5, 1899.

113. Lewis to Irwin.

114. Inez Milholland to the Dean and Faculty of Harvard Law School, [1909], box 2, folder 25, Milholland Papers.

115. Minutes of faculty meeting, Oct. 4, 1909, Minutes of Faculty Meetings, Harvard Law School, (Sept. 1870 to June 1928), p. 201, HLSL.

116. Henry L. Higginson to President A. Lawrence Lowell, Oct. 8, 1909, folder 959, Lowell Presidential Papers. See also George A. O. Ernst to Pres[ident] A. Lawrence Lowell, Oct. 8, 1909, folder 959, Lowell Presidential Papers.

117. Minutes of Faculty Meetings, Oct. 4, 1909, p. 201.

118. "Women in Law School," 13 *Law Notes* 165 (Dec. 1909).

119. A. Lawrence Lowell to Mr. George A. O. Ernst, Oct. 9, 1909, in Lowell Letters of the President, vol. 1: June 21, 1909, to Feb. 8, 1910, p. 159, Lowell Presidential Papers.

120. "Women in Law School."

121. Frederick C[harles] Hicks, *Yale Law School: 1869–1894, Including the County Court House Period* (New Haven, Conn.: Yale University Press, 1937), pp. 75–76.

122. On Fenberg, see "Her First Day at the Law School," 10 *Yale Law Report* 21–22 (1963).

123. "The Following Editorial from the *New York Evening Post* Is Interesting to Lawyers," 8 *Women Lawyers' Journal* 14 (1918).

124. See "Miss Ruth Dick Hall," *Chicago Legal News*, June 16, 1900, p. 361.

125. Quoted in Cynthia Fuchs Epstein, *Women in Law* (New York: Basic Books, 1981), p. 51.

126. "Columbia Law Department," 16 *Case and Comment* 293 (1910).

127. BVI questionnaire no. 12, Mar. 15, 1920, BVI Records.

128. Reprinted in *Shall Women Be Admitted to the Columbia Law School? Opinions of the Press and of Leading Lawyers* (New York: Women's City Club, 1917), box 9, folder 129, BVI Records.

129. *The Nation*, Oct. 5, 1916, reprinted in *Shall Women Be Admitted to Columbia Law School?*

130. *Shall Women Be Admitted to the Columbia Law School?*

131. "Woman in Law Faculty," *New York Times*, Oct. 27, 1917, p. 22.

132. "Women Seek Entry into Law School," *New York Times*, Nov. 28, 1920, p. 8. See also Julius Goebel, Jr., et al., *A History of the School of Law: Columbia University* (New York: Columbia University Press, 1955), p. 473.

133. "Women in Law School Asked of Columbia," *New York Times*, Dec. 11, 1924, p. 23.

134. Mae Viner, "Co-Education in the Law," *Transcript*, (Dixon, Ill.: Rogers Printing, 1925), pp. 136–139. All quotations are from pp. 137, 138.

135. Quoted in Karen Berger Morello, *The Invisible Bar: The Woman Lawyer in America: 1638 to the Present* (New York: Random House, 1986), p. 96.

136. "Report of Committee on Legal Education," 15 *Women Lawyers' Journal* 9 (1927). On the faculty vote at Columbia, see Goebel, *A History of the School of Law*, pp. 290–291, 473, 474.

137. Goebel, *A History of the School of Law*, pp. 90–91, 473–474, 490.

138. On Kappa Beta Pi, see "Kappa Beta Pi Sorority," *Transcript*, 1919, pp. 100–101; "Kappa Beta Pi Legal Sorority," *Transcript*, 1923, p. 88; and "The Woman's Page," 1 *Chicago Kent Review* 12 (1923). I would like to thank Ronald Chester for sharing with me his copies of the *Kappa Beta Pi Quarterly*. On Phi Delta Delta, see "What Is Phi Delta Delta?" *Phi Delta Delta*, Nov. 1924, pp. 22–25, esp. p. 22. Papers of Phi Delta Delta are in the University Research Library, UCLA. See also Ronald Chester, *Unequal Access: Women Lawyers in a Changing America* (South Hadley, Mass.: Bergin and Garvey, 1985), pp. 89–95.

139. See Laura Miller Derry, ed., *Digest of Women Lawyers and Judges: Biographical Sketches and Data of Women Lawyers and Judges of the United States and Its Possessions* (U.S.A.: Laura Miller Derry, 1949), pp. 431, 435.

140. *Kappa Beta Pi Quarterly* (Feb. 1926): 21.

141. Annett F. Hunley, "Early History of Phi Delta Delta," *Phi Delta Delta* (Nov. 1973): 6–8, reprinted from *Phi Delta Delta*, Nov. 1, 1925. See also Georgia Bullock to Mrs. Mildred Murphy, Sept. 23, 1925, in box 7, Bullock Papers.

142. *Kappa Beta Pi Quarterly* (Feb. 1926): 20.

143. *Kappa Beta Pi Quarterly* (May 1926): 76.

144. *Kappa Beta Pi Quarterly* (Feb. 1926): 23.

145. Flora Warren Seymour, "Indian Country," *Kappa Beta Pi Quarterly* (Mar. 1924): 41–53. Seymour was the first woman member of the United States Board of Indian Commissioners.

146. See, for example, "Phi Delta Deltas on the Bench," *Phi Delta Delta* (June 1925): 9–10; and "May Darlington Lahey, Judge of the Los Angeles Municipal Court," *Phi Delta Delta* (May 1929): 183–184.

147. "Maud Matley Shows Them That a Lawyer Can When She Wants To!!!!!" *Phi Delta Delta* (Jan. 1927): 111.

148. Eleanor Stuart Burch and Dorothy Ludington, "An Invitation," *Kappa Beta Pi Quarterly* (Mar. 1924): 69–70, quotation from p. 69.

149. "What Is Phi Delta Delta?" p. 24.

150. Allen, *To Do Justly,* p. 27.

151. Calculated from *Catalogue of the Graduates of the Boston University Law School, 1873–1905* (Boston: Boston University Press, 1905), and *Alumni Directory of Boston University,* pp. 137–181.

152. Calculated from Brown, *Legal Education at Michigan,* pp. 700–701.

6. "Primarily for Women"

1. Mary Roth Walsh, *"Doctors Wanted: No Women Need Apply": Sexual Barriers in the Medical Profession, 1835–1975* (New Haven, Conn.: Yale University Press, 1977), p. 180.

2. On the Washington College of Law, see Ronald Chester, *Unequal Access: Women Lawyers in a Changing America* (South Hadley, Mass.: Bergin and Garvey, 1985), esp. pp. 12–17, 53–86; Jean S. Schade, "The Washington College of Law: A History from the Founding of the College Until Its Merger with the American University, 1896–1949" (master's thesis, Department of Library Science, Catholic University of America, 1969), in WCLA; Ellen Spencer Mussey, "The Washington College of Law," 5 *Women Lawyers' Journal* 20 (1915); Susan A. Notar, "Grace Hays Riley and the Quest for ABA Approval," unpublished paper in WCLA; and Robert Stevens, *Law School: Legal Education in America from the 1850s to the 1980s* (Chapel Hill: University of North Carolina Press, 1983), pp. 83, 90, 91.

3. On Ellen Spencer Mussey, see Grace Hathaway, *Fate Rides a Tortoise: A Biography of Ellen Spencer Mussey* (Philadelphia: Winston, 1937); Edward T. James, ed., *Notable American Women, 1607–1950: A Biographical Dictionary* (Cambridge, Mass.: Harvard University Press, 1971), pp. 606–607; Patricia P. Bailey, "The Accomplishments of WCL Founder Ellen Spencer Mussey," 32 *American University Law Review* 619–621 (1983); Lisa M. Longo, "Ellen Spencer Mussey: An International Law Focus," 6 *Advocate* 11–12 (1987); and "Ellen Spencer Mussey Dies," *College Grit,* May 13, 1936, p. 1 in WCLA.

4. On Emma Gillett, see Virginia G. Drachman, *Women Lawyers and the Origins of Professional Identity in America: The Letters of the Equity Club, 1887 to 1890*

(Ann Arbor: University of Michigan Press, 1993), esp. pp. 96–97, 159–162, 184–185, 222–225; James, *Notable American Women*, pp. 36–37; *National Cyclopedia of American Biography* (Ann Arbor, Mich.: University Microfilms, 1967), vol. 17, p. 280; "Emma Melinda Gillett" 15 *Women Lawyers' Journal* (1927); and Hathaway, *Fate Rides a Tortoise*. Papers of Gillett are in the Dillon Collection.

5. *Washington College of Law, 1929–1930* (Washington, D.C.: Washington College of Law, 1929), p. 9.

6. Emma Gillett to Beatrice Doerschuk, Mar. 15, 1920, BVI Records.

7. See an announcement for the Washington College of Law in *Woman's Journal* 30 (1899): 264.

8. On the entry requirements at Washington College of Law, see "WCL Historical Summary," compiled by Audrey Pia, Di Horvath, and Lisa Longo, under direction of Paul P. Purta, WCLA; and Schade, "Washington College of Law," p. 15.

9. On tuition rates at various law schools, see 1 *Law Student's Helper* 138 (1893).

10. On enrollment figures, see "WCL Historical Summary"; Ronald Chester, "A Survey of WCL Women Graduates: The 1920s Through the 1940s," 32 *American University Law Review* 627–634 (1983); and Schade, "Washington College of Law," appendix 7: Degrees Conferred, 1898–1953.

11. "Women Lawyers," *Woman's Journal* 34 (1903): 204.

12. On Elizabeth Harris, see "Boston Girl Heads Law School: Miss Elizabeth C. Harris Elected Dean of the Washington College of Law," *Boston Sunday Globe*, Oct. 21, 1923, in Scrapbook no. 1, p. 82, PLSA; and Chester, *Unequal Access*, p. 54.

13. Typed letter from [Dean Emma Gillett] to the Board of Trustees of the Washington College of Law, Apr. 10, 1925, in WCLA.

14. "WCL Historical Summary."

15. On Boston University Law School, see *Catalogue of the Graduates of the Boston University Law School, 1873–1905* (Boston: Boston University, 1905); and *Alumni Directory of Boston University* (Boston: Boston University, 1924), pp. 137–181.

16. Papers of Annabel Matthews are at SL. On Alice Paul, see Alden Whitman, ed., *American Reformers* (New York: H. W. Wilson, 1985), pp. 640–642. On Sue Shelton White, see James, *Notable American Women*, pp. 590–592. Obituaries include "Miss Sue White, Women Voters' Leader, Dies," *Washington Post*, May 7, 1943; "Miss Sue S. White, Suffrage Leader, Dies in Alexandria," *Evening Star* (Washington, D.C.), May 7, 1943, both on file in Sue Shelton White Papers, box 1, folder 3, SL. For an analysis of White as part of a network of influential women in New Deal politics, see Susan Ware, *Beyond Suffrage, Women in the New Deal* (Cambridge, Mass.: Harvard University Press, 1981).

17. BVI questionnaire no. 195, Mar. 3, 1920. All BVI questionnaires are in the BVI Records.

18. BVI questionnaire no. 59, Mar. 4, 1920.

19. BVI questionnaire no. 54, Mar. 1, 1920.

20. BVI questionnaire no. 243, Mar. 17, 1920.

21. BVI questionnaire no. 247, Apr. 3, 1920.

22. "WCL Historical Summary."

23. On Portia Law School, see Stevens, *Law School*, pp. 83, 90, 194; Chester, *Unequal Access*, esp. pp. 9–12, 19–42; *New England School of Law, 1908 to 1983: A Look at Seventy-Five Years of Tradition* (Boston: New England School of Law, [1983]), pp. 4–21; Douglas Lamar Jones et al., *Discovering the Public Interest: A History of the Boston Bar Association* (Canoga Park, Calif.: CCA Publications, 1993), pp. 77–78; and "Portia Law School for Women Graduated Largest Class in History Last Commencement," *Cambridge Tribune*, July 31, 1926, in Portia Law School Scrapbook, vol. 2, p. 69, PLSA.

24. Stevens, *Law School*, p. 80.

25. Ibid., and Jones, *Discovering the Public Interest*, pp. 82–83, 77–78.

26. In 1931, Portia rescheduled evening classes to begin at 7:00 P.M., enabling working students to eat dinner before they went to class. See "Portia Law School," *Post* (Boston), Aug. 30, 1931, Portia Law School Scrapbook, vol. 5, p. 10, PLSA.

27. Chester, *Unequal Access*, p. 11; *New England School of Law, 1908 to 1983*, p. 7; "Portia Law School Asks Legal Right to Grant Master's Degree," *Transcript* (Boston), Feb. 2, 1926, Portia Law School Scrapbook, vol. 2, p. 40, PLSA; "Bill Reported to Grant Higher Portia Degrees," *Boston Morning Globe*, Mar. 10, 1926, Portia Law School Scrapbook, vol. 2, p. 42, PLSA.

28. "Women Lawyers Best in All Divorce Cases, College Head Holds," *Boston Telegram*, Sept. 11, 1922, Portia Law School Scrapbook, vol. 1, p. 60, PLSA; "Says Congress of Women Would Cure All Ills," *United News*, article syndicated in midwestern areas, Portia Law School Scrapbook, vol. 1, p. 69, PLSA; and "Women Are Best Law Students, Says Dean," *Sunday Advertiser* (Boston), Oct. 26, 1919, Portia Law School Scrapbook, vol. 1, p. 9, PLSA.

29. Chester, *Unequal Access*, p. 10.

30. Ibid., p. 24.

31. Only thirty-nine women had graduated from Boston University Law School by 1908. Calculated from *Alumni Directory of Boston University, 1924*.

32. "Women's Law School," *Christian Science Monitor*, Sept. 27, 1932, in Portia Law School Scrapbook, vol. 5, p. 91, PLSA; also Chester, *Unequal Access*, p. 10.

33. "Fourteen Points Relating to the Petition of Portia Law School for Authority to Grant the Degree of Master of Laws," unpublished document in Portia Law School Scrapbook, vol. 2, p. 58, PLSA.

34. Chester, *Unequal Access*, p. 12.

35. Virginia G. Drachman, *Hospital with a Heart: Women Doctors and the Paradox of Separatism at the New England Hospital, 1862–1969* (Ithaca, N.Y.: Cornell University Press, 1984), pp. 174–177.

36. On the Jama White incident at Portia, see "Says School Expelled Her, Negress Sues," *Advertiser* (Boston), Apr. 23, 1929; "Sues Law School," *Herald-*

News (Fall River, Mass.), Apr. 23, 1929; "Seeks $20,000 for Expulsion," *Herald* (Boston), Apr. 23, 1929, all in Portia Law School Scrapbook, vol. 3, p. 106, PLSA; and "Portia Law School Upheld in Dismissal of Student," *Boston Morning Globe*, Jan. 8, 1931, Portia Law School Scrapbook, vol. 4, p. 102, PLSA.

37. "Sues Law School."

38. "Portia Law School," *Post* (Boston), July 12, 1931, Portia Law School Scrapbook, vol. 5, p. 6, PLSA.

39. Chester, *Unequal Access,* pp. 27–29, quotation from p. 28.

40. Petition to the Corporation of Harvard University and the Faculty of Harvard Law School, Mar. 8, 1915, folder 324, Lowell Presidential Papers. See also A. Lawrence Lowell to Thomas Nelson Perkins, Esq., Feb. 24, 1915, Lowell Presidential Papers. The following discussion is based on materials in the Lowell Papers.

41. Meeting of the Law Faculty of Harvard University, Feb. 23, 1915, Minutes of Faculty Meetings, Harvard Law School, Sept. 1870–June 1928, p. 35, on microfilm, Harvard Law School Library.

42. Walter Lippman to President A. Lawrence Lowell, Apr. 19, 1915, folder 324, Lowell Presidential Papers.

43. A. Lawrence Lowell to [Walter] Lippman, Apr. 20, 1915, folder 324, Lowell Presidential Papers.

44. On Beale, see *Harvard Law School Year Book,* vol. 2; 1930–1931 (Cambridge, Mass.: Law School Year Book Committee of Phillips Brooks House Association, Harvard University), pp. 18–22.

45. "First Women's Law School Opens This Fall," *New York Times Magazine,* Oct. 3, 1915, p. 14.

46. Ibid.

47. Ibid.

48. Ibid.

49. See correspondence from L[e] B[aron] R[ussell] Briggs to [Joseph Henry] Beale, in Outgoing Letters, May 11, 1914 to Oct. 22, 1917, vol. 3, Briggs Papers. See esp. letters dated Nov. 24, 1914, p. 155; Dec. 2, 1914, p. 159; Dec. 8, 1914, p. 164; Mar. 18, 1915, pp. 268–269; June 5, 1915, p. 348; and June 19, 1915, p. 355.

50. A. Lawrence Lowell to Dean E. R. Thayer, Dec. 7, 1914, folder 324, Lowell Presidential Papers. See also L[e] B[aron] R[ussell] B[riggs] to [A. Lawrence] Lowell, Dec. 4, 1914, folder 324, Lowell Presidential Papers.

51. Joseph H. Beale to Prof. L. B. R. Briggs, June 3, 1915, Briggs Papers.

52. Meeting of the Radcliffe Council, Jan. 4, 1915, Radcliffe College Council Minutes, RCA.

53. L[e] B[aron] R[ussell] B[riggs] to Ezra [Thayer], June 5, 1915, Outgoing Letters, May 11, 1914 to Oct. 22, 1917, Briggs Papers.

54. Annual Report of Radcliffe College, 1914–1915, p. 25, RCA.

55. "First Women's Law School Opens This Fall."

56. Ibid. See also "Law School for Women," *New York Times,* Sept. 27, 1915,

p. 5; 5 *Women Lawyers' Journal* 15 (1915); and "Cambridge to Have Law School Exclusively for College Women," unidentified newspaper, [1915], RCA.

57. "The New Law School," *Radcliffe News*, Oct. 15, 1915, pp. 1, 4, RCA.

58. Some scholars believe that Beale lost interest in the Cambridge Law School when his daughter did. See Stevens, *Law School*, p. 90; and Chester, *Unequal Access*, p. 12. The wife of Gustavus Hill Robinson, who taught contracts at the Cambridge Law School, had this same impression. See anonymous letters, Mar. 24, 1981, and Mar. 26, 1981, box 1, folder 1, Ronald Chester Papers, SL. But evidence suggests that by 1920 Beale did in fact want to reopen the Cambridge Law School. See Marjorie Hurd to Beatrice Doerschuk, n.d., box 10, folder 145, BVI Records; and "What Are You Doing with Your A.B. Degree?" in Portia Law School Scrapbook, vol. 1, p. 40, PLSA.

59. Joseph H. Beale to Mr. [Manley O.] Hudson, Aug. 27, 1916, box 1, folder 6, Manley O. Hudson Papers, HLSL.

60. Richard Ames, secretary of the Harvard Law School, to Beatrice Doerschuk, Oct. 22, 1919, BVI Records.

61. "What Are You Doing with Your A.B Degree?" See also Hurd to Doerschuk, n.d.

62. Elizabeth Kemper Adams, *Women Professional Workers: A Study Made for the Women's Educational and Industrial Union* (Chautauqua, N.Y.: Chautauqua Press, 1921), p. 72.

7. "Woman's Position in the Profession"

1. Beatrice Doerschuk, *Women in the Law: An Analysis of Training, Practice, and Salaried Positions*, bulletin no. 3, The Bureau of Vocational Information, (New York, 1920).

2. Ibid., p. vii.

3. For background on the Bureau of Vocational Information, see my Appendix 2; *Bureau of Vocational Information*, Jan. 1925; and Beatrice Doerschuk to Mrs. Richard Borden, Director of the Radcliffe Women's Archives, May 7, 1953. The BVI survey questionnaires compiled by Doerschuk for *Women in the Law* discussed in this chapter, together with the pamphlets and letters cited, are all from the BVI Records.

4. Doerschuk, *Women in the Law*, pp. vii, 24–25, 63–65, 102–103.

5. Ibid., pp. 24–25, 61.

6. Ibid., pp. 16–19.

7. Ibid., pp. 17–18.

8. Alfred Zantzinger Reed, *Training for the Public Profession of the Law: Historical Development and Principal Contemporary Problems of Legal Education in the United States with Some Account of Conditions in England and Canada*, bulletin no. 15, Carnegie Foundation for the Advancement of Teaching (New York, 1921).

9. Doerschuk, *Women in the Law*, p. 32.

10. Calculated from Doerschuk, *Women in the Law*, table 2, pp. 114–124; and Reed, *Training for the Public Profession of the Law*, p. 441, appendix.

11. Doerschuk, *Women in the Law*, pp. 13–19.

12. Ibid., p. 33. For the elite, male model of law training and practice, see Jerold S. Auerbach, *Unequal Justice: Lawyers and Social Change in Modern America* (New York: Oxford University Press, 1976), pp. 23–24.

13. For a general discussion of meritocracy among professional women, see Nancy F. Cott, *The Grounding of Modern Feminism* (New Haven, Conn.: Yale University Press, 1987), pp. 233–235.

14. Doerschuk, *Women in the Law*, p. 38.

15. Ibid., p. 43.

16. Ibid., p. 44.

17. Ibid., p. 55.

18. Ibid., p. 54.

19. Ibid., p. 47.

20. Ibid., p. 52.

21. Ibid., p. vii.

22. Ibid., p. [viii].

23. BVI questionnaire 254, Apr. 22, 1920.

24. See also Cott, *Grounding of Modern Feminism*, pp. 217–221; and Cynthia Fuchs Epstein, *Women in the Law* (New York: Basic Books, 1981), p. 5.

25. Based on the BVI questionnaires, N = 200. See also Cott, *Grounding of Modern Feminism*, p. 226, for the view that women lawyers in 1920 were optimistic.

26. Doerschuk, *Women in the Law*, table 2, p. 124; Patricia M. Hummer, *The Decade of Elusive Promise: Professional Women in the United States, 1920–1930* (Ann Arbor, Mich.: UMI Research Press, 1979), p. 92.

27. Calculated from BVI questionnaires.

28. Elizabeth B. Smart, "The Women Lawyer and Country Practice," 7 *Women Lawyers' Journal* 10 (1917); "A Member Honored," 12 *Women Lawyers' Journal* 30 (1923).

29. Calculated from BVI questionnaires.

30. BVI questionnaire 93, n.d.

31. BVI questionnaire 131, Mar. 27, 1920.

32. BVI questionnaire 150, Mar. 1, 1920.

33. BVI questionnaire 6, Mar. 12, 1920.

34. BVI questionnaire 95, Apr. 3, 1920.

35. Regina Markell Morantz-Sanchez, in her *Sympathy and Science: Women Physicians in American Medicine* (New York: Oxford University Press, 1985), argues that between the late nineteenth century and 1940 the marital rates for women doctors were disproportionately higher than for all other women professionals—see table 5.1, pp. 135–137. Morantz-Sanchez's own data indicate a different conclusion than that which she suggests in her text; women lawyers

and women doctors had almost identical rates of marriage between 1920 and 1940. Morantz-Sanchez overstates the uniqueness of the marital patterns of women doctors compared with women lawyers, implying that the exceptional pattern of marriage of women doctors persisted until after World War II, "when professional women began to catch up." See Morantz-Sanchez, *Sympathy and Science*, pp. 136–137. Based on her Table 5.1, the marriage rates of women lawyers and doctors, according to the United States Census, were as follows:

	1900	1910	1920	1930	1940	1950
Lawyers	n.a.	28.7%	34.2%	33.1%	38.6%	44.2%
Doctors	31.9%	35.6%	32.9%	32.6%	37.2%	46.2%

On women scientists, see Margaret W. Rossiter, *Women Scientists in America: Struggles and Strategies to 1940* (Baltimore, Md.: Johns Hopkins University Press, 1982), table 6.3, pp. 140–141.

36. BVI questionnaire 6, Mar. 12, 1920.

37. BVI questionnaire 19, Mar. 19, 1920.

38. BVI interview with Alfred Z. Reed, Jan. 26, 1920, BVI Records.

39. BVI questionnaire 191, n.d., 1920.

40. BVI questionnaire 181, Apr. 16, 1920.

41. BVI questionnaire 180, Mar. 9, 1920.

42. Calculated from the BVI questionnaires.

43. Calculated from the *Martindale-Hubbell Law Directory, Seventy-First Annual Edition, 1939*, vol. 1 (New York: Martindale-Hubbell, 1939).

44. For example, see BVI questionnaire 146, Mar. 7, 1920; and BVI questionnaire 251, Mar. 1, 1920.

45. BVI questionnaire 306, Feb. 4, 1921.

46. BVI questionnaire 200, n.d.

47. BVI questionnaire 19, Mar. 19, 1920; and BVI questionnaire 175, Mar. 15, 1920.

48. BVI questionnaire 171, Mar. 10, 1920.

49. The percentage of women lawyers surveyed in 1920 who reported that they believed women lawyers were retaining women clients were as follows (N = 189; source: BVI questionnaires):

Women clients retaining women lawyers	53%
Women clients not retaining women lawyers	28%
Women clients may be retaining women lawyers	19%

50. The percentages of women clients of the women lawyers in 1920 were as follows (N = 121; source: BVI questionnaires)

	Percent	No.
0–33%	27%	(33)
34–50%	38%	(46)
50% +	35%	(42)

Cott, *Grounding of Modern Feminism*, p. 353, n. 34, calculates the data on women clients in a slightly different way but reaches essentially the same conclusion.

51. The annual income levels of women surveyed in 1920 are summarized as follows (N = 73):

	Percent	No.
$3,501–$6,000	14%	(10)
$2,000–$3,500	34%	(25)
$1,000–$1,999	36%	(26)
$100–$999	16%	(12)

52. The *Martindale-Hubbell Law Directory, 1939* reported the estimated net worth of women lawyers as follows (N = 482):

	Percent	No.
Over $100,000	1%	(6)
$50,000–$100,000	2%	(7)
$30,000–$50,000	3%	(12)
$20,000–$30,000	4%	(20)
$10,000–$20,000	9%	(43)
$5,000–$10,000	16%	(77)
Under $5,000	66%	(317)

53. Gerard W. Gawalt, "The Impact of Industrialization on the Legal Profession in Massachusetts, 1870–1900," in Gerard W. Gawalt, [ed.], *The New High Priests: Lawyers in Post–Civil War America* (Westport, Conn.: Greenwood, 1984), pp. 99–100.

54. Auerbach, *Unequal Justice*, p. 25.

55. Hummer, *Decade of Elusive Promise*, p. 97; and Doerschuk, *Women in the Law*, p. 57.

56. Elizabeth Kemper Adams, Ph.D., *Women Professional Workers: A Study Made for the Women's Educational and Industrial Union* (Chautauqua, N.Y.: Chautauqua Press, 1921), p. 69; and Hummer, *Decade of Elusive Promise*, p. 92.

57. Hummer, *Decade of Elusive Promise*, pp. 100–101.

58. Adams, *Women Professional Workers*, p. 380.

59. *Martindale-Hubbell Law Directory, 1939*.

60. The *Martindale-Hubbell Law Directory, 1939* yielded the following analysis of estimate of legal ability among women lawyers (total N = 3,461):

Rank	Percent	No.
a	2%	(74)
b	4%	(145)
c	9%	(293)
no rank	85%	(2,949)

61. Calculated from *Martindale-Hubbell Law Directory, 1939*.

62. Doerschuk, *Women in the Law*, pp. 73–101.

63. Ibid., p. 76.

64. Laura Miller Derry, ed., *Digest of Women Lawyers and Judges: Biographical Sketches and Data of Women Lawyers and Judges of the United States and Its Possessions, 1949* (U.S.A.: Laura Miller Derry, 1949), p. vi.

65. Angel Kwolek-Folland, *Engendering Business: Men and Women in the Corporate Office, 1870–1930* (Baltimore, Md.: Johns Hopkins University Press, 1994), pp. 3–4.

8. "The Golden Age of Opportunity for Women"

1. Rosalind Goodrich Bates, "Portia through the Centuries," 21 *Women Lawyers' Journal* 9–12 (1934).

2. On Emma Haddock, see Virginia G. Drachman, *Women Lawyers and the Origins of Professional Identity in America: The Letters of the Equity Club, 1887 to 1890* (Ann Arbor: University of Michigan Press, 1993), pp. 231–233.

3. Bates, "Portia through the Centuries," p. 12.

4. Ibid., p. 9.

5. Beatrice Doerschuk, *Women in the Law*, bulletin no. 3, Bureau of Vocational Information (New York, 1920), table 2, pp. 114–124; and Alfred Zantzinger Reed, *Training for the Public Profession of the Law: Historical Development and Principal Contemporary Problems of Legal Education in the United States with Some Account of Conditions in England and Canada*, bulletin no. 15, Carnegie Foundation for Advancement of Teaching (New York, 1921), appendix, p. 441; and Table 2.

6. J. Clay Smith, Jr., *Emancipation: The Making of the Black Lawyer, 1844–1944* (Philadelphia: University of Pennsylvania Press, 1993), p. 613.

7. See, for example, Nancy F. Cott, *The Grounding of Modern Feminism* (New Haven, Conn.: Yale University Press, 1987); Rosalind Rosenberg, *Beyond Separate Spheres: Intellectual Roots of Feminism* (New Haven, Conn.: Yale University Press, 1982); and Estelle B. Friedman, "The New Woman: Changing Views of Women in the 1920s," *Journal of American History* 61 (Sept. 1974): 372–393; J. Stanley Lemons, *The Woman Citizen: Social Feminism in the 1920s* (Chicago: University of Illinois Press, 1975); and William Henry Chafe, *The American Woman: Her Changing Social, Economic, and Political Roles, 1920–1970* (New York: Oxford University Press, 1972).

8. Edward A. Purcell, Jr., *The Crisis of Democratic Theory: Scientific Naturalism and the Problem of Value* (Lexington: University of Kentucky Press, 1973).

9. Rosenberg, *Beyond Separate Spheres;* Ellen Fitzpatrick, *Endless Crusade: Women Social Scientists and Progressive Reform* (New York: Oxford University Press, 1990); Regina G. Kunzel, *Fallen Women, Problem Girls: Unmarried Mothers and the Professionalization of Social Work, 1890–1945* (New Haven, Conn.: Yale University Press, 1993); and Patricia M. Hummer, *The Decade of Elusive Promise: Professional Women in the United States, 1920–1930* (Ann Arbor, Mich.: UMI Research Press, 1979).

10. On the meritocracy and professional women, see Cott, *Grounding of Mod-*

ern Feminism, pp. 213–249. On women doctors, see Virginia G. Drachman, *Hospital with a Heart: Women Doctors and the Paradox of Separatism at the New England Hospital, 1862–1969* (Ithaca, N.Y.: Cornell University Press, 1984), pp. 151–177; and Mary Roth Walsh, *"Doctors Wanted: No Women Need Apply": Sexual Barriers in the Medical Profession, 1835–1975* (New Haven, Conn.: Yale University Press),p. 180.

11. "Sane Suggestion," 14 *Women Lawyers' Journal* 8–9 (1926), quotation from p. 9.

12. Note on Alice M. Birdsall in 9 *Women Lawyers' Journal* 6 (1919). For other expressions of this view, see "Judge Emma Fall Schofield, Former Chelsean, Happy in Work as Mother-Lawyer," unidentified newspaper, Dec. 5, 1931, in Portia Law School Scrapbook, vol. 5, p. 38, PLSA; and "No Restless Sex, Says Woman Lawyer," *Boston Advertiser*, Dec. 5, 1926, in Portia Law School Scrapbook, vol. 2, p. 101, PLSA.

13. Jeannette Phillips Gibbs, *Portia Marries* (Boston: Little, Brown, 1926).

14. On Gibbs, see *Who's Who in Massachusetts, 1942–1943*, (Boston: Larkin, Roosevelt, and Larkin, 1942), p. 276; and "Marrying the Muse," *Independent*, Sept. 24, 1927, pp. 303–305.

15. Obituaries for Benjamin Phillips are in the *Boston Globe*, Feb. 12, 1917, p. 3, and *Boston Herald*, Feb. 12, 1917, p. 6.

16. Gibbs, *Portia Marries*, p. 32.

17. Ibid., p. 34.

18. Ibid., p. 19.

19. Ibid., p. 139.

20. Ibid., p. 207.

21. Ibid., p. 202.

22. Ibid., p. 203.

23. Ibid., p. 205.

24. Ibid., p. 473.

25. The character of Miss Padelford is in Charles C. Moore, "The Woman Lawyer," 5 *Green Bag* 525–531 (Dec. 1914). For a discussion of "Woman Lawyer," see Chapter 4.

26. *Saturday Review of Literature*, Oct. 9, 1926, p. 178; "A Feminine Gibbs," *Bookman*, Nov. 1926, pp. 350–351; *Independent*, Sept. 4, 1926, p. 276; *Outlook*, Sept. 29, 1926, p. 155; "She Got What Every Woman Wants: Career-Hubby-Money—and Babies!" *New York Evening Post*, Aug. 21, 1926, p. 2; *Wisconsin Library Bulletin*, Nov. 1926, p. 298; and *Boston Evening Transcript*, Aug. 25, 1926, p. 6.

27. The ninety-three women surveyed by the Bureau of Vocational Information believed that law offered general opportunities for women, as follows: to develop oneself, 66 percent (61); for financial gain, 25 percent (23); and to help society, 10 percent (9).

28. "Miss Helen Carloss Dies; Retired U.S Tax Attorney," *Washington Star* [Dec. 24, 1948]; unidentified article, *Washington Post* [Mar. 28, 1934]; and "As-

sistant to Attorney General Handles Much Work on Trains," *Washington Post* [Mar. 28, 1934], all in box 2, folder 23, A. Matthews Papers.

29. Unidentified article, *Washington Post* [Mar. 28, 1934].

30. "Assistant to Attorney General Handles Much Work on Trains."

31. Eleanor Rust Collier, "The Boston University School of Law, 1872–1960," unpublished paper, 1960, in Pappas Law Library, Boston University Law School, p. 43; and Eileen McCann, "Judge Emma Fall Schofield, Former Chelsean, Happy in Work as Mother-Lawyer," unidentified newspaper [Dec. 5, 1931], in Portia Law School Scrapbook, vol. 5, p. 38, PLSA.

32. Emma Fall Schofield, *Anna Christy Fall: My Remarkable Mother, April 23, 1855–January 13, 1930* (Malden, Mass.: published by the author, 1978); and Alice Parker Hutchins, "Anna Christy Fall," 18 *Women Lawyers' Journal* 36–37 (1930).

33. McCann, "Judge Emma Fall Schofield."

34. J. D. Ratcliff, "Justice—Edith Sampson Style," *Reader's Digest* (Nov. 1968): 168–174, in Employment Collection, box 40, Edith Sampson folder, Smith Collection; Darlene Clark Hine, ed., *Black Women in America: An Historical Encyclopedia* (Brooklyn, N.Y.: Carlson, 1993), pp. 1002–1003; Jessie Carney Smith, ed., *Notable Black American Women* (Detroit: Gale Research, 1991), pp. 969–973; *Negro Women in the Judiciary* (Chicago: Alpha Kappa Alpha Sorority, 1968), pp. 14–15; "Lady Lawyers Carry on Battle for Sex and Race Equality in Courts," *Ebony* (Aug. 1947): 18–21, esp. p. 19; Smith, *Emancipation*, pp. 37, 386, 433; and Dorothy Thomas, *Women Lawyers in the United States* (New York: Scarecrow Press, 1957), pp. 542–543.

35. Ratcliff, "Justice—Edith Sampson Style," p. 169.

36. 21 *Case and Comment* 353–394 (1914).

37. Isabel Giles, "The Twentieth Century Portia," 21 *Case and Comment* 353–356 (1914).

38. Ibid., p. 354.

39. Ibid.

40. Edith J. Griswold, "Interesting Features of Patent Law," 21 *Case and Comment* 358–360 (1914).

41. Marion Weston Cottle, LL.M., "The Prejudice against Women Lawyers: How Can It Be Overcome?" 21 *Case and Comment* 371–373 (1914), quotation from 371.

42. Ibid., p. 371.

43. Jean H. Norris, "The Women Lawyers' Association," 21 *Case and Comment* 364–366 (1914); and Jean H. Norris, LL.B., LL.M., "A New Future for Women at Law," *Association Monthly* [1920]: 286–287, in Employment Collection, box 40, folder 1, Smith Collection.

44. Nellie Carlin, "The Work of Public Guardian," 21 *Case and Comment* 374–375 (1914).

45. Other publications echoed *Case and Comment.* See "A Legal Panorama,"

Phi Delta Delta (May 1927): 195–214; and Zora Putnam Wilkins, "Portia Undisguised," *Woman Citizen*, Sept. 6, 1924, pp. 14–15, 25–26.

46. Rose Young, "Your Daughter's Career," *Good Housekeeping* (Oct. 1915): 470–477.

47. Ibid., p. 474.

48. Ibid., p. 473.

49. Helen Christine Bennett, "The Law Is Long—But It's Worth It!" *Green Book Magazine* (May 1920): 46–48.

50. Ibid., p. 47.

51. Ibid.

52. Ibid., p. 46.

53. Ibid., p. 48.

54. See *Green Book Magazine* (Nov. 1920): cover.

55. Helen Christine Bennett, "A Woman and the Law," *Green Book Magazine* (Nov. 1920): 14–15, 94, 96. On Janoer, see Rosalie F. Janoer, "The Practicing Woman Lawyer's Need," 9 *Women Lawyers' Journal* 12 (1920).

56. Bennett, "A Woman and the Law," p. 96.

57. Ibid.

58. Ibid.

59. Bureau of Vocational Information questionnaire 180, Mar. 9, 1920, BVI Records. All BVI questionnaires can be found in the BVI Records.

60. Nell B. Lynn, "Representative Women of the Golden West," *Business Woman's Magazine* (Dec. 1914): 31–32, quotation from p. 32, in Clipping Book, box 22, Bullock Papers. Also on Adams, see Barbara Sicherman and Carol Hurd Green, eds., *Notable American Women, the Modern Period* (Cambridge, Mass.: Harvard University Press, 1980), pp. 3–5; "Wins High Place in Federal Work," *Springfield Weekly Republican* Apr. 21, 1921, Employment Collection, box 40, folder 2, Smith Collection; and papers of Adams in various collections of the Bancroft Library, University of California, Berkeley.

61. The best source on Mabel Walker Willebrandt is Dorothy M. Brown, *Mabel Walker Willebrandt: A Study of Power, Loyalty, and Law* (Knoxville: University of Tennessee Press, 1984).

62. See Smith, *Emancipation*, pp. 384–385; 419; 432, n. 140; 557; 565; 575; 601, n. 212. See also Hine, *Black Women in America*, p. 35; and unidentified article in *Chicago Legal News*, July 15, 1920, p. 405.

63. Smith, *Emancipation*, p. 384.

64. Florence Ellinwood Allen, *To Do Justly* (Cleveland, Ohio: Case Western Reserve University Press, 1965), esp. pp. 63–72, 93–95; Jeanette E. Tuve, *First Lady of the Law: Florence Ellinwood Allen* (New York: University Press of America, 1984), esp. pp. 40–70, 102–110; Annabel Lee, "Her Honor, Judge Allen," *Independent Woman* (Dec. 1939): 385, 399–400; and Sicherman and Green, *Notable American Women, The Modern Period*, pp. 11–13.

65. *Negro Women in the Judiciary*, pp. 4–5; Hine, *Black Women in America*,

pp. 145–147; Smith, *Emancipation*, pp. 402, 405–406, 422; Smith, *Notable Black American Women*, pp. 94–95; "First Negro Woman Gets City Law Post," *New York Times*, Apr. 8, 1937, p. 3; Thomas, *Women Lawyers in the United States*, pp. 56–57; "Judge Jane Bolin to Be Honored by CUNY Law School," *New York Amsterdam News*, Mar. 5, 1994, p. 18.

66. Allen, *To Do Justly*, p. 95.

67. "Assistant to Attorney General Handles Much Work on Trains."

68. Ellamarye Failor, "Trial Practice," *Phi Delta Delta* (May 1932): 152–158, quotation from p. 157. Also on women attorneys challenging men in court, see Susan C. O'Neill, "Pioneer Practice in Connecticut," in 4 *Women Lawyers' Journal* 19–20 (1914), orig. printed in *Waterbury American* (Waterbury, Conn.), June 9, 1909.

69. Quoted in Mary C. Love Collins, "Some Suggestions," *Phi Delta Delta* (May 1927): 213–214, quotation from p. 213; see also "The Unsentimental Woman Juror," *Chicago Legal News*, Feb. 12, 1924, p. 237.

70. Mary G. Siegel, " 'Crossing the Bar': A 'She' Lawyer in 1917," *Women's Rights Law Reporter* (summer 1982): 357–363, quotation from p. 360.

71. Katherine Kilpatrick Makielski, "Fifty Years of Women in the Law," in Mary H. Zimmerman, ed., *Seventy-Five-Year History of National Association of Women Lawyers, 1899–1974* (Lansing, Mich.: Wellman, 1975), p. 146.

72. "Do Not Call Us Portias," 18 *Women Lawyers' Journal* 6 (1930); see also Failor, "Trial Practice," p. 158.

73. "Appropriate Attire for the Woman Court Lawyer," 1 *Women Lawyers' Journal* 34–35 quotation from 35 (1912).

74. "The Question of Cap and Gown," 6 *Women Lawyers' Journal* 69 (1914). See also "On Wearing Hats in Court by Women Lawyers," *Law Notes* (May 1914): 21.

75. See Jeanette C. Laver and Robert H. Laver, "The Language of Dress: A Sociohistorical Study of the Meaning of Clothing in America," *Canadian Review of American Sources* 10 (1979): 305–323.

76. Siegel, " 'Crossing the Bar,' " p. 360.

77. Tiera Farrow, *Lawyer in Petticoats* (New York: Vantage, 1953), pp. 70–71.

78. "Former St. Louisan, First Woman Judge," *St. Louis Dispatch*, Feb. 8, 1912, in Employment Collection, box 40, folder Bell, Smith Collection. On Whaley, see "New York Woman Lawyer Takes Off Her Hat to Argue Her Cases," *Afro-American Weekly*, July 25, 1931, p. 5, and Smith, *Emancipation*, pp. 404–405, 406–407. Georgia Bullock also wore no hat in court. See clipping from *Los Angeles Times*, Jan. 23, 1913, box 18, Bullock Papers.

79. "Eternal Question of Dress," 6 *Women Lawyers' Journal* 26 (1917).

80. Farrow, *Lawyer in Petticoats*, pp. 80–81.

81. "The Question of Cap and Gown," 3 *Women Lawyers' Journal* 69 (1914).

82. Susan C. O'Neill, "Pioneer Practice in Connecticut."

83. Percy T. Edrop, D.D., "New York's Family Court: A Study in Social Service," *Churchman*, Jan. 27, 1923, pp. 13–14, quotation from p. 13, in Em-

ployment Collection, box 40, folder Norris, Smith Collection; on Sampson, see Ratcliff, "Justice—Edith Sampson Style," p. 169.

84. Elizabeth Kemper Adams, Ph.D., *Women Professional Workers: A Study Made for the Women's Educational and Industrial Union* (Chautauqua, N.Y.: Chautauqua Press, 1921), p. 31; Virginia Collier, *Marriage and Careers: A Study of One Hundred Women Who Are Wives, Mothers, Homemakers, and Professional Women* (New York: Channel Bookshop, 1926). On the new views of marriage in the early twentieth century, see Cott, *Grounding of Modern Feminism*, pp. 156–159, 179–211; Elaine Tyler May, *Great Expectations: Marriage and Divorce in Post-Victorian America* (Chicago: University of Chicago Press, 1980); Elaine Showalter, ed., *These Modern Women: Autobiographical Essays from the Twenties* (Old Westbury, N.Y.: Feminist Press, 1978), pp. 3–29; Barbara Sicherman, "College and Careers: Historical Perspectives on the Lives and Work Patterns of Women College Graduates," in John Mack Faragher and Florence Howe, eds., *Women and Higher Education in American History* (New York: W. W. Norton, 1988), pp. 130–164; and Joyce Antler, *Lucy Sprague Mitchell: The Making of a Modern Woman* (New Haven, Conn.: Yale University Press, 1987). On marriage and career for contemporary women lawyers, see David Chambers, "Accommodation and Satisfaction: Women and Men Lawyers and the Balance of Work and Family," 14 *Law and Social Inquiry* 251–287 (1989); and Cynthia Fuchs Epstein, "Law Partners and Partial Partners: Strains and Solutions in the Dual-Career Family Enterprise," 24 *Human Relations* 549–564 (1971).

85. Showalter, *These Modern Women*, 91.

86. BVI questionnaire 147, Mar. 2, 1920.

87. BVI questionnaire 136, Mar. 12, 1920.

88. BVI questionnaire 17, Mar. 12, 1920; also BVI questionnaire 83, Apr. 4, 1920.

89. BVI questionnaire 123, Apr. 5, 1920; also BVI questionnaire 109, Apr. 3, 1920.

90. BVI questionnaire, 161, Mar. 2, 1920.

91. BVI questionnaire 172, Mar. 5, 1920.

92. BVI questionnaire 99, Mar. 22, 1920.

93. BVI questionnaire 171, Mar. 4, 1920.

94. "Judge Emma Fall Schofield."

95. BVI questionnaire 83, Apr. 4, 1920.

96. Smith, *Emancipation*, pp. 386, 406.

97. "Uses Maiden Name at Bar," *New York Times*, June 10, 1927, p. 11.

98. "Roger Nash Baldwin," in Alden Whitman, ed., *American Reformers* (New York: H. W. Wilson, 1985), pp. 45–48, quotation from p. 47. On marrying the "right man," see Cott, *Grounding of Modern Feminism*, p. 195.

99. Roger N. Baldwin, "Memo on Madeleine Zabriskie Doty," Oct. 1978, typed memo in Doty Papers. See also Peggy Lamson, *Roger Baldwin: Founder of the American Civil Liberties Union* (Boston: Houghton Mifflin, 1976), pp. 121–122.

100. Inez Milholland Boissevain to Eugen Jan Boissevain, Oct. 17, [1913],

in box 1, folder 2, Milholland Papers. On Milholland as a new woman, see Barbara Page, "Inez Milholland: Theorizing a Feminist Heroine," unpublished paper delivered at the Berkshire Conference on the History of Women, Douglass College, Rutgers University, June 1990.

101. Inez Milholland to Eugen Jan Boissevain, Oct. 18, [1913], in box 1, folder 2, Milholland Papers.

9. "Girl Lawyer Has Small Chance for Success"

1. " 'Girl Lawyer Has Small Chance for Success,' Says Mrs. Lesser," *Saturday Evening Traveller* (Boston), June 8, 1912, p. 2 of supplement.

2. On women doctors, see Virginia G. Drachman, "The Limits of Progress: Women Doctors' Professional Lives, 1881–1926," *Bulletin of the History of Medicine* 60 (1986): 58–72. On the decline of opportunity for doctors, academics, and lawyers in the 1920s, see Patricia M. Hummer, *The Decade of Elusive Promise: Professional Women in the United States, 1920–1930* (Ann Arbor, UMI Research Press, 1976).

3. Bureau of Vocational Information questionnaire 18, Mar. 2, 1920. All BVI questionnaires can be found in the BVI Records.

4. BVI questionnaire 131, Mar. 27, 1920.

5. Gertrude Smith to Inez Milholland, n.d., reel 2, folder 21, Milholland Papers.

6. On Kross, see "Seventy Thousand Work People Clients for Woman," *New York Times*, July 22, 1923, p. 7. On Schieber, see "Angel in Disguise," *People* (Dec. 18, 1995): 99.

7. BVI questionnaire 200, n.d.

8. BVI questionnaire 146, Mar. 7, 1920.

9. BVI questionnaire 199, Apr. 6, 1920.

10. BVI questionnaire 239, Mar. 13, 1920.

11. BVI questionnaire 95, Mar. 11, 1918.

12. BVI questionnaire 253, Apr. 22, 1920.

13. Ibid.

14. Tiera Farrow, *Lawyer in Petticoats* (New York: Vantage, 1953), pp. 61–66, 75–77.

15. Henrietta Dunlop Stonestreet, "Women Lawyers vs. the Baltimore Bar Association," 19 *Women Lawyers' Journal* 18–19 (1931).

16. See "Women Lawyers *vel non* in Georgia," 15 *Law Notes* 84 (1911); "Women Lawyers in Georgia? Not Yet," 15 *Law Notes* 102 (1911); and "Georgia Legislators Set Back the Clock of Progress," 1 *Women Lawyers' Journal* 17 (1911). Letter from Georgia McIntire-Weaver to Catharine Waugh McCulloch, Sept. 2, 1911, box 13, folder 309, McCulloch Papers, series 6, Dillon Collection.

17. Rose Young, "Your Daughter's Career," *Good Housekeeping* (Oct. 1915): 470–477. See also 1 *Women Lawyers' Journal* 57 (1913); 2 *Women Lawyers' Journal*

66 (1913); and "Woman Lawyer Follows Up Case," 3 *Women Lawyers' Journal* 29 (1914).

18. *Ex parte* Hale, 473 Ga. 216 (1916).

19. Betty Reynolds Cobb to Emma P. Hirth, Apr. 9, 1920, BVI Records. On the number of women lawyers in Georgia, see United States Bureau of the Census, *The Fourteenth Census of the United States*, vol. 4, (1920), pp. 70–71.

20. BVI questionnaire 251, Mar. 1, 1920.

21. "Women Lawyers," *Woman's Journal* 35 (1904): 153. On African-American women lawyers, see Darlene Clark Hine, ed., *Black Women in America: An Historical Encyclopedia* (Brooklyn: Carlson Publishing, 1993); Jessie Carney Smith, ed., *Notable Black American Women* (Detroit: Gale Research, 1992); Jessie Carney Smith, ed., *Notable Black American Women*, bk. 2 (Detroit: Gale Research, 1996); J. Clay Smith, Jr., *Emancipation: The Making of the Black Lawyer, 1844–1944* (Philadelphia: University of Pennsylvania, 1993); Dorothy C. Salem, ed., *African American Women: A Biographical Dictionary* (New York: Garland Press, 1993; "Lady Lawyers," *Ebony* (Aug. 1947): 18; and *Negro Women in the Judiciary*, Heritage Series no. 1, Alpha Kappa Alpha Sorority, Chicago, 1968.

22. "Lady Lawyers," p. 19.

23. Ibid.

24. Peter Wallenstein, " 'These New and Strange Beings': Women in the Legal Profession in Virginia, 1890–1990," *Virginia Magazine of History and Biography* (Apr. 1993): 193, 211.

25. Smith, *Emancipation*, pp. 300–303, 331, 351.

26. Ibid., p. 632.

27. By 1940, African-American women lawyers lived in the following parts of the country: ten in New York; eight in Illinois; three each in California and Virginia; two each in Indiana, Michigan, Ohio, and Pennsylvania; and only one each in Alaska, the District of Columbia, Florida, Iowa, Massachusetts, Minnesota, and Texas. There were no African-American women lawyers in thirty-four states. Smith, *Emancipation*, pp. 635–636.

28. "Is the Conviction of a Beautiful Woman an Impossibility?" 12 *American Lawyer* 391–392, quotation from 392 (1904).

29. James J. Montague, "It Can't Be Done," 6 *Women Lawyers' Journal* 53 (1917).

30. BVI questionnaire 81, Apr. 16, 1920; see also BVI questionnaire 150, Mar. 1, 1920.

31. Beatrice Doerschuk, *Women in the Law: An Analysis of Training, Practice, and Salaried Positions*, bulletin no. 3, The Bureau of Vocational Information, (New York, 1920), p. 48.

32. Bessie Isabel Giles, "The 'Eternal Feminine,' " 2 *Women Lawyers' Journal* 54 (1912).

33. BVI questionnaire 191, Apr. 24, 1920. See also "A Truer Perspective?" 4 *Women Lawyers' Journal* 47 (1915) and Young, "Your Daughter's Career," p. 470.

34. "Bar Group Assails Rivals of Lawyers," *New York Times*, Aug. 19, 1930, p. 16.

35. "Address of Hon. John M. Patterson, Associate Judge of the Court of Common Pleas, No. 1, of the County of Philadelphia, Made on the Occasion of the First Meeting of the Portia Club," 7 *Women Lawyers' Journal* 49, 64 (1918).

36. Vere Radir-Norton, "The Practice of Law from the Viewpoint of a Woman Lawyer," *Phi Delta Delta* (Jan. 1923): 14.

37. Ibid., p. 15.

38. Zora Putnam Wilkins, "Portias Undisguised," 9 *Woman Citizen* 14–15, 25–26 (1924).

39. On the link between capitalism and corporate law, see Auerbach, *Unequal Justice*, pp. 142–143; Morton J. Horwitz, *The Transformation of American Law, 1870–1960: The Crisis of Legal Orthodoxy* (New York: Oxford University Press, 1992), pp. 144–167; and Lawrence M. Friedman, *A History of American Law* (New York: Simon and Schuster, 1985), pp. 511–525.

40. William P. Rogers, "Is Law a Field for Woman's Work?" 24 *American Bar Association Reports* 548, 552 (1901).

41. Jessie Ashley, "Shall We Reverence the Law?" 2 *Women Lawyers' Journal* 37 (1912). On Jessie Ashley, see A. C. B., "Jessie Ashley," *Call* (New York) [1919]; "Friends Pay Tribute to Miss Ashley's Memory," *Call* [1919] and "Jessie Ashley a Victim of Pneumonia," *Call* Jan. 21, 1919, all in box 2, folder 30, Dennett Papers.

42. Ashley, "Shall We Reverence the Law?"

43. Elinor Byrns, "The Woman Lawyer," *New Republic*, Jan. 8, 1916, pp. 246–247.

44. Ibid., p. 246.

45. Ibid.

46. Ibid., p. 247.

47. Ibid.

48. Ibid.

49. Wilkins, "Portias Undisguised," p. 25.

50. Anna Moscowitz, "The Night Court for Women in NYC," 5 *Women Lawyers' Journal* 9 (1915).

51. On the juvenile courts, see David J. Rothman, *Conscience and Convenience: The Asylum and Its Alternatives in Progressive America* (Boston: Little, Brown, 1980), pp. 205–260; Estelle B. Freedman, *Maternal Justice: Miriam Van Waters and the Female Reform Tradition* (Chicago: University of Chicago Press, 1996), pp. 83–90; Michael Grossberg, *Governing the Hearth: Law and the Family in Nineteenth-Century America* (Chapel Hill: University of North Carolina Press, 1985), pp. 279, 303–304; Robyn Muncy, *Creating a Female Dominion in American Reform, 1890–1935* (New York: Oxford University Press, 1991), p. 18; and Edward T. James, ed., *Notable American Women, 1607–1905* (Cambridge, Mass.: Harvard University Press, 1971), p. 370.

52. Rothman, *Conscience and Convenience*, p. 253.

53. "Orfa Jean Shontz Referee Juvenile Court, Los Angeles," 6 *Women Lawyers' Journal* 30 (1917).

54. Grace Irene Rohleder, LL.M., *Woman on the Bench* (Washington, D.C.: Fairview, 1920), p. 16.

55. L. L. Fawcett, "Plea for Woman on the Bench," 6 *Women Lawyers' Journal* 37 (1917).

56. "The Woman Judge," 22 *Law Notes* 83 (1918). On Kathryn Sellers, see "What Our First Woman Judge Thinks of Judging," *Literary Digest*, May 9, 1925, p. 46, in Employment Collection, box 40, folder Sellers, Smith Collection.

57. Pat Noonan, "Her Honor, Georgia Bullock," pp. 6–7, unpublished essay in box 4, Bullock Papers. On Bullock in the Los Angeles Women's Court, see Beverly B. Cook, "Institution-Building: A New Public Role for Professional Women in the Los Angeles Women's Court," unpublished paper delivered at the Seventh Berkshire Conference, Wellesley College, Mass., June 19–21, 1987. On female prisoner see Georgia P. Bullock to Kate Crane-Gartz, May 24, 1927, box 9, Bullock Papers.

58. Rohleder, *Woman on the Bench*, p. 19. See also "Extracts from an Interview with Judge Reah Whitehead," 5 *Women Lawyers' Journal* 11 (1915); "Women Should Be Judged by Women," 4 *Women Lawyers' Journal* 45 (1915); Edith Meserve Atkinson, "Wanted—More Women Juvenile Judges," *Phi Delta Delta* (May 1927): 198–200; and Dorothy Dix, "The Case for Women Judges," *Good Housekeeping* (July 1914): 48–51.

59. Farrow, *Lawyer in Petticoats*, p. 170.

60. See Dix, "Case for Women Judges"; and Anne Shannon Monroe, "When Women Sit in Judgment," *Good Housekeeping* (Apr. 1920): 46–47, 145–161. See also Mildred Adams, "Can Women Make Good as Judges?" *Christian Advocate*, Dec. 10, 1925, pp. 1520–1522 in box 1, folder 3, Florence Allen Papers, Smith Collection.

61. Edward Bellamy, *Looking Backward* (New York: Signet, 1960), p. 37; and Charlotte Perkins Gilman, *Herland* (New York: Pantheon, 1979).

62. On the Women Lawyers' Association, see Jean H. Norris, LL.M., "The Women Lawyers' Association," 4 *Women Lawyers' Journal* 28 (1915); Sarah Stephenson, "Cooperation of Women Lawyers," 7 *Women Lawyers' Journal* 68 (1918); and "Annual Banquet of the Women Lawyers' Association," 11 *Women Lawyers' Journal* 17 (1922). On the Women's Bar Association of the District of Columbia, see Clarice F. Hens, *Women's Bar Association, The First Fifty Years . . ., 1917–1967: A Brief History of the Women's Bar Association of the District of Columbia* (Washington, D.C.: Women's Bar Association, 1967); Ida Moyers McElroy and Edwina Austin Avery, "The Women's Bar Association of the District of Columbia," 21 *Women Lawyers' Journal* 21–26 (1935). On the Women's Bar Association of Illinois (WBAI), see *Women's Bar Association of Illinois: Twentieth Anniversary Journal and Directory, 1934–1935*, ([Chicago: Women's Bar Association], 1914). Pa-

pers of the WBAI are available at the Chicago Historical Society, Chicago, Illinois. On the Portia Club of Milwaukee, see "The Portia Club of Milwaukee," 53 *Chicago Legal News*, Sept. 9, 1920, p. 53.

63. Norris, "Women Lawyers' Association"; Stephenson, "Cooperation of Women Lawyers"; and "Annual Banquet of the Women Lawyers' Association."

64. McElroy and Avery, "The Women's Bar Association of the District of Columbia," 21.

65. "Women Lawyers' Association Dinner," 3 *Women Lawyers' Journal* 62 (1914).

66. On the National Association of Women Lawyers, see Mary H[elen] Zimmerman, ed., *Seventy-Five Years of National Association of Women Lawyers, 1899–1974* (Lansing, Mich.: Wellman, 1975); Katharine R. Pike, "The National Association of Women Lawyers," 18 *Women Lawyers' Journal* 14–15 (1930); Lillian D. Rock, "The Need for and the Purpose of the National Association of Women Lawyers," 18 *Women Lawyers' Journal* 15–17 (1930); Marion Gold Lewis, "Minutes of the National Association of Women Lawyers, Atlantic City," 19 *Women Lawyers' Journal* 10–16 (1931); and Burnita Shelton Matthews, "Why an Association of Women Lawyers," 21 *Women Lawyers' Journal* 32 (1935).

67. 9 *Women Lawyers' Journal* 6 (1919).

68. L. H. Shoemaker, "Sane Suggestion," 14 *Women Lawyers' Journal* 9 (1926).

69. See Rosalind Goodrich Bates, "Loyalty and the Woman Lawyer," 19 *Women Lawyers' Journal* 29–30, 33 (1932); and Florence Thacker, "The Married Woman Worker," 19 *Women Lawyers' Journal* 32–33 (1932).

70. Matthews, "Why an Association of Women Lawyers."

71. Lillian D. Rock, "The Need for and the Purpose of the National Association of Women Lawyers." See also Katherine R. Pike to Georgia P. Bullock, Dec. 30, 1926, box 9, Bullock Papers. On a similar plea by women doctors to join the all-women's medical associations, see Drachman, *Hospital with a Heart*, pp. 178–195.

72. Georgia P. Bullock to Nellie Brewer Pierce, July 12, 1924, box 14, Bullock Papers; reelection card, n.d., box 18, Bullock Papers.

73. Various Supporters to Mrs. Bullock, June 21, 1923, box 14, Bullock Papers.

74. Georgia P. Bullock to Caroline P. Kelly, [undated], box 10, Bullock Papers; Georgia P. Bullock to Maury Maverick, Aug. 27, 1928, box 10, Bullock Papers.

75. Endorsement of Georgia P. Bullock by Phi Delta Delta, 1927; Annette [Hunley] to Georgia P. Bullock, Apr. 5, 1927; Georgia P. Bullock to Annette Hunley, Apr. 13, 1927; all in box 9, Bullock Papers.

76. Georgia P. Bullock to T. S. Moodie, May 3, 1929, Bullock Papers.

77. J. M. Fursee to Olive Scott Gabriel, Aug. 1, 1925; Olive Scott Gabriel to Georgia P. Bullock, n.d.; Georgia P. Bullock to Olive Scott Gabriel, Sept. 23, 1925, box 8; all in Bullock Papers. See also miscellaneous correspondence

in box 14, folder on elections, Bullock Papers. The quotation is from Gabriel to Bullock, n.d.

78. Rock, "The Need for and the Purpose of the National Association of Women Lawyers."

79. On Matthews, see Burnita Shelton Matthews, "Women Should Have Equal Rights with Men: A Reply," 11 *American Bar Association Journal* 117 (1926); "The Status of Women," typed report prepared by Burnita Shelton Matthews, 1927, in box 2, folder 51, B. Matthews Papers; Burnita Shelton Matthews, "Women Lawyers and Lawmaking," *Kappa Beta Pi Quarterly*, Mar. 1927, pp. 11–13, in box 2, folder 33, B. Matthews Papers; Burnita Shelton Matthews, *The Equal Rights Amendment* (Washington, D.C.: National Woman's Party, 1934), in box 2, folder 50, B. Matthews Papers; Burnita Shelton Matthews, "Glimpse of Laws Shows Need for Equal Rights," n.d., reprinted from National Women's Party, *Equal Rights*, in box 2, folder 50, B. Matthews Papers; and "Burnita Shelton Matthews," *Current Biography* (Apr. 1950): 35–37. See generally B. Matthews Papers.

80. Susan Ware, *Beyond Suffrage: Women in the New Deal* (Cambridge, Mass.: Harvard University Press, 1981), pp. 60–67.

81. Mary Connor Myers, "Women Lawyers in Federal Positions," 19 *Women Lawyers' Journal* 19–20, quotation from 19 (1932).

82. Mary Connor Myers, "Women Lawyers in the Department of Justice," 21 *Women Lawyers' Journal* 13–16, quotations from 13, 16 (1935).

83. Farrow, *Lawyer in Petticoats*, p. 170. On the new companionate marriage, see generally Elaine Tyler May, *Great Expectations: Marriage and Divorce in Post-Victorian America* (Chicago: University of Chicago Press, 1980); Nancy F. Cott, *Grounding of Modern Feminism* (New Haven, Conn.: Yale University Press, 1987), pp. 175–211; Elaine Showalter, ed., *These Modern Women: Autobiographical Essays from the Twenties* (Old Westbury, N.Y.: Feminist Press, 1978), pp. 3–29; and Joyce Antler, *Lucy Sprague Mitchell: The Making of a Modern Woman* (New Haven, Conn.: Yale University Press, 1978), pp. 161–169, 256–262.

84. On Willebrandt, see Dorothy M. Brown, *Mabel Walker Willebrandt: A Study of Power, Loyalty, and Law* (Knoxville: University of Tennessee Press, 1984).

85. Mabel Walker Willebrandt, "Give Women a Fighting Chance!" *Smart Set* (Feb. 1930): 24–26, 106–107, quotations from pp. 24, 25; see also Brown, *Mabel Walker Willebrandt*, pp. 19–34. On the more general problem of the lack of companionship women endured in the modern marriage, see R. Le Clerc Phillips, "Getting Ahead of the Joneses," *Harper's Magazine* (Apr. 1927): 579–585.

86. Roger Nash Baldwin, Memo on Madeliene Zabriskie Doty (Oct. 1978), box 1, folder 4, Doty Papers. See also Peggy Lamson, *Roger Baldwin, Founder of the American Civil Liberties Union* (Boston: Houghton Mifflin, 1976), pp. 121–122; and Alden Whitman, ed., *American Reformers* (New York: H. W. Wilson, 1985), pp. 45–48.

87. Lamson, *Roger Baldwin*, p. 151.

88. Baldwin, Memo on Doty; see also Lamson, *Roger Baldwin*, pp. 150–154, 210.

89. In answer to the question of how to solve the paradox of vocation versus marriage, the women surveyed revealed the following results: Choose Marriage over Career, 37% (71); Choose Either Marriage or Career, 10% (20); Balance Marriage and Career, 44% (83); and Not Sure or Can't Advise, 8% (16). N = 190. BVI questionnaires, all from BVI Records.

90. BVI questionnaire 26, n.d.

91. BVI questionnaire 190, Apr. 19, 1920.

92. BVI questionnaire 95, Apr. 3, 1920.

93. BVI questionnaire 150, Mar. 1, 1920.

94. BVI questionnaire 95.

95. BVI questionnaire 254, Aug. 10, 1920.

96. BVI questionnaire 142, Mar. 5, 1920.

97. BVI questionnaire 148, Mar. 2, 1920.

98. BVI questionnaire 152, Mar. 20, 1920.

99. BVI questionnaire 136, Mar. 2, 1920.

100. BVI questionnaire 26 n.d.; also BVI questionnaire 242, Apr. 26, 1920.

101. BVI questionnaire 189 n.d.

102. BVI questionnaire 131, Mar. 27, 1920.

103. BVI questionnaire 6, Mar. 12, 1920.

104. BVI questionnaire 156, Mar. 8, 1920.

105. BVI questionnaire 145, Mar. 7, 1920.

106. BVI questionnaire 146, Mar. 1, 1920.

107. BVI questionnaire 19, Mar. 19, 1920.

108. BVI questionnaire 304, July 20, 1920; also BVI questionnaire 122, n.d.

109. BVI questionnaire 134, n.d.

110. BVI questionnaire 144, Mar. 31, 1920.

111. Lucy R. Tunis, "I Gave Up My Law Books for a Cook Book," *American Magazine* (July 1927): 34–35, 172–177, quotation from p. 173; see also Jane Allen, "You May Have My Job: A Feminist Discovers Her Home," *Forum* (Apr. 1932): 228–231.

112. Showalter, *These Modern Women*, p. 52.

113. "Bar Group Assails Rivals of Lawyers."

114. Matthews, "Why an Association of Women Lawyers."

Index